workbook

FOR LECTORS AND GOSPEL READERS

Martin Connell

LTP

LITURGY
TRAINING
PUBLICATIONS

WORKBOOK FOR LECTORS AND GOSPEL READERS 2006, UNITED STATES EDITION © 2005 Archdiocese of Chicago. All rights reserved.

Liturgy Training Publications, 1800 North Hermitage Avenue, Chicago IL 60622-1101; 1-800-933-1800, fax 1-800-933-7094, orders@ltp.org, www.ltp.org

Editor: Paul A. Zalonski
Production editor: Audrey Novak Riley
Typesetter: Jim Mellody-Pizzato
Original book design: Jill Smith
Revised design: Anna Manhart and Jim Mellody-Pizzato
Cover art: Barbara Simcoe
Interior art: Steve Erspamer, SM

Printed in Canada.

ISBN 1-56854-533-9
WL06

Nihil Obstat
Reverend Brian J. Fisher, STL
Censor Deputatus
April 19, 2005

Imprimatur
Reverend George J. Rassas
Vicar General
Archdiocese of Chicago
April 20, 2005

The *Nihil Obstat* and *Imprimatur* are official declarations that a book is free of doctrinal and moral error. No implication is contained therein that those who have granted the *Nihil Obstat* and *Imprimatur* agree with the content, opinions, or statements expressed. Nor do they assume any legal responsibility associated with publication.

CONTENTS

The Author

Martin Connell is a professor of liturgical studies at Saint John's University in Collegeville, Minnesota, where he teaches the history and sources of the liturgy, the rites of Christian initiation, and the liturgical year. His most recent books are *Workbook for Lectors and Gospel Readers 2006* (Chicago: LTP, 2005), and *Church and Worship in Fifth-Century Rome: The Letter of Innocent I to Decentius of Gubbio*, Joint Liturgical Studies #52 (London: Alcuin/GROW, 2002). Martin has just finished writing *Eternity Today: A Theology of the Liturgical Year*. His recent articles have appeared in *America, Worship, Studia Liturgica, Theological Studies*, the *GIA Quarterly*, and *U.S. Catholic*. By God's grace, the ideas for these works usually occur while he is jogging long distances or knitting.

Dedication

Martin dedicates this book to his friends Patricia and Philip Rosini, of Glen Mills, Pennsylvania, who embody the living Christ every day in the sacrament of Marriage. They celebrated the sacrament of unity in Our Lady of Angels Church in Philadelphia on June 3, 1961, and in them God's love is tangible. Their love and unity are manifest in their three children (Andrea, Philip, and Danielle), with their spouses (Harry, Susan, and Gregory), and seven grandchildren (Amanda, Nicholas, and Patricia [+1992]; Christopher and Eric; Carmen and Gregory). Pat (née Pirocchi) is an image of God's compassion and embrace, and Phil of God's word and wisdom in all things (except political affiliation).

INTRODUCTION

Words Today

In contemporary culture, words are cheap. The advent of the computer has occasioned a nearly constant barrage of words in ever brasher and more dazzling advertisements and solicitations sent to homes, families, and religious communities. The sheer quantity of words is ever more distracting as advertisers, creative consultants, and eloquent salespeople compete with one another for viewers' and hearers' attention. The result is that as words multiply astronomically, they depreciate.

As a minister of God's word, you, with the Church, are called to be a sign of contradiction in a world buried under this avalanche of words. Long before the computer and long before the printing press—the two inventions that immeasurably magnified the avalanche of words in which we live and under which we buckle, bend, and thrash—the Gospel of John promulgated the fundamental fact of Christian faith: "In the beginning was the Word, and the Word was with God, and the Word was God" (John 1:1).

When that Gospel was written down, written words were expensive, for the process of making written words involved raising the animals whose skins would be made into manuscript pages—*manu-*, "by hand," *-script*, "written"—and writing each word by the hand of a human being, not by a machine. The poignant and fundamental theology of Jesus Christ as the Word of God was first proclaimed in the context of cultures where the written word was expensive and greatly valued. A Bible was the result of an unimaginable amount of time, effort, and expense. One Bible was used in most assemblies for the proclamation of the word, so that God's word was revered not only for its message, but also for the rarity of its medium, the manuscript.

Now the opposite is true, for, in the world we know, making words and reproducing them is cheap. Part of the lectors' vocation is to be people of the Word of God, people whose own words are trusted by spouses, children, parents, friends, workmates, and even strangers. This is no small accomplishment in a world where talk is cheap. In his preface to a tenth-anniversary edition of a Church teaching on evangelization, "Go and Make Disciples" (1992, henceforth referred to as GMD), Cardinal Francis George, OMI, the Archbishop of Chicago, helped evangelizers and lectors recognize potential difficulties they face as ministers of the word as they compete with the ever louder, faster, and more frenetic pace of communications in contemporary society. His words are addressed to all the Catholic faithful, but to lectors in particular: "Do not let the problems, the obstacles [of today] discourage you. On the contrary, may they force you to open your hearts to divine grace so that, with the strength of the word of Christ, you can sow the joy and newness of the Gospel with your presence and your action." No human life, individual or communal, is without problems, yet, as the cardinal says, this omnipresence of obstacles is not an impediment to "the strength of the word" of God, for, "[e]vangelization is the essential mission of the Church" (GMD, #8). In accepting the call to proclaim God's word in

Church and in life, "we must let our faith shine on the world around us, radiating the love of Jesus by the everyday way we speak, think, and act" (GMD, #17).

Though Pope Paul VI—who was born in northern Italy in 1897 and was pope from 1963 until 1978—might never have imagined the world of communications today when he wrote on evangelization thirty years ago, he was already seeing how valueless words become when they are constant and overwhelming. In his teaching on "Evangelization in the Modern World," of December 8, 1975—before the omnipresence of computers, the Internet, and e-mail—he wrote: "We know that there are today many men who are wearied of talk, who often seem to be tired of listening and, which is more serious, to have closed their minds to the spoken word" (#42). As a proclaimer of God's word in the Sunday assembly of the body of Christ, you can be a sign of contradiction to those many who are weary and tired of listening.

Evangelization

In spite of the Church's teaching about evangelization, it is not often talked about in Roman Catholic parishes in North America. Evangelization—the process of spreading the Good News of salvation in God's Word, Jesus Christ—has carried great importance in the official teachings of the Church, but at the parish level this message is muted. Catholics in general—and lectors in particular—might be surprised to discover with what strength the bishops advocate evangelization as a necessary way to build up the Church.

The *great* importance accorded the issue of evangelization for the Church at large should be ratcheted up to *supreme* importance in the lives of ministers of God's word in the sacred scriptures that you proclaim to your community of faith. Pope Paul VI was the Bishop of Rome at the closing of Vatican II (1962–1965), and ten years after the Council's end he delivered an important teaching on evangelization entitled *Evangelii Nuntiandi* (henceforth EN). In 1992, in their teaching about evangelization, the bishops of the United States looked with hope at how a dedication to evangelization would animate humanity: "We pray that our Catholic people will be set ablaze with a desire to live their faith fully and share it freely with others. May their eagerness to share the faith bring a transformation to our nation and, with missionary dedication, even to the whole world. We ask God to open the heart of every Catholic, to see the need for the Gospel in each life, in our nation and on our planet" (GMD #138). As a minister of God's word, you can meditate on the Church's assessment of spreading the Good News in God's gift of his Son.

Parishes are encouraged to support lectors in their work with the Bible and their study of the Lectionary. Paul VI taught about how ministers need to be trained for their proclamation: "Careful preparation is essential for all workers in the field of evangelization and it is especially necessary for those who devote themselves to the ministry of the Word. Inspired by an ever deeper appreciation of the nobility and richness of the word of God, they whose function it is to proclaim the Word must exercise every care to ensure that their words are dignified, well-chosen and adapted to their audience. . . . It is our earnest desire that in every church the bishops provide suitable instruction for all the ministers of the Word. If this education is undertaken seriously it will not only develop their self-confidence but will also serve to increase their zeal to preach Jesus Christ in our times" (EN, #73).

As a minister of God's word in your parish, you can be an advocate for such instruction and training, perhaps contacting the worship office of your diocese to find out what resources are available for you and your fellow ministers as a way to deepen your understanding of God's word and your ability to deliver that word confidently in the Sunday assembly of Christ's body, the Church. Such training is in line with Pope Paul VI's inspiring message for those who are evangelists in the modern world: "May [evangelization] be a great source of joy to us who have dedicated our lives to the task. And may the world of our time which is searching, now in anguish and now in hope, receive the gospel not from evangelizers who are dejected or dispirited, not from those who are impatient or anxious; let them hear it from ministers of the gospel whose lives are aglow with fervor, from those who, having received the joy of Christ into their own hearts, are ready to risk their lives so that the kingdom may be proclaimed and the church established throughout the world" (EN, #80). The Church is obliged to call forth and train those "whose lives are aglow with fervor" for God's word.

By God's grace, you yourself are such an evangelizer, but this vocation is not without demands or expectations. Below you will find a few significant points from the teachings on evangelization by Pope Paul VI and the U.S. bishops, included as a way for you to consider and deepen your vocation in prayer and contemplation. These also provide a format with which you and your fellow ministers of the word can support one another with discussion and prayer. We believe and proclaim that "God, whose love is unconditional, offers us divine life even in the face of our sins, failures, and inadequacies" (GMD, #20). As a group, ministers of the Church are stronger than any one as an individual can be.

However, our own individual lives contribute to the ministry, for "[w]e all have—and are—stories of faith, for through the Spirit, the Gospel of Jesus Christ takes hold of us in the proclamation of his Word, and Jesus touches us in the celebration of his sacraments. When this genuinely happens, we are all set ablaze by his love" (GMD, #7). Claim your story and God's role in it so that you can confidently proclaim God's story to the Church.

The Vocation of Invitation and Hospitality

Having led the Church through the tumult after Vatican II, Pope Paul VI knew how many Catholics felt disenfranchised by the changes in the liturgy and the Church. As he wrote to the Church at large on evangelization, he highlighted the need for the Church's mission to those who had left, and earnestly extended a new invitation to those who had departed, to "those who do not practice their religion" (EN, #56). As a minister of God's word, you too are called to be an evangelizer by inviting back to the Church those who have left. He wrote that "[t]here are great numbers of people who have been baptized and, while they have not formally renounced their membership of the church, are, as it were, on the fringe of it and do not live according to her teaching." He knew that the Church as institution would not be able to reach these people, for "[t]he only true form of evangelization is that by which the individual communicates to another those truths of which he is personally convinced by faith" (EN, #46).

You are such an individual. Part of your vocation is to be the voice of the Church to those who have left the communion of the Church, not in a coercive manner, but simply to let them know that they are missed. As the U.S. bishops wrote, "We want to let our inactive brothers and sisters know that they always have a place in the Church and that we are hurt by their absence—as they are" (GMD, #40). Your proclamations will be powerful when you participate in carrying this message of Good News to those who had found only news of gloom, doom, and dissolution. In this you can be an example of that which all believers are called to be: "Every Catholic can be a minister of welcome, reconciliation, and understanding to those who have stopped practicing the faith" (GMD, #40).

The experience of manifesting God's word in bringing back those who have been hurt by the Church or by ministers of the Church is not simple, but it is a primary call for ministers of the word in the Church in North America at the start of the twenty-first century. To be a bearer of this message of reconciliation, you must earnestly consider how your life has been formed and transformed by membership in the Church and participation in its liturgy.

Moreover, both Pope Paul VI and the U.S. bishops encouraged care for the poor, not simply because the Church ministers to those in need but because Christ is found among them, as Jesus of Nazareth was in his incarnate life in first-century Palestine. As the bishops teach, "[t]he validity of our having accepted the Gospel . . . comes from the way we serve others, especially the poorest, the most marginal, the most hurting, the most defenseless, and the least loved" (GMD, #18).

This formation and transformation of you, a minister of God's word, will echo through the world, and your response to this vocation, consonant with God's grace and love, will change the world: "The transformation of our society in Christ particularly calls for the involvement and skills of lay men and women who carry the values of the Gospel into their homes,

Consonance of Word and Life

Finally, the ministry of proclaiming the word of God is not for Sundays only. As you are transformed by God's love and word, the power of your ministry will be apparent from the example you set for the members of your Church with your life, from the decisions you make day after day, by the reconciliation you seek from and offer to those you love, and by how God's love shines forth in your days. The power of this witness flows from your own experience and therefore will vary from one lector to the next. As the U.S. bishops write—"[t]he ministry of evangelization does not consist in following a recipe but in letting the Spirit open our hearts to God's Word so that we can live and proclaim God's Word to others. So let the Spirit work!" (GMD, #79)

Support for this vocation of the word should be sought out with others in the ministry. Consult friends who share the faith and a passion for the word. Pray in the liturgy and with the scriptures you practice in preparation for your ministry. Speak with other ministers of the word. Seek direction and spiritual guidance from your pastor and the pastoral leaders of your community of faith. In so doing you can "[d]iscover how the Spirit is leading you to evangelize" (GMD, #131). One basic challenge for you as a lector is to have a fundamental consonance between what you believe and how you live, for—just as in the Incarnation the Son reflected the life of God in the world in word and deed—your faith forms your life, and the words you proclaim will be grounded in the choices you make and others witness day by day.

Though you might not be aware of how others perceive you as a minister of the Church, you must be aware that expectations of ministers are high. All ministers must consider their own integrity as it will be assessed by those who measure the balance of word and deed in their lives. Pope Paul VI recognized this about his own ministry, about the role of the bishops, and indeed about those who seek to evangelize and proclaim the word. His teaching on evangelization challenged preachers in particular, but this is clearly applicable to your role in the Church as well: "We are continuously being questioned, sometimes tacitly, sometimes openly: Do you believe yourselves what you are saying to us? Is your life in accord with your beliefs? Is your preaching in accord with your life?

workplaces, areas of recreation—indeed, into all aspects of life" (GMD, #119).

In the Sunday assembly, those who—needing the Church's sacraments and embrace, but in an anonymous way—tiptoe in after the entrance procession and bolt out after communion are often the poor, though perhaps not the poorest in material possessions. These last-pew participants are among those to whom God is nearest, and, both socially and in proclaiming the word, lectors need to address the word to these most fragile and vulnerable, frightened and alone. They are no less members of the Church than any other baptized or ordained ministers of the faith. Your convictions and strengths need to be put in balance with your vulnerabilities and weaknesses so that you will be an instrument of God's word to those for whom it is a lifeline. Acknowledging the transformative power of grace in your own story, you will be able to look at the broken and marginalized edge and know that God is near. Gazing into their eyes and addressing the word to their ears in particular, you carry on the work of evangelization in the Church and the world.

More than ever before the witness of our life has become an essential requirement if our preaching is to be fully effective. Accordingly, the development and the effectiveness of our preaching of the gospel depends in a large measure on ourselves who are preaching it" (EN, #76).

Consonance between one's word and one's life is shown when you, as a minister of the word, are present to members of the Church in good times and in bad, when you bear God's word in times of plenty and in need, in times of celebration and loss, in health and sickness, even to the end, when death is near and the Good News is a consolation when there is nothing else to offer. You are called to deliver God's word in the Church, and also to make that word incarnate in your daily living and in the lives of those to whom you bring the word.

This balance of faith and action for ministers of God's word is reflected in the prayer from the "Order for the Blessing of Readers." The presiding minister prays:

> Everlasting God,
> when he read in the synagogue at Nazareth,
> your Son proclaimed the good news of salvation
> for which he would give up his life.
> Bless these readers.
> As they proclaim your words of life,
> strengthen their faith

that they may read with conviction and boldness, *and put into practice what they read.*
We ask this through Christ our Lord. Amen.

This aspect of your vocation is as important as the moment you step up for the proclamation of God's word to the Sunday assembly, for your word in the assembly is only as clear, profound, and welcome as your word to those you meet outside the Church's walls.

The Proclaimer and the Hearer

The liturgy of the word is the Church's proclamation of God's life in us, and it is mediated by the gifts you have (or will learn) as a good and effective minister of the word. Whether you have been in the ministry for a long time or are relatively new, you can always work on your ability to proclaim. It is difficult to prescribe the best way to proclaim, for so many of the tools are unique to each person as a unique creation of God. But there are guidelines that you can attend to as a newcomer or as a renewed comer.

Aelred Rosser, an eminent teacher of proclaiming the word and former author of the *Workbook*, wrote of the characteristics of human speech and the vocal variety that helps hearers attend to the proclamation of the scriptures. Among the qualities you can consider and practice are melody, rate, pause, volume change, and articulation. Each minister employs such qualities differently, uniquely, but each minister can benefit from the help of others by having them listen to proclamations and evaluate them. The characteristics of bad proclamations are easier to identify than those of good ones. Bad proclamations are dull, boring, monotonous, hasty, unclear, mumbled, and easily forgettable, or stiff, stagey, pompous, exaggerated, and annoying. That is not what the Church seeks in its proclamation of God's word! The most important recommendation is that you seek help from trained proclaimers, from those whose proclamations you yourself find strong and convincing, from those whose readings have a balance of power of faith and strength of the delivery, from those who can give criticism that is both gentle and direct.

Practical Matters of the Word and Its Delivery

In addition to your own natural instrument, your voice, there are the practical tools of your church building. You need to be comfortable with the sound system, with the right position for the microphone, and with the height of the bookstand, as well as with the Lectionary itself. If the church is relatively small, perhaps it does not have a sound system; in this case, you should ask a friend to help you determine the volume that you need to use so that the people in the last places hear your proclamation clearly. If your parish does not routinely offer help in acclimating you to these practical matters, you can and indeed must ask for help.

Moreover, in addition to the practical matters, the text that you will be proclaiming calls for a different voice than everyday speech. The Bible is a complex book. In fact, it is not merely *a* book, but a *library* of books, with many different authors who wrote in many different genres and styles, from many different places and different centuries. Part of your task in taking on the ministry of the reader is to engage in Bible study. This will give you tools that will help you with the readings you are assigned. It is important that your proclamations be confident and convincing, and these qualities come from your own understanding of the word and its intricacies. The *Workbook* is one tool, and there are many others that you can consult. (The list in "Recommended Works," below, offers some suggestions.)

A final practical note about what you should wear for your service as a reader. In a place as large and varied as North America that it is virtually impossible to speak specifically about what a reader should wear or not wear, but some general guidelines might help as you stand in front of the closet on Sunday morning wondering what to wear. It is not necessary to wear the color of the liturgical season or day, but do your best *not* to wear a color that contradicts the liturgical color of the season or day. For example, since purple is the color for Lent, purple is not a good choice the Easter season. Similarly, since the liturgical color of Advent is purple, wearing purple during the actual season of Christmas would be a little odd at best, contradictory at worst. Black is relatively neutral, but during the Easter season, when white is the liturgical color, black too might look out of place.

We have all proclaimed the word and come away thinking that we could have done a much better job, only to find that it was one of the most well-received reading we had ever proclaimed. At the same time, we can remember times when we had studied the passage closely, rehearsed well, dressed appropriately, and proclaimed our text without mistake or impediment, only to find out that no one seemed to have noticed. The work of the ministry is a process, one that takes time and attention, and having the *Workbook* in hand, as you do, is a good start.

Whether the assembly to whom you proclaim has the printed text of the scriptures to read as you proclaim, you need to prepare and proclaim as if no one in the assembly has the text before them. Indeed, your proclamation should be so sharp and so instrumental a tool of God's word that those who picked up the booklet when they came in will never glance at it because your delivery is so clear and animated.

As a minister, your apparel should be dignified, perhaps a step up in formality from the ordinary dress of the members of the assembly. Ministers of the word should not proclaim the word with outdoor clothes on. Even if there is no place for the assembly to hang their coats, you should not minister the word wearing yours. Ultimately, we recommend that you follow the guidelines established by your bishop and yoru pastor about the type of clothing to be worn while serving in the Sacred Liturgy. Attention to the dignity of serving as a lector is not merely aesthetic; it honors the revelation of God.

Pronunciation Key

Most consonants in the pronunciation key are straightforward: The letter B always represents the sound B and D is always D, and so on. Vowels are more complicated. Note that the long I sound (as in kite or ice) is represented by *ī* while long A (as in skate or pray) is represented by *ay*; long A followed by an R (as in prayer or Samaritan) is represented by *ai*. Long E (as in beam or marine) is represented by *ee*; long O (boat, coat), *oh*; long U (sure, secure) by *oo* or *yoo*. Short A (cat), E (bed), I (slim), and O (dot) are represented by *a*, *e*, *i*, and *o* except in an unstressed syllable, when E and I are signified by *eh* and *ih*. Short U (cup) is represented by *uh* or sometimes *u*. An asterisk (*) indicates the *schwa* sound, as in the last syllable of the word

"stable." The letters *oo* and *th* can each be pronounced in two ways (as in *cool* or *book*; *thin* or *they*); underlining differentiates between them. Stress is indicated by the capitalization of the stressed syllable in words of more than one syllable.

bait = bayt	finesse = fih-NES
cat = kat	thin = thin
sang = sang	vision = VIZH*n
father = FAH-<u>ther</u>	ship = ship
care = kair	sir = ser
paw = paw	gloat = gloht
jar = jahr	cot = kot
easy = EE-zee	noise = noyz
her = her	poison = POY-z*n
let = let	plow = plow
queen = kween	although = ahl-<u>TH</u>OH
delude = deh-L<u>OO</u>D	church = cherch
when = hwen	fun = fun
ice = īs	fur = fer
if = if	flute = fl<u>oo</u>t
	foot = foot

Recommended Works

Guides for Proclaiming God's Word:

Martin Connell, *Guide to the Revised Lectionary* (Chicago, LTP, 1998).

Susan E. Myers, *Pronunciation Guide for the Sunday Lectionary* (Chicago: LTP, 1998).

Aelred R. Rosser, *A Well-Trained Tongue: Formation in the Ministry of Reader* (Chicago: LTP, 1996).

Biblical Studies

Raymond E. Brown, *Introduction to the New Testament* (Anchor Bible, 1997).

Pheme Perkins, *Reading the New Testament: An Introduction* (Paulist Press, 1988).

Gospel of Mark

Eugene LaVerdiere, sss, *The Beginning of the Gospel: Introducing the Gospel of Mark* (Collegeville: Liturgical Press, 1999).

Donald Senior, *The Passion of Jesus in the Gospel of Mark* (Wilmington: Glazier, 1984).

John R. Donahue, sj, and Daniel J. Harrington, sj, *The Gospel of Mark* (Sacra Pagina Series) (Collegeville: The Liturgical Press, 2005).

1ST SUNDAY OF ADVENT

Lectionary #2

READING I   Isaiah 63:16b–17, 19b; 64:2b–7

Isaiah = ī-ZAY-uh

A reading from the Book of the Prophet Isaiah

> **You**, LORD, are our **father**,
>   our **redeemer** you are named **forever**.
> Why do you let us **wander**, O LORD, from your ways,
>   and harden our **hearts** so that we fear you not?
> **Return** for the sake of your **servants**,
>   the tribes of your **heritage**.
> Oh, that you would **rend** the heavens and come **down**,
>   with the mountains **quaking** before you,
> while you wrought **awesome** deeds we could not **hope** for,
>   such as they had not heard of from of **old**.
> No **ear** has ever **heard**, no **eye** ever **seen**, any God but **you**
>   doing such deeds for those who **wait** for him.
> Would that you might meet us doing **right**,
>   that we were **mindful** of you in our ways!
> **Behold**, you are **angry**, and we are **sinful**;
>   all of us have become like unclean people,
>   all our **good** deeds are like polluted **rags**;
> we have all **withered** like **leaves**,
>   and our **guilt** carries us away like the **wind**.
> There is **none** who calls upon your name,
>   who **rouses** himself to cling to you;

Here the Advent theology is important and hopeful: the Lord *will* return to the people of Israel.

A shift in tone, as the prophet recounts transgressions of the past and present.

READING I The words of the prophet Isaiah have echoed through the season of Advent for centuries. The prophet looked forward to a time when Israel, then crushed by its enemies, would be restored and regain its strength. In these weeks when the Church anticipates the birth of the Messiah, Jesus Christ, she too longs for a restoration, a re-strengthening.

The passage you prepare for proclamation captures various aspects of the experience of ancient Israel, and the mood of the reading changes a few times. The opening and closing verses are consoling and hopeful.

Cataclysmic indictments, such as "you were angry, and we sinned," are broken up by consolations like "God . . . works for those who wait." The rhetoric is a bit complex, and you need to know how the message progresses in order to be ready for the changes in direction. You need to know when it is indicting and when consoling, when it is gloomy and when trusting.

Even in its darker aspects, the reading has potent poetry, with such images as "one who is unclean," "a filthy cloth," "a leaf," and "the wind." Take your time over these so they will be appreciated.

The final metaphor—"we are the clay, and you are the potter"—is familiar to many believers. Therefore, pause slightly before beginning it so that the hearers are poised to receive this clearly. The prophet wanted his listeners to recognize the profound truth that, though we have strayed, God is the creator of all good things and sustainer of all we do.

READING II Commit the opening verse to memory, so that after naming the reading, you can look up and

for you have hidden your **face** from us
and have **delivered** us up to our **guilt**.
Yet, O LORD, **you** are our **father**;
we are the **clay** and **you** the **potter**:
we are all the **work** of your **hands**.

This final verse is key, so pause before it and proclaim it slowly, clearly, boldly, as a message of hope for your community.

READING II 1 Corinthians 1:3–9

Corinthians = kor-IN-thee-unz

This opening greeting is a prime opportunity for you to address the assembly before you directly and with conviction.

Pause to have the assembly poised for the first-person address. Here you begin a long and complex sentence. You need to understand its shifts and turns in order to proclaim it confidently.

A reading from the first Letter of Saint Paul to the Corinthians

Brothers and sisters:
Grace to you and **peace** from God our **Father**
and the Lord Jesus **Christ**.
I give **thanks** to my God **always** on your account
for the grace of God **bestowed** on you in Christ **Jesus**,
that in him you were enriched in **every** way,
with all **discourse** and all **knowledge**,
as the **testimony** to Christ was **confirmed** among you,
so that you are not lacking in **any** spiritual gift
as you **wait** for the revelation of our Lord Jesus **Christ**.
He will keep you **firm** to the end,
irreproachable on the day of our Lord Jesus **Christ**.
God is **faithful**,
and by him you were **called** to fellowship with his **Son**,
Jesus **Christ** our **Lord**.

make eye contact with your "brothers and sisters" as you pray for them for God's gifts of grace and peace.

Verses from Saint Paul are often the ancient sources of texts used in the liturgy yet today, so proclaim "The grace and peace of God our Father . . ." so that the assembly recognizes the link between the words of Paul and those of the liturgy. Paul's letters are always a gift to the reader, for his use of first- and second-person pronouns enables the proclaimer to stand in Paul's place and address the faithful directly, as in this wonderful sentence: "I give thanks to my God

always for you." Good eye contact will make your hearers recognize themselves in that "you."

Notice that the middle of this reading is one long sentence. Be prepared for the complexity of this sentence so you can proclaim it smoothly. Examine it and understand it thoroughly, for if you do not, neither will the assembly. Your confident delivery will go far to make it it clear.

The Advent season's mood of waiting is captured in the second half of the passage, and this is likely why the Letter found its place on this First Sunday of Advent, for it

leads the Church into anticipation of the revelation of our Lord.

The readings of the opening weeks of Advent point to the Lord's coming at the end of time, and the later weeks are about the Lord's coming in the Incarnation. The reference to the "day of our Lord Jesus Christ" is the end-time theology of the Advent readings.

As ever, pause before you deliver the liturgical closing: "The word of the Lord."

GOSPEL In Advent, the metaphor of the journey is applied to both God's life and humanity's. God waits for

GOSPEL   Mark 13:33–37

A reading from the holy Gospel according to Mark

Jesus said to his **disciples**:
"Be **watchful**! Be **alert**!
You **do** not know when the time will **come**.
It is like a man traveling **abroad**.
He leaves **home** and places his **servants** in charge,
      each with his own **work**,
      and orders the **gatekeeper** to be on the **watch**.
Watch, therefore;
      you do not **know** when the **lord** of the house is **coming**,
      whether in the **evening**, or at **midnight**,
      or at **cockcrow**, or in the **morning**.
May he not come **suddenly** and find you **sleeping**.
What I say to **you**, I say to **all**: 'Watch!'"

Except for these opening five words, the entire passage is from the lips of Jesus. Deliver these commands as commands.

A short parable of Advent vigilance.

This final verse with its command is a concise summary of the theology of Advent. Pause before you deliver it.

humanity to recognize the fullness of life; humanity waits for the revelation of God. As a metaphor, the householder "traveling abroad" may be applied to the whole Church as she journeys through this season of the liturgical year watching for the Lord, as the gatekeeper is on the watch in today's Gospel.

The reading's basic message appears a number of times, each time with the imperative form of a command: "Be watchful," "keep alert," and "keep awake." Practice to find the best way to proclaim the two repetitions of the key command: "Watch!"

Because the theology of the whole passage is wrapped up in this command, deliver it in a way that can be heard well and received clearly.

Many of the early Christians expected the Lord's imminent return, based on many of Jesus' words. And yet his parables sometimes speak of the slow growth of the kingdom in this world, and neither Jesus nor his apostles gives a precise timetable for the Parousia. Instead, they exhort us to watchfulness—after all, our own lives will end one day, as surely as the world must come to its consummation as well.

The season of anticipation of Christmas emerged in the fifth century, and ever since then, the season has retained its theological structure. The opening few weeks are about the Lord's coming at the end of time and the later weeks are about the Lord's coming in the Incarnation. The message of vigilance in the imperatives of the Gospel is linked to the end-time theology of the first and second Sundays of Advent, a further reason for you to make the imperatives about vigilance clear.

2ND SUNDAY OF ADVENT

Lectionary #5

READING I   Isaiah 40:1–5, 9–11

Isaiah = ī-ZAY-uh

The first section is a message of soothing consolation after a hard experience. Note that this is from God, and its verbs are commands.
Jerusalem = juh-ROO-suh-lem

A reading from the Book of the Prophet Isaiah

Comfort, give **comfort** to my people,
    says your God.
Speak **tenderly** to **Jerusalem**, and proclaim to her
    that her **service** is at an **end**,
    her **guilt** is **expiated**;
indeed, she has received from the hand of the LORD
    double for all her **sins**.

    A **voice** cries out:
In the **desert prepare** the way of the **Lord**!
    Make **straight** in the **wasteland** a **highway** for our **God**!
Every **valley** shall be filled **in**,
    every **mountain** and **hill** shall be made **low**;
the **rugged** land shall be made a **plain**,
    the **rough** country, a broad **valley**.
Then the **glory** of the LORD shall be **revealed**,
    and all **people** shall see it **together**;
    for the **mouth** of the LORD has **spoken**.

Now a "voice" speaks, indeed cries out. This anticipates the Gospel passage that centers on the Baptist. The poetic images from nature are beautiful. Accentuate them.

You return to the voice of God, and to the imperative verbs: "Go up," "cry out," "fear not." Perhaps imagine exclamation points to capture the imperative tone.
Zion = ZĪ-ahn

Go **up** on to a high **mountain**,
    Zion, herald of glad **tidings**;
cry **out** at the top of your **voice**,
    Jerusalem, herald of good **news**!

READING I   The theology of the prophet Isaiah is apt for the season of Advent, for the prophet preached to the ancient Israelites about the redemption that would accompany the coming of the Lord. The people of Israel knew that this coming of the Lord would be the dawn of a new age, the start of a season of consolation and rejoicing. The word Advent means a "coming (-venire) to (ad-)," for this coming of the Lord to his people.

The consolation that the prophet Isaiah proclaimed—and that you in his stead announce to a new people of God—revealed to them that the hardships of the past are about to end: "[Jerusalem's] service is at an end," "her guilt is expiated," and the people of Israel have already paid "double" for all their sins. The first part of the reading, therefore, should be proclaimed as consoling, as from someone who comes to tell prisoners that their sentence has come to an end.

Since the early Middle Ages when Advent was first celebrated, there has always been a Sunday before Christmas that centers John the Baptist, the "forerunner." This text from Isaiah was picked up almost word for word by the Gospels, as you can see if you flip ahead and consider the Gospel that will be proclaimed today. Because this Second Sunday of Advent has a particular focus on the Baptist, deliver the second section of the passage ("A voice cries out") with emphasis. If you can, commit some of it to memory so that you can make eye contact as you announce the prophet's words, especially the metaphors from the terrain of the land of Israel, such as "every valley shall be

Judah = JOO-duh

This final verse highlights the familiar
and wonderful image of the shepherd
caring for the lamb in his arms. Proclaim
it confidently, and capture its tenderness.

Fear **not** to cry out
    and say to the cities of **Judah**:
      Here is your **God**!
Here comes with power
    the Lord **God**,
    who **rules** by his strong arm;
here is his **reward** with him,
    his **recompense** before him.
Like a **shepherd** he feeds his **flock**;
    in his **arms** he gathers the **lambs**,
carrying them in his **bosom**,
    and leading the **ewes** with **care**.

READING II   2 Peter 3:8–14

Because the New Testament book
2 Peter is not heard often in the liturgy, be
measured and emphatic in the identifying
line at the start.

Advent is a season of renewal and repentance in anticipation of Christmas joy.

A reading from the second Letter of Saint Peter

Do **not** ignore this one **fact**, beloved,
    that with the Lord one **day** is like a thousand **years**
    and a thousand **years** like one **day**.
The Lord does not **delay** his promise, as **some** regard "delay,"
    but he is **patient** with you,
    not wishing that **any** should perish
    but that **all** should come to **repentance**.
But the day of the **Lord** will come like a **thief**,
    and then the **heavens** will pass away with a mighty **roar**
    and the **elements** will be dissolved by **fire**,
    and the **earth** and everything **done** on it will be found **out**.

filled in, and every mountain and hill shall
be made low."
    The last verse is beautiful, and though
its images — of flock, shepherd, and
lambs — may not be part of the daily life of
the members of your community, they are
universally understood. The image of Christ
as the shepherd — who cares for the lamb
that he carries in his arms, close to his
bosom, his heart — is so deep in Christian
theology that you can linger over its message of intimacy and nurturing. Take your
time with this significant image of Advent
so that your hearers can catch Isaiah's

poignant consolation as delivered through
your voice to your people.

READING II For centuries the first half of
the season of Advent has
focused on the final advent of God at the end
of time. The second half of the season centers
on the advent of Jesus Christ at a particular
time, but for now the Church encourages her
people to consider not only that first coming,
but the final coming, when all things come
together according to God's plan.

    There are some end-time images in this
reading that might be disconcerting: "the
heavens will pass away with a mighty roar,"
"the elements will be dissolved by fire,"
"everything . . . will be found out," and
"the heavens will be dissolved in flames."
Consider what — for yourself and for the
liturgical assembly before you — will be the
best way to proclaim such anticipations of
a stormy apocalypse.
    Some people may imagine the end as
violent, frightening, unfamiliar, and unpre-
dictable. Yet for most people of faith, that
end is not to be feared, for they will have

This longer middle section is a little frightening with its end-of-the-world imagery. Consider what voice, in light of the experience and faith of those in your community, would be best for reading these elements.

The final section is soothing, so match your voice to the content.

Since **everything** is to be dissolved in this way,
    what sort of persons ought you to **be**,
    conducting yourselves in **holiness** and **devotion**,
    waiting for and **hastening** the coming of the day of **God**,
    because of which the **heavens** will be dissolved in **flames**
    and the **elements** melted by **fire**.
But according to his **promise**
    we await **new** heavens and a **new** earth
    in which **righteousness** dwells.
Therefore, beloved, since you **await** these things,
    be **eager** to be found without **spot** or **blemish** before him,
      at **peace**.

GOSPEL   Mark 1:1–8

A reading from the holy Gospel according to Mark

The **beginning** of the gospel of Jesus **Christ** the Son of **God**.

As it is **written** in Isaiah the **prophet**:
    *Behold, I am sending my **messenger** ahead of you;*
      he will prepare your way.
    *A **voice** of one crying out in the **desert**:*
      *"**Prepare** the way of the **Lord**,*
      *make **straight** his **paths**."*
John the **Baptist** appeared in the **desert**
    proclaiming a baptism of **repentance** for the forgiveness of **sins**.

Isaiah = ī-ZAY-uh

This verse comes from the Isaiah text we heard in the first reading today. A clear proclamation will help people recognize the link between these books.

been waiting for God's reign all their lives. It will be consistent with the experience of faith in their own lives.

The Advent season is a time of waiting, so this passage's message about time and about people's experience of time as passing swiftly or laboriously slowly is fitting for the season. Consider your own experiences of hours or days or years flying by or dragging on, and hold those experiences in your imagination as you prepare to proclaim this word to your community.

Recognize the imperative mood of a number of the passage's verbs—"do not

ignore," "be eager"—and encourage your hearers with such directive verbs. Coming after the apocalyptic elements in the middle of the passage, the verses at the end are not threatening but consoling. Make sure to proclaim the calming elements—the patience of the Lord, "new heavens" and "new earth," being found "without spot or blemish," at peace—with the voice of a consoler, instilling confidence in the believers as they stand before God, as you proclaim or at the end of the world.

GOSPEL   Notice the citation in the Lectionary at the start of this reading: Mark 1:1–8. We often think of the Gospel account beginning with Jesus' infancy, with magi and a heavenly host (as in Matthew), or with a manger and shepherds (as in Luke). But the Gospel of Mark does not have a narrative of Jesus' infancy or childhood; the account begins with an adult John the Baptist anticipating an adult Jesus coming to his people.

In the narrative of the Gospel of Mark, this passage anticipates Jesus' appearance

Judean = joo-DEE-un

Jerusalem = juh-R<u>OO</u>-suh-lem

Jordan = JOR-d*n

The image of John's ascetic diet and clothing is deeply embedded in the Christian imagination. Most will recognize him from the description even if they do not hear his name.

Highlight this final emphasis on baptism.

People of the **whole** Judean countryside
and **all** the inhabitants of **Jerusalem**
were going **out** to him
and were being **baptized** by him in the Jordan **River**
as they acknowledged their **sins**.
John was clothed in **camel's** hair,
with a leather **belt** around his waist.
He fed on **locusts** and wild **honey**.
And **this** is what he **proclaimed**:
"One **mightier** than I is coming **after** me.
I am not worthy to **stoop** and loosen the **thongs** of his **sandals**.
I have baptized you with **water**;
he will baptize you with the Holy **Spirit**."

on the scene, his preaching, healing, and ministry among the people. Yet equally important in this Gospel are the repeated references to Baptism, in the name of John the *Baptist,* of course, but also in John's work of baptizing, mentioned in terms of John's message and his ritual practice.

Advent's second Sunday is always dedicated to John the Baptist and his work among God's people. There is an important link to be made between the anticipation of Christmas, the celebration of the manifestation of Jesus in the flesh, and the anticipation of the celebration of the sacrament of Baptism in the Church, where we find new members of the Church also in the flesh.

As you prepare to proclaim this reading, therefore, emphasize the references to Baptism in the second half of the passage, and particularly in the final verse. The familiar juxtaposition of John's Baptism "with water" and Jesus' Baptism "with the Holy Spirit" closes the proclamation, and your emphasis will enable the assembly to recognize that their birth into the body of Christ (in the sacrament of Baptism) is important to us, just as the birth of Jesus to the world two millennia ago is.

IMMACULATE CONCEPTION

Lectionary #689

READING I   Genesis 3:9 – 15, 20

Genesis = JEN-uh-sis

A reading from the Book of Genesis

After the man, **Adam**, had eaten of the **tree**,
  the LORD God **called** to the man and **asked** him,
    "Where **are** you?"
He answered, "I **heard** you in the garden;
  but I was **afraid**, because I was **naked**,
  so I **hid** myself."
Then he asked, "Who **told** you that you were **naked**?
You have eaten, then,
  from the **tree** of which I had **forbidden** you to eat!"
The man replied, "The **woman** whom you put here with me —
  she gave me **fruit** from the tree, and so I **ate** it."
The LORD God then asked the **woman**,
  "Why did **you** do such a thing?"
The **woman** answered, "The **serpent** tricked me into it,
    so I ate it."

Then the LORD God said to the **serpent**:
  "Because you have **done** this, you shall be **banned**
    from **all** the animals
    and from **all** the wild **creatures**;
  on your **belly** shall you **crawl**,
    and **dirt** shall you **eat**
    all the **days** of your **life**.

Pause after the first exchange between the Lord and Adam.

Pause again after the exchange between the Lord and the woman.

Proclaim this long quote clearly so that imaginations of the assembly will be engaged by the description of the serpent crawling on its belly and dining on dirt.

Mary is the "new Eve," so this description of Eve in relation to the serpent is important to the theology of the day and of Mary's place in the tradition.

READING I For the solemnity of the Immaculate Conception, the first reading comes from the beginning of the Bible, a passage familiar to many. This narrative has a number of characters, and three of them—God, the man, and the woman—have speaking parts. The fourth character of consequence, the serpent, does not have a speaking part, but does have a significant role.

Keep the difference between a *drama* and a *proclamation* in mind as you prepare for this proclamation. If this were a dramatic reading, you would work at finding a unique voice for each character, and you would recite all the words of the one character in that unique voice, as in a play on stage. With the ministry of the word, however, a dramatic reading is not the goal. The liturgy is not an imitation of something that happened in the past: God is active in the lives of human beings as much in our own day as in the past, especially in the reading of the scriptures.

This is a *proclamation,* a reading that is not merely a reminder of a past; it is a communal experience in which the hearts and minds of the faithful are engaged in a common experience of hearing a text. You are the minister of the word, and for this feast your ministry is to bring the word of God to life in the community of faith by a well-prepared and well-proclaimed text. This particular reading will take some preparatory attention because it is fairly complex.

You might mark or highlight in this *Workbook* the words of the three different speakers with different colors, one for what

I will put **enmity** between **you** and the **woman**,
> and between **your** offspring and **hers**;
he will strike at your **head**,
> while **you** strike at his **heel**."
The man called his wife **Eve**,
> because she became the **mother** of **all** the **living**.

READING II   Ephesians 1:3 – 6, 11 – 12

Ephesians = ee-FEE-zhunz

A reading from the Letter of Saint Paul to the Ephesians

Brothers and sisters:
Blessed be the **God** and **Father** of our **Lord** Jesus **Christ**,
> who has **blessed** us in **Christ**
> with **every** spiritual blessing in the **heavens**,
> as he **chose us** in him, before the foundation of the world,
> to be **holy** and without **blemish** before him.
In **love** he destined us for **adoption** to himself
> through Jesus **Christ**,
> in accord with the **favor** of his **will**,
> for the **praise** of the **glory** of his **grace**
> that he granted **us** in the **beloved**.

In **him** we were also **chosen**,
> **destined** in accord with the **purpose** of the One
> who accomplishes **all** things according to the intention
> of his **will**,
> so that we might **exist** for the praise of his **glory**,
> we who **first hoped** in Christ.

Notice that this reading is only three sentences long, but each of them is complex. This first one is a blessing, in praise of God but not addressed directly to God. You are proclaiming praise on behalf of the assembly.

The familial images in the middle of this passage—"adoption," "beloved," "chosen"—are engaging and potent. Proclaim with clarity.

---

is said by the Lord God, another for what is said by the man, and the third for what is said by the woman. The woman has the briefest part, with that single line, "The serpent tricked me into it, so I ate it," but theologians over the centuries have reflected on that one line.

Your task is to make the account engaging, and you can do that best by being animated as you proclaim the well-known tale to the assembly on this day of the Immaculate Conception.

READING II This passage starts with a hymn of praise to God, a beautiful and theologically powerful one that opens the letter to the Ephesians. The reading has three basic parts: the first is the blessing; the second and third parts speak, respectively, of how Christians have become God's children by Christ, the "Beloved," and of how as God's children they have gained an inheritance in Christ.

This dense passage is quite relevant for this solemnity of Mary. What can most fruitfully be emphasized in your proclamation is what humanity has gained by the saving life of Christ, which has come from Mary's cooperation with grace and in which we believers share.

As a member of a particular community of faith, you might imagine as you proclaim that you are in fact ministering to the living body of Christ, and that this ecclesial

GOSPEL Luke 1:26–38

A reading from the holy Gospel according to Luke

The angel **Gabriel** was sent from **God**
  to a town of **Galilee** called **Nazareth**,
  to a virgin betrothed to a man named **Joseph**,
  of the house of David,
  and the virgin's name was **Mary**.
And coming to her, he said,
  "**Hail**, full of **grace**! The **Lord** is with you."
But she was greatly **troubled** at what was said
  and **pondered** what sort of greeting this might be.
Then the angel said to her,
  "Do not be **afraid**, **Mary**,
  for you have found **favor** with God.
Behold, you will conceive in your womb and bear a **son**,
  and you shall **name** him **Jesus**.
He will be **great** and will be called **Son** of the **Most High**,
  and the Lord God will give him the **throne** of **David** his father,
  and he will **rule** over the house of **Jacob forever**,
  and of his Kingdom there will be **no end**."
But **Mary** said to the **angel**,
  "How can this **be**,
  since I have **no** relations with a **man**?"
And the angel said to her in reply,
  "The **Holy Spirit** will come upon you,
  and the **power** of the Most **High** will **overshadow** you.
Therefore the **child** to be **born**
  will be called **holy**, the Son of **God**.

These are among the most beloved persons of our tradition, so proclaim their names with care.
Galilee = GAL-ih-lee
Nazareth = NAZ-uh-reth

This is the scriptural source of the beginning of the familiar prayer, "Hail, Mary, full of grace, the Lord is with thee."

Jacob = JAY-kub

This section of the reading is fitting for Advent, so take your time and let the assembly catch the Advent echoes here.

---

assembly—however great or small, however lively or quiet, however active or contemplative in the celebration of the Lord's Supper, is made up of children adopted by God because of Christ's life. If you know and trust this to be so by God's love, your proclamation will reveal this by the freshness of your voice. You can depend on the words of the text so that the assembly can trust your living words mediating the scriptures to them, the living body of Christ.

It might seem a little odd to have a second reading on a solemnity of Mary in which Mary is not even mentioned. Yet because she is indeed the Mother of God, she is also the mother of the Church. In its teaching on the Church, the Second Vatican Council found in Mary a model for the Church. So what you proclaim here about believers sharing in the adoption and inheritance of Christ does have a revelatory theology about Mary, though it is not explicit in the passage. Mary's role is far more significant in the Gospels than in the letters of the New Testament. Your task here is to be clear about the Church as children of God, as those who have inherited God's grace from Christ's purpose and life.

GOSPEL Many believers do not understand what is celebrated on the Solemnity of the Immaculate Conception, thinking that it celebrates the conception of Jesus in the womb of Mary. But the feast actually celebrates the conception of Mary in the womb of her mother, Saint Ann. (The tradition of the saints gives us the name of Mary's parents, Ann and Joachim; they are not named in scripture.) The Church's Lectionary uses this account to show God's presence in a conception.

One of the most beloved parts of the Bible, this description of Mary's connection to her relative Elizabeth. Proclaim this part with care.

And **behold**, **Elizabeth**, your relative,
    has **also** conceived a son in her old age,
    and this is the **sixth** month for her who was called **barren**;
    for **nothing** will be **impossible** for **God**."
Mary said, "**Behold**, I am the **handmaid** of the Lord.
May it be **done** to me according to your **word**."
Then the angel **departed** from her.

The narrative has two basic parts, the setting of the context and the conversation between Gabriel and Mary. The first part introduces the main characters of the account—Gabriel, Mary, and Joseph—and the location, Nazareth. Take your time with this reading, for it can be both a blessing and a curse to proclaim a familiar narrative.

The second part is the dialogue between the angel and Mary, with their words and some identifying interjections. The assembly's grasp of the scene and its implications depend on your clear pronunciation of the proper names and accessible presentation of the course of the conversation. You have the printed text with its punctuation marks before you, and can use it to determine how to distinguish direct discourse from narrative in your proclamation so that even someone who does not know the story could follow the conversation clearly.

In addition to its connection to the solemnity, the Gospel passage today is fitting for Advent. Near the end of the passage the evangelist includes details about the Holy Spirit's role in the conception of Jesus and about Elizabeth's conceiving in her old age.

3RD SUNDAY OF ADVENT

Lectionary #8

READING I   Isaiah 61:1–2a, 10–11

Isaiah = ī-ZAY-uh

This is the part that Jesus reads in the synagogue at the beginning of his public ministry in the Gospel of Luke.

A reading from the Book of the Prophet Isaiah

The **spirit** of the Lord GOD is upon me,
    because the LORD has **anointed** me;
he has sent me to bring glad **tidings** to the **poor,**
    to **heal** the **brokenhearted,**
to proclaim **liberty** to the **captives**
    and **release** to the **prisoners,**
to announce a year of **favor** from the LORD
    and a day of **vindication** by our **God.**

The clothing images are lovely as they describe how the servant of the Lord has been adorned.

I rejoice **heartily** in the LORD,
    in my **God** is the joy of my **soul;**
for he has **clothed** me with a robe of **salvation**
    and **wrapped** me in a mantle of **justice,**
like a **bridegroom** adorned with a **diadem,**
    like a **bride** bedecked with her **jewels.**

Completing the beauty of the passage from Isaiah is this image of plants springing up in a garden.

As the **earth** brings forth its **plants,**
    and a **garden** makes its **growth** spring up,
so will the Lord GOD make **justice** and **praise**
    spring **up** before all the **nations.**

READING I Often as lector of the second reading on a Sunday, you will find a reading from the apostle Paul in which he has used first-person ("I," "me," "my") and second-person ("you," "your") pronouns. Paul personally knew many of the people to whom he wrote these letters and therefore wrote in this direct way. Now in this first reading, you find an equally personal statement.

   With this reading, you stand in the place of the prophet, and his words are realized by your voice as you minister to the Church. So when you proclaim such sentences as "The spirit of the Lord GOD is upon me," and I rejoice heartily in the LORD," and "in my God is the joy of my soul," imagine that you are delivering a passage of joy in your own experience of God's power in the world and in your life.

   In the second part of the reading, the servant of the Lord describes how God has clothed and adorned him as befits any child of God, ennobled by God's grace and favor. As you prepare, imagine yourself—and other members of your community—so clothed and adorned. The more vivid this description is to you, the more vivid it will be to those who listen to your proclamation.

READING II For centuries, one Sunday of Advent has been designated Gaudete Sunday. the Latin word *gaudete* is the imperative second-person plural form of the verb *gaudare,* "to rejoice," so it means, roughly, "all of you, rejoice!" You can see where this imperative from comes in the second line of the passage you prepare from 1 Thessalonians: "Rejoice always!" Saint Paul is addressing the community at

READING II   1 Thessalonians 5:16–24

A reading from the first Letter of Saint Paul to the Thessalonians

Brothers and sisters:
Rejoice **always**. Pray without **ceasing**.
In **all** circumstances give **thanks**,
    for this is the will of **God** for you in Christ **Jesus**.
Do not **quench** the Spirit.
Do not **despise** prophetic **utterances**.
Test everything; **retain** what is **good**.
Refrain from every kind of **evil**.

May the God of **peace** make you **perfectly** holy
    and may you **entirely**, **spirit**, **soul** and **body**,
    be preserved **blameless** for the coming of our Lord Jesus **Christ**.
The one who **calls** you is **faithful**,
    and he will also **accomplish** it.

Thessalonians = thes-uh-LOH-nee-unz

Here you start with commands: "rejoice!" "pray!" and "give thanks!"

The negative commands of this section, "do not quench," "do not despise," or its encouragement of discipline, "test!" "retain!" and "refrain!" are all toward the same end, waiting, as we do in Advent.

Read below on how to consider this passage and proclaim it as your prayer for your community of faith.

GOSPEL   John 1:6–8, 19–28

A reading from the holy Gospel according to John

A man named **John** was sent from **God**.
He came for **testimony**, to testify to the **light**,
    so that all might **believe** through him.
He was **not** the light,
    but came to **testify** to the light.

Emphasize the "light" imagery at this opening, for it might connect with the experience of those in the assembly who have decorated their homes and trees with lights.

Thessalonica, and encouraging them to rejoice as they await their sanctification. The tone of your proclamation should be joyful to reflect the apostle's command: rejoice!

The solemnity the Church awaits in Advent, Christmas, did not emerge in the Christian tradition until the fourth century, so the rejoicing that the apostle encouraged at Thessalonica in the middle of the first century was not about Christmas, even though they, like us, were waiting for "the coming of our Lord Jesus Christ." The coming the apostle wrote of was the coming of Christ at the end of time. In those days the followers

of Christ in the ministry of Paul were expecting the imminent return of Jesus, and this would happen at the end of the world.

Notice a few literary characteristics in the passage. The first section is positive, commanding the brothers and sisters about what they ought to do. The second section complements the first for it introduces the negatives, what the believers ought not do as they wait. The last section is a wonderful ending, for here the apostle offers a prayer on behalf of the community. As you proclaim, you offer the same prayer today on behalf of your community gathered before

you as you serve. If you can do so comfortably, commit the final three or four lines to memory, so that you can engage the liturgical assembly with eye contact as you offer this prayer on their behalf.

GOSPEL In the four weeks of Advent, the first two Sundays are traditionally about the coming of the Lord not at the birth of Jesus, but at the end of the world. Bernard of Clairvaux's First Sermon for Advent is helpful for reflection. He says

Levites = LEE-vīts
Jerusalem = juh-ROO-suh-lem

And **this** is the testimony of John.
When the Jews from Jerusalem sent **priests** and **Levites** to him
    to ask him, "Who **are** you?"
    he **admitted** and did not **deny** it,
    but admitted, "I am **not** the Christ."

The main part of the reading is this
exchange between the Jewish leaders
and the Baptist. Its theology is important,
but it is not an easy narrative to proclaim.
Elijah = ee-LĪ-juh

So they asked him,
    "What **are** you then? Are you **Elijah**?"
And he said, "I am **not**."
"Are you the **Prophet**?"
He answered, "**No**."
So they said to him,
    "Who **are** you, so we can give an **answer** to those who **sent** us?
What do you have to **say** for yourself?"
He said:
    "I am *the* **voice** *of one crying out in the* **desert**,
    make **straight** *the way of the* **LORD**,
    as Isaiah the **prophet** said."

Pharisees = FAIR-uh-seez

Some **Pharisees** were **also** sent.
They asked him,
    "Why then do you **baptize**
    if you are not the **Christ** or **Elijah** or the **Prophet**?"
John **answered** them,
    "**I** baptize with **water**;

This final piece from the lips of John is the
capstone of the passage.

    but there is one **among** you whom you do not **recognize**,
    the one who is coming **after** me,
    whose **sandal** strap I am not worthy to **untie**."
This happened in **Bethany** across the **Jordan**,
    where John was **baptizing**.

Bethany = BETH-uh-nee
Jordan = JOR-d*n

---

that in Advent we celebrate three "comings" of Christ: his coming in the flesh at the Incarnation, his coming into our hearts in the present, and his coming at the end of time. As Advent progresses, the season moves to the coming of Jesus in salvation history two millennia ago, and this takes up the last two Sundays, one dedicated to the coming of John the Baptist, the final one to the manifestation of God's Son in the birth of Jesus to Mary and Joseph. Though this last is usually what believers think we wait for when we observe Advent, we are really as much looking forward to the final coming

as we are looking back at the manger in Bethlehem.

In many Christian homes in North America, believers and their families have already decorated a tree or will soon do so. A traditional ingredient in the decorations are the lights, which symbolize the light that Jesus was for the world at his coming. This Gospel passage begins with distinguishing John from the "light." The link between the Gospel and the cultural practice would be strengthened by your own clear proclamation of this element.

Be careful as you study and prepare the middle verses of the passage, for it is a complex exchange between Jewish leaders and the Baptist, as they try to figure out why he is baptizing if he is neither a prophet nor the Messiah. Careful reading will help you grasp the back and forth exchange so that you can proclaim it effectively.

The summary is what has the closest implications for the Church as it remembers Jesus' coming, as John speaks of his ministry and of his relationship to Jesus. So after the final question from the leaders, pause before you deliver John's response.

4TH SUNDAY OF ADVENT

Lectionary #11

READING I   2 Samuel 7:1–5, 8b–12, 14a, 16

A reading from the second Book of Samuel

When King **David** was settled in his **palace**,
  and the LORD had given him **rest** from his **enemies** on
    every **side**,
  he said to **Nathan** the **prophet**,
  "Here **I** am living in a house of **cedar**,
  while the ark of **God** dwells in a **tent**!"
Nathan answered the king,
  "Go, do **whatever** you have in mind,
  for the **LORD** is with you."
But that night the LORD **spoke** to Nathan and said:
  "**Go**, tell my servant **David**, '**Thus** says the LORD:
  Should **you** build **me** a house to dwell in?'

"'It was **I** who took you from the **pasture**
  and from the care of the **flock**
  to be **commander** of my people **Israel**.
I have **been** with you **wherever** you went,
  and I have destroyed all your **enemies** before you.
And I will make you **famous** like the **great** ones of the **earth**.
I will fix a place for my people **Israel**;
  I will **plant** them so that they may **dwell** in their place
  without further **disturbance**.

Samuel = SAM-yoo-ul

This is a long reading from a historical book of the Old Testament. In preparation, be attentive to any words that are unfamiliar to you.

Nathan = NAY-thun

A large part of the reading includes direct discourse, from King David, from the prophet Nathan, and from the Lord. Consider how you will distinguish the various speakers by your tone.
cedar = SEE-der

Israel = IZ-ree-ul

READING I The historical books of the Old Testament are not generally well known. The first five books of the Old Testament, the Pentateuch, are proclaimed in the liturgy much more frequently.

The reading you prepare is powerful in itself and fitting for the end of Advent, the Sunday before Christmas, which this year falls on Sunday. In terms of the history of Israel, this passage is keen for its presentation of the multiple meanings of "house."

King David's house was made of precious wood, cedar, and the king had his idea because he lived in a house of precious materials while the ark of the covenant was housed in a mere tent.

Then the word of the Lord comes to the prophet Nathan, recalling how the Lord raised up David from shepherd to king, a "great one" of the earth. The message from the Lord expands the notion of "house," and it points to the people Israel as God's dwelling place, a dwelling place built up by David's ancestors and a dwelling place that endures in his descendants, the Jews yet in our own time. The word of the Lord foretells the eternity of David's "house," that is, the Lord's protection of his people Israel.

Mary was herself a dwelling place for the Son of God. We can pray the Litany of the Blessed Virgin Mary, in which the Mother of God is praised under the various names that have been taken into the litany. One of these names is "the Ark of the Covenant," for as the ark was the dwelling place of the law of Moses, so was the womb of Mary the dwelling place of the new law, that is, Jesus, the Son of God, whom she bore to the world for its salvation. In the reading, you hear the author's words about the "ark of

Neither shall the **wicked** continue to **afflict** them as they did
  of **old**,
  since the time I first appointed **judges** over my people Israel.
I will give you **rest** from all your enemies.
The LORD **also** reveals to you
  that **he** will establish a **house** for you.
And when your **time** comes and you rest with your **ancestors**,
  I will raise up your **heir** after you, sprung from your **loins**,
  and I will make his kingdom **firm**.
I will be a **father** to him,
  and he shall be a **son** to me.
Your **house** and your **kingdom** shall endure **forever** before me;
  your **throne** shall stand firm **forever**.' "

A summary of David's vocation and rise to kingship.

Pause at the end of this section, as the Lord turns from the past to Israel's future.

You might commit the last few sentences to memory, so that you can look up on the assembly as you speak of "your house" and "your kingdom."

READING II Romans 16:25–27

A reading from the Letter of Saint Paul to the Romans

Brothers and sisters:
To him who can **strengthen** you,
  according to my **gospel** and the proclamation of Jesus **Christ**,
  according to the revelation of the **mystery** kept **secret**
    for long ages
  but now **manifested** through the prophetic **writings** and,
  according to the **command** of the eternal **God**,
  made known to all nations to bring about the **obedience**
    of **faith**,
  to the only **wise** God, through Jesus **Christ**
  be **glory** forever and **ever**. **Amen**.

Romans = ROH-munz

Notice that the reading is one long sentence. See below for some thoughts about its meaning and your delivery.

Pause after "obedience of faith," for the remainder can be proclaimed as an exclamatory prayer which you yourself close with the "Amen." End the hymn of praise on a rousing note, for it is indeed a laudatory song to God. Put an exclamation point in your voice, your tone!

God," a metaphor that came to be adopted and applied to Mary in the litany.

READING II This passage from the letter to the Romans is an ancient literary form, a doxology, a hymn of praise and thanksgiving to God. In it the apostle Paul describes some of the many ways that God has acted on behalf of this Church at Rome and, in general, on behalf of all people. This doxology mentions God at the beginning and then proceeds to praise God by going into detail about how the Gospel

has been made manifest to all for salvation through Jesus.

It was a common device in antiquity to use the end of a letter to praise and thank the recipient for the ways the sender's life has been blessed by the presence and beneficence of the recipient.

You can see by the chapter and verse numbers of this reading that this is the very end of the letter to the Romans, for 16:27 is the last verse. Paul has already thanked many of the particular members of the Church at Rome, his fellow believers, ministers, and apostles in the proclamation of the

Gospel. So, having thanked the individuals and their work for the Church, the apostle turns to the source of all ministries and vocations, the source of the Church and of salvation—God—and delivers his final words of thanks and praise to the Creator of all things.

Notice that the reading is only one sentence. And that is not precisely true, for the text does not have the subject-verb-object form of a sentence. It is basically "to God be glory forever" with specifics included in a

GOSPEL   Luke 1:26–38

A reading from the holy Gospel according to Luke

The angel **Gabriel** was sent from God
    to a town of **Galilee** called **Nazareth**,
    to a **virgin** betrothed to a man named **Joseph**,
    of the house of **David**,
    and the **virgin's** name was **Mary**.
And coming to her, he said,
    "**Hail**, full of **grace**! The **Lord** is with you."
But she was greatly **troubled** at what was said
    and **pondered** what sort of **greeting** this might be.
Then the angel said to her,
    "Do not be **afraid**, Mary,
    for you have found **favor** with God.

"**Behold**, you will **conceive** in your womb and bear a **son**,
    and you shall name him **Jesus**.
He will be **great** and will be called Son of the Most **High**,
    and the Lord God will give him the **throne** of David his **father**,
    and he will **rule** over the house of Jacob **forever**,
    and of his **kingdom** there will be no **end**."
But Mary said to the angel,
    "How can this **be**,
    since I have no **relations** with a man?"
And the angel said to her in **reply**,
    "The Holy **Spirit** will come **upon** you,
    and the power of the Most **High** will **overshadow** you.

Gabriel = GAY-bree-ul
Galilee = GAL-ih-lee
Nazareth = NAZ-uh-reth
These are among the most beloved persons in the tradition, so proclaim the names with care.

This is the scriptural source of the beginning of the familiar prayer, "Hail, Mary, full of grace, the Lord is with thee."

Jacob = JAY-kub

This section is most fitting for Advent, so take your time and let the assembly hear the echoes of Advent in this passage.

long parenthetical list in the middle. Keep this literary structure in mind as you prepare and as you deliver the passage. Parse it out for yourself ahead of time in order to keep an unhurried pace as you proclaim, to know where you might pause for breath, and to know where you should put the emphases.

GOSPEL   This is one of the most familiar passages of the New Testament. It is the narrative of the conception of Jesus in the womb of Mary, and so leads the Church into the proper

chronology as we await the proclamation of Jesus' birth at Christmas. The theology of this narrative is what most believers think of during Advent, but the fact is that the first half of this season concentrates on the final coming of Christ at the end of time, not the first coming of Christ as a human being. Last week we heard about John the Baptist (as an adult) anticipating the coming of the Lord, and now, still moving backward in time as the season moves forward, we move to the conception of Jesus.

The narrative has two parts: the setting of the scene and the conversation between Gabriel and Mary. The first part introduces the characters of the account—Gabriel, Mary, and Joseph—and the location, Nazareth. Take your time with this, for it can be a blessing and a curse to proclaim such a familiar text.

The second part of the reading is the dialogue between the angel and Mary. Your listeners' understanding of the scene and its implications depend on your clear and comprehensible proclamation of the familiar

Mary's connection to her relative Elizabeth is one of the most beloved aspects of the Bible. Proclaim this part with care.

Therefore the **child** to be born
   will be called **holy**, the Son of **God**.
And **behold**, Elizabeth, your relative,
   has **also** conceived a son in her old **age**,
   and this is the sixth month for her who was called **barren**;
   for **nothing** will be impossible for **God**."
Mary said, "**Behold**, I am the **handmaid** of the Lord.
May it be **done** to me according to your word."
Then the angel **departed** from her.

names. Distinguish the words of the speakers from narrative with your tone so that someone who does not know the story would understand it.

You have an important task in preparing this passage, for the coming of Christ is a message of great consolation and hope to believers. It also helps them with their own preparations for the great feast a week from now. Proclaim this passage from your own conviction about the dawn of the new age that accompanied the Holy Spirit's message to the young Mary.

NATIVITY OF THE LORD: VIGIL

Lectionary #13

READING I   Isaiah 62:1–5

Isaiah = ī-ZAY-uh

Proclaim this pronoun, "I," as if the words were written to those to whom you proclaim, who are the "you" and "your" of the passage.
Zion = ZĪ-an
Jerusalem = juh-ROO-suh-lem

A reading from the Book of the Prophet Isaiah

For **Zion's** sake I will **not** be silent,
    for **Jerusalem's** sake I will **not** be quiet,
until her **vindication** shines forth like the dawn
    and her **victory** like a burning **torch**.

Nations shall **behold** your vindication,
    and **all** the kings your **glory**;
you shall be called by a **new** name
    pronounced by the mouth of the LORD.
You shall be a **glorious crown** in the hand of the LORD,
    a royal **diadem** held by your **God**.
No **more** shall people call you "**Forsaken**,"
    or your land "**Desolate**,"
but you shall be called "My **Delight**,"
    and your land "**Espoused**."
For the LORD **delights** in you
    and makes your land his **spouse**.
As a **young man** marries a **virgin**,
    your **Builder** shall marry **you**;
and as a **bridegroom** rejoices in his **bride**
    so shall **your** God rejoice in you.

Enunciate the phrases as if they were a single name. It might be easier to imagine the third one as "My-Delight," to help you do this.

Proclaim the Marriage and wedding images so that they come through clearly.

READING I   The prophet Isaiah guides us every Advent in our anticipation of the great solemnity of Christmas. And now on the feast itself, the prophet has the first word from scripture for all four Masses of Christmas—the vigil, at midnight, at dawn, and Christmas Day. Such a preponderance of the prophet Isaiah's words confirms how much this Old Testament book has contributed to the Gospel tradition of the birth of Jesus as well as how much the prophet has shaped the liturgical tradition of this solemnity.

The prophet's message that you will proclaim is a weighty and beautiful text, but its literary style and devices would have been more familiar to the Israelites than it is for your assembly. You might practice this passage a number of times to appropriate the content for a strong proclamation, particularly with the names in the third section.

Take your time and be clear with the middle verse, "You shall be a glorious crown," and then again toward the end of the passage, for the last part is striking. In it the relationship between God and God's people is compared to the intimate union of bride and groom. The intimacy suggested by the prophet for this celebration of the Incarnation can feel almost unnerving, yet God does indeed know us and love us this well.

READING II   Acts 13:16–17, 22–25

A reading from the Acts of the Apostles

When **Paul** reached **Antioch** in Pisidia and entered
   the **synagogue**,
  he **stood** up, **motioned** with his hand, and **said**,
   "Fellow **Israelites** and you others who are God-fearing, **listen**.
The God of this people **Israel** chose our ancestors
  and exalted the people during their **sojourn**
   in the land of **Egypt**.
With **uplifted** arm he **led** them out of it.
Then he removed **Saul** and raised up **David** as king;
  of him he **testified**,
   'I have found **David**, son of **Jesse**, a man after my own **heart**;
  he will carry out my **every** wish.'
From this man's **descendants** God, according to his promise,
  has brought to Israel a **savior**, **Jesus**.
John heralded his coming by proclaiming a **baptism** of **repentance**
  to all the people of **Israel**;
  and as John was completing his course, he would say,
   '**What** do you suppose that I **am**? I am **not** he.
Behold, one is coming **after** me;
  I am not **worthy** to unfasten the **sandals** of his **feet**.'"

This opening sets the context for what follows.
Antioch = ANN-tee-ahk
Pisidia = pih-SID-ee-uh
synagogue = SIN-uh-gog

From here forward it is Paul's speech to the assembly in the synagogue.
Israelites = IZ-ree-uh-līts
Egypt = EE-jipt

Jesse = JES-ee

This gives the excerpt a Christmas bearing.

This is familiar to us from the Gospels, where we hear John use this image of the sandals.

For yourself as the lector and medium of this beautiful scripture message, perhaps it would make for a more vital proclamation if you, like the prophet, imagine the love between yourself and someone you love. How much like home is it for you to be in the presence of your beloved? So it is to be in the Lord's presence, particularly in this time of celebrating the Incarnation, the Word made flesh and dwelling with us.

READING II As the proclaimer of this passage from Acts, you have two points to make. First, you set the scene for Paul's speech to his fellow Israelites. Then, you stand in Paul's stead and proclaim the words that Paul himself spoke in that ancient assembly of the synagogue. Although you want the congregation to hear the identification of character and place clearly, you might be even more animated, engaged, and engaging when you move to the speech itself, which begins, "Fellow Israelites and you others who are God-fearing, listen."

Paul's speech is more appropriate for the Christmas solemnity than one might at first realize, for the birth of Christ in these attentive people of faith is as vibrant an aspect of the Incarnation as is the birth to Mary and Joseph.

GOSPEL   Matthew 1:1–25

A reading from the holy Gospel according to Matthew

The book of the **genealogy** of Jesus **Christ**,
    the son of **David**, the son of **Abraham**.

Abraham became the father of **Isaac**,
    Isaac the father of **Jacob**,
    Jacob the father of **Judah** and his brothers.
Judah became the father of **Perez** and **Zerah**,
    whose **mother** was **Tamar**.
Perez became the father of **Hezron**,
    Hezron the father of **Ram**,
    Ram the father of **Amminadab**.
Amminadab became the father of **Nahshon**,
    Nahshon the father of **Salmon**,
    Salmon the father of **Boaz**,
    whose **mother** was **Rahab**.
Boaz became the father of **Obed**,
    whose **mother** was **Ruth**.
Obed became the father of **Jesse**,
    Jesse the father of **David** the king.

David became the father of **Solomon**,
    whose mother had been the **wife** of Uriah.
Solomon became the father of **Rehoboam**,
    Rehoboam the father of **Abijah**,
    Abijah the father of **Asaph**.
Asaph became the father of **Jehoshaphat**,
    Jehoshaphat the father of **Joram**,
    Joram the father of **Uzziah**.

This is the most challenging passage of the whole three-year Lectionary cycle to proclaim because of the many difficult names. Practice them so that you can proclaim them smoothly.
Abraham = AY-bruh-ham
Isaac = Ī-zik
Jacob = JAY-kub
Judah = JOO-duh
Perez = PAIR-ez
Zerah = ZEE-rah
Tamar = TAY-mar
Hezron = HEZ-run
Aram = AIR-um
Aminadab = uh-MIN-uh-dab
Nahshon = NAH-shun
Salmon = SAL-mun
Boaz = BOH-az
Rahab = RAY-hab
Obed = OH-bed
Ruth = rooth
Jesse = JES-ee

Solomon = SOL-uh-mun
Uriah = yoo-RĪ-uh
Rehoboam = ree-huh-BOH-um
Abijah = uh-BĪ-juh
Asaph = AY-saf
Jehoshaphat = jeh-HOH-shuh-fat
Joram = JOR-um
Uzziah = uh-ZĪ-uh

On the historical level, this speech can be taken as an anticipation of the Gospel reading of the long genealogy that follows. Paul's mention of God's mighty works among the Jews—that God "chose our ancestors," and "exalted the people during their sojourn in the land of Egypt," who "raised up David as king," and so on—these are episodes in the history of Israel that is implicit in the genealogy in the Gospel.

As you review this reading and anticipate your service as lector on Christmas Eve, be decisive about how you will stand in Paul's place and recount the history of the Jews, and how you will stand in the place of John the Baptist, saying, "I am not worthy," and so on. This is a key reading on a very solemn feast. You, like Paul, stand in an assembly of faith to deliver an important message.

GOSPEL   In the middle of this reading from Matthew there is a numerical symbolism. The genealogy is divided into three sections of 14 generations each—from Abraham to David, then from David to the Babylonian captivity (called "exile"), then from the captivity to Jesus, "who is called the Christ." You might similarly divide up the reading for your practicing. Get the first set down pat before you

22

NATIVITY OF THE LORD: VIGIL ■ DECEMBER 24, 2005

Jotham = JOH-thum
Ahaz = AY-haz
Hezekiah hez-eh-KĪ-uh
Manasseh = muh-NAS-uh
Amos = AY-m*s
Josiah = joh-SĪ-uh
Jechoniah = jek-oh-NĪ-uh
Babylon = BAB-ih-lon

Salathiel = suh-LAY-thee-ul
Zerubbabel = zuh-ROOB-uh-b*l
Abiud = uh-BĪ-uhd
Eliakim = ee-LĪ-uh-kim
Azor = AY-zor
Zadok = ZAD-dok

Slow down so that any whose attention may have wandered during the names will perk up and realize the evangelist's point about God's plan.

Uzziah became the father of **Jotham**,
   Jotham the father of **Ahaz**,
   Ahaz the father of **Hezekiah**.
Hezekiah became the father of **Manasseh**,
   Manasseh the father of **Amos**,
   Amos the father of **Josiah**.
Josiah became the father of **Jechoniah** and his brothers
   at the time of the **Babylonian exile**.

After the **Babylonian exile**,
   Jechoniah became the father of **Shealtiel**,
   Shealtiel the father of **Zerubbabel**,
   Zerubbabel the father of **Abiud**.
Abiud became the father of **Eliakim**,
   Eliakim the father of **Azor**,
   Azor the father of **Zadok**.
Zadok became the father of **Achim**,
   Achim the father of **Eliud**,
   Eliud the father of **Eleazar**.
Eleazar became the father of **Matthan**,
   Matthan the father of **Jacob**,
   Jacob the father of **Joseph**, the **husband** of **Mary**.
Of her was born **Jesus** who is called the **Christ**.

Thus the **total** number of generations
   from **Abraham** to **David**
   is **fourteen** generations;
   from **David** to the **Babylonian exile**,
   fourteen generations;
   from the **Babylonian exile** to the **Christ**,
   fourteen generations.

move on to the second, and so on to the third. It is imperative that you be familiar with the names so that you (the messenger) not become the center of attention and distract from the message (the word of God). As you prepare for the proclamation, take one of these sections at a time and practice it until you have proclaim it smoothly, even the more difficult names, like "Aminadab," "Rehoboam," and "Zerubbabel."

This is surely one of the most difficult and most beautiful Gospels in the Lectionary. Most will opt for the shorter version, presuming that the assembly will be bored with the proclamation of these many ancestors. But think about the quirky and odd and unique characters in your own family's history. Though the names in this Jewish genealogy might sound boring, even a little research into the characters and stories of those who bore these names will reveal that this family is just as vivid and strange as all families!

There are some well-known figures of Israel's history here, with Abraham, Isaac, Jacob, Solomon, and David, and these you need to pronounce accurately. But most of the names here are not as familiar. With these, it is as important that you proclaim them confidently as that you proclaim them accurately. The women in the genealogy are very important: Tamar, Rahab, Ruth, the wife of Uriah, and of course, Mary, Jesus' mother. Scripture scholar Raymond Brown suggests

Be emphatic here with this first line that establishes the narrative setting.

Matthew fashions Joseph after the patriarch Joseph (of the end of the book of Genesis).

Emphasize the role of the Holy Spirit.

Because so much of our Christmas hymnody uses the word Emmanuel and its meaning, "God is with us," proclaim this part of the reading with clarity.

The ending is a calm resolution.

Now **this** is how the **birth** of Jesus Christ came about.
When his mother **Mary** was betrothed to **Joseph**,
 but **before** they lived together,
 she was found with **child** through the Holy **Spirit**.
Joseph her **husband**, since he was a **righteous** man,
 yet unwilling to expose her to **shame**,
 decided to divorce her quietly.
Such was his intention when, **behold**,
 the **angel** of the Lord **appeared** to him in a **dream** and said,
 "**Joseph**, son of **David**,
 do **not** be afraid to take Mary your **wife** into your home.
For it is through the Holy **Spirit**
 that this child has been **conceived** in her.
She will bear a **son** and you are to name him **Jesus**,
 because he will save his **people** from their **sins**."
All this took place to **fulfill**
 what the **Lord** had said through the **prophet**:
 *Behold, the **virgin** shall **conceive** and bear a **son**,*
 *and they shall name him **Emmanuel**,*
 which means "**God** is **with** us."
When Joseph **awoke**,
 he did as the angel of the Lord had **commanded** him
 and took his wife into his home.
He had **no** relations with her until she bore a **son**,
 and he **named** him Jesus.

[Shorter: Matthew 1:18–25]

that these women appear because their unions with their partners was irregular or extraordinary, or perhaps because the women demonstrated initiative as instruments of God's plan in salvation, or even that these women were Gentiles or associated with Gentiles, and thus demonstrate that God goes outside the expected boundaries to establish his people. Whatever the combination of reasons for their place, do them justice in highlighting their role in salvation according to the family tree of Jesus.

NATIVITY OF THE LORD: MIDNIGHT

Lectionary #14

READING I   Isaiah 9:1–6

Isaiah = Ī-ZAY-uh

The metaphors of light and darkness are important to the rituals and theology of Advent and Christmas.

A reading from the Book of the Prophet Isaiah

The people who walked in **darkness**
    have seen a great **light**;
upon those who **dwelt** in the land of **gloom**
    a **light** has **shone**.
You have brought them **abundant** joy
    and great **rejoicing**,
as they **rejoice** before you as at the **harvest**,
    as people make **merry** when dividing spoils.
For the **yoke** that **burdened** them,
    the **pole** on their **shoulder**,
and the **rod** of their **taskmaster**
    you have **smashed**, as on the day of Midian.
For **every** boot that tramped in **battle**,
    every cloak rolled in **blood**,
    will be burned as **fuel** for **flames**.
For a **child** is **born** to us, a **son** is **given** us;
    upon his shoulder **dominion** rests.
They name him Wonder-**Counselor**, God-**Hero**,
    Father-**Forever**, Prince of **Peace**.
His dominion is **vast**
    and forever **peaceful**,

Midian = MID-ee-un

This part of Isaiah's prophecy is foundational for much of what became central to the Christian tradition and theology of the Savior.

Each of these phrases with dashes is a name.

READING I   The lights of Christmas trees are reflections of the theology of light at the heart of this great solemnity, and indeed part of the Christian tradition at all times. The many lights are images of the one great Light of our lives, the gift of God's life in us, Emmanuel, God-with-us. This is the gift of grace in the incarnate life of Jesus of Nazareth, the light of the world. The opening prayer for this Mass at midnight or Mass during the night says of God, "Father, / you make this holy night radiant / with the splendor of Jesus Christ our Light," and at all the liturgies of this great feast the image of light is central.

Christmas found its place in the calendar because it was a consolation at the darkest time of the year, near the winter solstice (December 21). When the days are shortest, the Church looks for its light, in the lengthening of the days and in the coming of Christ. Calendar and theology work together, at least in the northern hemisphere, where the nativity feast comes during the darkest days of winter.

This image of light comes from Isaiah: "The people who walked in darkness have seen a great light." The same verse lists the names by which the prophet suggests the Messiah be called.

From the historical point-of-view, one might think of this deed of salvation as already accomplished in Christ and in the Church, which is so, but the Gospel needs to be proclaimed and heard again and again, year after year, in each community of faith and in each Christian life. Your ministry as reader is part of this hearing and manifestation of Christ.

from David's **throne**, and over his **kingdom**,
    which he confirms and sustains
by **judgment** and **justice**,
    both now and **forever**.
The **zeal** of the LORD of **hosts** will **do** this!

READING II   Titus 2:11–14

Titus = Tī-tus

A reading from the Letter of Saint Paul to Titus

Beloved:
The **grace** of **God** has **appeared**, saving **all**
    and training us to reject **godless** ways and **worldly** desires
    and to live **temperately**, **justly**, and **devoutly** in this age,
    as we await the **blessed** hope,
the **appearance** of the **glory** of our great **God**
and savior Jesus **Christ**,
who gave himself for us to **deliver** us from all **lawlessness**
and to **cleanse** for himself a people as his own,
eager to do what is **good**.

Emphasize "appeared" for its Christmas significance.

Another strong phrase for the feast is this "appearance of the glory . . ." Make your reading capture a tone of joyful wonder and awe fitting for announcing a manifestation of God.

GOSPEL   Luke 2:1–14

A reading from the holy Gospel according to Luke

In those days a **decree** went out from Caesar **Augustus**
    that the whole **world** should be **enrolled**.
This was the **first** enrollment,
    when **Quirinius** was governor of **Syria**.

There are many proper names in these few verses. Do not rush through them.
Caesar = SEE-zer
Augustus = aw-GUS-tus
Quirinius = kwih-RIN-ee-us
Syria = SEER-ee-uh

The reading from the prophet is not only key to the Christmas tradition, but probably contributed to the shaping of that tradition because it would have influenced the writers of the Gospels. Your clear and confident proclamation can also shape and refresh the hearts and souls of the assembly.

READING II   We do not hear much from the letter of Paul to Titus in the Lectionary. This reading you are preparing for tonight is one instance, and there is another short excerpt assigned for the

Christmas Mass at dawn. The same two passages are combined into a single reading for the Baptism of the Lord in Year C.

There is no one named Titus mentioned in the Acts of the Apostles, but there is a companion of Paul named Titus in the letter to the Galatians and also in the second letter to the Corinthians.

Because the feast and context are so grand and this passage is so short, consider how to begin and end the reading with a dignified, prayerful pause to gather the attention of the assembly. The reading should not disappear because of its brevity.

This reading is very fitting for the celebration of Christmas, and the exhortation to the people of God is as appropriate in our time as it was when written many centuries ago. It makes a connection between the manifestation of the grace of God and the moral life, between the gift of salvation in Christ and the transformation of human ways. Rejecting worldly desires doesn't always come to mind when we think of the celebration of this holiday, but these are the words you will proclaim.

Pause here to allow for the transition
from the universal ("all the world")
to the particular in the persons of Joseph
and Mary.
Galilee = GAL-ih-lee
Judea = joo-DEE-uh

So all went to be enrolled, each to his own town.
And **Joseph** too went up from **Galilee** from the town of **Nazareth**
   to **Judea**, to the city of **David** that is called **Bethlehem**,
   because he was of the house and family of **David**,
   to be enrolled with **Mary**, his **betrothed**, who was with **child**.
While they were there,
   the **time** came for her to **have** her child,
   and she gave **birth** to her **firstborn son**.
She **wrapped** him in **swaddling** clothes and **laid** him in a **manger**,
   because there was no **room** for them in the **inn**.

The shepherds are important characters in
the story of Christmas.

Now there were **shepherds** in that region living in the **fields**
   and keeping the **night** watch over their **flock**.
The **angel** of the Lord **appeared** to them
   and the **glory** of the Lord shone **around** them,
   and they were struck with great **fear**.
The **angel** said to them,

Proclaim this announcement of the angel
with clarity and without haste.

   "Do **not** be **afraid**;
   for **behold**, I proclaim to you good **news** of great **joy**
   that will be for **all** the **people**.
For **today** in the city of **David**
   a **savior** has been born for you who is **Christ** and **Lord**.
And **this** will be a **sign** for you:
   you will find an **infant** wrapped in **swaddling** clothes
   and **lying** in a **manger**."
And **suddenly** there was a multitude of the heavenly **host**
      with the angel,
   praising **God** and saying:
      "**Glory** to God in the **highest**

Take your time here and be clear, for the
connection between the liturgical hymn of
"Glory to God in the highest" and this
verse can be effective.

      and on earth **peace** to those on whom his favor **rests**."

Be most forthright when Paul speaks of the appearance of God's glory and our savior Jesus Christ.

GOSPEL Luke included the detail about the vast census to emphasize the universal significance of the birth of this child. Since his Gospel was written, the account of the life of Jesus has indeed been heard around the globe. From the universality at the start of the passage, the account narrows down quickly to the main characters: Joseph, Mary, and the child they were about to have.

One of the wonderful literary qualities of the Christmas account is that each hope or joy is set next to something scary or grim. In this Christmas Gospel, the joy of the birth is set in balance with the travelers with no room in the inn. The shepherds are at first terrified by the angel; then the angel gives them good news of great joy. The Savior whose birth is heralded by angels is lying in a manger, a feeding trough for animals.

In all, this is a great account, and your proclamation of the Gospel is so important for this feast, as well as the keystone for the seasons of Advent and Christmas that precede and follow. The passage ends with the heavenly host praising God, and as proclaimer you stand in the place of that multitude of angels. End your proclamation with joy in the words from the Gospel and the liturgy: "Glory to God in the highest."

NATIVITY OF THE LORD: DAWN

Lectionary #15

READING I   Isaiah 62:11–12

Isaiah = Ī-ZAY-uh

Proclaim with joy what the Lord has proclaimed to the ends of the earth.

See the recommendation below on how to deal with this verse.

A reading from the Book of the Prophet Isaiah

See, the LORD proclaims
   to the **ends** of the **earth**:
say to daughter **Zion**,
   your **savior** comes!
Here is his **reward** with him,
   his **recompense** before him.
They shall be called the **holy** people,
   the **redeemed** of the LORD,
and you shall be called "**Frequented**,"
   a city that is **not forsaken**.

READING I   As throughout the season of Advent and for each of the liturgies of this great solemnity of Christmas, the reading that you prepare is from the prophet Isaiah. Unlike most of the other readings, this one is short, so you will need to communicate its message as it bears on the feast and on the Gospel as clearly as possible, without rushing.

   The brevity of the passage calls you to pause after the identification opening— "A reading from the book of the Prophet Isaiah"—so that the assembly is poised to hear the word as you begin to proclaim the biblical words right from the start.

   The meaning of the passage is not readily clear, so consider its theology first. The last sentence is the one that is a little tricky. The prophet was telling the people Israel that the coming of the Lord would change the fortunes of the people, and that as a result not only would the people be redeemed, but the beloved city itself would be regarded in a new way. Their city had been sacked, abandoned, forsaken. With the coming of the savior, it would be inhabited once again, even a place for visitors, that is, "Frequented."

   Don't be distracted by the capital letter in "Frequented". It merely signifies that this is a name, not a description. The action of the Lord will give the city a new name, just as Abram was given a new name.

**Titus is unfamiliar to many. Be clear as you read the name of the book.
Titus = Tī-tus**

Stress this mention of Baptism, so important to the mission of the Church and the theology of Christmas.

READING II   Titus 3:4–7

A reading from the Letter of Saint Paul to Titus

Beloved:
When the **kindness** and **generous** love
of **God** our savior **appeared**,
not because of any righteous deeds **we** had done
but because of his **mercy**,
he **saved** us through the **bath** of rebirth
and **renewal** by the Holy **Spirit**,
whom he **richly** poured out on us
through Jesus Christ our **savior**,
so that we might be **justified** by his **grace**
and become **heirs** in **hope** of eternal **life**.

READING II See the commentary on Reading II at the Mass at midnight, page 25. Because this passage is so short, be mindful of how you begin the reading so that the assembly is poised to hear it right from the start.

This reading makes explicit the connection between the appearance of the Savior and the "bath of rebirth," a clear reference to Baptism. Not many Christians think of their own Baptism as participating in the Paschal Mystery in as serious a way as the birth of Christ, or that their Baptism has salvific consequences for the world around them. Since the reading makes this link, make the most of this mention of Baptism on the solemnity of Christmas.

At Mary's conception of Jesus, the Holy Spirit was sent to begin the Incarnation of the Savior. Likewise, according to the passage you proclaim, the Holy Spirit is poured out on the Church and on each of us at this feast of Christmas as a continuation of that salvation long ago.

GOSPEL Each of the Christmas liturgies—vigil, night, dawn, and day—has its own Gospel narrative, and in the dawn liturgy, the shepherds of the Gospel of Luke are featured. For people who live in places where there are no sheep and no shepherds, one can imagine the shepherds as romantic figures. But tending sheep was not then and is not now a romantic business, and, for the original community for

GOSPEL   Luke 2:15–20

A reading from the holy Gospel according to Luke

When the **angels** went away from them to **heaven**,
   the **shepherds** said to one another,
   "Let us go, then, to **Bethlehem**
   to see this thing that has taken place,
   which the **Lord** has made known to us."
So they went in haste and found **Mary** and **Joseph**,
   and the **infant** lying in the **manger**.
When they saw this,
   they made known the **message**
   that had been told them about this **child**.
All who heard it were **amazed**
   by what had been told them by the **shepherds**.
And **Mary** kept all these things,
   reflecting on them in her **heart**.
Then the shepherds returned,
   glorifying and **praising** God
   for all they had **heard** and **seen**,
   just as it had been told to them.

Pause between the various elements of
the narrative.

Because the mother of Jesus is so beloved
and this passage reflects her feelings,
emphasize this sentence.

The shepherds, as they proclaim and
praise, are a model for you who do
the same.

which the Gospel was written, the shepherds would not have been attractive. They were outsiders, and dirty ones at that. The account is spare, and so we don't get the details of their appearance and their place in society, details that might keep us from romanticizing the holy family and their visitors gathered around the crib.

Moreover, the nativity sets and crèches in our homes are often set up with the shepherds already present at the birth, but Gospel here reveals that the angel tells them of the great event only after it "has taken place."

The Christmas Gospel is a very familiar narrative. Prepare for it so that you can proclaim it with freshness, so that those listening might hear it as if for the first time.

The passage has four basic elements that move the account along. The shepherds set out, they find the family and report what the angel told them, Mary takes all this to heart, and the shepherds return. That's a lot of action for such a short passage, so take your time. Proclaim it with the exuberance and joy of this great feast.

NATIVITY OF THE LORD: DAY

Lectionary #16

READING I Isaiah 52:7–10

A reading from the Book of the Prophet Isaiah

How **beautiful** upon the **mountains**
    are the **feet** of him who brings glad **tidings**,
announcing **peace**, bearing good **news**,
    announcing **salvation**, and saying to **Zion**,
    "Your God is **King**!"

Hark! Your **sentinels** raise a cry,
    together they shout for **joy**,
for they see **directly**, before their eyes,
    the LORD **restoring** Zion.
Break out together in **song**,
    O **ruins** of Jerusalem!
For the LORD **comforts** his people,
    he **redeems** Jerusalem.
The LORD has **bared** his holy arm
    in the sight of all the nations;
all the **ends** of the **earth** will **behold**
    the **salvation** of our God.

Each of the words ending in "-ing" is describing "him who bring glad tidings." Do not rush through these even though they are grammatically similar; make each a clear description of the messenger.
Isaiah = Ī-ZAY-uh
Zion = ZĪ-ahn
sentinels = SEN-tih-nuls

The first half of the reading is more exuberant than the second. This part connects well with the acclamation about the messenger.
Jerusalem = juh-ROO-suh-lem

Continue the positive tone, but be aware of the sad history that preceded the Lord's comfort, redemption, and restoration.

READING I This reading gives a boost to ministers of the word. It begins with this compliment: "How beautiful upon the mountain are the feet" of the messenger who brings glad tidings, and so on. Though you will not actually be standing "upon the mountains" as you proclaim, you are bringing good news and announcing salvation. Take the compliment from the prophet to heart for this Christmas liturgy, and let it refresh you in your work for the Church.

The joy and good news for the people of Israel did not come out of their own history, for life had indeed been painful and their hopes dashed. The prophecy is addressed directly to the "ruins of Jerusalem," to a glory that had been destroyed. As you prepare this passage, keep that in mind alongside the fact that for many in your parish community, the celebration of a grand holiday may not be so joyous this year. These people might be more attentive to Isaiah's address to the "ruins" than to the exuberance of the message. You can echo the Lord as described here and bring comfort to the people.

The reading has two basic elements. The first part is more exuberant. As you prepare, think of the glad tidings as the Christmas message in our time, for we know that the Lord is present among us today, as he was on the day of his birth.

The second element encourages the people after their time of strife and sorrow. The prophet calls the people to join in

READING II   Hebrews 1:1–6

Hebrews = HEE-brooz

This is an overview of God's speaking to humanity in history, culminating in the "word" of the Son.

This section is quite dense, so do not rush through it.

This final part can be difficult because of the string of three quotations. Be careful with this so that the assembly is not lost.

A reading from the Letter to the Hebrews

Brothers and sisters:
In times **past**, God spoke in partial and various ways
    to our **ancestors** through the **prophets**;
      in these **last** days, he has spoken to us through the **Son**,
      whom he made **heir** of all things
      and **through** whom he created the **universe**,
      who is the **refulgence** of his **glory**,
      the very **imprint** of his **being**,
      and who **sustains** all things by his mighty **word**.
When he had accomplished **purification** from **sins**,
    he took his **seat** at the right hand of the **Majesty** on high,
    as far **superior** to the **angels**
    as the **name** he has inherited is more **excellent** than theirs.

For to **which** of the angels did God ever say:
    *You are my son; **this** day I have **begotten** you?*
Or again:
    *I will be a **father** to him, and **he** shall be a **son** to me?*
And again, when he leads the **firstborn** into the world, he says:
    *Let all the **angels** of God **worship** him.*

singing because the Lord has rescued them. Announce this good news as if for the first time.

READING II You can see from the citation that this reading is the very beginning of the letter to the Hebrews. This book of the New Testament is wonderful in many ways, theologically complex and with a unique vocabulary. For this reason this reading is not an easy one for proclamation. Before practicing it aloud, consider its meaning so that it will be familiar to you

before you start practicing the physical and mechanical aspects of the delivery.

The first part of the reading is a kind of theological overview, acknowledging that God has spoken in different ways and people over the centuries, but that these have all been fulfilled in what has been spoken in the Son. (This is unique at Christmas because it sees the birth of Christ in God's speaking as well as in the manger at Bethlehem.)

The passage then moves on to a description of who this Son is and what is accomplished in his very existence. As you

consider this part, you will see that it is is theologically rich but rhetorically difficult.

Finally, the passage shifts. Here the writer is asking questions, citing scripture. The scripture passages he quotes are not themselves questions; the questions are about the passages.

As always, prepare the reading as if those hearing you will not have the text and its punctuation marks in front of them. Let your tone make it clear when you are reading the cited passages in quotation marks. It might be helpful to highlight the three passages in your *Workbook* to remind you to

The philosophical theology of this opening prologue is dense, but preparation will enable you to read it with clarity and conviction.

This metaphor of light begins a more concrete narrative.

Later in the Gospel of John, Jesus squarely declares, "I am the light of the world." This anticipates that image.

GOSPEL   John 1:1–18

A reading from the holy Gospel according to John

In the **beginning** was the **Word**,
   and the Word was **with God**,
   and the Word **was** God.
He was in the **beginning** with God.
All things came to be **through** him,
   and **without** him **nothing** came to be.
What came to be through him was **life**,
   and this life was the **light** of the human **race**;
the **light** shines in the **darkness**,
   and the **darkness** has not overcome it.
A man named **John** was sent from God.
He came for **testimony**, to testify to the **light**,
   so that **all** might **believe** through him.
He was **not** the light,
   but came to **testify** to the light.
The **true** light, which enlightens **everyone**,
   was coming into the world.
He was **in** the world,
   and the world came to be **through** him,
   but the world did not **know** him.
He came to what was his own,
   but his **own** people did **not** accept him.

find a way to capture the difference between the words of the author of Hebrews and the words that the author cites.

GOSPEL The Gospel of John does not have a nativity narrative as do the Gospels of Matthew and Luke. But it does have a narrative of Jesus' origins, and it begins with those very words, "In the beginning." Though the narrative may not be as engaging as those infancy stories of Matthew and Luke, it has contributed enormously to the Christian theological tradition.

Be assertive with it, even with its philosophical vocabulary. The end of the opening section comes together with the metaphor of light, which will occupy the next section.

Recall that the Gospel of John alone includes the saying of Jesus, "I am the light of the world." That comes later in the Gospel, but here already the evangelist has introduced light and darkness. Light and darkness play key roles throughout the Gospel, beginning with this prologue.

The next section is a summary of the Gospel's start, about Jesus' coming into the world and the world not receiving him. The

use of the first-person plural—"made his dwelling among us," "we saw," and "we have all received"—enables you, as the proclaimer, to bring this ancient text up to the present. Proclaim it as if it were written for your community, and as if it were written for the proclamation that you deliver.

But to those who **did** accept him
 he gave **power** to become **children** of **God**,
 to those who believe in his name,
 who were born not by **natural** generation
 nor by **human** choice nor by a **man's** decision
 but of **God**.
 And the Word became **flesh**
  and made his **dwelling** among us,
  and we saw his **glory**,
  the glory as of the Father's only **Son**,
  full of **grace** and **truth**.
John **testified** to him and cried out, saying,
 "**This** was he of whom I said,
 'The one who is coming **after** me ranks **ahead** of me
 because he existed **before** me.'"
From his **fullness** we have **all received**,
 grace in place of **grace**,
 because while the **law** was given through **Moses**,
 grace and **truth** came through Jesus **Christ**.
No one has ever **seen** God.
The only **Son**, God, who is at the Father's **side**,
 has **revealed** him.

[Shorter: John 1:1–5, 9–14]

MARY, MOTHER OF GOD

Lectionary #18

READING I   Number 6:22 – 27

A reading from the Book of Numbers

The LORD said to **Moses**:
"**Speak** to **Aaron** and his sons and **tell** them:
    This is how you shall **bless** the Israelites.
Say to them:
    The LORD **bless** you and **keep** you!
    The LORD let his face **shine** upon you,
        and be **gracious** to you!
    The LORD look upon you **kindly**
        and give you **peace**!
So shall they invoke my **name** upon the **Israelites**,
    and I will **bless** them."

The commentary below identifies the layers of this reading. Pause at each transition from one speaker to the next.
Moses = MOH-ziz
Aaron = AIR-un
Israelites = IZ-ree-uh-līts
Take your time with this blessing to help the assembly appreciate its beauty.

This is a summary verse after the blessing.

READING II   Galatians 4:4 – 7

A reading from the Letter of Saint Paul to the Galatians

Brothers and sisters:
When the **fullness** of time had **come**, **God** sent his **Son**,
    born of a **woman**, born under the law,
    to **ransom** those under the law,
    so that **we** might receive **adoption** as **sons**.

Galatians = guh-LAY-shunz

This "born of a woman" is the kernel of this passage for this solemnity. Proclaim it with deliberateness.

READING I There are a number of layers to this reading, and it will help your proclamation if you are aware of these layers. The innermost core is the blessing itself, and this core will sound familiar. This is what Aaron and his sons will say to the Israelites.

Moving outward, the next layer identifies Moses as the one who will tell Aaron and his sons what to say.

The next layer moving still further out identifies the Lord as the one telling Moses. This makes the reading a bit complex, for you are telling the assembly what the Lord told Moses to tell Aaron and his sons to say to the people. You might pause slightly between these layers so that there is less chance for confusion. It is a relatively short reading, but read it with a deliberate pace.

At the end of the reading is a kind of summary wrapping up the proclamation.

READING II This passage is assigned to this solemnity of Mary, Mother of God, because of four words in the English translation of Paul, "born of a woman."

A good emphasis for your proclamation would be to highlight the juxtaposition of "woman," referring to Mary, and "Father!," referring to God. This balance of the feminine and masculine in the passage is lovely, for it both exalts the role of Mary, as the one chosen by God, and appreciates the gift of life and faith given by the generosity of God the Father.

Overall, the passage is short, only three sentences. There is absolutely no reason to rush. If you tend to deliver the readings too quickly, a short reading such as this is a prime opportunity to practice pacing, so

As **proof** that you are sons,
God sent the **Spirit** of his **Son** into our **hearts**,
crying out, "**Abba**, **Father!**"
So you are no longer a **slave** but a **son**,
and if a **son** then also an **heir**, through **God**.

This verse has great theological weight, for it reveals that each of us is a a child of God, and therefore like the Son.

GOSPEL Luke 2:16 – 21

A reading from the holy Gospel according to Luke

**As this reading reminds us, we are still in the Christmas season.
Bethlehem = BETH-luh-hem**

The **shepherds** went in **haste** to **Bethlehem**
and found **Mary** and **Joseph**,
and the **infant** lying in the **manger**.
When they saw this,
they made **known** the message
that had been **told** them about this child.
All who **heard** it were **amazed**
by what had been **told** them by the **shepherds**.
And **Mary** kept all these things,
reflecting on them in her **heart**.

Emphasize this verse for in this the Church, like the shepherds, is prompted to be "glorifying and praising God for all they had heard and seen."

Then the **shepherds** returned,
glorifying and **praising** God
for all they had **heard** and **seen**,
just as it had been told to them.

The focus shifts in this final verse. Pause before it to mark the transition from the scene with the shepherds to the action of the naming and circumcision.

When **eight** days were completed for his **circumcision**,
he was named **Jesus**, the name given him by the **angel**
before he was **conceived** in the womb.

---

that you can proclaim a short passage in the most fruitful way for the building up the Church.

GOSPEL This solemnity focuses not on one particular event in the life of Jesus but on the maternity of Mary. It arose from fifth-century contentions about Mary's role in salvation history. The debate took place in the year 431 in the city of Ephesus, the same place to which the New Testament letter to the Ephesians was written.

In terms of the proclamation, this account has a few different narrative elements, characters, and places. Notice the changes, and pause slightly as the focus shifts. First there are angels and shepherds, next the holy family, then Mary herself, back to the shepherds, and finally on to the circumcision and naming.

On this solemnity, when we remember and celebrate the maternity of Mary—in the life of Jesus, in the life of the Church, and in the life of the world—proclaim the reading by highlighting the Mother of God.

EPIPHANY OF THE LORD

Lectionary #20

READING I Isaiah 60:1–6

Isaiah = Ī-ZAY-uh

From its earliest days, the feast has carried images of light and darkness. Emphasize these elements in the first section.

A reading from the Book of the Prophet Isaiah

Rise up in splendor, Jerusalem! Your light has come,
    the glory of the LORD shines upon you.
See, darkness covers the earth,
    and thick clouds cover the peoples;
but upon you the LORD shines,
    and over you appears his glory.
Nations shall walk by your light,
    and kings by your shining radiance.
Raise your eyes and look about;
    they all gather and come to you:
your sons come from afar,
    and your daughters in the arms of their nurses.

Then you shall be radiant at what you see,
    your heart shall throb and overflow,
for the riches of the sea shall be emptied out before you,
    the wealth of nations shall be brought to you.
Caravans of camels shall fill you,
    dromedaries from Midian and Ephah;
all from Sheba shall come
    bearing gold and frankincense,
    and proclaiming the praises of the LORD.

This final verse will please listeners who have camels in their nativity sets at home.
Midian = MID-ee-un
Ephah = EE-fah
Sheba = SHEE-buh
frankincense = FRANK-in-sens

READING I The account we know from the Gospel of Matthew has precedents in the Old Testament, and this is one of them.

Notice that the reading has three basic parts. In your proclamation, emphasize in particular the imagery of light and dark, for the prayers for this day draw on these metaphors. Today's opening prayer prays, "Father, . . . Lead us to your glory in heaven by the light of faith" and the preface for the eucharistic prayer says, "his glory has shone among us." If you are clear in proclaiming these images of light and radiance and brightness on the one hand, and darkness and thick clouds at the other, the prayer texts will have the chance to sink into the liturgical experience of the assembly more deeply.

Be careful, as ever, with the place names. It is more important that you proclaim them with confidence than with exact accuracy.

READING II Since the Gospel has the wise men and the first reading has gold and frankincense, their relation to this day is clear. But the purpose in having the letter to the Ephesians on Epiphany is not as apparent.

The early tradition of the Church found in the wise men examples of strangers and foreigners who would find the faith attractive even though they were from faraway places with strange-sounding names. The feast of Epiphany was a celebration, among other things, of the universality of the Christian message. Look, the feast exclaims, even wise men from the east are on their way!

In the first century, the biggest social challenge to the Church was not Magi

READING II   Ephesians 3:2–3a, 5–6

Ephesians = ee-FEE-zhunz

The author assumes that readers (and hearers) have heard someone addressing this topic already.

Pause slightly before "It was not made known . . ."

Gentiles = JEN-tils
coheirs = co-airs

A reading from the Letter of Saint Paul to the Ephesians

Brothers and sisters:
You have **heard** of the **stewardship** of God's **grace**
    that was given to me for your **benefit**,
    namely, that the **mystery** was made **known** to me
        by **revelation**.
It was not made known to people in **other** generations
    as it has **now** been revealed
    to his **holy** apostles and **prophets** by the **Spirit**:
    that the **Gentiles** are **coheirs**, **members** of the **same body**,
    and **copartners** in the **promise** in Christ **Jesus**
        through the **gospel**.

GOSPEL   Matthew 2:1–12

Bethlehem = BETH-luh-hem
Judea = joo-DEE-uh
Herod = HAIR-ud

This opening sets the stage for what is to happen.

A reading from the holy Gospel according to Matthew

When **Jesus** was born in **Bethlehem** of Judea,
    in the days of King **Herod**,
    behold, **magi** from the **east** arrived in **Jerusalem**, saying,
    "**Where** is the newborn **king** of the Jews?
We saw his **star** at its **rising**
    and have **come** to do him **homage**."

on camels, but Gentiles, non-Jews, who wanted to join. The issue of whether Gentile Christians should have to accept the whole of the Mosaic law in their life with Christ was splitting the Church in its earliest days. The reading you will proclaim comes out of this challenge.

The Church in Ephesus was far from the birthplace of Christianity in Jerusalem and Palestine, so the message about welcoming and receiving Gentiles would have been very important in that time and place. The apostle makes the point very clear: "The Gentiles have become fellow heirs, mem-

bers of the same body, and sharers in the promise." They are not to be excluded or discriminated against, the apostle commands his fellow Jewish Christians. This would have been hard for many of them to hear, because many were not receptive to Gentiles as members.

Your proclamation of this message can be vibrant if you think of its scope more broadly than its first-century history. The message about receiving those unlike ourselves is so fundamental that the reading is meaningful even without the link to the early division.

GOSPEL   This is a long and familiar account from the Gospel of Matthew, among the best known of all the stories from the Gospels. Artists have long depicted the Magi bearing their gifts to the infant Christ in romantic settings amidst rejoicing and glad tidings, but the darker angle of the story is that King Herod is afraid of the newborn Messiah and wants to kill him. This is a foreshadowing of the Passion and death at the other end of the Gospel.

The narrative has a few different parts to consider as you prepare. The first part introduces the wise men, who are neither

This large portion of the reading reveals the king's evil design on the infant savior. Your tone can match the darkness and calculation of the king's scheming.

When King **Herod** heard this,
  he was greatly **troubled**,
  and **all Jerusalem** with him.
Assembling all the chief priests and the scribes of the people,
  he inquired of them where the **Christ** was to be **born**.
They said to him, "In **Bethlehem** of Judea,
  for **thus** it has been **written** through the **prophet**:

This is a quotation from the Old Testament.

  *And **you**, **Bethlehem**, land of Judah,*
    *are by no means **least** among the **rulers** of **Judah**;*
  *since from you shall **come** a **ruler**,*
    *who is to **shepherd** my people **Israel**."*
Then Herod **called** the **magi** secretly
  and ascertained from them the **time** of the star's **appearance**.
He sent them to **Bethlehem** and said,
  "**Go** and search **diligently** for the **child**.
When you have found him, **bring** me word,
  that I **too** may go and **do** him **homage**."
After their **audience** with the **king** they set **out**.

Take your time with this most familiar scene.

And **behold**, the **star** that they had **seen** at its **rising**
    preceded them,
  until it **came** and **stopped** over the place where the **child** was.
They were **overjoyed** at seeing the **star**,
  and on entering the house
  they saw the **child** with **Mary** his **mother**.
They **prostrated** themselves and did him **homage**.
Then they **opened** their **treasures**
  and **offered** him gifts of **gold**, **frankincense**, and **myrrh**.

frankincense = FRANK-in-sens
myrrh = mer
Let your voice highlight this ominous echo of the king's plot.

And having been **warned** in a dream **not** to return to **Herod**,
  they **departed** for their **country** by another **way**.

named nor numbered as three. Immediately the king's fear and plotting is brought into the picture. Do not read too hastily through this part.

The next part is the one beloved of artists, when the child and his mother are visited by the Magi, who open up their "treasures" for the newborn Savior. The evangelist does not close the account with that scene; rather, we are told that the Magi learn in a dream to avoid Herod on their return trip.

The challenge when reading a familiar passage is to keep a balance between knowing that the hearers know the story and proclaiming it so that the listeners can appreciate the beloved story as if hearing it for the first time.

2ND SUNDAY IN ORDINARY TIME

Lectionary #65

READING I   1 Samuel 3:3b–10, 19

Samuel = SAM-yoo-ul

A reading from the first Book of Samuel

Samuel was **sleeping** in the temple of the LORD
    where the **ark** of God was.
The LORD called to Samuel, who answered, "**Here** I am."
Samuel ran to **Eli** and said, "**Here** I am. You **called** me."
"I did **not** call you," Eli said. "Go back to **sleep**."
So he went back to sleep.
Again the LORD called **Samuel**, who **rose** and went to **Eli**.
"**Here** I am, " he said. "You **called** me."
But Eli answered, "I did **not** call you, my **son**. Go back to **sleep**."

Eli = EE-lī

At **that** time **Samuel** was not **familiar** with the LORD,
    because the LORD had not **revealed** anything to him as yet.
The LORD called Samuel **again**, for the **third** time.
Getting **up** and going to **Eli**, he said, "**Here** I am. You **called** me."
Then Eli understood that the LORD was calling the youth.
So he said to Samuel, "Go to **sleep**, and **if** you are called, reply,
    '**Speak**, LORD, for your servant is **listening**.'"
When Samuel went to **sleep** in his place,
    the LORD **came** and **revealed** his presence,
    calling out as **before**, "**Samuel, Samuel!**"
Samuel answered, "**Speak**, for your servant is **listening**."

Samuel grew **up**, and the LORD was with him,
    not permitting any **word** of his to be without **effect**.

End of part one, so insert a significant pause.

End of part two. Another a significant pause.

End of part three; pause before going on to the conclusion.

This last sentence reveals the change in Samuel that came from his experience of vocation, as well as the Lord's care for him.

READING I This reading has five clear parts. The first three all have a similar structure. Each contains four sub-parts: 1) the call of the Lord; 2) Samuel's response, which is exactly the same each time: "Here I am. You called me"; 3) advice from Eli; 4) Samuel's response to the exchange.

To have hearers recognize the Lord's persistence in revealing a vocation, proclaim the three so that each follows a recognizable pattern. The recognition will occur more easily if you take a significant pause after each of these three parts.

The fourth and fifth parts are the resolution of the narrative. For this reason you should pause after Eli's final recommendation: "Reply, 'Speak, Lord, for your servant is listening.'" A significant pause there will signal the change in Samuel's reception to the Lord's call, for, heeding Eli's advice, he has come to recognize the Lord's voice and is prepared to listen. Proclaim this final call, "Samuel, Samuel!," with vigor, and be clear as you deliver the response of Samuel, newly instructed by Eli.

Finally, the Lectionary skips ahead to a verse that brings the story to a satisfying close. Samuel grows up, and the Lord is vigilant in caring for him. You want the Lord's love and vigilance for Samuel—and for each member of your parish family—to be the message heard from the passage.

It is a long reading, but its narrative structure and engaging account will have the assembly following your proclamation closely, receiving the theology of vocation.

READING II Here at the start of this short span of Ordinary Time between the Christmas season and Ash

Corinthians = kor-IN-thee-unz

Be careful here to proclaim "immorality" clearly.

Pause before and after you proclaim this important question.

Be resolute and direct here in delivering Paul's words.

Again, pause before the question. Read below for more.

This final command is very important, so proclaim it boldly, perhaps imagining an exclamation point: "Glorify God in your body!"

READING II 1 Corinthians 6:13c–15a, 17–20

A reading from the first Letter of Saint Paul to the Corinthians

Brothers and sisters:
The **body** is not for **immorality**, but for the **Lord**,
    and the **Lord** is for the **body**;
    God raised the **Lord** and will **also** raise **us** by his **power**.

Do you not **know** that your **bodies** are members of **Christ**?
But whoever is **joined** to the Lord becomes one **Spirit** with him.
Avoid immorality.
Every **other** sin a person commits is **outside** the body,
    but the **immoral** person sins against his **own** body.
Do you not **know** that your body
    is a **temple** of the Holy **Spirit** within you,
        whom you have from **God**, and that you are not your **own**?
For you have been **purchased** at a price.
Therefore **glorify** God in your **body**.

Wednesday, the Church proclaims a series of second readings from 1 Corinthians. Your proclamation begins this series.

As you can see by the identifying line, "A reading from . . ." the author of this letter is the apostle Paul. First Corinthians is one of the earliest books of the New Testament, written by the apostle to the community at Corinth in about the year 56, 20 years or so before the writing of the Gospels. It captures the time in the Church between the Crucifixion and the writing of the Gospels.

As you prepare the reading, notice that when the apostle uses the pronoun "you," it is a plural pronoun. Imagine yourself in Paul's position: He told the members of a local community of faith about their responsibilities to one another as the "body" of Christ, as "a temple of the Holy Spirit." So too will you, proclaiming to your community of faith with the same gravity, care, and passion of the apostle Paul.

The sentences of the reading have different moods: There are questions, commands, and simple statements. The tone of your voice will let the assembly know that

you are asking a question when you say, "Do you not know . . . ?" twice. The two imperatives should also be recognizable not just from the words but from how you deliver them.

The second question is powerful, and fairly complex. Practice this carefully, for there is a natural inclination to have the question end at the end of ". . . Holy Spirit within you," but the inquiry continues for two more lines.

The reading is not long, so do not rush. Insert significant pauses, particularly to

GOSPEL   John 1:35–42

A reading from the holy Gospel according to John

John was standing with **two** of his disciples,
    and as he watched **Jesus** walk by, he said,
    "Behold, the **Lamb** of God."
The two disciples **heard** what he said and **followed** Jesus.
Jesus **turned** and **saw** them following him and said to them,
    "What are you **looking** for?"
They said to him, "**Rabbi**"—which translated means **Teacher**—
    "where are you **staying**?"
He said to them, "**Come**, and you will **see**."
So they **went** and **saw** where Jesus was staying,
    and they **stayed** with him that day.
It was about four in the afternoon.
Andrew, the brother of Simon **Peter**,
    was **one** of the two who heard **John** and **followed** Jesus.
He **first** found his own brother Simon and told him,
    "We have found the **Messiah**"—which is translated **Christ**.
Then he **brought** him to Jesus.
Jesus looked at him and said,
    "You are **Simon** the son of **John**;
    you will be called **Cephas**"—which is translated **Peter**.

See below on the necessity of emphasizing this liturgical phrase in your proclamation.

Rabbi = RAB-ī

Pause after the time reference to mark the shift to Andrew's spreading the news to his brother.
Simon = SĪ-mun

Messiah = meh-SĪ-uh

This connection between the two names "Cephas" and "Peter" is important.
Cephas = SEE-fus

frame the questions and the commands from the apostle. You stand in his place, so your words and passion need to be as evocative and clear as when he wrote them two millennia ago.

GOSPEL This year, when Christmas fell on a Sunday, the liturgical calendar had more celebrations than Sundays, so the Baptism of the Lord fell on a Monday. So Ordinary Time begins this year not with the Gospel of Mark but with the Gospel of John. Next Sunday, we turn to

Mark and stay with that Gospel until Ash Wednesday.

The scriptural passage you proclaim is a good one for the start of the Gospels for Ordinary Time, for it tells the vocation story at the start of the Gospel. The Gospel has already introduced John the Baptist, and this passage tells of the two disciples with John, Simon Peter, and his brother Andrew.

It might be surprising to realize that the other three Gospels do not emphasize the theology of Jesus as the "Lamb of God" as John does. In the others it is indirect, but in John, it is emphatic. This Gospel was written at

least half a century after the death and Resurrection of Jesus, and the evangelist's use of the phrase "Lamb of God" likely reflects the use of that phrase in the liturgy of his community. So emphasize the phrase—"Behold, the Lamb of God"—so that the assembly will hear it echoed in the communion litany "Lamb of God."

The presence of Simon Peter in this reading from the first chapter of John is complemented by his presence on the shore with the risen Christ in the final scene of the last chapter of the Gospel of John.

3RD SUNDAY IN ORDINARY TIME

Lectionary #68

READING I   Jonah 3:1–5, 10

Be clear with the announcement of the book of Jonah, for he is a popular figure of the Old Testament, and this book of the Bible does not appear often in the Lectionary.
Jonah = JOH-nuh
Nineveh = NIN-uh-vuh
Pause at the break.

Have your tone reflect the voice of Jonah announcing his prophecy to the great city.

Another pause for the shift to how the people's action moved God.

A reading from the Book of the Prophet Jonah

The **word** of the LORD came to **Jonah**, saying:
   "Set out for the great city of **Nineveh**,
      and **announce** to it the message that I will tell you."
So Jonah made **ready** and went to **Nineveh**,
   according to the LORD's bidding.
Now **Nineveh** was an **enormously** large city;
   it took three days to go through it.
Jonah **began** his journey through the city,
   and had gone but a single day's **walk** announcing,
   "**Forty** days more and **Nineveh** shall be **destroyed**,"
when the **people** of Nineveh **believed** God;
   they proclaimed a **fast**
   and **all** of them, **great** and **small**, put on **sackcloth**.

When God **saw** by their actions how they **turned** from their
      evil way,
   he **repented** of the evil that he had **threatened** to do to them;
   he did **not** carry it out.

READING I   If you asked people to name a few memorable Bible stories, Jonah and the whale—actually a big fish, according to modern translations—would probably come up often. Many of these witnesses might be surprised at how short the book of Jonah is (only 47 verses) and how infrequently it is proclaimed in the liturgy of the word at Sunday Mass.

Because of Jonah's rare appearance, you can engage the sacred assembly as you announce the reading at the start. Since the prophet is linked with the big fish, perhaps the assembly's interest will be piqued, but they will soon realize that the dramatic scene is not included in the narrative for this Sunday picks it up. Nevertheless, you can seize on the recognition of Jonah's name so that the assembly will be attentive to your proclamation about how the citizens of Nineveh listened and acted on the prophecy.

In some Churches in antiquity, this passage was proclaimed during Lent, for "forty days," the donning of sackcloth, and the proclamation of a fast were all part of these Churches' practice in the season of repentance. The Church itself prepared as the people of Nineveh had.

READING II   This passage continues the series of readings from 1 Corinthians that began last week. The start and end of the passage form a kind of

READING II   1 Corinthians 7:29–31

A reading from the first Letter of Saint Paul to the Corinthians

I **tell** you, brothers and sisters, the **time** is running **out**.
From now **on**, let those having **wives** act as **not** having them,
    those **weeping** as **not** weeping,
    those **rejoicing** as **not** rejoicing,
    those **buying** as not **owning**,
    those **using** the world as not using it **fully**.
For the world in its **present** form is passing **away**.

Corinthians = kor-IN-thee-unz

Emphasize this statement. Make a full stop at the end of this sentence.

Read below for suggestions about the structure of these phrases.

Another pause to signal to the assembly that this last line is key. The point of Paul's message is here, and the pause will gather your listeners' attention for it. As ever, pause before "The word of the Lord."

embrace, with the basic point that time is short and this world passing. So it might be best to imagine the reading as three parts, with a significant pause between them. The first is the direct address, "Brothers and sisters," with its statement, "the time is running out."

Then after a breath and pause, consider "from now on" as the start of the second part, and this has a unique literary device. Notice the five structured parallels in the

lines in the middle of the reading. In each of the five the apostle starts by describing how some might be living, and then he suggests that they live to the contrary. With each of these, the apostle was telling his readers that the ways of the world are different from the ways of God. So they (and we) should not be deceived by the world's ways, but should live the life of God rather than the life of the world.

You do not want to proclaim the strong message of the structured phrases in a "sing-song" sort of way, for Paul's message is yet timely. Take advantage of the parallels by making the contradictions resound in your voice.

GOSPEL | In the other two synoptic gospels, Matthew and Luke, this call story comes much later, in the fourth chapter of each. But in Mark, because

GOSPEL   Mark 1:14–20

A reading from the holy Gospel according to Mark

After **John** had been **arrested**,
     Jesus came to **Galilee** proclaiming the gospel of **God**:
     "**This** is the time of **fulfillment**.
The kingdom of **God** is at **hand**.
Repent, and **believe** in the **gospel**."

As he passed by the Sea of **Galilee**,
     he saw **Simon** and his brother **Andrew** casting their **nets** into
          the sea;
     they were **fishermen**.
Jesus said to them,
     "Come after **me**, and **I** will make you fishers of **men**."
Then they **abandoned** their nets and **followed** him.
He walked along a little farther
     and saw **James**, the son of **Zebedee**, and his brother **John**.
They **too** were in a boat mending their nets.
Then he **called** them.
So they **left** their father **Zebedee** in the boat
     along with the hired men and **followed** him.

These are the first words that Jesus speaks in the Gospel of Mark.

Galilee = GAL-ih-lee
Simon = SI-mun
Zebedee = ZEB=eh-dee

Emphasize the immediacy of their response to Jesus' command.

This mention of the sons leaving their father reflects the high price of following Jesus in the earliest days of his ministry and of the Church.

there is no genealogy or infancy narrative, the call of the first followers of Jesus comes very early. As you can see by the citation, the account is in the middle of the first chapter, just after the appearance of John the Baptist, the Baptism of Jesus by John, the temptation in the desert. (All that in just 14 verses!)

     Throughout Mark, Jesus speaks with power and authority, and this power is apparent in his ministry, his voice, from the start. Here we find a number of commands

from Jesus: "Repent!" "Believe in the gospel!" "Come after me!" Because this is so early in Mark's narrative, the presence of Jesus radiates strength, and you match that strength with your proclamation.

     The narrative you prepare has three basic sections. The first eclipses John the Baptist as Jesus comes to Galilee, and then we find Jesus' first words in this Gospel, the three lines in quotation marks.

     The second part has Jesus call Simon (Peter) and his brother Andrew as they fish. The call continues into the third part, wherein Jesus calls another pair of brothers, this time James and John, the sons of Zebedee.

     This is not a complicated narrative, and it will be familiar to most of your hearers. Mark's powerful narrative is unique, so step up to proclaim the story with the immediacy of the disciples' response to Jesus' call.

4TH SUNDAY IN ORDINARY TIME

Lectionary #71

READING I   Deuteronomy 18:15 – 20

A reading from the Book of Deuteronomy

Moses spoke to **all** the people, saying:
"A **prophet** like me will the LORD, your **God**, raise **up** for you
from among your own **kin**;
to **him** you shall **listen**.
This is **exactly** what you **requested** of the LORD, your God,
at **Horeb**
on the **day** of the assembly, when you **said**,
'Let us not **again** hear the voice of the LORD, our **God**,
nor see this great **fire** any more, lest we **die**.'
And the LORD said to me, 'This was **well** said.
I will **raise** up for them a **prophet** like you from among their **kin**,
and will put my **words** into his **mouth**;
he shall tell them **all** that I **command** him.'
Whoever will **not** listen to my words which he speaks
in my **name**,
I **myself** will make him **answer** for it.
But **if** a prophet presumes to speak in my name
an **oracle** that I have **not** commanded him to **speak**,
or **speaks** in the name of **other** gods, he shall **die**."

Deuteronomy = doo-ter-AH-nuh-mee

The first line of the reading is the only place where the speaker and the hearers are identified. Pause slightly before you begin so that the assembly is ready to hear this.
Moses = MOH-ziz

Horeb = HOH-reb

The promise of the Lord to deliver a prophet is strong.

The final section proclaims the fate of false prophets.

READING I Notice at the start of your preparation that all but the first line of this passage is the words of Moses as he addresses the people of Israel, and he relays the words of God. Because of this, you might pause after you announce the reading so that the assembly is ready to hear that short introduction that identifies the speaker and to whom he is speaking.

The Pentateuch traces the salvation history of Israel, God's Chosen People, from Creation to the establishment of the covenant and the nation. In this passage Moses, and through him the Lord, foretells the prophet who will be raised up to speak the word of the Lord to the people once again. For Christians, this points to the coming of Jesus Christ; for Jews it points to the prophetic books of the Old Testament that follow in the Bible and to the Messiah, the Lord's messenger who speaks the words of truth and redeems the people Israel.

In spite of this wonderful reflection of both the Jewish and Christian traditions, the reading does not end on the optimism you proclaim in the middle section, "I will raise up . . . a prophet like you from among their own kin"; rather, the final two verses speak of false prophets who speak "in the name of other gods." The reading ends with the dark promise that such a prophet will die. Discern for yourself how best to deliver the positive and warning messages, but, whatever kind of proclamation you choose, be clear and unhurried.

Corinthians = kor-IN-thee-unz

Engage the assembly with this direct address, and continue to demonstrate your encouragement through this sentence.

As described below, these middle two sections are similarly structured.

Pause before you return to the first-person "I," so that the assembly is attentive as you address them with the apostle's intentions.

READING II   1 Corinthians 7:32 – 35

A reading from the first Letter of Saint Paul to the Corinthians

Brothers and sisters:
I should like you to be free of **anxieties**.
An **unmarried** man is anxious about the things of the **Lord**,
    how he may please the **Lord**.
But a **married** man is anxious about the things of the **world**,
    how he may please his **wife**, and he is **divided**.
An **unmarried** woman or a **virgin** is anxious about the things
        of the **Lord**,
    so that she may be **holy** in both **body** and **spirit**.
A **married** woman, on the other hand,
    is anxious about the things of the **world**,
    how she may please her **husband**.
I am telling you this for your own **benefit**,
    not to impose a **restraint** upon you,
    but for the sake of **propriety**
    and **adherence** to the Lord without **distraction**.

READING II We continue the series of second readings from 1 Corinthians. This letter is well-known for its theology of the body of Christ (chapters 6 and 12), for its account of the supper with Jesus and the disciples (chapter 11), and its "love" passage (chapter 13), proclaimed at many weddings. Other parts of the letter are less familiar, where the apostle takes up some of the social issues of the Church in that time, regarding clothing, food, and relations between men and women, as well as

the state of life of the married and the unmarried. The passage you will proclaim deals with these.

The style of Paul's writing here enables you, indeed invites you, to proclaim this to the assembly as if you yourself had written it. When you get up to read the scripture, engage your community with a direct address to your "brothers and sisters."

You can see from the Lectionary that there are four parts, and the middle two in particular discuss the social issues of the unmarried and the married in relation to the world and to the Lord. Each of these sections, the first about men and the second about women, has the same structure. Within each, Paul remarks on the differences between the concerns of the unmarried and the married. Learn and appropriate what Paul is saying, and proclaim it clearly and with conviction.

GOSPEL Mark 1:21–28

A reading from the holy Gospel according to Mark

Then they came to **Capernaum**,
    and on the **sabbath** Jesus entered the **synagogue** and **taught**.
The people were **astonished** at his teaching,
    for he taught them as one having **authority** and not as the
        scribes.
In their synagogue was a man with an **unclean** spirit;
    he cried out, "What have you to do with **us**, Jesus of
        Nazareth?
Have you come to **destroy** us?
I know who **you** are—the **Holy** One of **God**!"
Jesus **rebuked** him and said,
    "**Quiet!** Come **out** of him!"
The unclean spirit **convulsed** him and with a loud cry
        came **out** of him.
All were **amazed** and asked one another,
    "What **is** this?
A new teaching with **authority**.
He commands even the **unclean** spirits and they **obey** him."
His **fame** spread **everywhere** throughout the **whole** region
        of **Galilee**.

Capernaum = kuh-PER-n*m
sabbath = SAB-uth
synagogue = SIN-uh-gog

Pause here as the narrative shifts from the general setting to the particular story of the man possessed.

The words from the man can be proclaimed boldly.
Nazareth = NAZ-uh-reth

These are commands from Jesus; proclaim them with authority.

Pause before this summary conclusion.
Galilee = GAL-ih-lee

GOSPEL   Although we are already at the Fourth Sunday in Ordinary Time, we have not yet exhausted the first chapter of the Gospel of Mark. The evangelist's opening chapters are packed with exciting narratives and fast-paced action, and this is so of the passage you are preparing. As you prepare your proclamation, consider how your tone and style will carry Mark's exciting narrative.

You could not be assigned a more dramatic narrative for this day. The man with the unclean spirit cries out to Jesus, and the voice he employs is plural: "Have you come to destroy us?" The chilling words are complemented by action, for the man convulses as the unclean spirit is driven out, and then the spirit itself cries out in a loud voice.

While you do not want to re-enact the story in your proclamation, you can take full possession of the details. Also, deliver the speeches—from the man, the spirit, from

Jesus, and from the crowd—vibrantly, for the words and the actions are well balanced.

The reading ends with the subtle acknowledgment of the impact of Jesus' ministry and fame. News of his work on behalf of the sick, the possessed, and the poor is beginning to spread, and the Gospel of Mark is filled with the tension of the spreading fame of Jesus' good works and of his desire for solitude and silence.

5TH SUNDAY IN ORDINARY TIME

Lectionary #74

READING I Job 7:1–4, 6–7

A reading from the Book of Job

Job spoke, saying:
Is not man's life on **earth** a **drudgery**?
    Are not his **days** those of **hirelings**?
He is a **slave** who longs for the **shade**,
    a **hireling** who waits for his **wages**.
So I have been assigned months of **misery**,
    and troubled **nights** have been **allotted** to me.
If in **bed** I say, "When shall I **arise**?"
    then the night **drags** on;
    I am filled with **restlessness** until the **dawn**.
My days are **swifter** than a weaver's **shuttle**;
    they come to an end without **hope**.
Remember that my life is like the **wind**;
    I **shall** not see **happiness** again.

Job = johb

The announcement of the book and the first line are very important, for once the speech begins, there are no more indications of the speaker.

Pronounce these time references, clearly.

Though Job speaks of the speed of time, your proclamation will suffer if you read this too fast.

READING I The story of Job is well known, and the poetry of this man's tale of sorrow and heavy burdens is beautiful. It draws the hearer or reader into Job's plight, and your job as the proclaimer of Job's story is to make this speech of Job vibrant to your assembly.

The book of Job is long, 42 chapters, and the excerpt you prepare comes relatively early in the account. The book introduces Job as "blameless and upright, one who feared God and turned away from evil," with "seven sons and three daughters," yet calamity after calamity befalls him. In just two verses, we hear that a great wind blows through the house where his children were having a party, and the house collapses, killing them all. This only one of Job's many sorrows; knowing this will prepare you for the speech of the faithful man whose words you will share with your community.

There is deep and gripping poetry in this passage. Attend to the specific images of this short reading, the "months of misery" and "troubled nights," the "slave who longs for the shade" and the speed of the "weaver's shuttle." This is the voice of experience, of someone who had actually watched a weaver at work, been astounded at the speed of the tool, and linked it to his experience of time.

Job's experience is that of someone who has suffered and tried to make sense of it in faith. You today will stand in Job's place as a person of faith recounting human experience; be true to his experience by proclaiming the passage with sincerity.

READING II   1 Corinthians 9:16–19, 22–23

Corinthians = kor-IN-thee-unz

A reading from the first Letter of Saint Paul to the Corinthians

Brothers and sisters:
If I preach the **gospel**, this is no **reason** for me to **boast**,
> for an obligation has been **imposed** on me,
> and **woe** to me if I do **not** preach it!
If I do so **willingly**, I have a **recompense**,
> but if **unwillingly**, then I have been entrusted with
> > a **stewardship**.
What then is my **recompense**?
That, when I **preach**,
> I **offer** the gospel **free** of charge
> so as not to make full use of my **right** in the gospel.

Although I am **free** in regard to all,
> I have made myself a **slave** to all
> so as to win over as many as **possible**.
To the **weak** I became **weak**, to win **over** the weak.
I have become all things to all, to save at least **some**.
All this I do for the sake of the gospel,
> so that I **too** may have a **share** in it.

recompense = REH-kum-pens

The rhetoric of the passage shifts here, so pause before you launch into the question.

These final lines are powerful, so be bold with your delivery.

READING II   It is amazing that the message of the apostle Paul is both so ancient and so contemporary, so refreshing. With passages like the one that you will proclaim, it is hard to believe that he was writing only a short time after the death and Resurrection of Jesus. It can be proclaimed as if written by you for your own community!

Because of its timelessness, consider committing a few parts to memory, so that you might look up and deliver Paul's words with conviction and gravity. Statements like "when I preach, I offer the gospel free of charge" and "I have become all things to all, to save at least some" are examples in which the first-century Greek message can be proclaimed boldly to a twenty-first-century assembly in North America.

Notice that, the apostle asks a question, "What then is my recompense?" and answers it, "That, when . . ." Capture the question-answer style with your tone of voice.

This is a key passage, but it may not come easily. Practice it until you are comfortable with Paul's words, so that you can be utterly confident standing in the apostle's place. As Paul was familiar to those to whom he wrote, so are you and your ministry familiar to your community. Pray for the confidence to proclaim such powerful words forthrightly.

Each of the first three sections starts with a time reference. The evangelist employed this as a way of moving the narrative, here focusing on the particular woman with a fever.
synagogue = SIN-uh-gog
Simon = SĪ-mun
Galilee = GAL-ih-lee

Pause before the next time reference, as the narrative broadens from the cure of one person to the "whole town" gathering at the door.

Another pause before the time reference, this time to reveal Jesus' withdrawal.

Finally, the revelation of Jesus' purpose, to preach God's word, a purpose in which you share as a minister of the word today.

GOSPEL   Mark 1:29–39

A reading from the holy Gospel according to Mark

On leaving the **synagogue**
    Jesus entered the house of **Simon** and **Andrew**
        with **James** and **John**.
Simon's **mother**-in-law lay sick with a **fever**.
They **immediately** told him about her.
He **approached**, grasped her hand, and helped her **up**.
Then the fever **left** her and she **waited** on them.

When it was **evening**, after **sunset**,
    they brought to him all who were **ill** or possessed by **demons**.
The whole **town** was gathered at the **door**.
He cured many who were **sick** with various **diseases**,
    and he drove out many **demons**,
        not **permitting** them to speak because they **knew** him.

Rising very **early** before dawn, he **left**
    and went off to a **deserted** place, where he **prayed**.
Simon and those who were with him **pursued** him
    and on **finding** him said, "**Everyone** is **looking** for you."
He **told** them, "Let us go **on** to the nearby **villages**
    that I may preach **there also**.
For this purpose have I **come**."
So he went into their **synagogues**,
    preaching and driving out **demons** throughout the **whole**
        of Galilee.

GOSPEL   This passage has four basic parts: 1) a particular healing, 2) the effect on Jesus' reputation, 3) Jesus' withdrawal, and 4) his statement of the purpose and wider scope of his ministry. Consider each of the units as a narrative piece with its own contribution to the whole; the first three are begun with particular time references—"On leaving," "evening, after sunset," and "very early, before dawn"— and these supply a chance for a break in your proclamation as the scene shifts.

The first account is about the apostle Peter's wife's mother, who was sick. Her friends give voice to the situation to Jesus and he acts on it. Human words move him to act, an inspiration you can take as a charge for your own ministry.

Mark frequently mentions Jesus' withdrawal to deserted, solitary places. As often as the crowds seek him out, Jesus seeks a place to be alone. In spite of the wonder of the miracles he worked and the many demons he cast out, the final summary of this passage does not highlight these wonders, as he encourages his followers to move on, "that I may preach there also. For this purpose have I come." As proclaimer of the Gospel, you carry on this purpose of the Lord. Trusting in the Lord's power, step up to proclaim the truth of salvation made known in the work of Jesus.

6TH SUNDAY IN ORDINARY TIME

Lectionary #77

READING I   Leviticus 13:1—2, 44—46

Leviticus = lih-VIT-ih-kus

The first line is the only place where the speaker, the Lord, and the hearers, Moses and Aaron, are identified. Pause before you begin so that the assembly is ready for this opening.
Moses = MOH-ziz
Aaron = AIR-un
leprosy = LEP-ruh-see

A reading from the Book of Leviticus

The LORD said to Moses and Aaron,
    "If someone has on his skin a scab or pustule or blotch
    which appears to be the sore of leprosy,
    he shall be brought to Aaron, the priest,
    or to one of the priests among his descendants.
If the man is leprous and unclean,
    the priest shall declare him unclean
    by reason of the sore on his head.

"The one who bears the sore of leprosy
    shall keep his garments rent and his head bare,
    and shall muffle his beard;
    he shall cry out, 'Unclean, unclean!'
As long as the sore is on him he shall declare himself unclean,
    since he is in fact unclean.
He shall dwell apart, making his abode outside the camp."

The physical manifestations of leprosy were hard enough for those afflicted, but the social excision of the leper made it harder.

READING II   1 Corinthians 10:31—11:1

Corinthians = kor-IN-thee-unz

The apostle alludes to Jewish dietary laws in the first sentence.

A reading from the first Letter of Saint Paul to the Corinthians

Brothers and sisters,
whether you eat or drink, or whatever you do,
    do everything for the glory of God.

READING I This reading about how lepers were required to mark themselves off from the rest of society is paired with the Gospel reading in which a leper comes to Jesus to be made clean.

The reading reveals a lot about the fears of the society from which it sprang. Scripture ought to lead to conversion of hearts and mind. Feelings of self-righteousness need to be examined and changed according to how God views people who are sick. Though they may be in nursing homes, hospitals, or care facilities of various kinds (if they are well off), our culture often shuts them off from daily life because we are uncomfortable with the weak and vulnerable.

As you prepare and step up to proclaim, imagine the "one who bears the sore of leprosy" as those whom our culture ignores or excises. Your words will be more engaging and impassioned.

READING II In the first part of the reading, Paul is referring to the Jewish dietary laws. He is advocating that believers consider these issues from the point of view of those with whom they sit at table. The moral principle is clear: We need to consider not only ourselves when making decisions, but our social and religious contexts. We need to attend not only to our own consciences, but to the consciences of those around us.

The final part of the reading contains a number of commands: "Do everything for the glory of God," "Avoid giving offense," and "Be imitators of me." These are apt opportunities for you to look up at the assembly and

Here Paul points to a potential contemporary witness, who might object to what other believers have on their plates.

This final line is the summary.

Avoid giving **offense**, whether to the **Jews** or **Greeks** or
the church of **God**,
just as **I** try to please **everyone** in **every** way,
not seeking my **own** benefit but that of the **many**,
that they may be **saved**.
Be imitators of **me**, as **I** am of **Christ**.

GOSPEL Mark 1:40–45

A reading from the holy Gospel according to Mark

This is a short passage punctuated with direct discourse. Use the interplay of narrative and quotations to sustain the attention of your assembly.
leper = LEP-er

leprosy = LEP-ruh-see

Moses = MOH-ziz

A **leper** came to Jesus and kneeling down **begged** him and said,
"If you **wish**, you can make me **clean**."
Moved with **pity**, he **stretched** out his hand,
touched him, and said to him,
"I **do** will it. Be made **clean**."
The **leprosy** left him **immediately**, and he was made **clean**.
Then, warning him **sternly**, he **dismissed** him at **once**.

He said to him, "See that you tell **no** one **anything**,
but **go**, show yourself to the **priest**
and **offer** for your cleansing what Moses prescribed;
that will be **proof** for them."

The man went **away** and began to **publicize** the whole matter.
He **spread** the report abroad
so that it was **impossible** for Jesus to enter a town **openly**.
He remained **outside** in **deserted** places,
and people kept **coming** to him from **everywhere**.

---

speak as if you yourself had written these commands. You and the apostle share in the ministry of the word, even over the centuries and continents, so you are called to make these words a living word for your community of faith.

GOSPEL Much of this reading is punctuated with direct dialogue: the leper's plea, Jesus' response, and finally Jesus' warning that the man not say anything to anyone. Consider what tone of voice you will use for these words from Jesus and the man and how you will distinguish the narration from the spoken lines.

We do not often attend to the physical contact between Jesus and those to whom he ministers, but the contact between him and the other tells us how the sacraments are to be celebrated by "two or three gathered in my name." Since the reform of the liturgy, this corporal contact among believers at prayer has improved, for we share the sign of peace. The link between this reading and the sacramental tradition is clear. Be clear as you relate the healing miracle to those assembled so that they too can appreciate the human contact at the heart of our sacramental experience.

7TH SUNDAY IN ORDINARY TIME

Lectionary #80

READING I   Isaiah 43:18–19, 21–22, 24b–25

Isaiah = ī-ZAY-uh

Pause before you start the reading, for only this opening line identifies the speaker.

This metaphor emphasizes the theology of newness; proclaim it clearly.

Jacob = JAY-kub
Israel = IZ-ree-ul

See below on the double pronoun here.

A reading from the Book of the Prophet Isaiah

Thus says the LORD:
Remember **not** the events of the **past**,
    the things of **long** ago **consider** not;
see, I am doing something **new**!
    Now it springs forth, **do** you not perceive it?
In the **desert** I make a **way**,
    in the **wasteland**, **rivers**.
The **people** I formed for **myself**,
    that they might **announce** my praise.
Yet you **did** not call upon me, O **Jacob**,
    for you grew **weary** of me, O **Israel**.
You **burdened** me with your **sins**,
    and **wearied** me with your **crimes**.
It is I, **I**, who wipe out,
    for my **own** sake, your **offenses**;
    your **sins** I remember no **more**.

READING I Pause slightly after announcing that the reading is "from the book of the prophet Isaiah" so that the members of the assembly are poised to hear who the speaker is, "the Lord," for there are no explicit indications after the first line.

This reading's main issue for this Sunday is the Lord's words at the end: "I . . . wipe out . . . your offenses," "your sins I remember no more." Stress these elements of forgiveness in your proclamation, for they are connected to the Gospel reading, in which Jesus speaks of himself as "the Son

of Man [who] has authority to forgive sins on earth."

The main subject of the passage is newness, manifest in welcome surprises, as the opening says explicitly and as the metaphors capture, such as rivers in the desert. Be forward in the proclamation for many believers have hope in the future, that things will be new and their own sins will not impede them from life with God. Your forthright proclamation will offer consolation.

The sentence starting "The people" is arranged in a poetic way, with the object ("people") before the subject ("I"). As you

study the reading for its meaning, consider the sentence in a more mundane arrangement: "I formed the people for myself, that they might announce my praise."

The double pronoun in the last verse— "I, I"—is meant to emphasize the identity of the one doing this, and the gravity of what the Lord does.

READING II Since the end of the Christmas season, the second readings have been from 1 Corinthians; at this point we move on to 2 Corinthians.

Corinthians = kor-IN-thee-unz

The key elements, "yes" and "no," need to be proclaimed clearly and with conviction.

Silvanus = sil-VAY-nus

Take a significant pause after this poignant line.

The consonance of "Amen" in the reading and the amens of the liturgy is important.

The sacramental link between this anointing, the "seal," and the Spirit needs to be heard clearly.

READING II   2 Corinthians 1:18–22

A reading from the second Letter of Saint Paul to the Corinthians

Brothers and sisters:
As God is **faithful**,
    our word to you is not **"yes"** and **"no."**
For the Son of **God**, Jesus **Christ**,
    who was **proclaimed** to you by us, **Silvanus** and
        Timothy and **me**,
    was **not** "yes" **and** "no," but **"yes"** has been in him.
For **however** many are the promises of **God**, their **Yes** is in **him**;
    therefore, the **Amen** from us **also** goes through him to God
        for **glory**.
But the one who gives us **security** with you in **Christ**
    and who anointed **us** is God;
    he has **also** put his **seal** upon us
    and given the **Spirit** in our **hearts** as a first **installment**.

GOSPEL   Mark 2:1–12

A reading from the holy Gospel according to Mark

When Jesus returned to **Capernaum** after some days,
    it became **known** that he was at **home**.
Many gathered **together** so that there was no longer **room**
        for them,
    not **even** around the **door**,
    and he preached the word to them.

This opening part supplies the setting.
Capernaum = kuh-PER-n*m

This book is not well known or as frequently proclaimed in the liturgy. The theology heard today is powerful.

For clarity, look carefully at the second sentence. Perhaps it would be easier to ascertain its meaning and grammatical structure if you first consider it in its sparest meaning: "For the Son of God, Jesus Christ . . . was not 'yes' and 'no,' but 'yes.'" The other elements are qualifiers of that essential kernel on the Son's ministry of proclamation, in

his word and his life. Into the simple declaration the apostle inserts more detail about Jesus Christ, namely, "who was proclaimed to you by us," and more detail about who make up the "we," namely, "Silvanus and Timothy and me." After examining it thoroughly, you can return to the way it is printed in the Lectionary and be more confident in proclaiming it.

Be most emphatic with the phrases in quotation marks: "Yes and No," "Yes," and "Amen." These are key to understanding the apostle's purpose. Also, because the Church says "Amen" so many times in the Sacred

Liturgy, be as clear as possible where the apostle links the "Amen" to the "Yes" of God's promises.

When we are confirmed, the Church uses the perfumed oil named chrism. That word is related to the words "Christ" and "anointed" in the last sentence of the passage. The further mention of the "Holy Spirit" and the "seal" in the same sentence ties the theology of the ritual action together even more closely, though this is not as evident in the translation.

The second part narrates the joyful support that the friends play in the healing miracle.

The largest part is this exchange between the authorities and Jesus, who recognize that Jesus is contesting their power.

This final verse is a summary, and it weds the conclusion of the miracle story with the confrontation with the scribes.

They came **bringing** to him a **paralytic** carried by **four men**.
Unable to get near **Jesus** because of the **crowd**,
    they opened up the **roof** above him.
After they had broken **through**,
    they let down the **mat** on which the paralytic was **lying**.
When **Jesus** saw their **faith**, he said to the **paralytic**,
    "**Child**, your sins are **forgiven**."
Now some of the **scribes** were sitting there **asking** themselves,
    "**Why** does this man **speak** that way? He is **blaspheming**.
Who but God **alone** can forgive **sins**?"
Jesus immediately knew in his mind
    what they were thinking to themselves,
    so he said, "Why are you **thinking** such things in your **hearts**?
Which is **easier**, to say to the paralytic,
    'Your **sins** are forgiven,'
    or to say, '**Rise**, pick up your **mat** and **walk**?'
"But that you may **know**
    that the Son of Man has **authority** to forgive sins on **earth**"
    —he said to the **paralytic**,
    "I **say** to you, **rise**, pick up your **mat**, and go **home**."
He **rose**, picked up his mat at **once**,
    and went **away** in the sight of **everyone**.
They were all **astounded**
    and **glorified** God, saying, "We have **never** seen **anything**
        like this."

GOSPEL The wonder-working of Jesus is enough for our edification and salvation, but we cannot help but be impressed by the dedication of these four friends of the paralyzed man, who "opened up the roof" and let the mat down on which the man was lying. Moreover, it is the faith of the four friends that moves Jesus to act on behalf of the paralyzed man.

Too often believers think of their faith as something between themselves and God alone, without the need for fellow believers, fellow worshipers, fellow children of God. But at every step of its development, from the early Church to today, faith is nurtured by the courageous example and support of others, and your strong proclamation of this narrative might sink in as an example of the communal, ecclesial dimension of God's healing touch.

The account you prepare has various parts and elements. The first part supplies the general setting; pause at the break to mark the shift to the particular narrative of the man paralyzed. This is the touching account of the man and his friends, and it is interrupted by the complaining of the scribes, which is the third part and occupies a good part of the account.

The final part brings together the healing of the man and the sanctioning of Jesus' authority in the face of those questioning him. The final verse is strong in confirming the healing and in anticipating the popularity of Jesus' healing ministry.

As you read the narrative, anticipate the transitions from section to section, and pause between them to mark the transitions in place, actions, audience, and exchanges.

8TH SUNDAY IN ORDINARY TIME

Lectionary #83

READING I   Hosea 2:16b, 17b, 21–22

The passage is short, so pause between the identifying line and the beginning of the reading. Similarly, pause significantly between sentences.
Hosea = hoh-ZAY-uh

A reading from the Book of the Prophet Hosea

Thus says the LORD:
I will **lead** her into the **desert**
    and speak to her **heart**.
She shall respond there as in the days of her **youth**,
    when she came **up** from the land of **Egypt**.
I will **espouse** you to me **forever**:
    I will **espouse** you in **right** and in **justice**,
    in **love** and in **mercy**;
I will espouse you in **fidelity**,
    and **you** shall know the LORD.

Egypt = EE-jipt
See below for the shift of pronouns and how this will affect your understanding of the passage.

READING II   2 Corinthians 3:1b–6

Corinthians = kor-IN-thee-unz

A reading from the second Letter of Saint Paul to the Corinthians

Brothers and sisters:
Do **we** need, as **some** do,
    letters of **recommendation** to you or **from** you?
You are our letter, **written** on our **hearts**,
    known and **read** by **all**,
    shown to be a letter of **Christ** ministered by us,

Be animated as you read the phrase "letters of recommendation," as its relevance for job applications still today will engage the hearers. Capture the question mark in your proclamation.

READING I This is a short passage, and it is quite beautiful in the way it casts the relationship of the Lord and Israel as that between spouses.

As you prepare, pay attention to the pronouns. Throughout the entire passage, the Lord is speaking in the first person: "I will lead," and "*I* will espouse." It is your charge to deliver the Lord's words directly.

In literary terms, however, the one about whom the Lord speaks shifts from third person to second person. You will be able to proclaim the passage more confidently if you are aware of the literary device

employed in identifying the one to whom the Lord speaks.

Notice that in the first half of the reading speaks *about* Israel in the third person: "I will lead *her*," "in the days of her *youth*." In the second half the speaker remains constant ("I") but the other changes from the third-person "her" to the second-person "you." The Lord speaks no longer about Israel, as in the first half of the reading, but *to* Israel: "I will espouse *you* to me," and "*you* shall know." The change happens exactly at the mid-point.

After the shift, you can address the assembly more directly, for you stand in the prophet's place speaking the words of the Lord to the community of believers. It's a familiar change in biblical texts, but this shift does not often happen in the middle of a passage chosen for the Lectionary, as here.

READING II The connection between Paul's mention of "letters of recommendation" in the first-century Mediterranean world he know and "letters of recommendation" as we know them in

Take your time and be clear with these beautiful metaphors of writing.

Significant pause here.

Deliver the juxtaposition of these contrary elements, the "letter" and the "spirit," so that the assembly picks up the opposition between the two from the tone of your voice.

written not in **ink** but by the **Spirit** of the living **God**,
not on tablets of **stone** but on tablets that are hearts of **flesh**.

Such **confidence** we have through Christ toward **God**.
Not that of **ourselves** we are qualified
to take **credit** for anything as coming from **us**;
rather, our **qualification** comes from **God**,
who has indeed **qualified** us as **ministers** of a new **covenant**,
not of **letter** but of **spirit**;
for the letter brings **death**, but the Spirit gives **life**.

GOSPEL Mark 2:18–22

A reading from the holy Gospel according to Mark

**The opening line supplies characters and context.
Pharisees = FAIR-uh-seez**

The disciples of **John** and of the **Pharisees** were accustomed
to **fast**.
People **came** to him and **objected**,
"Why do the disciples of **John** and the disciples of the
Pharisees fast,
but your disciples do **not** fast?"
Jesus answered them,
"Can the **wedding** guests **fast** while the **bridegroom** is
with them?
As long as they have the bridegroom **with** them they **cannot** fast.
But the days will **come** when the bridegroom is taken **away** from
them,
and **then** they will **fast** on that day.

---

the business world now make this a delightful phrase. This passage is still near the beginning of the letter, so Paul is describing the relationship between himself and this community of faith. They, the living people of Corinth, are "letters" written by the Holy Spirit! Read these metaphors of correspondence carefully, so that you understand what the apostle intends with them, and thereby the assembly before you can appreciate their richness.

A word sometimes used for a letter is "missive," which literally means "something sent." Its origins are linked to the word "missionary," or "someone sent." The members of the Church at Corinth were Paul's "letters" and missionaries in bearing the Good News in their lives, news written "on the tablets of human hearts." The metaphors are rich. Take your time in proclaiming them.

Usually Paul speaks in terms of "I" (singular) and "you" (plural), but here it is "we" and "you" (both plural). In your proclamation you are not only giving life to an ancient text; you are animating the text as the word of God for your own parish. With your voice, let the community of faith know that these holy words are applicable to your own assembly, brought together for this liturgy in the power of the Holy Spirit, the gift of the living God for us today.

The reading can provide a lesson for you in your own ministry of the word, for the gifts and competence that you bring to the work of the word are not from yourself; such competence "is from God." Your task is to develop the gifts and keep your ministry ever fresh for Christ's Church.

Jesus' discourse about fasting and his followers is followed by two more sayings. Pause between each of these, for they are adages from an older tradition put into the story by the evangelist.

No one sews a piece of **unshrunken** cloth on an old **cloak**.
If he **does**, its fullness pulls **away**,
  the **new** from the **old**, and the tear gets **worse**.
Likewise, **no** one pours **new** wine into **old** wineskins.
Otherwise, the wine will **burst** the skins,
  and both the **wine** and the **skins** are **ruined**.
Rather, **new** wine is poured into **fresh** wineskins."

GOSPEL In the early Church's Easter season, as the Church celebrated the Baptism of new members at the Easter Vigil, the Church's leaders preached about the mark of the Easter season: the Alleluia was to be sung (it is omitted during Lent), there was to be no kneeling, and there was to be no fasting. As the leaders spoke of not fasting in the Easter season, they drew from this passage, for while the risen Christ, the bridegroom, was with them "they

cannot fast." Once he is taken away, "then they will fast." The passage itself does not speak of the risen Christ and the Easter season, but the practices of the Easter season were echoes of this passage on the presence or absence of the bridegroom.

The passage is not long; it has three distinguishable parts. The first leads up to the people's inquiry about the disciples' behavior. Jesus answers them with sayings that were likely of a tradition older than the Gospel itself, and the evangelist puts them in the context of the narrative.

The rest of the passage is from Jesus' lips. Even after the second part on fasting, he adds a few sayings, and these constitute the third part, with the sayings about cloth and wineskins. These sayings also likely existed before Mark put them in his Gospel. Deliver them as discrete sayings, of course, but do so confidently in the voice of Jesus.

ASH WEDNESDAY

Lectionary #219

READING I   Joel 2:12–18

Joel = JOH-*l

Be clear with this "says the Lord," so that the assembly is able to distinguish between the words of the prophet and the words of the Lord.

As you practice and then as you proclaim, pause slightly at these breaks in the printed text so that the assembly can let the words sink in.

Be bold as you read these imperative verbs; these are commands, and they rally the Church for the disciplines of Lent.

A reading from the Book of the Prophet Joel

Even **now**, says the LORD,
  return to me with your whole **heart**,
  with **fasting**, and **weeping**, and **mourning**;
Rend your **hearts**, not your **garments**,
  and **return** to the LORD, your **God**.
For **gracious** and **merciful** is he,
  slow to **anger**, **rich** in **kindness**,
  and **relenting** in punishment.
Perhaps he will again relent
  and leave behind him a **blessing**,
Offerings and **libations**
  for the LORD, your **God**.

Blow the **trumpet** in **Zion**!
  proclaim a **fast**,
  call an **assembly**;
Gather the **people**,
  notify the congregation;
Assemble the **elders**,
  gather the **children**
  and the **infants** at the **breast**;
Let the **bridegroom** quit his room,
  and the **bride** her **chamber**.

READING I   This is a day of the liturgical year that has always drawn people to church. The rite of the ashes draws from the minor prophet Joel, who prophesied to Israel in exile. His inspired words capture some of the ritual traditions of the people, including this proclamation of a time of fasting.

As the proclaimer of the word, consider yourself as a prophet in a new place and a new time, for with the reading of the text you will proclaim the period of fasting and penitence.

Ash Wednesday has been the day that begins the period of preparation for Easter for many centuries. This period is not a time of merely individual penitence, but of communal observance and penitence. So your assertive proclamation—"Blow the trumpet!""Proclaim a fast!" "Call an assembly!" "Gather the people!"—will help the assembly before you recognize the importance of this communal endeavor of preparation for the celebration of the death and Resurrection of Christ.

Notice the many imperative phrases in the reading, how many times the prophet takes up the words of the Lord, who declares to the people, "Return to me!" "Rend your hearts!" "Gather! Notify! Assemble!" Your proclamation here can be bold. This prepares the way for the Gospel passage, in which fasting is also a focus.

Between the porch and the altar
  let the **priests**, the **ministers** of the LORD, **weep**,
And say, "**Spare**, O LORD, your **people**,
  and make not your **heritage** a **reproach**,
  with the nations **ruling** over them!
Why should they say among the **peoples**,
  '**Where** is their **God**?'"

Then the Lord was stirred to concern for his land
  and took pity on his people.

Note that the last verse is not the words *of* the Lord, but words *about* the Lord. The passage comes to a gentle ending. Soften your voice a little as you read this final sentence.

| READING II | 2 Corinthians 5:20—6:2 |

A reading from the second Letter of Saint Paul to the Corinthians

Brothers and sisters:
We are **ambassadors** for **Christ**,
  as if God were **appealing** through us.
We **implore** you on behalf of Christ,
  be **reconciled** to God.
For our sake he made him to **be** sin
    who did not **know** sin,
  so that we might become the **righteousness**
    of God in him.

This short passage is very important to the Church's theology of Lent.

READING II Saint Paul's second letter to the Corinthians does not come up in the Lectionary nearly as often as the first letter. Here is one of the strongest passages from this lesser-known letter. The concept of believers as "ambassadors for Christ" is important because of the role of the laity in social and family life, prayer, works of charity, and the witness of faith. Think of how, in the secular realm, a nation's

ambassadors go to foreign places to talk about their experience and to advocate for the leaders back home. So, too, then and now, Christians are called to give witness to their own experience of the risen Christ in the Church and to be advocates for that risen Christ in the world.

There are two important theological notions that this reading contributes to our experience of Lent. First, that for our sake God made Christ "to be sin who did not know sin," so that we might be saved. Second, the very end of the reading with its emphasis on *now* is important. None of us knows how long we will live. Though we try to avoid thinking about death, we must be

Working **together**, then,
  we appeal to you **not** to receive the grace
    of God in **vain**.
For he says:

  In an **acceptable** time I **heard** you,
    and on the day of **salvation** I **helped** you.

Behold, **now** is a very acceptable time;
  behold, **now** is the day of salvation.

The reading has a climax at the end. Emphasize the word "now" in its two places in the final verse.

GOSPEL   Matthew 6:1–6, 16–18

A reading from the holy Gospel according to Matthew

Jesus said to his **disciples**:
  "Take care **not** to perform righteous deeds
  in order that people may **see** them;
    otherwise, you will have **no** recompense
      from your heavenly **Father**.
When you give **alms**,
  do not blow a **trumpet** before you,
    as the **hypocrites** do in the **synagogues**
      and in the **streets**
  to win the praise of others.
Amen, I say to you,
  they have **received** their reward.
But when **you** give alms,
  do not let your **left** hand know what your **right** is doing,
    so that your almsgiving may be **secret**.
And your Father who **sees** in secret will **repay** you.

Except for these few opening words, the entire passage is made up of Jesus' words. Pause slightly before this line so that the assembly hears this identification of who speaks and to whom he speaks.

hypocrites = HIP-uh-crits
synagogues = SIN-uh-gogz

prepared for the end. Lent is the season of the year when the Church dedicates itself to preparing for meeting God face-to-face.

The progress of those who will be baptized and confirmed at the Easter Vigil offers us a witness of the importance of faith in turning people away from sin and toward the Good News. A strong proclamation that "now is a very acceptable time" and that "now is the day of salvation" will help the assembly recognize this importance.

The passage is short, so take your time and be well prepared. That will allow your hearers to recognize the gravity of this decisive time in the liturgical year.

GOSPEL   The exhortation of the Gospel prompts every believer to recognize our tendency to sin and to recognize Lent as the opportunity to confess and make reparation for the ways in which our sins drag down the Church and the society in which we live. Your service contributes to prompting us all to this recognition.

Ash Wednesday gives those who participate a distinctive and visible mark so that others do indeed recognize them as believers. The challenge the ashes might provide, then, is to let our faith so shape our attitudes and actions that people will recognize us as Christians even when we do not have the black smudge on our foreheads.

The Gospel of Matthew is the text for Ash Wednesday every year because the passage mentions fasting explicitly and

"When **you** pray,
    do not be like the **hypocrites**,
    who love to stand and pray in the **synagogues**
        and on **street corners**
    so that others may see them.
Amen, I say to you,
    they have **received** their reward.
But when **you** pray, go to your inner **room**,
    close the **door**, and pray to your Father in **secret**.
And your Father who **sees** in secret will **repay** you.

"When **you** fast,
    do not look **gloomy** like the **hypocrites**.
They neglect their **appearance**,
    so that they may **appear** to others to be fasting.
Amen, I say to you, they have **received** their reward.
But when **you** fast,
    anoint your **head** and wash your **face**,
    so that you may **not** appear to be fasting,
    except to your **Father** who is hidden.
And your Father who **sees** what is hidden
        will **repay** you."

In these last verses the reading names the practice many associate with the season of Lent, fasting. To unite the words of Jesus with the practice, be clear with this imperative about fasting.

because it exhorts us not to think that we earn God's favor by our public good works. By faith working through charity, we become a new creation in Christ and, therefore, become fruitful in the works of love. Saint James tells us that such love covers a multitude of sins because it is a participation in the infinite charity of Christ. But all is of grace, from start to finish.

This is a moderately long passage, and almost all of it is a quotation of Jesus' words to the disciples, delivered after the Sermon on the Mount. This is one of the few times when what is described in the Gospel anticipates what the members of the parish community might do in the weeks to come. (Perhaps some members of your parish walk on water or calm the sea, but in my community of faith, at least so far, that hasn't happened . . . yet.) Here the exhortations to almsgiving, prayer, and fasting will be taken up by believers between today and Holy Thursday, the end of Lent. For this reason, be measured and clear in your proclamation so that this link is made between Gospel and Church.

1ST SUNDAY OF LENT

Lectionary #23

READING I   Genesis 9:8–15

Genesis = JEN-uh-sis

Notice that most of the reading is from the mouth of God. This line identifies the speaker and the hearers, so be clear as you begin the passage.
Noah = NOH-ah

Imagine for yourself the covenant with nature that is captured here.

Pause here.

The nature imagery continues, here with the bow as the sign of the covenant, a wonderful and powerful image. ("Bow" is pronounced as in "rainbow," which is what it refers to, not what actors do after a performance!)
bow = boh

A reading from the Book of Genesis

God said to **Noah** and to his **sons** with him:
"**See**, I am now establishing my **covenant** with you
    and your descendants **after** you
    and with every living **creature** that was **with** you:
    all the **birds**, and the various tame and wild **animals**
    that were **with** you and came out of the **ark**.
I will establish my **covenant** with you,
    that never **again** shall all bodily creatures be **destroyed**
    by the waters of a **flood**;
    there shall not be another **flood** to devastate the **earth**."
God added:
"**This** is the **sign** that I am **giving** for all ages to come,
    of the covenant between **me** and **you**
    and **every** living creature **with** you:
    I set my **bow** in the clouds to serve as a **sign**
    of the covenant between **me** and the **earth**.
When I bring **clouds** over the earth,
    and the **bow** appears in the clouds,
    I will **recall** the covenant I have made
    between **me** and **you** and **all** living beings,
    so that the **waters** shall **never** again become a flood
    to destroy **all** mortal **beings**."

READING I   The familiar account of Noah and the flood occupies a large span of the book of Genesis. The narrative that you prepare for this First Sunday of Lent comes after the flood, just after Noah and his family and the animals have left the ark. This will help you understand the viewpoint of the Church in putting this at the start of the penitential season of renewal. Humanity was brought low by its sins in the time of Noah. So now at the start

of Lent we pause to consider how we have not lived up to our baptismal vocation as the people of God.

At Baptism we were brought into God's people, and in that rite we were cleansed of sin by God's grace. Lent gives the opportunity for renewal and for the restoration of our baptismal promises and purity in preparation for Easter. The covenant about which God speaks in this passage is the word of God to us in the Church now with no less promise, hope, or power.

Notice that all but a few words in the reading are in quotation marks as from the mouth of God. Yet, even though it is such a monologue from God's lips, there is a lot of action and drama in the passage. So do not read it as a news report of something that has already taken place. God speaks of the present, "I am now establishing my covenant," and of the future, "I will recall," and mediated by your well-prepared proclamation, these will apply today as vibrantly as they did to the Jews in antiquity.

Notice the tenses of the verbs in the reading. The first part is in the past tense, looking back to the Passion and to Christ's descent to the dead.

The backward look continues to the great flood. Pause significantly at the break. Noah = NOH-ah

Here the verbs shift significantly and consequentially into the present tense: "baptism, which saves *you now.*" Make eye contact with your hearers to emphasize that this means *you!* This final section is one sentence. Examine the sentence's structure so that you will be well prepared for delivering its hopeful message. Proclaim it slowly and clearly, rising toward the glory at the end.

READING II 1 Peter 3:18–22

A reading from the first Letter of Saint Peter

Beloved:
Christ **suffered** for sins **once**,
    the **righteous** for the sake of the **unrighteous**,
    that he might lead you to **God**.
Put to **death** in the **flesh**,
    he was brought to **life** in the **Spirit**.
In it he **also** went to preach to the spirits in **prison**,
    who had once been **disobedient**
    while God **patiently** waited in the days of Noah
    during the **building** of the **ark**,
    in which a **few** persons, **eight** in all,
    were **saved** through **water**.
This prefigured **baptism**, which saves you **now**.
It is not a removal of **dirt** from the body
    but an **appeal** to God for a clear **conscience**,
    through the **resurrection** of Jesus **Christ**,
    who has gone into **heaven**
    and is at the right hand of **God**,
    with **angels**, **authorities** and **powers** subject to him.

The nature images—of creatures, birds, animals, clouds, waters, and especially the bow (the rainbow)—are wonderful in the passages, so describe the world from God's vantage point in order to engage the imaginations of those to whom you proclaim.

READING II One of the most prominent icons of the Eastern Church is that of Jesus Christ's descent to the dead, to those who had died before the advent of our Savior. The meaning is that salvation is not only for all people in all places, but for all people of all times.

This descent is described uniquely in this passage of 1 Peter. It captures a central theological tenet of Christ proclaiming the Good News to those who lived before the Incarnation. Two further aspects of the passage warrant your attention. First, the passage is linked to the first reading because of the mention of "the days of Noah."

Second, at this First Sunday of Lent, we as the body of Christ have started to renew our baptismal dedication to God. The reading is explicit with its theology of Baptism, a fitting proclamation for this start of the Church's season of renewal.

You have every reason to be bold and emphatic with this passage. It is not an easy passage to prepare or to proclaim, but your clear delivery offers the community to which you proclaim the opportunity to understand itself in the line of tradition from the waters of the flood, to the waters of its Baptisms in the past, and forward to the Baptisms that will be celebrated at Easter.

GOSPEL   Mark 1:12–15

A reading from the holy Gospel according to Mark

The **Spirit** drove **Jesus** out into the **desert**,
　　and he remained in the desert for **forty** days,
　　　　tempted by **Satan**.
He was among wild **beasts**,
　　and the angels **ministered** to him.

After John had been **arrested**,
　　Jesus came to **Galilee** proclaiming the gospel of **God**:
　　"**This** is the time of **fulfillment**.
The **kingdom** of God is at **hand**.
Repent, and **believe** in the gospel."

The passage is both brief and filled with important symbols at the start of Lent.

Satan = SAY-t*n

Pause as the focus shifts.

Galilee = GAL-ih-lee

Pause before you proclaim the words of Jesus.

GOSPEL │ The three readings of Sundays are not usually so tightly linked as they are on this First Sunday of Lent. The metaphors of water and Baptism bring the three together as the Church begins its preparations for Easter.

　　Notice how brief the passage is. You can take your time and be deliberate with the important emphases. The symbolism of the number 40 is important in the tradition. We remember the 40 years that the Israelites

spent wandering in the wilderness on their way to the Promised Land. In today's passage we find the "forty days" of Jesus' time in the desert. And we are beginning to observe the "forty days" of Lent, and for this reason you can proclaim the imperative verbs, "Repent!" and "Believe!" The symbol of the "forty days" is as strong now as in the past, for God is ever with us as we prepare for Easter.

　　Because the passage is quite short, pause where the printed text has a break, for at this point in the short reading the focus shifts from Jesus in the desert to the link between the arrest of John and the beginning of Jesus' public ministry, proclaiming the Good News of God.

2ND SUNDAY OF LENT

Lectionary #26

READING I   Genesis 22:1–2, 9a, 10–13, 15–18

Genesis = JEN-uh-sis

This call sequence appears twice in the passage, once between God and Abraham and later between the angel and Abraham. **Abraham = AY-bruh-ham**

Here God commands Abraham with imperative verbs. Sound commanding. **Isaac = Ī-zik**
Moriah = moh-RĪ-uh

This section is the action of the narrative, important for capturing the imaginations of those hearing you.

A reading from the Book of Genesis

God put **Abraham** to the **test**.
He called to him, "**Abraham**!"
"**Here** I am!" he replied.
Then God said:
  "Take your son **Isaac**, your **only** one, whom you **love**,
    and **go** to the land of **Moriah**.
There you shall **offer** him up as a **holocaust**
  on a height that I will point **out** to you."

When they **came** to the place of which God had told him,
  Abraham built an **altar** there and arranged the **wood** on it.
Then he reached **out** and took the **knife** to **slaughter** his son.
But the LORD's **messenger** called to him from **heaven**,
  "**Abraham, Abraham**!"
"**Here** I am!" he answered.
"Do not lay your **hand** on the **boy**," said the messenger.
"Do not do the least **thing** to him.
I **know** now how **devoted** you are to God,
  since you did not **withhold** from me your **own** beloved son."
As Abraham looked **about**,
  he spied a **ram** caught by its **horns** in the **thicket**.
So he went and took the **ram**
  and offered it up as a holocaust in place of his son.

READING I This account of the near-sacrifice of Isaac at the hand of his father Abraham was very frequently taken up in the preaching and theology of the early Church and the Middle Ages. It was seen as a precedent for God the Father's sacrifice of his Son, Jesus Christ, on the cross.

From a rhetorical point of view, it is important for you to be aware of how much of the reading is from the mouths of the characters in the story, and their parts are varied. There are God's and the angel's calls to Abraham by name, and the imperative verbs, "Take your son . . . go to the land . . ." from God, and "Do not lay your hand on the boy" from the angel. There are Abraham's two replies, identical in form, "Here I am." Finally, there are the words of the Lord that come from the angel at the end of the reading. This is a long quotation. Examine it and parse it out for yourself so that you can deliver it with confidence and sustain the interest of those listening to you.

The variety of speakers and verb forms can be good and bad. They are good because they challenge you to vary your voice according to the speaker and what is being said. They are hard because you have to be mindful of the shifts in the text before you come to them. You should therefore know the structure of the reading thoroughly. This will take a bit of preparation time, but the assembly hearing you will benefit from your dedication.

Again the LORD's messenger called to Abraham
    from heaven and said:
"I **swear** by **myself**, declares the LORD,
that **because** you acted as you **did**
in not **withholding** from me your beloved **son**,
I will **bless** you **abundantly**
and make your **descendants** as countless
as the stars of the **sky** and the sands of the **seashore**;
your descendants shall take **possession**
of the gates of their **enemies**,
and in your **descendants** all the nations of the earth
    shall find **blessing**—
all this because you **obeyed** my command."

Here begins the final speech from the angel of the Lord.

READING II   Romans 8:31b–34

Romans = ROH-munz

A reading from the Letter of Saint Paul to the Romans

Brothers and sisters:
If God is **for** us, who can be **against** us?
He who did not **spare** his own Son
    but handed him **over** for us **all**,
    how will he not **also** give us **everything** else along with him?

Who will bring a **charge** against God's **chosen** ones?
It is God who **acquits** us, who will **condemn**?
Christ **Jesus** it is who **died**—or, rather, was **raised**—
    who also is at the right hand of **God**,
    who indeed **intercedes** for us.

The reading starts with a gripping rhetorical question. Deliver it as a true question addressed to those who are present.

The questions continue; pause after each to give your hearers a chance to consider their answer.

READING II This is a unique passage from the hand of the apostle Paul, not only because of the richness of its theology in the context of the letter to the Romans, but because of the many questions contained in it.

I recommend that you pause before and after each question as a way to give the community of faith before you a chance to consider what their own answers would be: "Who can be against us?" "Who will bring a charge?" "Who will condemn?" Because of the number and depth of these questions, they can be punctuated on each side with silence.

The point of the reading is that *nothing* can separate us from the love of Christ, not even our own sinfulness. Paul reminds us that the love of Christ conquers all things. The final sentence is a summary. This reading fits the time of the liturgical year most aptly, for in Lent believers consider what in their lives has tried to turn them away from the love of Christ. The Church once again considers the source of her faith, hope, and love, which are always from God, mediated by the Holy Spirit, and inspired by the example of Jesus Christ. The last sentence puts the reason for the questions into a light leading the Church through Lent to the Paschal Mystery.

GOSPEL   Mark 9:2–10

A reading from the holy Gospel according to Mark

Jesus took **Peter, James** and **John**
   and led them up a **high** mountain apart by **themselves**.
And he was **transfigured** before them,
   and his **clothes** became dazzling **white**,
   such as no fuller on earth could **bleach** them.
Then **Elijah** appeared to them along with **Moses**,
   and they were **conversing** with Jesus.
Then **Peter** said to Jesus in **reply**,
   "**Rabbi**, it is **good** that we are **here**!
Let us make three **tents**:
   one for **you**, one for **Moses**, and one for **Elijah**."
He hardly knew what to say, they were so **terrified**.
Then a **cloud** came, casting a **shadow** over them;
   from the cloud came a **voice**,
   "**This** is my beloved **Son. Listen** to him."
Suddenly, looking **around**, they no longer saw **anyone**
   but Jesus **alone** with them.

As they were coming **down** from the mountain,
   he **charged** them not to relate what they had seen to **anyone**,
   except when the Son of **Man** had **risen** from the **dead**.
So they **kept** the matter to **themselves**,
   questioning what rising from the dead **meant**.

See below for the reason why the details of Jesus' garments should be proclaimed very clearly.

Elijah = ee-LĪ-juh
Moses = MOH-ziz

Rabbi = RAB-ī

Pause here at the break for the assembly to be poised for the voice from the cloud. These words from above are the crux of the narrative.

This is the typical Marcan element of the "messianic secret."

GOSPEL   The evangelist's description of the color of Jesus' garments here is quite detailed, not merely "white," but "dazzling white," and "such as no fuller on earth could bleach them."

Mark is often very concise, not including much detail. Clearly here, in the experience of the evangelist and his community, the whiteness of the garments meant something, something too important to leave out.

Although we cannot know for certain if there was an especially *baptismal* significance to these white garments, it is not unlikely. Notice that the voice from above here is also present at the Baptism of Jesus and uses similar phrases, "my Son" and "Beloved."

As the living body of Christ moving closer to the celebration and renewal of initiation at Easter, we make a link between the experience of Christ and his followers in the first century and our experience as believers

now, two millennia later. So, this echo of the early community's baptismal practice is a direct link between what they did in the past and what we do in the Church today.

If your parish is blessed with catechumens and elect, or with candidates for reception into full communion or for completion of initiation, address these details to them. They can see that the tradition has been maintained from the earliest days.

3RD SUNDAY OF LENT

Exodus = EK-suh-dus

Lines two and four are the parts of the first commandment with which people are familiar.
Egypt = EE-jipt

Here is a further elaboration on the first commandment.

Like the first, the third commandment has commentary accompanying it here.
sabbath = SAB-uth

Lectionary #29

READING I   Exodus 20:1–17

A reading from the Book of Exodus

In **those** days, God **delivered** all these **commandments**:
   "**I**, the **LORD**, am your **God**,
      who **brought** you out of the land of **Egypt**, that place
         of **slavery**.
You shall not have **other** gods besides **me**.
You shall not carve **idols** for yourselves
      in the shape of **anything** in the sky **above**
      or on the earth **below** or in the waters **beneath** the earth;
      you shall not bow **down** before them or **worship** them.
For **I**, the LORD, your **God**, am a **jealous** God,
      inflicting **punishment** for their fathers' **wickedness**
      on the **children** of those who **hate** me,
      down to the **third** and **fourth** generation;
      but bestowing **mercy** down to the **thousandth** generation
      on the children of those who **love** me
         and keep my **commandments**.

"You shall **not** take the name of the LORD, your God, in **vain**.
For the LORD will **not** leave **unpunished**
      the one who **takes** his name in **vain**.

Remember to keep **holy** the sabbath day.
Six days you may **labor** and do all your **work**,
      but the **seventh** day is the **sabbath** of the LORD, your **God**.

On the Third, Fourth, and Fifth Sundays of Lent in Years B and C, there are two sets of readings assigned by the Church and therefore two sets in the *Workbook.* If the parish has catechumens and people elected for initiation or full communion at the Easter Vigil, it's likely that you will use the readings from Year A. Check with the person who coordinates the schedule of readers to find out which readings to prepare.

READING I   There are two basic characteristics of this passage for which you will need to prepare: it is fairly long and it will be familiar to most listeners. Consider how you, as a hearer of another person proclaiming, would be engaged by such a passage.

Notice that far more of the passage is dedicated to the first three commandments than to the remaining seven, which are simply listed, with a little elaboration for the tenth. The first and third commandments are by far the longest, nearly half the passage as a whole.

Because of its relative length, prepare your proclamation of the first commandment as a unit unto itself, then the next two as a unit, and finally the last seven as a unit.

Although many people might not be able to list all Ten Commandments in order, they are all familiar. Emphasize the commandments themselves by pausing as you move from one to the next, even in the final section where some of the commandments are quite short, "you shall not steal," for example.

No **work** may be done then either by **you**, or your
    son or **daughter**,
    or your **male** or **female** slave, or your **beast**,
    or by the **alien** who lives with you.
In **six** days the LORD made the **heavens** and the **earth**,
    the **sea** and all that is **in** them;
    but on the **seventh** day he **rested**.
That is why the LORD has **blessed** the sabbath day and
    made it **holy**.

"Honor your **father** and your **mother**,
    that you may have a long life in the land
    which the LORD, your **God**, is **giving** you.
You shall not **kill**.
You shall not commit **adultery**.
You shall not **steal**.
You shall not bear false **witness** against your **neighbor**.
You shall not **covet** your neighbor's **house**.
You shall not **covet** your neighbor's **wife**,
    nor his male or female **slave**, nor his **ox** or **ass**,
    nor anything **else** that **belongs** to him."

[Shorter: Exodus 20:1–3, 7–8, 12–17]

From here to the end, the commandments are sparely listed.

In our culture and even in the courts, the Ten Commandments have been quite important in debates about separation of church and state. Whatever you think about the issue, proclaim the commandments well, for they are a central part of our faith.

READING II Although the letters of Paul were written before the Gospels, his theology of the cross and its power is potent and tangible. This passage is short but its message is deep.

During the season of Lent—as the Church, universal and local, prepares for the celebration of Easter—we need to consider how the cross of Christ is sometimes misunderstood by believers and nonbelievers alike.

Saint Paul knew the risen Christ, not Jesus of Nazareth, as he himself says explicitly. It is important to realize that he writes about the cross not in the past tense, but in the present: "the cross . . . is the power of God." The historical moment of the Crucifixion was indeed past as the apostle Paul wrote these words, so how can he write in the present tense about a past historical event? Because the suffering of the body of Christ—in the life of Jesus, in the ministry of Paul and the communities he founded, and today in your own parish—are all joined in the Paschal Mystery of God's life in us, then, now, and in the future.

Corinthians = kor-IN-thee-unz

READING II   1 Corinthians 1:22–25

A reading from the first Letter of Saint Paul to the Corinthians

Brothers and sisters:
Jews demand **signs** and Greeks look for **wisdom**,
    but we proclaim Christ **crucified**,
    a **stumbling** block to **Jews** and **foolishness** to **Gentiles**,
    but to those who are **called**, Jews and Greeks **alike**,
    Christ the **power** of God and the **wisdom** of God.
For the **foolishness** of God is **wiser** than human **wisdom**,
    and the **weakness** of God is **stronger** than human **strength**.

If possible, memorize this key line and
proclaim it while looking at the assembly.
Gentiles = JEN-tils

The artistry of the apostle's rhetoric is
manifest here in his skillful use of paradox.

GOSPEL   John 2:13–25

A reading from the holy Gospel according to John

Since the **Passover** of the Jews was **near**,
    Jesus went up to **Jerusalem**.
He found in the **temple** area those who sold **oxen**,
        sheep and **doves**,
    as well as the **money** changers seated there.
He made a **whip** out of **cords**
    and **drove** them all **out** of the temple area,
        with the **sheep** and **oxen**,
    and **spilled** the coins of the **money** changers
    and **overturned** their **tables**,
    and to those who sold **doves** he said,
    "Take these **out** of here,
    and **stop** making my Father's **house** a **marketplace**."

Jerusalem = juh-ROO-suh-lem
Attend to the details here by proclaiming
them deliberately. These will engage
those who listen to your delivery.

Paradox is hard to capture well in proclamations of scripture. Their subtleties are perhaps not as easily understood as other literary techniques. The end of this reading is a paradox, as the apostle speaks of *foolishness* being "wiser," and of *weakness* being "stronger." God's ways are never fully understood by human beings, so the apostle is able to write about the juxtapositions of "God's" and "human" wisdom, "God's" and "human" strength.

For a short reading, this passage is not the easiest you might have been assigned. Be convinced of its significance for the Church here and now, in your community on this Third Sunday of Lent, and you can boldly proclaim the apostle's theology of the cross. The key line for your proclamation is this: "Christ is the power of God and the wisdom of God."

GOSPEL Although we are in Year B of the Lectionary's three-year cycle, and therefore concentrating on the Gospel of Mark, during Lent and Easter the Gospel of John appears frequently. The theology of the Gospel of John is uniquely suited to the Church's season of preparation for and celebration of Easter.

His **disciples** recalled the words of **Scripture**,
>   *Zeal for your house will* **consume** *me.*
At **this** the Jews answered and said to him,
>   "What **sign** can you show us for **doing** this?"
Jesus answered and said to them,
>   "**Destroy** this temple and in **three** days I will raise it **up**."
The Jews said,
>   "This **temple** has been under construction for **forty-six years**,
>   and **you** will raise it up in **three days**?"
But **he** was speaking about the temple of his **body**.
Therefore, when he was raised from the **dead**,
>   his disciples **remembered** that he had said this,
>   and they came to believe the **Scripture**
>   and the **word** Jesus had **spoken**.

While he was in **Jerusalem** for the feast of **Passover**,
>   **many** began to believe in his **name**
>   when they saw the **signs** he was doing.
But Jesus would not **trust** himself to them because he **knew**
>   them all,
>   and did not need **anyone** to testify about human **nature**.
He **himself** understood it **well**.

Here the evangelist is taking up a passage from Psalm 69:9. Pause after the action and quotation, for the tone shifts after this. zeal = zeel

This whole section is a kind of parenthetical comment.

Your tone of voice can supply a clear conclusion.

The passage you prepare is the account of Jesus' overturning the tables in the temple. The first half has the action; the second half interprets the action. It is a unique moment in the ministry of Jesus, for, even knowing that his death was drawing nearer, Jesus was justly angry and indignant in the temple here. Your proclamation can capture some of the drama of the scene.

We know from biblical studies that the Gospels were all written years after the events they narrate. For instance, here, Jesus in the Gospel of John speaks of the imminent destruction of the temple. When the evangelist wrote his Gospel, the temple had indeed been destroyed by the Romans in the year 70. So the evangelist takes recent history and interprets it theologically and christologically, as in the parenthetical remark, "Jesus was speaking of the temple of his body."

That link between the temple and the body of Christ is the crux of your proclamation, for on it rests the significant point that the Church is not a building, but an assembly, a body not of stone, but of human flesh united as the body of Christ in the sacraments of initiation. In the season of Lent, this interpretation is more than fitting because the Church is reviewing how it has fallen short of the lavishness of God's grace.

As you prepare, seek a good balance in the presentation of the two parts of the reading, for the engaging action is narrated at the start, and the end of the reading is more explanatory than action-packed.

3RD SUNDAY OF LENT, YEAR A

Lectionary #28

READING I   Exodus 17:3–7

A reading from the Book of Exodus

In those days, in their thirst for **water**,
   the people **grumbled** against Moses,
   saying, "**Why** did you ever make us leave **Egypt**?
Was it just to have us **die** here of **thirst**
   with our **children** and our **livestock**?"
So Moses cried out to the LORD,
   "What shall I **do** with this people?
A little **more** and they will **stone** me!"
The LORD answered Moses,
   "Go over there in front of the **people**,
   along with some of the **elders** of Israel,
   holding in your hand, as you go,
   the **staff** with which you struck the **river**.
I will be standing there in **front** of you on the rock in Horeb.
Strike the rock, and the **water** will flow from it
   for the people to drink."
This Moses **did**, in the presence of the **elders** of Israel.
The place was called Massah and Meribah,
   because the Israelites **quarreled** there
   and **tested** the LORD, saying,
   "Is the LORD **in** our midst or **not**?"

In Lent we should emphasize any references to water (or dryness or thirst) in anticipation of the Easter Baptisms!

This is a complaint. Although you don't want to whine, make it sound like a serious complaint.

Moses = MOH-ziz

The Lord's instructions again emphasize water. This is a significant moment in the history of Israel, as the people are despairing and the Lord provides.

Horeb = HOH-reb

Massah = MAS-ah
Meribah = MAIR-ih-bah

READING I This reading anticipates the Gospel reading's image of water, and the Gospel anticipates the use of water in the rites of Christian initiation, toward which the Forty Days of Lent are directed. So this reading you will proclaim from the book of Exodus is part of an interwoven net of texts, practices, and theology for this season. Keep that in mind as you prepare.

This narrative is part of the long journey of the Israelites from slavery in Egypt to the Promised Land. From the earliest days of the Church, that trek from Egypt to Israel was taken up as a metaphor for the Paschal Mystery and the narrative of the Gospels, moving from Christ's death to his Resurrection. The most engaging part of the journey of the Israelites is their walking on dry land through the Red Sea, and so the bishops of the early Church took up that journey through water as a metaphor for the catechumens' journey from unbelief to faith, and of the Christian's journey from sin to salvation gained in the death of Jesus.

Overall, the reading is laced with speeches. First the people complain to Moses, then Moses cries out to the Lord, then the Lord instructs to Moses, and finally we return to the complaining Israelites. Make sure that the liturgical assembly can

Proclaim with the directness of Paul's words.

READING II   Romans 5:1–2, 5–8

A reading from the Letter of Saint Paul to the Romans

Brothers and sisters:
Since we have been justified by **faith**,
  we have **peace** with God through our Lord Jesus **Christ**,
  through whom we have gained **access** by faith
  to this **grace** in which we stand,
  and we **boast** in **hope** of the glory of **God**.

This is a profound theological truth.

And **hope** does not **disappoint**,
  because the love of **God** has been poured **out** into our **hearts**
  through the Holy **Spirit** who has been **given** to us.
For **Christ**, while we were still **helpless**,
  died at the appointed **time** for the **ungodly**.
Indeed, only with difficulty does one die for a **just** person,
  though perhaps for a **good** person one **might** even
    find courage to **die**.
But God **proves** his love for us
  in that while we were still **sinners** Christ **died** for us.

---

distinguish from the tone of your voice the context and the speeches. By your very proclamation, those who hear you should be able to recognize what is a quotation and what is not.

READING II   As he often does, Paul writes in an engaging literary form, employing first-person pronouns—"we," "our," "us." Sometimes when he does so, he is speaking only of himself or his life. More

often, as here in the letter to the Romans, he writes in the plural form. He is speaking to members of the Church at Rome, and the literary form he employs puts him and the believers in Rome together in understanding the ways of God in human salvation.

With this in mind, then, it might be best not to think of your proclamation as an imitation of Paul, for your assembly is far from the city of Rome and our century far from the first. Yet, even with these distinctions, you and the assembly to which you will proclaim share a fundamental experience with

Paul and the ancient Roman Christian assembly to which he wrote, and that experience is Baptism.

Baptism has made each member inextricably linked to all. While you and the other members of your parish, whether infants or adults, were still sinners (by original sin for the infants, original and personal sin for the adults), Christ saved you, just as he saved Paul and the people of the ancient

GOSPEL   John 4:5–42

A reading from the holy Gospel according to John

Jesus came to a town of **Samaria** called **Sychar**,
near the plot of land that **Jacob** had given to his son **Joseph**.
Jacob's **well** was there.
Jesus, tired from his **journey**, sat down there at the **well**.
It was about noon.

A woman of **Samaria** came to draw **water**.
Jesus said to her,
"**Give** me a drink."
His disciples had gone into the town to buy food.
The Samaritan woman said to him,
"How can **you**, a **Jew**, ask **me**, a **Samaritan** woman,
for a **drink**?"
—For Jews use **nothing** in common with Samaritans.—
Jesus answered and said to her,
"If you knew the **gift** of God
and who is saying to you, '**Give** me a drink,'
you would have asked him
and he would have given you **living** water."
The woman said to him,
"**Sir**, you do not even have a **bucket** and the cistern is **deep**;
where then can you **get** this living water?
Are you greater than our father **Jacob**,
who **gave** us this cistern and **drank** from it **himself**
with his **children** and his **flocks**?"

This opening sets the scene by providing the details of place and time for the long narrative to follow.
Samaria = suh-MAIR-ee-uh
Sychar = SĪ-kar
Jacob = JAY-kub

This social transgression—a Jew interacting with a Samaritan—is foundational to the passage and key in Jesus' ministry to Gentiles.
Samaritan = suh-MAIR-uh-tun

Pause slightly as you move from one speaker to the other so that the assembly can feel the shift.

Church from whose letter you read. In this, what Paul wrote and what you proclaim are intimately connected, and, across the continents and centuries, we are connected to that ancient Christian assembly in Rome and to Paul himself. "We," like they, "have gained access by faith to this grace in which we stand," in which the assembly before you exists and have been set free by the unimaginable gift of God.

If, as a minister of God's word, you truly believe this gift to be yours from God's generosity, "because the love of God has been poured out into our hearts," then proclaim Paul's words as your own. Those before you will accept the words as true if you, from your faith and your experience, believe them to be so.

GOSPEL This long reading from chapter 4 of the Gospel of John has been associated with the formation of catechumens for Baptism since the earliest times. Indeed, it can be placed in the liturgical calendar of the early Church, for its theology was then, as now, related to its place in the Church's conception of time and the Church.

A reader can see how the faith of the Samaritan woman deepens from unbelief to belief, and then to the point where we hear that she herself is testifying to the good things that Jesus has done. This progress in faith is similar to the experience each year when the faith of the newly baptized at the Vigil awakens the faith of the entire Church.

Although the reading does not mention Baptism, imagine the rite as celebrated in your own parish, and know that this metaphor of water is deep in the Church's memory and experience, particularly during Lent.

Jesus answered and said to her,
  "Everyone who drinks **this** water will be thirsty **again**;
  but whoever drinks the water **I** shall give will **never** thirst;
  the water I shall give will become in him
  a **spring** of water welling up to eternal **life**."
The woman said to him,
  "Sir, **give** me this water, so that **I** may not be thirsty
  or have to keep coming **here** to draw **water**."

Jesus said to her,
  "**Go** call your **husband** and come **back**."
The woman answered and said to him,
  "I do not **have** a husband."
Jesus answered her,
  "You are **right** in saying, 'I do not have a husband.'
For you have had **five** husbands,
  and the one you have now is **not** your husband.
What you have said is **true**."
The woman said to him,

Jesus speaks the truth about her life, yet it does not impede his conversation with her.

  "Sir, I can see that you are a **prophet**.
Our **ancestors** worshiped on this **mountain**;
  but you people say that the place to worship is in **Jerusalem**."
Jesus said to her,

Jerusalem = juh-ROO-suh-lem

  "**Believe** me, woman, the hour is coming
  when you will worship the Father
  neither on this mountain **nor** in Jerusalem.
You people worship what you do not understand;
  we worship what we understand,
  because **salvation** is from the **Jews**.

It is similar too to the progress and perseverance in faith of each Christian from Baptism until death, whether that span is a century or a few hours.

Whether or not the account is a reflection of baptismal formation in the community of John's Gospel, it is for the Church today a brilliant account of faith development. The narrative can deepen the faith not only of those about to be baptized, but of all members of the sacred assembly.

We see the faith of the woman grow, from her opening line to Jesus about the practical matters at hand—"Sir, you do not even have a bucket"—to what, after her conversion, she tells her neighbors: "He told me everything I have done." Between these two her faith deepens from skepticism to trust.

For you, the Gospel reader preparing such a narrative for proclamation, particularly with the long liturgies of the Three Days on the horizon, there might be a temptation to think, "Hmm, this is a long reading; I should keep up a good pace here so that the assembly does not get bored." If that is your concern, it would be better to use the abbreviated version than to rush through the long version. With a long reading, it is

Messiah = meh-SĪ-uh

But the hour is **coming**, and is now **here**,
    when **true** worshipers will worship the Father
        in **Spirit** and **truth**;
    and indeed the Father seeks such people to worship him.
God is **Spirit**, and those who worship him
    must worship in **Spirit** and **truth**."
The woman said to him,
    "I know that the **Messiah** is coming, the one called the **Christ**;
    when he **comes**, he will tell us **everything**."
Jesus said to her,
    "**I** am he, the one **speaking** with you."

Jesus often scandalizes his own followers.

At that moment his disciples returned,
    and were **amazed** that he was talking with a **woman**,
    but still no one said, "What are you **looking** for?"
    or "Why are you talking with **her**?"
The woman **left** her water jar
    and went into the town and said to the people,
    "Come see a man who told me **everything** I have **done**.
Could he possibly be the **Christ**?"
They went out of the town and came to him.

Rabbi = RAB-ī

Meanwhile, the disciples urged him, "Rabbi, **eat**."
But he said to them,
    "I have food to eat of which you do not know."
So the disciples said to one another,
    "Could someone have **brought** him something to eat?"
Jesus said to them,
    "**My** food is to do the will of the one who **sent** me
    and to finish his **work**.
Do you not say, 'In four months the harvest will be here'?
I tell you, look **up** and see the fields ripe for the **harvest**.

This is a difficult section, for the passage is already long and a new set of images is introduced—food, sowing, harvesting, reaping.

always better to give a strong proclamation that takes a little more time than to give a speedy version with little of it heard or well received.

As you prepare, notice the narrative breaks. The first part sets the scene, and next is the opening exchange about water. This metaphor is, of course, very important as the catechumens and the Church anticipate Easter Baptisms and renewal of baptismal promises.

In the next part, Jesus reveals his knowledge of the complexity of her life. The details are important not to cast blame on the woman, for Jesus himself does not do this, but to demonstrate that this person with whom Jesus had such a long conversation was a person of whom many would disapprove. Her faith deepens during this exchange, for she calls him "a prophet" and then he reveals to her that he is the Messiah.

Then their conversation is broken by the return of the disciples.

The last section is a summary, in a way, but it reveals also that her word about Jesus brings many to faith, just as the deepening faith of the catechumens enriches the faith of the Church into which they are welcomed. Your proclamation of this long narrative is a opportunity for strengthening faith and for making a link between the faith of the Samaritan woman, the faith of those being brought to the Church, and the faith of those who have been members for nearly their entire lives.

The **reaper** is already receiving **payment**
  and gathering **crops** for eternal **life**,
  so that the **sower** and **reaper** can rejoice **together**.
For here the saying is verified that '**One** sows and **another** reaps.'
I sent you to **reap** what you have not **worked** for;
  others have done the work,
  and **you** are sharing the **fruits** of their work."

The woman's "evangelizing" to her neighbors, testifying to Jesus' word, brings many of her people to belief.

Many of the Samaritans of that town began to **believe** in him
  because of the word of the woman who testified,
  "He told me **everything** I have done."
When the Samaritans **came** to him,
  they invited him to **stay** with them;
  and he stayed there two days.
Many more began to believe in him because of his **word**,
  and they said to the **woman**,
  "We no longer believe because of **your** word;
  for we have heard for **ourselves**,
  and we know that this is **truly** the savior of the **world**."

[Shorter: John 4:5–15, 19b–26, 39a, 40–42]

4TH SUNDAY OF LENT

Lectionary #32

READING I   2 Chronicles 36:14–16, 19–23

A reading from the second Book of Chronicles

In **those** days, all the **princes** of Judah, the **priests**, and the **people**
    added **infidelity** to **infidelity**,
    practicing **all** the abominations of the **nations**
    and **polluting** the LORD's **temple**
    which he had **consecrated** in **Jerusalem**.

Early and **often** did the LORD, the God of their **fathers**,
    send his **messengers** to them,
    for he had **compassion** on his people and his **dwelling** place.
But they **mocked** the messengers of God,
    despised his warnings, and **scoffed** at his prophets,
    until the **anger** of the LORD against his people was so **inflamed**
    that there was no **remedy**.
Their enemies **burnt** the house of God,
    tore **down** the walls of **Jerusalem**,
    set all its **palaces** afire,
    and **destroyed** all its precious objects.
Those who escaped the **sword** were carried **captive** to **Babylon**,
    where they became **servants** of the king of the **Chaldeans** and
        his **sons**
    until the **kingdom** of the **Persians** came to power.

Chronicles = KRAH-nih-k*ls

The opening sets the stage for the disaster that will strike Israel.
Judah = JOO-duh

The Israelites would not pay attention to the warnings delivered by God's messengers.

Jerusalem = juh-ROO-suh-lem

This section is a summary of that critical moment of Israel's history when the Jews were defeated and taken into captivity. Be clear with the details.
Babylon = BAB-ih-lon
Chaldeans =kal-DEE-unz

On the Third, Fourth, and Fifth Sundays of Lent in Years B and C, there are two sets of readings assigned by the Church and therefore two sets in the *Workbook*. If the parish has catechumens and people elected for initiation or full communion at the Easter Vigil, it's likely that you will use the readings from Year A. Check with the person who coordinates the schedule of readers to find out which readings to prepare.

READING I Today's reading is from a book of the Hebrew Scriptures that is proclaimed only once in the whole three-year Lectionary cycle. Enunciate the identification line clearly, for many of those assembled will not be familiar with the name.

We know from the Gospels—most often in Mark, this year's Gospel—how often Jesus is helped by or finds favor with the most unexpected characters—tax collectors, sinners, prostitutes—rather than those whom most of his followers might have expected him to associate. In this

Jesus was following an ancient Jewish theological line of unexpected events and characters who mediate God's presence, message, providence, and indeed salvation to God's people.

This account has one of those unexpected characters who fulfills God's plan. Here it is no ordinary passerby or Roman citizen; it is the pagan king of Persia, a distant land, and this king's name was Cyrus.

The author declares the problem from the first line: the princes, priests, and people had "added infidelity of infidelity." Not just your ordinary lack of faith, but infidelity to

All this was to fulfill the **word** of the LORD spoken by **Jeremiah**:
 "Until the land has retrieved its lost sabbaths,
 during all the time it lies **waste** it shall have **rest**
 while **seventy** years are **fulfilled**."

In the first year of **Cyrus**, king of **Persia**,
 in order to fulfill the **word** of the LORD spoken by **Jeremiah**,
 the LORD **inspired** King Cyrus of **Persia**
 to issue this **proclamation** throughout his **kingdom**,
 both by word of **mouth** and in **writing**:
 "Thus says **Cyrus**, king of **Persia**:
 All the kingdoms of the **earth**
 the LORD, the God of **heaven**, has **given** to me,
 and he has **also** charged me to build him a **house**
 in **Jerusalem**, which is in **Judah**.
Whoever, therefore, among you belongs to **any** part of his **people**,
 let him go **up**, and may his **God** be **with** him!"

Persia = PER-zhuh
Jeremiah = jair-uh-MĪ-uh
Cyrus = SĪ-rus

This final portion reveals the main message of the passage for relation to the Gospel; the people's devotion is encouraged by an unexpected person, the pagan king of a foreign nation.

READING II Ephesians 2:4–10

Ephesians = ee-FEE-zhunz

A reading from the Letter of Saint Paul to the Ephesians

Brothers and sisters:
God, who is rich in **mercy**,
 because of the great **love** he had for us,
 even when we were **dead** in our **transgressions**,
 brought us to life with **Christ**—by **grace** you have
  been **saved**—,
 raised us **up** with him,

This opening sentence is long. Examine it and parse it out for yourself so that you can proclaim it smoothly.

---

an appalling degree! God sent prophets to call them to change their ways before it was too late—but "too late" arrived and they were conquered and the survivors carried into exile in Babylon. (This is the "Babylonian captivity.") The familiar prophet Jeremiah is named here, for he prophesied to the people in Babylon.

Decades later comes this pagan king Cyrus. The one who finally restored Israel was not a fellow Israelite, it was the Persian king. God commanded Cyrus to build him a house in Jerusalem (for the previous house of God, Solomon's temple, was destroyed as

the people were carried off), and Cyrus set Israel free to go up to Jerusalem. As a result of Cyrus's obedience of God, the house of worship was restored and the people had the place for worship that they had ignored before their captivity.

Be careful and close with your preparation, for the account is long and fairly complex; moreover, it has a few strange names. Spending some time in studying the passage will be worthwhile for you and the congregation you serve.

READING II At important moments in the Church's history, the debate about the relationship of faith and works has been taken up with passion. It characterized the debate between Peter and Paul in the middle of the first century and the debate between the Catholic Church in Rome and Martin Luther, and it still goes on among many Christians. This tension is evident in this beautiful excerpt from Paul's letter to the Ephesians.

Paul was the advocate for faith over works in our salvation, and the letter is clear on this—"by grace you have been

and **seated** us with him in the **heavens** in Christ **Jesus**,
that in the ages to **come**
he might show the **immeasurable** riches of his **grace**
in his **kindness** to us in Christ **Jesus**.
For by **grace** you have been **saved** through **faith**,
and this is not from **you**; it is the **gift** of God;
it is not from **works**, so no one may **boast**.
For we are his **handiwork**, created in Christ **Jesus** for the
good **works**
that God has prepared in **advance**,
that we should **live** in them.

Pause at the break in preparation for the strong second half.

The message of the final verse is powerful; proclaim it with comparable strength.

GOSPEL   John 3:14–21

A reading from the holy Gospel according to John

Jesus said to **Nicodemus**:
"Just as **Moses** lifted up the **serpent** in the **desert**,
so must the Son of **Man** be lifted up,
so that **everyone** who **believes** in him may have eternal **life**."
For God so **loved** the world that he gave his only **Son**,
so that everyone who **believes** in him might not **perish**
but might have eternal **life**.
For God did **not** send his Son into the world
to **condemn** the world,
but that the world might be **saved** through him.
Whoever **believes** in him will not be condemned,
but whoever does **not** believe has **already** been condemned,
because he has not believed in the name of the only Son of **God**.

Nicodemus = nik-oh-DEE-mus

This reading contains one of the most well-known verses in scripture, John 3:16. Proclaim it with confidence. Pause at the end of the verse before you continue.

saved"—without ignoring the important of works. You find at the end of the passage that "we are his handiwork, created in Christ Jesus for the good works that God has prepared." Thus we are God's creation, gifted by God's grace, and from this will flow the good works with which we thank God and contribute to the wellbeing of society and the world.

Although the theological point might seem like obvious, it is still poignant in the Catholic faith, for many believers still operate in faith as if God only loves them if they

are doing good works, as if they could earn God's love. Rather, God first loves us, and for this we give thanks and from that flows our contribution to the Church, to society, to humanity, to Creation.

Take advantage of the first-person plural pronouns throughout the passage—"we," "us," "our"—to engage the assembly. You stand in Saint Paul's stead as you deliver God's word, so address the congregation as Paul addressed the Ephesians, with confidence and love.

GOSPEL John 3:16 is one of the most well-known sentences from the lips of Jesus in the whole of the New Testament: "God so loved the world that he gave his only Son." That all Christians share the faith and confidence of this verse is important, so proclaim it with conviction and ecumenical confidence.

The entire reading is the words of Jesus to Nicodemus, yet because here Jesus speaks of himself in the third person, "God did not send the Son . . . to condemn the world," rather than in the first person, "God did not send me . . ." you can proclaim

And **this** is the **verdict**,
    that the **light** came into the world,
    but **people** preferred **darkness** to **light**,
    because their works were **evil**.
For **everyone** who does **wicked** things **hates** the light
    and does not come **toward** the light,
    so that his **works** might not be **exposed**.
But whoever lives the **truth comes** to the light,
    so that his **works** may be clearly seen as done in **God**.

them as if they are indeed your own testimony to the love of God for the salvation of the world. You offer this testimony from the Gospel of John to your fellow believers.

The reading is from the start of the Gospel, in chapter 3, and Nicodemus appears again at the other end of the Gospel, after Jesus has died on the cross. There Nicodemus comes with Joseph of Arimethea to give Jesus a proper burial. The relevant part of that reading is how Nicodemus is introduced, as the one "who had at first come to Jesus at night." By this we know

that the tension between day and night, light and darkness, are important to this formerly secret follower.

Knowing this will help you understand better the final section of the reading you prepare, for it speaks of Jesus as "the light [that] came into the world." And that is spoken to Nicodemus, who has moved from darkness into light. Testify to his conversion with a strong proclamation of the reading.

4TH SUNDAY OF LENT, YEAR A

Lectionary #31

Samuel = SAM-yoo-ul

This reading alternates between narrative and direct discourse. Mark in your *Workbook* who the speakers are so that you know their roles in the progress of this story of election. Pause as speakers change so that the assembly can sense the change.
Jesse = JES-ee
Bethlehem = BETH-luh-hem

Consider how you will proclaim *thoughts* differently than spoken words. Will this difference be understood by the assembly?
Eliab = ee-LĪ-ub

Can the assembly know from your voice that the Lord's words are different from those of Samuel?

READING I   1 Samuel 16:1b, 6–7, 10–13a

A reading from the first Book of Samuel

The LORD said to **Samuel**:
   "Fill your horn with **oil**, and be on your **way**.
I am sending you to **Jesse** of Bethlehem,
   for I have chosen my **king** from among his **sons**."

As Jesse and his sons came to the **sacrifice**,
   Samuel looked at **Eliab** and thought,
   "**Surely** the LORD's **anointed** is here before him."
But the LORD said to Samuel:
   "Do not judge from his **appearance** or from his lofty **stature**,
   because I have rejected him.
Not as **man** sees does **God** see,
   because **man** sees the **appearance**
   but the LORD looks into the **heart**."
In the same way Jesse presented **seven** sons before Samuel,
   but Samuel said to **Jesse**,
   "The LORD has not chosen **any** one of these."
Then Samuel asked Jesse,
   "Are these **all** the sons you **have**?"
Jesse replied,
   "There is still the **youngest**, who is tending the **sheep**."
Samuel said to Jesse,
   "**Send** for him;
   we will not begin the sacrificial **banquet** until he arrives **here**."

READING I   A Lenten reading about election—like the one you are preparing in which David is chosen from among the sons of Jesse—cannot help but have different layers of interpretations in the minds, hearts, and experiences of the Church. One might think, first, of the life of Christ, the savior for whom the Church and the world wait—the only-begotten of the Father, the chosen one of God. Second, one might think of the elect of the catechumenate, those in formation who will be brought into the Church and baptized at the Easter Vigil. Third, one might think of the community of faith in which you minister, for they, as a whole, are the people of God, the incarnate and risen body of Christ in the Church. They, too, are the chosen of God. Fourth, one might think of all people, those who by the gift of life, which has its origin in God, were chosen to have life and enjoy the company of family and friends and time and space. Finally, one can think of all living things, of all creation, which exists also as a gift of God.

As you read this reading from 1 Samuel and think about what will best bring it forth for the community, notice that David was at first overlooked by his family. His father has

From this point, the reading focuses on David. Be clear in reading the descriptions of him.

This is a rite of election in which David is marked with distinction.

Jesse sent and had the young man brought to them.
He was **ruddy**, a youth **handsome** to behold
    and making a **splendid** appearance.
The LORD said,
    "There—anoint **him**, for **this** is the one!"
Then **Samuel**, with the horn of oil in **hand**,
    anointed **David** in the presence of his **brothers**;
    and from that day **on**, the spirit of the LORD
        rushed upon David.

READING II Ephesians 5:8–14

Ephesians = ee-FEE-zhunz

These opening two lines are extremely important.

The next few verses are encouragements to the Church.

The final part, the quotation, is a rallying cry. It is an imperative, a command: wake up!

A reading from the Letter of Saint Paul to the Ephesians

Brothers and sisters:
You were once **darkness**,
    but **now** you are **light** in the **Lord**.
Live as children of **light**,
    for **light** produces every kind of **goodness**
    and **righteousness** and **truth**.
Try to learn what is **pleasing** to the Lord.
Take no part in the **fruitless** works of **darkness**;
    rather **expose** them, for it is **shameful** even to **mention**
    the things done by them in **secret**;
    but **everything** exposed by the **light** becomes **visible**,
    for **everything** that becomes visible is **light**.
Therefore, it says:
    "**Awake**, O sleeper,
    and **arise** from the **dead**,
    and Christ will give you **light**."

seven sons pass before Samuel without giving any thought to the possibility that the Lord might want David. He was merely the youngest, the keeper of the sheep. Who would want the little sheep-keeper?

Few of use are chosen for greatness in the eyes of the world, in the eyes of the Church, or in the eyes of our parish. Yet we are magnificent in the eyes of God, because he made us and we belong to him, whatever our state in life, whatever our abilities or

disabilities. David was a man of his family's disregard, yet, as Jesse met him, he was ruddy, with beautiful eyes, and handsome to boot! What is not appreciated in the world is often appreciated in the sight of God, and what God appreciates is often never even noticed in the world.

As you prepare and as you proclaim, keep this message in your mind and heart, and deliver the reading to those in your assembly who are not appreciated in the eyes of the world.

READING II | The meaning of this passage rests on the contrast between light and darkness. Your own reflection on these images in the life of the Church during Lent will embolden your proclamation, so listen for readings with such images in the weeks leading up to this Sunday. Consider the various levels of the symbols to animate your delivery of the word, especially the image of light.

GOSPEL John 9:1–41

A reading from the holy Gospel according to John

As Jesus passed by he saw a man **blind** from **birth**.
His disciples asked him,
    "**Rabbi**, who **sinned**, this **man** or his **parents**,
    that he was born **blind**?"
Jesus answered,
    "**Neither** he **nor** his parents sinned;
    it is so that the works of **God** might be made **visible**
        through him.
We have to do the works of the one who sent me while it is day.
Night is coming when **no** one can work.
While I am in the **world**, I am the **light** of the world."
When he had said this, he **spat** on the ground
    and made **clay** with the **saliva**,
    and **smeared** the clay on his **eyes**, and said to him,
    "Go **wash** in the Pool of Siloam"—which means **Sent**.
So he **went** and **washed**, and came back able to **see**.

His **neighbors** and those who had seen him earlier
    as a **beggar** said,
    "Isn't **this** the one who used to sit and **beg**?"
Some said, "It **is**,"
    but **others** said, "**No**, he just **looks** like him."
He said, "I **am**."
So they said to him, "How were your eyes **opened**?"
He replied,
    "The man called Jesus made **clay** and **anointed** my eyes
    and told me, 'Go to Siloam and **wash**.'
So I **went** there and **washed** and was able to **see**."

The opening question, "who sinned?" is very important.
Rabbi = RAB-ī

That Jesus Christ is himself the light is a key metaphor of the Gospel of John.

This tactile sign performed by Jesus is beautiful.

Siloam = sih-LOH-um

First, throughout Lent, the contrast between the ways of the Lord and the ways of the devil and sin is captured in the rhetoric of illumination by the light and overshadowing and obscuring by the darkness. The formation of the Church is the work of Lent, as it is reshaped and reoriented to the Lord's light and revelation.

Second, think about the formation of catechumens for initiation at the Easter Vigil. The intense formation of the catechumens during Lent is another manifestation of

the darkness being vanquished and the light realized. For the individuals so formed, this is the true experience, and for the rest of the Church praying for them and supporting them, they are a sign of the life and light of Christ in the world.

Third, the symbol of light will be manifest throughout the Fifty Days of the Easter season. At the Easter Vigil, as the people of God enter the darkened Church in procession from the outdoors to the place for the assembly, the increase in the light as flame of the Easter candle is shared is a sign of the

light of Jesus Christ defeating the darkness of sin. This reading anticipates and contributes to the depth of that symbol at Easter.

Proclaim this reading with power so that the reality and sign of light in darkness is awakened in the experience of the Church.

GOSPEL   Coming as it does between the narrative of the Samaritan woman and the narrative of the raising of Lazarus, both in the Gospel of John and in

**The authorities are determined to get to
the bottom of this change!
Pharisees = FAIR-uh-seez**

And they said to him, "Where **is** he?"
He said, "I don't know."

They brought the one who was once blind to the **Pharisees**.
Now Jesus had made clay and opened his eyes on a **sabbath**.
So then the Pharisees **also** asked him how he was able to see.
He said to them,
     "He put **clay** on my eyes, and I **washed**, and now I can **see**."
So some of the Pharisees said,
     "This man is **not** from God,
     because he does not keep the **sabbath**."
But **others** said,
     "How can a **sinful** man do such signs?"
And there was a division among them.
So they said to the blind man **again**,
     "What do you have to say about him,
     since he opened your eyes?"
He said, "He is a **prophet**."

Now the Jews did not believe
     that he had been **blind** and gained his **sight**
     until they summoned the **parents** of the one
          who had gained his sight.
They asked them,
     "Is this your **son**, who you say was born **blind**?
How does he now **see**?"
His parents answered and said,
     "We **know** that this is our **son** and that he was born **blind**.
We do **not** know how he **sees** now,
     nor do we know who opened his eyes.
Ask **him**, he is of age;
     he can speak for **himself**."

the season of Lent, this account is some-times overshadowed. But the narrative and its theology are wonderful and ancient parts of the Church's penitential season.

As you prepare for the proclamation, know that the healing of the man is the central physical change in the account, but the moral and theological issue of sin in human life is as important. At the start, for example, the disciples' question ("who sinned?") is

important. Throughout the reading, this issue of the relationship of sickness and sin persists, and the authorities opposed to Jesus want to attribute the man's blindness to sin.

This is an age-old issue. Think of the many people in the Church whose lives have been touched by sickness and death. Think of those who have lost a child. Think of those who are widowed. Think of those whose own chronic illnesses make them wonder if God is somehow punishing them.

Or think even of those who attribute their own slight illnesses—colds, sniffles, and so on—to lack of exercise, to lack of sleep.

Jesus' answer, "Neither this man nor his parents sinned," is no less important and no less Good News for the people of God today than it was when written by the evangelist John centuries ago. Your vocation is to proclaim it as Good News.

His parents said this because they were afraid
    of the Jews, for the Jews had already agreed
    that if anyone **acknowledged** him as the **Christ**,
    he would be **expelled** from the **synagogue**.
For this reason his parents said,
    "**He** is of age; question **him**."

So a **second** time they called the man who had been **blind**
    and said to him, "Give **God** the praise!
We know that this man is a **sinner**."
He replied,
    "If he is a **sinner**, I do not **know**.
One thing I **do** know is that I was **blind** and now I **see**."
So they said to him,
    "What did he **do** to you?
    How did he open your eyes?"
He answered them,
    "I told you **already** and you did not **listen**.
Why do you want to hear it **again**?
Do **you** want to become his disciples, too?"
They **ridiculed** him and said,
    "**You** are that man's disciple;
    we are disciples of **Moses**!
We know that God spoke to Moses,
    but we do **not** know where this one is from."
The man answered and said to them,
    "This is what is so **amazing**,
    that you do not know where he is from,
        yet he opened my eyes.
We **know** that God does not listen to **sinners**,
    but if one is **devout** and does his **will**, he **listens** to him.

The obstinacy of the authorities is growing.

Notice that this reading, as with stories of the woman at the well (last week) and the raising of Lazarus (next week), is filled with dialogue. As you practice, it might be helpful to highlight the speeches of each person in a distinct color so that you can be confident about the relationship of the actions and words in the account.

The reading does not finish on the most powerful note. Do your best to engage the assembly's attention throughout.

The theological point about sickness and sin emerges again, this time with the authorities contradicting what Jesus said at the beginning of the reading.

It is **unheard** of that anyone ever opened the eyes
    of a person **born** blind.
If this man were not from **God**,
  he would not be able to do **anything**."
They answered and said to him,
  "You were born **totally** in sin,
  and are **you** trying to teach **us**?"
Then they threw him out.

When Jesus heard that they had thrown him out,
  he found him and said, "Do you **believe** in the Son of **Man**?"
He answered and said,
  "Who **is** he, sir, that I **may** believe in him?"
Jesus said to him,
  "You have **seen** him,
  the one speaking with you is he."
He said,
  "I **do** believe, Lord," and he **worshiped** him.
Then Jesus said,
  "I came into this world for **judgment**,
  so that those who do **not** see **might** see,
  and those who **do** see might become **blind**."

During Lent, the catechumens and candidates are formed to follow the example of the man born blind. With him they say, "I do believe, Lord."

Some of the Pharisees who were with him heard this
  and said to him, "Surely **we** are not also blind, **are** we?"
Jesus said to them,
  "If you **were** blind, you would have no **sin**;
  but now you are saying, 'We **see**,' so your sin **remains**."

[Shorter: John 9:1, 6–9, 13–17, 34–38]

5TH SUNDAY OF LENT

Lectionary #35

READING I   Jeremiah 31:31–34

Jeremiah = jair-uh-MĪ-uh

In the first-person phrases, you speak not the words of Jeremiah, but the words of the Lord. Be confident.
Israel = IZ-ree-ul
Judah = J<u>OO</u>-duh
Egypt = EE-jipt

A beautiful image of the hearts on which God writes.

The final line should be proclaimed boldly.

A reading from the Book of the Prophet Jeremiah

The **days** are **coming**, says the LORD,
    when I will make a **new** covenant with the house of **Israel**
    and the house of **Judah**.
It will **not** be like the covenant I made with their **fathers**
    the day I **took** them by the **hand**
    to lead them forth from the land of **Egypt**;
    for they broke my **covenant**,
    and I had to show myself their **master**, says the LORD.
But **this is** the covenant that I will **make**
    with the house of Israel **after** those days, says the LORD.
I will **place** my law **within** them and **write** it upon their **hearts**;
    I will be their **God**, and **they** shall be my **people**.
No **longer** will they have need to teach their **friends** and **relatives**
    how to know the LORD.
All, from **least** to **greatest**, shall **know** me, says the LORD,
    for I will forgive their **evildoing** and remember their sin
        no more.

On the Third, Fourth, and Fifth Sundays of Lent in Years B and C, there are two sets of readings assigned by the Church and therefore two sets in the *Workbook.* If the parish has catechumens and people elected for initiation or full communion at the Easter Vigil, it's likely that you will use the readings from Year A. Check with the person who coordinates the schedule of readers to find out which readings to prepare.

READING I   This week's first reading, like last week's, testifies to Israel's unfaithfulness, its breaking of the solemn covenant between the Lord and Moses, the leader and spokesperson of the people Israel. Yet this broken relationship is not the final word with God, then or now. This is the hope that the reading you prepare will bear to the members of your community. It is a powerful proclamation if you take it to heart, as the prophet encouraged the Israelites to write the law on their hearts.

The season of Lent is the span when the Church pares away the sinfulness of the year gone by since last Easter season. Or, in other words, the span when the Church is renewed in its positive dedication to the ways of God. So here we stand just two weeks before Easter, recognizing that we have not kept our word and recognizing as well that God will "make a new covenant."

Pause before beginning the passage; the opening words are significant.

Because this is a relatively short passage, you can afford to make significant pauses at the period and semicolon.

READING II   Hebrews 5:7–9

A reading from the Letter to the Hebrews

In the **days** when Christ **Jesus** was in the **flesh**,
    he offered **prayers** and **supplications** with loud **cries** and **tears**
    to the one who was able to **save** him from **death**,
    and he was **heard** because of his **reverence**.
Son though he **was**, he learned **obedience** from what he **suffered**;
    and when he was made **perfect**,
    he became the **source** of eternal salvation for **all** who
        obey him.

The opening verses mention a variety of characters: the Greeks, Philip, Andrew, and Jesus himself.
Bethsaida = beth-SAY-ih-duh
Galilee = GAL-ih-lee

GOSPEL   John 12:20–33

A reading from the holy Gospel according to John

Some **Greeks** who had come to **worship** at the Passover Feast
    came to **Philip**, who was from **Bethsaida** in **Galilee**,
    and asked him, "**Sir**, we would like to see **Jesus**."
Philip went and told **Andrew**;
    then **Andrew** and **Philip** went and told **Jesus**.
Jesus answered them,
"The **hour** has come for the **Son** of Man to be **glorified**.
Amen, amen, I **say** to you,
    unless a grain of **wheat** falls to the ground and **dies**,
    it **remains** just a grain of **wheat**;
    but if it **dies**, it produces much **fruit**.

Look at this part as a series of sayings and pause after each of them for emphasis.

READING II The letter to the Hebrews interprets the life of Christ in terms of Jewish ritual practices, and sometimes the vocabulary and imagery feel unfamiliar. But the Letter as a whole and this passage in particular are rich in meaning. The passage is short and needs to be delivered slowly and deliberately. The most engaging element of the passage is at the start, with the portrayal of Jesus "in the flesh." (Unlike the letters of Paul, where the word "flesh" often carries a negative meaning, here in Hebrews the meaning is positive.)

This passage will spark interest because of its specific images: "prayers and supplications," "loud cries and tears," and "what he suffered." In this description is an important theology of this season as the Church moves toward the Passion accounts of the Gospel of Mark next Sunday (Passion Sunday) and of the Gospel of John on Good Friday.

We are the inheritors of Jesus' obedience to the Father, and like him we are not therefore immune from suffering.

Render this passage accessibly, and highlight the physical elements as a vehicle for the theological element. Take significant pauses at the end of each verse, at each period and semicolon, and engage the assembly with eye contact to punctuate the gravity of the author's meaning.

GOSPEL We do not hear much about the apostle Philip in the Lectionary. He is mentioned by name in the lists of the apostles at Matthew 10:3, Mark 3:18, and Luke 6:14, but most of what we

The voice from heaven comes between
the two sections from Jesus, as does
the crowd's misunderstanding of the voice
as thunder.

Whoever **loves** his life **loses** it,
  and whoever **hates** his life in this world
  will **preserve** it for **eternal** life.
Whoever **serves** me must **follow** me,
  and where **I** am, there also will my **servant** be.
The **Father** will honor whoever **serves** me.

"I am **troubled** now. Yet what should I say,
'Father, **save** me from this **hour**'?
But it was for **this** purpose that I **came** to this hour.
Father, **glorify** your **name**."
Then a **voice** came from **heaven**,
"I **have** glorified it and will **glorify** it again."
The crowd there **heard** it and said it was **thunder**;
  but **others** said, "An **angel** has spoken to him."
Jesus answered and said,
"This voice did not come for **my** sake but for **yours**.
Now is the time of **judgment** on this world;
  now the **ruler** of this world will be driven **out**.
And when I am **lifted** up from the **earth**,
  I will draw **everyone** to myself."
He said this indicating the **kind** of death he would die.

know about him is from the Gospel of John. In John he acts explicitly in the ministry. Just before the multiplication of the loaves and fishes, Philip mentions how much it would cost to feed the crowd. Later, he tells Jesus, "Lord, show us the Father, and we will be satisfied."

The passage you prepare is one of those where the Church can get a sense of Philip's role in the community of Jesus. It's possible that the Greeks mentioned here knew Philip, since they approach him to ask about seeing Jesus.

Most of this passage is from the lips of those in the scene, with Jesus having the largest portion of spoken words. Jesus' portion is interrupted by the voice from heaven and by the crowd that thought the voice was thunder or an angel.

The words of Jesus before the words of the voice from heaven are best taken as a series of sayings, and you would do well to pause between the sayings. The final part from Jesus is more consonant, so this may be proclaimed without much separation between sentences.

Because this passage is not a narrative or a parable or even the theological discourse, it is not easy. But a little study and understanding of its rhetorical path will help you to deliver it well.

5TH SUNDAY OF LENT, YEAR A

Lectionary #34

READING I   Ezekiel 37:12–14

Ezekiel = ee-ZEE-kee-ul

Pause briefly after the introductory identification of the Lord God as the speaker.

Israel = IZ-ree-ul

This is dramatic. Proclaim it with conviction and authority.

A reading from the Book of the Prophet Ezekiel

Thus says the Lord **GOD**:
O my **people**, I will open your **graves**
    and have you **rise** from them,
    and bring you **back** to the land of **Israel**.
Then you shall know that **I** am the **LORD**,
    when I **open** your graves and have you **rise** from them,
    O my **people**!
I will put my **spirit** in you that you may **live**,
    and I will **settle** you upon your **land**;
    thus you shall know that **I** am the LORD.
I have **promised**, and I will **do** it, says the LORD.

READING I This proclamation from the prophet Ezekiel was surely chosen for this Sunday because it goes so beautifully with the raising of Lazarus in today's Gospel. Your assignment is to get the assembly's ears and hearts prepared for that narrative by a strong proclamation of the excerpt from Ezekiel.

The passage from Ezekiel is brief but packed with a powerful message. Recall that the prophet Ezekiel is both indicting and consoling God's people after their captivity in Babylon, and this reading contains key components of the consolations and of God's amazing promises to the people of Israel: "I will open your graves and have you rise from them," and "bring you back to the land of Israel." "I will put my spirit in you that you may live."

As you proclaim, be mindful of expressing clearly the communal character of God's promise in this reading. Believers can sometimes think of Lent as an individual preparation for Easter more than as a renewal, rebirth, and replenishment for the whole people of God. But from its earliest days Lent has been a spiritually powerful time for the

READING II   Romans 8:8–11

A reading from the Letter of Saint Paul to the Romans

Brothers and sisters:
Those who are in the **flesh** cannot **please** God.
But **you** are **not** in the **flesh**;
    on the **contrary**, **you** are in the **spirit**,
    if only the Spirit of **God dwells** in you.
Whoever does **not** have the Spirit of **Christ**
        does **not belong** to him.
But **if Christ** is in you,
    although the **body** is **dead** because of **sin**,
    the **spirit** is **alive** because of **righteousness**.
If the **Spirit** of the **one** who raised **Jesus** from the **dead**
        dwells in you,
    the **one** who raised **Christ** from the **dead**
    will give **life** to **your** mortal bodies **also**,
    through his **Spirit** dwelling in **you**.

GOSPEL   John 11:1–45

A reading from the holy Gospel according to John

Now a man was **ill**, **Lazarus** from **Bethany**,
    the village of **Mary** and her sister **Martha**.
Mary was the one who had **anointed** the Lord with perfumed **oil**
    and dried his **feet** with her **hair**;
    it was her **brother** Lazarus who was ill.

As ever, address the "brothers and sisters" of your community of faith as if they were the ones to whom the letter was written.

The contrast set up by Paul is between the "spirit," on the one hand, and the "flesh" or "mortal bodies," on the other.

These opening verses introduce the names of the major characters in the long narrative. Start your proclamation slowly and clearly so that the assembly knows who's who.
Lazarus = LAZ-uh-rus
Bethany = BETH-uh-nee

rebirth of the Church, not just of the individuals within the Church. The prophet's words, "O my people," capture this sense well, and as proclaimer you can capture the prophet's sense and share it with the community.

The prophecy is framed by an introductory identification of "the Lord God" as the speaker of the words delivered by the

prophet and by a simple closing, "says the Lord." Use these as framing identifiers, but leave a little space between them and the words of the Lord. That will allow the assembly to be alert and poised for the dramatic prophecy.

READING II The theology of the body in the letters of Paul is quite complex. In 1 Corinthians we hear, "Do you not know that you are members of the body of Christ?" where "body" has a positive connotation. Here in the reading from Romans that you are preparing, the body is associated with sin and death. In the former, the

Jesus' affection for the siblings is strong.

Judea = joo-DEE-uh

Rabbi = RAB-ī

Last Sunday's Gospel revealed that Jesus himself is the "light of the world," so here he is referring to himself. The juxtaposition of light and darkness is a Lenten theme.

Be careful and clear with the dialogue in this section.

So the sisters sent word to Jesus saying,
  "**Master**, the one you **love** is ill."
When Jesus heard this he said,
  "This illness is **not** to end in **death**,
  but is for the glory of **God**,
  that the Son of God may be **glorified** through it."
Now Jesus **loved** Martha and her **sister** and **Lazarus**.
So when he heard that he was **ill**,
  he remained for **two days** in the place where he was.
Then after this he said to his **disciples**,
  "Let us go back to **Judea**."
The disciples said to him,
  "**Rabbi**, the Jews were just trying to **stone** you,
  and you want to go **back** there?"
Jesus answered,
  "Are there not twelve hours in a **day**?
If one walks during the **day**, he does not **stumble**,
  because he sees the **light** of this world.
But if one walks at **night**, he **stumbles**,
  because the **light** is not **in** him."
He said this, and then told them,
  "Our friend Lazarus is **asleep**,
  but I am going to **awaken** him."
So the disciples said to him,
  "**Master**, if he is **asleep**, he will be **saved**."
But Jesus was talking about his **death**,
  while they thought that he meant ordinary **sleep**.
So then Jesus said to them **clearly**,
  "Lazarus has **died**.
And I am **glad** for you that I was not **there**,
  that you may **believe**.

body is the community of faith at Corinth, and here the body is the flesh, that which is inclined toward sin rather than salvation.

The important comparison in this passage from Romans is between life in the Holy Spirit and life in the flesh, and it is by the power of the Holy Spirit that the mortal body, the body of flesh, can be an instrument of new life. As you prepare for your proclamation, highlight the contrast between Spirit and flesh, for the former does not annihilate the latter; we still live in the flesh even after we have received the Holy Spirit. But the indwelling of the Holy Spirit vivifies the mortal flesh so that it is not an impediment to salvation but an instrument of grace.

If, in your community, there are catechumens and candidates for initiation into the Catholic Church at the Easter Vigil, you might bear in mind the changes that these people have experienced as their lives have been transformed through their formation for Baptism. Their sacrifices and preparations are examples of the kind of conversion about which Paul writes. On this scrutiny Sunday, consider the examples of faith in those who have joined or will join your parish, and the meaning of the reading will be more clear.

GOSPEL Since the restoration of the catechumenate and the promulgation of the RCIA, the rituals and the readings have been brought together for the

Didymus = DID-ih-mus

The detail of "four days" is incredible, so make sure it is heard clearly.

Jerusalem = juh-ROO-suh-lem

This promise of Lazarus' rising anticipates Christ's Resurrection at Easter.

Another of the theologically important "I am" sayings of Jesus in the Gospel of John.

Let us go to him."
So **Thomas**, called Didymus, said to his fellow **disciples**,
    "Let us also go to **die** with him."

When Jesus **arrived**, he found that Lazarus
    had already been in the **tomb** for **four days**.
Now Bethany was near **Jerusalem**, only about two miles away.
And many of the Jews had come to Martha and Mary
    to **comfort** them about their **brother**.
When **Martha** heard that Jesus was coming,
    she went to **meet** him;
    but **Mary** sat at home.
Martha said to Jesus,
    "Lord, if you had **been** here,
    my brother would not have **died**.
But even now I **know** that **whatever** you ask of God,
    God will **give** you."
Jesus said to her,
    "Your brother will **rise**."
Martha said to him,
    "I **know** he will rise,
    in the **resurrection** on the last **day**."
Jesus told her,
    "I am the **resurrection** and the **life**;
    whoever believes in **me**, even if he **dies**, will **live**,
    and everyone who lives and believes in me will **never** die.
Do you **believe** this?"
She said to him, "**Yes**, Lord.
I have come to believe that you are the **Christ**, the Son of **God**,
    the one who is **coming** into the world."

first time in centuries. The Church is still learning what the catechumenate means for its growth and self-understanding and what it means as a ritual way of welcoming people who want to be members of the Catholic Church. As proclaimer of this key Gospel of the raising of Lazarus, you are contributing toward the learning and experience of the

Church in these rites of Lent and of the formation of the elect. You will need to be clear about the ritual and theological underpinnings so that the richness of this marvelous account can be brought to its fullest.

  This Gospel, as with the Gospels of the previous two Sundays, accompanies a scrutiny. The narrative gives meaning to a ritual action, the last of the three scrutinies. On the Third, Fourth, and Fifth Sundays of

Lent, the length of the scrutiny Gospels enables the Church to hear the changes in the main characters of the stories: the woman at the well, the man born blind, and Lazarus. These stories are not merely remembrances of things past, for the changes in the characters capture the changes in those being prepared for the sacraments in your parish.

When she had said this,
     she went and called her sister Mary **secretly**, saying,
     "The **teacher** is here and is **asking** for you."
As soon as she **heard** this,
     she rose **quickly** and went to him.
For Jesus had not yet come into the **village**,
     but was still where Martha had **met** him.
So when the Jews who were with her in the house **comforting** her
     saw Mary get up quickly and go **out**,
     they **followed** her,
     presuming that she was going to the **tomb** to **weep** there.
When Mary came to where Jesus was and saw him,
     she **fell** at his feet and said to him,
     "Lord, if **you** had been here,
     my **brother** would not have **died**."
When Jesus saw her **weeping** and the Jews who had come
          with her weeping,
     he became **perturbed** and deeply **troubled**, and said,
     "Where have you **laid** him?"
They said to him, "Sir, come and **see**."

One of the shortest verses in the whole Bible, and one of the most moving.

And Jesus **wept**.
So the Jews said, "See how he **loved** him."
But some of them said,
     "Could not the one who opened the eyes of the **blind** man
     have done something so that this man would not have **died**?"

So **Jesus**, perturbed **again**, came to the **tomb**.
It was a **cave**, and a **stone** lay across it.
Jesus said, "Take away the **stone**."
Martha, the dead man's **sister**, said to him,

Another arresting detail.

     "Lord, by **now** there will be a **stench**;
     he has been **dead** for **four days**."

They have experienced sacrifice and transformation, so as you proclaim, be alert for the ways the narrative reflects what these people have been going through.

Of the many elements in this reading, you should place emphasis on those with a strong bearing on initiation and formation. These would be the theology of illness, death, and Resurrection; the familial and communal relationships—brother, sisters,

loved ones; light and darkness; being awake and sleeping; and the strips of cloth in which Lazarus is bound. From parish to parish, different parts of the rites of the catechumenate may be carried out slightly differently, and you can emphasize those elements in the Gospel that most clearly parallel your community's ritual.

The Gospel you will proclaim is gripping, both because of the inconceivable act performed by Jesus and because of the details that the evangelist employs. The

details are essential to the success of your ministry with the Gospel. It is a long narrative, but you can make the account your own by becoming familiar with its progress and by relating it to your own experience of faith. The more intimately related the Gospel is to your own faith experience, the more engaging, persuasive, and inspiring your proclamation will be.

Jesus said to her,
    "Did I not **tell** you that if you **believe**
    you will see the glory of **God**?"
So they took away the **stone**.
And Jesus raised his eyes and said,
    "**Father**, I **thank** you for **hearing** me.
I know that you **always** hear me;
    but because of the **crowd** here I have said this,
    that they may **believe** that you **sent** me."
And when he had said this,
    he cried **out** in a loud **voice**,
    "**Lazarus**, come **out**!"
The dead man came **out**,
    tied hand and foot with **burial** bands,
    and his **face** was wrapped in a **cloth**.
So Jesus said to them,
    "**Untie** him and let him **go**."

Now **many** of the Jews who had come to **Mary**
    and **seen** what he had done began to **believe** in him.

[Shorter: John 11:3–7, 17, 20–27, 33b–45]

Be bold as you proclaim this. Though you are not acting the part of Jesus, you do want the gravity of his command, "Lazarus, come out!" to be clear.

PALM SUNDAY OF THE LORD'S PASSION

Lectionary #37

GOSPEL AT THE PROCESSION   Mark 11:1–10

A reading from the holy Gospel according to Mark

When **Jesus** and his **disciples** drew near to **Jerusalem**,
  to **Bethphage** and **Bethany** at the Mount of **Olives**,
  he sent **two** of his disciples and **said** to them,
  "Go into the village **opposite** you,
  and immediately on **entering** it,
  you will find a **colt** tethered on which no one has ever **sat**.
Untie it and **bring** it **here**.
If anyone should **say** to you,
  'Why are you **doing** this?' reply,
  'The **Master** has **need** of it
  and will send it **back** here at **once**.'"
So they went **off**
  and **found** a colt tethered at a **gate** outside on the **street**,
  and they **untied** it.
Some of the **bystanders** said to them,
  "What are you **doing**, untying the **colt**?"
They **answered** them just as Jesus had **told** them to,
  and they **permitted** them to **do** it.
So they **brought** the colt to Jesus
  and put their **cloaks** over it.
And he **sat** on it.

Because it interrupts the usual order of the rite, this Gospel at the start of the liturgy may be confusing. Be confident as you step up to proclaim.

As ever with place names, correct pronunciation is important, but not as important as confident pronunciation.
Jerusalem = juh-ROO-suh-lem
Bethphage = BETH-fayj
Bethany = BETH-uh-nee

There is a choice of Gospels at the procession today.

PROCESSION GOSPEL Passion Sunday is an extraordinary day for many reasons, not least because such a fullness of the word of God is proclaimed. Unlike Good Friday, which has the same Passion account proclaimed every year (from the Gospel of John),

Passion Sunday follows the three-year Lectionary cycle. In this Year B, the Passion is taken from Mark. The shorter Gospel passage at the procession, which narrates the triumphal entry of Jesus into Jerusalem, may be taken from either Mark or John.

The opening Gospel account, though considerably shorter than the Passion to come, is as full a Gospel passage as those the Church often proclaims on Sundays in Ordinary Time. Here it accompanies the ritual action of the distribution of palm branches to the assembly outside the gathering place. This gesture, in the Gospel and

in your community, is one of prophetic fulfillment and kingship.

MARK. One of Mark's characteristic elements is the insertion of prophetic texts from the Hebrew Scriptures to show how Jesus fulfilled them. Here we see that this entrance into the city on a donkey is a fulfillment of Zechariah 9:9, and how this fulfillment is itself a foundation for the kingship of Jesus.

A more explicit connection is with the assembly with their palm branches. In the narrative, we find people who "spread leafy

Here the narrative turns quickly from the mission of the two disciples to the crowd with the branches and Jesus' entry into the city. Pause between these two parts.

Take your time with this acclamation that is repeated at every eucharistic liturgy. Hosanna = hoh-ZAH-nah

Many people spread their **cloaks** on the **road**,
and **others** spread leafy **branches**
that they had cut from the **fields**.
Those **preceding** him as well as those **following** kept crying **out**:
"**Hosanna!**
Blessed is he who **comes** in the name of the **Lord**!
Blessed is the **kingdom** of our father **David** that is to **come**!
Hosanna in the **highest**!"

Or:

GOSPEL AT THE PROCESSION   John 12:12–16

A reading from the holy Gospel according to John

When the great **crowd** that had come to the **feast** heard
that **Jesus** was coming to **Jerusalem**,
they took **palm** branches and went out to **meet** him,
and cried **out**:
"**Hosanna!**
Blessed is he who **comes** in the name of the **Lord**,
the king of **Israel**."
Jesus found an **ass** and **sat** upon it, as is **written**:
*Fear no **more**, O daughter **Zion**;*
*see, your king **comes**, seated upon an **ass's** colt.*
His disciples did not **understand** this at first,
but when **Jesus** had been **glorified**
they **remembered** that these things were **written** about him
and that they had **done** this for him.

It is not necessary to imitate the shouts of the crowds. Only a slight increase in intensity is sufficient.

branches that they had cut from the fields," another sign of the kingship of Christ.

As a liturgical link, you might be particularly clear with the crowd's cry of "Hosanna," since it links the community of Mark's Gospel with the liturgical tradition of the Church yet today. The "Holy, Holy" has been passed down for centuries and centuries, and your clear proclamation will help the community appreciate for how long this acclamation has been sung about the coming of the Lord.

JOHN. This brief Gospel passage that recounts the triumphal entry of Jesus into Jerusalem prepares us for the proclamation of his suffering and death to come later. In the book of the prophet Zechariah we find the image that is fulfilled in Jesus' entering the city riding a donkey.

John's account of the entry into Jerusalem is unique. In verses just before and after the excerpt here, he relates that the crowds wanted to see Jesus because they had heard that he raised Lazarus from the dead. They also wanted to see Lazarus.

And the leaders who wanted Jesus dead wanted Lazarus dead, too.

Be particularly clear with the crowd's cry of "Hosanna," and so on. This acclamation is still sung in our liturgy today, and it will capture your assembly's hearts to hear about the crowd so long ago shouting these inspired words as they went out to meet the Lord.

Lectionary #38

READING I   Isaiah 50:4–7

Isaiah = Ī-ZAY-uh

This first line from the prophet is indeed a good word for lectors. Proclaim it with confidence.

A reading from the Book of the Prophet Isaiah

> The Lord **GOD** has **given** me
> a **well**-trained **tongue**,
> that I might **know** how to **speak** to the **weary**
> a **word** that will **rouse** them.
> **Morning** after **morning**
> he opens my **ear** that I may **hear**;
> and I have not **rebelled**,
> have not turned **back**.
> I **gave** my back to those who **beat** me,
> my **cheeks** to those who plucked my **beard**;
> my **face** I did not **shield**
> from **buffets** and **spitting**.

The description of the indignities suffered by the prophet is sharp and detailed.

The passage ends with a note of hope and rescue, a sign of good things to come, even for those who suffer.

> The Lord **God** is my **help**,
> **therefore** I am not **disgraced**;
> I have set my **face** like **flint**,
> **knowing** that I shall **not** be put to shame.

READING II   Philippians 2:6–11

Philippians = fih-LIP-ee-unz

A reading from the Letter of Saint Paul to the Philippians

Christ **Jesus**, though he was in the **form** of **God**,
did **not** regard **equality** with God
something to be **grasped**.

READING I This passage from the Suffering Servant portion of the prophet Isaiah is well suited for the day of the Passion from the Gospel of Mark, for its description of the servant who "gave my back to those who beat me" is realized in the way of the cross of Jesus.

With two Gospel readings today, you might be inclined to run through this reading from the prophet as quickly as possible. Resist the temptation. It has a beautiful message for ministers of the word as it declares, "The Lord GOD has given me a well-trained tongue, that I might know how to speak to the weary a word that will rouse them."

You can be inspired and encouraged in your service as lector by this passage, for the liturgy of the word does indeed provide guidance and consolation to many believers. This is why it is important to take the vocation and practice of the ministry to heart.

It is the second half of the prophecy that makes the passage most fitting for this Passion Sunday. Many of the indignities suffered by the prophet as he spoke the Lord's unwelcome words to the people of Israel were visited on our Lord as well. And we remember too that there are many in our Church who have suffered for their work, ministry, and for speaking truths that are not welcomed in the world.

READING II The importance of this text is not simply because of its antiquity; its theology is rich and beautiful. Before the reform at the Second Vatican Council, this text was a kind of stational hymn, a text that unfolded as the days of Holy Week passed. The first part of the text would have been sung on the first day,

Pause slightly at the break.

Rather, he **emptied** himself,
taking the form of a **slave**,
coming in **human** likeness;
and found **human** in **appearance**,
he **humbled** himself,
becoming **obedient** to the point of **death**,
even death on a **cross**.
Because of this, God greatly **exalted** him
and **bestowed** on him the **name**
which is above **every** name,
that at the name of **Jesus**
every **knee** should **bend**,
of those in **heaven** and on **earth** and **under** the earth,
and every **tongue confess** that
Jesus **Christ** is **Lord**,
to the glory of **God** the **Father**.

Pause again between the downward and upward movements. When you continue your proclamation, have your voice capture this downward and upward movement.

PASSION   Mark 14:1—15:47

Pause briefly after the introduction identifying it as the Passion according to Mark. The time references here are not as vital to us as they were to Mark's community.

The Passion of our Lord Jesus Christ according to Mark

(1) The **Passover** and the Feast of Unleavened **Bread**
were to take **place** in two days' **time**.
So the chief **priests** and the **scribes** were seeking a way
to **arrest** him by **treachery** and put him to **death**.
They said, "**Not** during the **festival**,
for fear that there may be a **riot** among the **people**."

another part added the following day, and so on. In this way the movement of the Church through time was accompanied by the movement of the praying Church through the text. It would have been complemented by movement, a procession most likely, as there were and are many practices involving the movement of the ministers or assembly to symbolize a spiritual reality. The most common of these, and still practiced in many parishes during Lent, is the Stations of the Cross.

Although the Church does not punctuate the Holy Week liturgies with this text as was done decades ago, this text does have a central place in our theology of the Passion and the relationship between Jesus Christ and God the Father. For this reason your proclamation should not be rushed, and you can pause between the significant parts as a reminder to those who remember the old practice and as catechesis on the Three Days for those preparing to participate in them for the first time.

PASSION Although Mark is the shortest of the four Gospels, Mark's Passion narrative is almost as long as those of the others. Moreover, because of the looming foreshadowings of the Passion through the whole of Mark's work, some scholars have described it as a "Passion account with a long introduction."

This looming Passion is not only because the suffering and the cross are deeply embedded in Mark's theology; it is quantitative as well, for the narrative of the Passion takes up nearly one-fifth (18%) of the Gospel!

Pause significantly before you begin this
section, for this is a change of scene.
Bethany = BETH-uh-nee
Simon = SĪ-mun
alabaster = AL-uh-bas-ter
As mentioned in the commentary below,
some of these ritual actions and signs
might well have reflected the worship
traditions of Mark's community.

Jesus' retort to them is long. You, the
proclaimer of this passage in a distant
land and distant time, are an embodiment
of Jesus' foretelling.

(2) When he was in **Bethany** reclining at **table**
in the house of **Simon** the **leper**,
a **woman** came with an alabaster **jar** of perfumed **oil**,
costly genuine **spikenard**.
She **broke** the alabaster jar and **poured** it on his **head**.
There were **some** who were **indignant**.
"Why has there been this **waste** of perfumed **oil**?
It could have been **sold** for more than three **hundred** days' **wages**
and the **money** given to the **poor**."
They were **infuriated** with her.
Jesus said, "Let her **alone**.
Why do you make **trouble** for her?
She has done a **good** thing for me.
The poor you will **always** have with you,
and whenever you **wish** you can do **good** to them,
but you will **not** always have **me**.
She has done what she **could**.
She has **anticipated** anointing my **body** for **burial**.
Amen, I **say** to you,
wherever the **gospel** is **proclaimed** to the whole **world**,
what she has **done** will be **told** in **memory** of her."

Another interesting fact about the Passion of Mark is that it was unheard in the liturgy for centuries before Vatican II. Between the reforms of the Lectionary in the sixteenth century after the Council of Trent (1570) and in the twentieth after Vatican II (1969), the cycle of readings was only one year long, and there were only two readings proclaimed each Sunday. In that Lectionary there were 24 readings from the Gospel of Matthew, 21 from Luke, 17 from John, and only *four* readings from the Gospel of Mark. Less than five percent of the Gospel of Mark was proclaimed for centuries. In proclaiming Mark's Passion, you are giving voice to a text that had been silent for a long, long time.

There are a number of reasons why this was so. One was that the disciples of Jesus are not shown in a good light in this Gospel, and their behavior at the time of the arrest and suffering of Jesus is especially disturbing. In the other Gospels, the disciples do some of the same ignoble things, but in those Gospels the disciples appear later, after Jesus has died and risen, and rehabilitate themselves. In Mark, however, the last word on the disciples does not put them in a good light. In the end Peter denies Jesus, Judas betrays him, and Peter, James, and John fall asleep on him in one of the most vulnerable times in Jesus' Passion, in the garden of Gethsemane.

Before you look at the individual sections of the Passion reading, it is important that you be familiar with the evangelist's unique theology of Jesus Christ as reflected in the Gospel in general and in Jesus' way to the cross in particular. We will consider the Passion narrative under four headings: 1) insiders out, 2) outsiders in and the unexpected followers of Jesus, 3) the liturgical

Pause after the previous section, for again there is a change of scene. Proclaim the name of "Judas Iscariot" clearly, for he plays a major part in the narrative.
Judas = JOO-dus
Iscariot = is-KAIR-ee-ut

The time reference will not have the significance today that it had in the first century. No need to emphasize it. The "Passover lamb," however, does still carry meaning for us.

Study this discourse carefully before proclaiming it, as described below.

(3) Then Judas **Iscariot**, one of the **Twelve**,
    went off to the chief **priests** to hand him **over** to them.
When they **heard** him they were **pleased**
        and promised to pay him **money**.
Then he looked for an **opportunity** to hand him **over**.

(4) On the first **day** of the Feast of Unleavened **Bread**,
    when they **sacrificed** the Passover **lamb**,
    his **disciples** said to him,
    "Where do you want us to **go**
    and **prepare** for you to eat the **Passover**?"
He **sent** two of his disciples and said to them,
    "Go into the **city** and a man will **meet** you,
    carrying a jar of **water**.
Follow him.
Wherever he **enters**, say to the **master** of the house,
    'The **Teacher** says, "Where is my **guest** room
    where I may eat the **Passover** with my **disciples**?"'
Then he will **show** you a large upper room **furnished** and **ready**.
Make the **preparations** for us **there**."
The disciples then went **off**, **entered** the city,
    and **found** it just as he had **told** them;
    and they prepared the **Passover**.

elements in the Passion, and 4) proclaiming the Passion.

INSIDERS OUT. Mark highlights the contrast between the people who are faithful to Jesus in his suffering and those who abandon him. There is a reversal, in a way, for those who were "insiders" in the early part of the Gospel—that is, the disciples and family members—are not so constant when the threats of the leaders are pressing on Jesus; the disciples become outsiders when the Passion is imminent.

This brings up another characteristic of the Twelve throughout Mark's Gospel, their

repeated misunderstanding and perplexity at things Jesus tried to teach them. We find Jesus asking them over and over, "Do you still not understand?"

As with the disciples, so with family in the Gospel of Mark. A few times in the Gospel someone approaches Jesus to tell him that his family is nearby, as at the end of chapter 3: "Your mother and your brothers and your sisters are outside asking for you." His answer? "Whoever does the will of God is my brother and sister and mother." The same issue comes up in what Jesus says later: "A prophet is not without honor except

in his native place and among his own relatives and in his own house."

For Jesus and those who followed him, blood connections are not the ones that endure; rather, commitment to following the will of God is what makes a disciple in this Gospel. Mark is unique in this, for we know that Jesus' mother is present at his death in the Gospel of John, but Mark does not name her specifically as being at the foot of the cross. In this Gospel, Jesus' closest followers hand him over, betray him, and fall asleep. Even at the empty tomb, they run away in fear.

As always, members of the assembly might not be reading the text along with you, so let your voice distinguish what is context and what is dialogue.

(5) When it was **evening**, he came with the **Twelve**.
And as they reclined at **table** and were **eating**, Jesus said,
  "**Amen**, I **say** to you, **one** of you will **betray** me,
  one who is **eating** with me."
They began to be **distressed** and to **say** to him, one by **one**,
  "**Surely** it is not **I**?"
He said to them,
  "One of the **Twelve**, the one who **dips** with me into
    the **dish**.
For the Son of **Man** indeed **goes**, as it is **written** of him,
  but **woe** to that man by **whom** the Son of **Man** is **betrayed**.
It would be **better** for that man if he had never been **born**."

The familiarity of these words should not prompt you to rush through this section.

(6) While they were **eating**,
  he took **bread**, said the **blessing**,
  broke it, and **gave** it to them, and said,
  "**Take** it; **this** is my **body**."
Then he took a **cup**, gave **thanks**, and **gave** it to them,
  and they all **drank** from it.
He said to them,
  "**This** is my **blood** of the **covenant**,
  which will be **shed** for **many**.
Amen, I **say** to you,
  I shall not drink **again** the fruit of the **vine**
  until the day when I drink it **new** in the kingdom of **God**."

OUTSIDERS IN. Throughout the Gospel of Mark, and in a more concentrated way in the Passion you prepare, those who are faithful to Jesus to the very end are those one might not expect. We see in Mark that Jesus not only attends to the outsiders, but the outsiders attend to him. They help Jesus; Jesus helps them. This pattern is especially evident in the Passion. Outsiders are the insiders in the moment of Jesus' suffering.

Among the outsiders who attend to Jesus during the Passion are Simon of Cyrene, the Roman centurion, Joseph of Arimathea, and Mary Magdalene and the other women.

LITURGICAL ELEMENTS IN THE PASSION. One dimension of the Passion that you can emphasize in the proclamation is its liturgical elements, for in these we still hear, taste, feel, and imagine what happened in the Passion and what the members of Mark's community heard, tasted, felt, and imagined as it was proclaimed to them.

The members of the community of Mark's Gospel in the first century had not likely witnessed the Crucifixion themselves, but they had the memories and words of those who had. In the decades between the historical events and the Gospel-writing, the risen Christ was present to them in worship. We can see this in the Gospel itself, where some liturgical elements are reflected in the text. It will contribute to the life-giving quality of your proclamation if you are aware of the elements of that first-century community's worship that are still part of our experience today.

The very words "Christ" and "Messiah" mean "anointed," and so the words carry an echo of a liturgical action. At the start of the Passion narrative, you will proclaim the

Those who were Jesus' closest followers earlier in the Gospel are those who fail in the Passion.

Galilee = GAL-ih-lee

Let this prediction be heard clearly, for the threefold denial by Peter is not proclaimed for a while.

(7) **Then**, after singing a **hymn**,
  they went out to the Mount of **Olives**.

Then Jesus said to them,
  "**All** of you will have your **faith** shaken, for it is **written**:
  I will strike the **shepherd**, *and the* **sheep** *will be* **dispersed**.
But after I have been **raised up**,
  I shall go **before** you to **Galilee**."
Peter said to him,
  "Even though **all** should have their faith shaken,
  mine will **not** be."
Then Jesus said to him,
  "**Amen**, I **say** to you,
  this very **night** before the **cock** crows **twice**
  you will **deny** me three **times**."
But he **vehemently** replied,
  "Even though I should have to **die** with you,
  I will not **deny** you."
And they **all** spoke **similarly**.

account of the woman with an alabaster jar who poured perfumed oil on his head. Our own liturgical anointing with oil—for catechumens, in the rites of initiation, in Confirmation, at ordinations, and with the sick—continues this ancient ritual sign of God's presence.

Holy Thursday is the day for celebrating the Mass of the Lord's Supper, with the account of Jesus' washing the disciples' feet from John's Gospel. The disciples are gathered before the betrayal, arrest, and Passion, but at this gathering there are no eucharistic elements. The only Last Supper

scene that the Church will proclaim and hear during Holy Week is the one that you will proclaim in the Markan account of the Passion. The sacrament of body and blood of Christ that we share is another link with the community of Mark's Gospel and with Jesus and his disciples.

Another liturgical element is the presence of an enigmatic character in the Gospel of Mark, one who does not appear in any of the other Gospels, a certain "young man." He appears in only two scenes, one in today's Passion reading and the other at the Easter Vigil, when the Mark's story of the

empty tomb is read. The detail of the evangelist's description of the "young man" that bears on the liturgy, particularly at the Easter Vigil, is his clothing.

Here is all that the Passion text says about this young man. Notice what he is wearing: "Now a young many followed [Jesus] wearing nothing but a linen cloth about his body. They seized him, but he left the cloth behind and ran off naked." Considering the two mentions of the cloth and his leaving it behind, some have supposed the young man to represent a person to be baptized, who like him would have left

**This is an important place name, so pronounce it clearly.
Gethsemane = geth-SEM-uh-nee**

These are the same three disciples who accompanied Jesus at the Transfiguration.

(8) Then they came to a place named **Gethsemane**,
  and he said to his disciples,
    "Sit **here** while I **pray**."
He **took** with him **Peter**, **James** and **John**,
  and began to be **troubled** and **distressed**.
Then he said to them, "My **soul** is **sorrowful** even to **death**.
Remain here and keep **watch**."
He **advanced** a little and fell to the **ground** and **prayed**
  that if it were **possible** the hour might **pass** by him;
  he said, "**Abba**, **Father**, all things are possible to **you**.
Take this cup **away** from me,
  but not what **I** will but what **you** will."
When he **returned** he found them **asleep**.
He said to **Peter**, "**Simon**, are you **asleep**?
Could you not keep **watch** for one **hour**?
Watch and **pray** that you may not undergo the **test**.
The **spirit** is **willing** but the **flesh** is **weak**."
Withdrawing **again**, he **prayed**, saying the same **thing**.
Then he returned once **more** and found them asleep,
  for they could not keep their **eyes** open
  and did not **know** what to **answer** him.

their old "garment" behind as they moved on to following the way of Christ.

As you prepare for the proclamation, imagine this young man as any one of the candidates for initiation at the Easter Vigil. Consider how nervous and vulnerable they feel. Think about those who had been members of other Christian churches and felt called to Catholic faith, for they, like the young man, must have felt afraid of the consequences of such a change.

The flight of the young man, however, is not the final word in the Gospel of Mark or in the Christian life. The young man appears

again in the proclamation of the Gospel at the Easter Vigil: "On entering the tomb [the women] saw a young man sitting on the right side, clothed in a white robe, and they were utterly amazed." Like the young man who was afraid and fled only to return as the bearer of the Good News of the risen Christ, the people seeking membership in the Catholic Church and those who will profess their baptismal vows anew at the Vigil are born again by the sacraments of the Church. Think of them as you prepare, and proclaim the Passion of Mark with strength as if to one who had not heard the account before.

It is our experience of the Passion, death, and Resurrection of Jesus Christ that brings us to the sacraments at this key time of the liturgical year. Even in solemn liturgical moments like the proclamation of two long Passion readings in one week— Mark on Passion Sunday and John on Good Friday—we come back because we know the story and we are part of that story, for we are indeed the body of Christ. As Christ's story is our story, so is Christ's Passion our passion. The Passion and Resurrection became our story at our Baptism, and become

As with Peter's denial yet to take place, the disciples' fail three times to carry out Jesus' request that they "keep watch."

Judas = JOO-dus

Emphasize Judas' instructions, for his betrayal of "the man I shall kiss" reveals the gravity of his deed.

After Judas' intimate action comes the change in the narrative. Jesus is under arrest.
Rabbi = RAB-ī

He returned a **third** time and said to them,
    "Are you still **sleeping** and taking your **rest**?
It is **enough**. The hour has **come**.
Behold, the Son of **Man** is to be handed **over** to **sinners**.
Get **up**, let us **go**.
See, my **betrayer** is at **hand**."

(9) **Then**, while he was still **speaking**,
    Judas, one of the **Twelve**, **arrived**,
    accompanied by a **crowd** with **swords** and **clubs**
    who had come from the chief **priests**,
    the **scribes**, and the **elders**.
His **betrayer** had arranged a **signal** with them, saying,
    "The man I shall **kiss** is the one;
    arrest him and lead him away **securely**."
He came and **immediately** went over to him and said,
    "**Rabbi**." And he **kissed** him.
At this they laid **hands** on him and **arrested** him.
One of the **bystanders** drew his **sword**,
    struck the high priest's **servant**, and cut off his **ear**.
Jesus said to them in **reply**,
    "Have you come out as against a **robber**,
    with **swords** and **clubs**, to seize me?

our story again and again each year during Holy Week.

   PROCLAIMING THE PASSION. As you know, the Gospels are not a script for a drama. If you look at the script of a play as it is to be performed on a stage, most of the page is taken up by the words to be spoken by the actors. Playwrights give only the barest attention to the context in which the spoken words will be delivered. This is not what we find in the Gospels, in which there is a balance of setting and dialogue, a balance of the actions described and the words

spoken. This is particularly apparent in the Passion accounts.

   Some liturgists have thought that the members of the assembly might be more attentive if they were able to participate in the narration somehow. While this is not a bad inclination, it does require that printed parts be prepared and distributed, and the assembly's attention will be divided between coming in at the right time and listening with engagement to the Passion. The idea needs to be evaluated in light of the other demands of the liturgy, and particularly the many liturgical exceptions of Holy Week.

   For the Passion, this year or any year, a balance needs to be found between having the long proclamation seem interminable and having it turn into a kind of entertainment. The Church's liturgy is not entertainment. Engaging and inspiring, yes; entertaining or amusing, no.

   We have a lot in common with this evangelist and his Church. Mark's Gospel came from the memories of eyewitnesses and his community's own experience of the risen Christ. That experience transformed his own life so deeply that he was called to write a Gospel, reflecting the experiences

There is no line break in the Lectionary before the appearance of the "young man," but pause before and after this short scene to highlight this uniquely Markan character.

Sanhedrin = san-HEE-drin

The injustice of the events to take place are clear.

Day after **day** I was **with** you **teaching** in the **temple** area,
  yet you did **not** arrest me;
  but that the **Scriptures** may be **fulfilled**."
And they all **left** him and **fled**.
Now a **young man** followed him
  wearing nothing but a linen **cloth** about his body.
They **seized** him,
  but he left the cloth **behind** and ran off **naked**.

(10) They led Jesus away to the **high** priest,
  and all the chief **priests** and the **elders** and the **scribes**
    came **together**.
Peter followed him at a **distance** into the high priest's **courtyard**
  and was seated with the **guards**, **warming** himself at the **fire**.
The chief **priests** and the entire **Sanhedrin**
  kept trying to obtain **testimony** against Jesus
  in order to put him to **death**, but they found **none**.
Many gave **false** witness against him,
  but their **testimony** did not **agree**.
Some took the **stand** and testified **falsely** against him,
  alleging, "We heard him say,
  'I will **destroy** this **temple** made with **hands**
  and within three **days** I will build **another**
  not made with hands.'"
Even so their testimony did not **agree**.

of the community of faith to which he belonged. That is what we do; having been incorporated into the Church at Baptism, whether as infants or as adults, and having experienced the life of faith in our community, we participate in the liturgy because there we meet the risen Christ.

1) The coincidence of the Passover and Jesus' death is an integral part of the chronology of the synoptic Gospels. Here that chronology is brought to the fore with the mention of the "Feast of Unleavened Bread." This detail would have had more relevance to Mark's first readers, when the

Church was made up of believers from both Jewish and Gentile backgrounds.

For us today, the detail adds a kind of ratification of the reality of the unfolding Passion, but it will not be as engaging to the assembly as the details of the betrayal and suffering, which are universal. As you prepare and proclaim, be discerning as you consider the elements to stress in your reading.

2) Here are two outsiders (see above), and you can see how their presence upsets the disciples. The fact that Jesus accepted the hospitality of a leper, Simon, would have

been unimaginable to many. So too with the woman with the alabaster jar of perfumed oil. Her ministry to Jesus by anointing infuriates the disciples. As you proclaim, recall Mark's point: the Good News comes from the most unexpected sources. The Passion reveals how much of an outsider Jesus was in his own social and political setting.

3) Juxtaposed to the hospitality of Simon the leper and the ministry of the woman, here we find one of the insiders scheming to betray Jesus. The narrative will continue with the failures of those who should have been strong, as with Judas here

(11) The **high** priest **rose** before the **assembly** and **questioned** Jesus,
   saying, "Have you no **answer**?
What are these men **testifying** against you?"
But he was **silent** and answered **nothing**.
Again the high priest asked him and said to him,
   "Are you the Christ, the son of the **Blessed** One?"
Then Jesus **answered**, "I **am**;
   and 'you will see the Son of Man
     seated at the right hand of the Power
     and coming with the clouds of heaven.'"
At **that** the high priest tore his **garments** and said,
   "What further **need** have we of **witnesses**?
You have **heard** the **blasphemy**.
What do you **think**?"
They all **condemned** him as deserving to **die**.
Some began to **spit** on him.
They **blindfolded** him and **struck** him and said to him,
   "**Prophesy!**"
And the **guards** greeted him with **blows**.

"Prophesy" is easy to stumble over.
prophesy = PROF-uh-sī

as he sells the one he loves. The support that comes from the outsiders makes Judas' betrayal stand out in contrast.

4) As the Passover lamb is being prepared, so Jesus, the Lamb of God, prepares for his Passion and death. He has spoken of it throughout the Gospel, and now the moment for his sacrifice presses upon him.

Attend to this complex section carefully. The evangelist offers the words of Jesus instructing the disciples what to say to a particular man. They are to quote Jesus, that is, "the Teacher." So the layers are evangelist > Jesus > disciples > "Teacher."

It is simpler than it sounds, but it will take attention to proclaim it with ease.

5) The injustice of what is to happen is clear. One of Jesus' followers, one with whom he dips into the dish, will hand him over to death. This section has two parts, the first with the exchange between Jesus and the Twelve, the second with Jesus' specific prediction of the betrayal and the fate of that disciple. The first part reveals that Jesus knows that his closest supporters will fail him, and the distress of the disciples reveals their own fear.

We who partake of the Eucharist are in communion with the faith of the Church, yet notice: the betrayer continues to share the sacrifice with the one he will betray.

6) The weekly assembly hears this section every Sunday in the eucharistic prayer. To allow them to feel the connection between the ritual action and its Passion context, pause at the start and end of this section. The eucharistic scene is so basic to our sacramental life, yet we find it bracketed here by the betrayal of Christ by Judas on the one side and the denial of Christ by Peter on the other. Pauses between the

Now comes Peter's threefold denial predicted by Jesus. Pause slightly after each so that each of the three denials is heard.

Nazarene = naz-uh-REEN
Pause before beginning this section to mark the change of day at its opening.

Galilean = gal-ih-LEE-un

(12) While **Peter** was below in the **courtyard**,
  one of the high priest's **maids** came along.
Seeing Peter **warming** himself,
  she looked **intently** at him and said,
  "You **too** were with the **Nazarene**, **Jesus**."
But he **denied** it saying,
  "I neither **know** nor **understand** what you are **talking** about."
So he went **out** into the outer **court**.
Then the **cock** crowed.
The maid **saw** him and began **again** to say to the **bystanders**,
  "**This** man is **one** of them."
Once **again** he denied it.
A little **later** the bystanders said to Peter once **more**,
  "**Surely** you are **one** of them; for you **too** are a **Galilean**."
He began to **curse** and to **swear**,
  "I do not **know** this man about whom you are talking."
And **immediately** a **cock** crowed a **second** time.
Then Peter **remembered** the word that **Jesus** had **said** to him,
  "Before the **cock** crows **twice** you will **deny** me three **times**."
He broke **down** and **wept**.

scenes will give a transition from the dark scenes of betrayal and denial to the intimate context of the eschatological banquet.

The actions of the Eucharist are as central to the tradition as the words that accompany the actions: Jesus *took* bread, *blessed* it, *broke* it, and *gave* it to his followers; he *took* the cup, *gave thanks,* and *gave* it to them. The link between this sacrificial meal Jesus shared with his disciples and the Passion about to unfold contributes to Christian sacramental theology. In the Eucharist, our participation in the death of Christ is unmistakable.

7) We know that the evangelist does not cast Jesus' disciples in a flattering light. Already he has predicted the betrayal by Judas, and here is a stark prediction: "All of you will have your faith shaken." Peter contradicts Jesus: "I will not deny you," and, following their leader, the other disciples say the same. Emphasize the gravity of these lines from the lips of Jesus and Peter.

8) The place name "Gethsemane" tells us of the imminence of Jesus' suffering, and the narrative again presents the disciples failing their Teacher.

At the start of this section Jesus asks them to "sit here while I pray," yet even this is beyond their abilities. Jesus returns to find them asleep.

The symbol of the cup is to be emphasized, for the cup is a symbol of Christ's Passion, and he asks his father with an intimate term, "Abba," to take the cup away. Twice more he finds his followers asleep, with the threefold repetition foreshadowing the threefold denial on the horizon. The section ends with Jesus predicting the betrayal once again.

Pilate = PĪ-lut

The dramatic irony of the exchange
between the man in power questioning
Jesus about being a king is sharp. We
know what Pilate doesn't.

Barabbas = buh-RAB-us

(13) As soon as **morning** came,
   the chief **priests** with the **elders** and the **scribes**,
   that is, the whole **Sanhedrin** held a **council**.
They **bound** Jesus, led him **away**, and handed him **over** to **Pilate**.
(14) Pilate **questioned** him,
   "**Are** you the **king** of the **Jews**?"
He said to him in **reply**, "**You** say so."
The chief **priests** accused him of **many** things.
Again Pilate questioned him,
   "Have you no **answer**?
See how many things they **accuse** you of."
Jesus gave him no further **answer**, so that **Pilate** was **amazed**.

Now on the occasion of the **feast** he used to **release** to them
   one **prisoner** whom they **requested**.
A man called **Barabbas** was then in prison
   along with the **rebels** who had committed **murder** in
      a **rebellion**.
The crowd came **forward** and began to **ask** him
   to **do** for them as he was **accustomed**.

9) That predicted betrayal comes to its climax here, with the kiss as the signal. In your proclamation, be clear with the shocking juxtaposition of "a crowd with swords and clubs" and the kiss.

We can be inclined to assign responsibility for both wonderfully good and horribly bad things to individuals, rather than realizing that groups of people contribute to most significant events. Here as you proclaim the betrayal, it is easy to cast Judas as the sole villain. But there is a kind of inevitability to the betrayal, that it had to be done by someone who loved Christ and whom Christ loved. The betrayal is followed by the striking detail of violence against the slave of the high priest.

The final two verses of this section have the enigmatic young man, described above as one who represents an inquirer who flees in the face of violence.

10) Pause before turning to the new scene in which Jesus is brought before the high priest. Be careful as you prepare this section, for there are some complex layers in the dialogue. In a number of places the speakers are citing other sources or things that Jesus had predicted earlier in the narrative.

In addition to the scriptural citations in this section, there is quite a lot of dialogue, from the crowd, from the high priest, from Jesus, and from those who taunt Jesus to prophesy. (Be careful with the imperative verb, "prophesy," pronounced PROF-uh-sī. It is not the same as the noun, "prophecy," pronounced PROF-uh-see.)

Be clear about who the speakers are so that you will be confident with the narrative you will proclaim. The best preparation for sections like this is simply to be familiar

Still one more piece of evidence of the injustice of the event about to unfold.

Pilate answered,
"Do you want me to **release** to you the **king** of the **Jews**?"
For he **knew** that it was out of **envy**
that the chief **priests** had handed him **over**.
But the chief priests **stirred** up the crowd
to have him release **Barabbas** for them **instead**.
Pilate **again** said to them in **reply**,
"Then what do you want me to **do**
with the man you call the **king** of the **Jews**?"
They shouted again, "**Crucify** him."
Pilate said to them, "**Why**? What **evil** has he done?"
They only shouted the **louder**, "**Crucify** him."
So Pilate, wishing to **satisfy** the crowd,
released **Barabbas** to them and, after he had Jesus **scourged**,
handed him **over** to be **crucified**.

Do not rush through the indignities of this scene and the soldiers' mockery.

(15) The **soldiers** led him **away** inside the **palace**,
that is, the **praetorium**, and **assembled** the whole **cohort**.
They **clothed** him in **purple** and,
weaving a crown of **thorns**, **placed** it on him.
They began to **salute** him with, "**Hail**, King of the **Jews**!"
and kept striking his **head** with a **reed** and **spitting** upon him.

with the account; if you know how the story unfolds, you will read with assurance.

11) Now the scene shifts again, to the courtyard below. We have already seen Peter falling asleep on Jesus three times, and now we have another threefold manifestation of the chief disciple's failings. The details of this poignant scene are important for the engagement of the assembly's imagination. For this reason, be clear with the details, the characters—the high priest's maid and the bystanders.

The crowing cock proves Jesus' earlier prediction: "before the cock crows twice you will deny me three times." All of us have had to face our failings in trying to follow the Gospel, and so we can relate to Peter as he weeps bitter tears, a striking detail of this stalwart disciple's realization of his own contribution to the Passion unfolding.

12) The exchange between Pilate and Jesus is ironic: The powerless innocent man and the powerful Roman governor are talking about power. The Roman starts the exchange, asking, "Are you the king of the Jews?"

The Church has had a feast celebrating Christ's kingship for many years (the last Sunday of Ordinary Time), and this dialogue with Pilate reveals that the theology of this feast has been part of the tradition from the start. Pilate's power over Jesus is highlighted by the governor's custom of releasing a prisoner on this feast.

The choice between the innocent Jesus and Barabbas, "who had committed murder in a rebellion," highlights the injustice even more, heightening Mark's emphasis of Jesus' desperate situation.

Another outsider steps up to help this suffering, friendless man being taunted by the soldiers.
Simon = SĪ-mun
Cyrenian = si-REE-nee-un
Rufus = ROO-fus

As with Gethsemane, this place name bears a tradition as a signifier of the Passion.
Golgotha = GOL-guh-thuh
myrrh = mer

They **knelt** before him in **homage**.
And when they had **mocked** him,
   they **stripped** him of the purple **cloak**,
   dressed him in his own **clothes**,
   and led him **out** to **crucify** him.

(16) They pressed into **service** a **passer**-by, **Simon**,
   a **Cyrenian**, who was coming in from the **country**,
   the father of **Alexander** and **Rufus**,
   to **carry** his cross.

They **brought** him to the place of **Golgotha**
   —which is translated Place of the **Skull**—.
They gave him **wine** drugged with **myrrh**,
   but he did not **take** it.
Then they **crucified** him and divided his **garments**
   by casting **lots** for them to see what each should **take**.

It was **nine o'clock** in the **morning** when they **crucified** him.
The **inscription** of the **charge** against him read,
   "The **King** of the **Jews**."

Pilate will play a large role in the Passion of Good Friday from the Gospel of John, but it is quite different there than here in Mark. Pilate's character has been interpreted widely since the earliest days, and here in the second Gospel we get a sense that Pilate is trying to let Jesus go free: "Why? What evil has he done?" he asks.

As you proclaim this sequence, try to be true to the double role in which Pilate is cast here, as the governor who is responsible and will hand Jesus over, yes, but also as one who made an effort to act justly by having Barabbas taken away and Jesus set free. Make this section particularly accessible because the issues of authority and earthly power and kingship are important not only in the Passion narrative but in the theology of the Church through the ages.

13) Now comes another change of scenery, to the inside of the palace. The description of the soldiers' mocking Jesus is distressing, and even more painful to read aloud in the knowledge of his innocence.

The soldiers dress Jesus in a parody of regal finery so that they can mock him bitterly. However, this is no indication of the soldiers' power; it is evidence of the rulers' insecurity in the precarious social and political scene that the evangelist describes. If Jesus had truly been a man of no importance, there would have been no need for such displays.

The symbolism of the clothes he was decorated with—the purple cloak and crown of thorns—while it might not have the depth for us that it did for the original community for which it was written, still

This "Aha!" captures the original Greek. You might proclaim it in a muted way.

With him they crucified two **revolutionaries**,
    one on his **right** and one on his **left**.
Those passing by **reviled** him,
    shaking their **heads** and saying,
    "Aha! **You** who would **destroy** the **temple**
    and **rebuild** it in three **days**,
    save yourself by coming **down** from the **cross**."
Likewise the chief **priests**, with the **scribes**,
    mocked him among themselves and said,
    "He saved **others**; he cannot save **himself**.
Let the **Christ**, the King of Israel,
    come **down** now from the **cross**
    that we may **see** and **believe**."
Those who were **crucified** with him **also** kept **abusing** him.

Eloi, Eloi, lema sabachthani = ee-loh-ee, ee-loh-ee, luh-mah sah-bahk-TAH-nee

(17) At **noon darkness** came over the whole **land**
    until **three** in the **afternoon**.
And at three o'clock Jesus **cried out** in a loud **voice**,
    "Eloi, Eloi, lema sabachthani?"
    which is **translated**,
    "My **God**, my **God**, **why** have you **forsaken** me?"
Some of the **bystanders** who heard it said,
    "**Look**, he is calling **Elijah**."
One of them **ran**, soaked a **sponge** with **wine**, put it on a **reed**
    and gave it to him to **drink** saying,
    "**Wait**, let us see if **Elijah** comes to take him **down**."
Jesus gave a loud **cry** and breathed his **last**.

Another of the strangers, outsiders, who testify to Jesus' holiness, a valiant profession of faith.
Elijah = ee-LĪ-juh

[Here all kneel and pause for a short time.]

bears the weight of embarrassment and grief. Do not rush through the details of this mockery of Jesus on the way of the cross.

14) Here we find an outsider, an unexpected character, coming to Jesus' aid. This is not simply a historical fact; it contains a theological truth as well. God is often found in unexpected places.

Simon from Cyrene is on the scene only briefly. (Some Catholics might be more familiar with him from the Stations of the Cross than from the Gospels.) The evangelist is not only emphasizing that someone was pressed into service to help Jesus, but that this

someone was from far away. Cyrene was located in North Africa.

The other place name in this section is "Golgotha," defined here as meaning "Place of the Skull." For centuries, the artistic tradition has imagined this as the skull of Adam. In Paul's theology, Christ is the new Adam. As death came from one man, so has new life come from one man. In paintings and sculptures of the Crucifixion, the old Adam is often symbolized by a skull at the foot of the cross.

15) The change of scene in next two sections begin with references not to place, but to time. Here "it was nine o'clock in the morning."

Most crucifixes have an inscription on the cross above Jesus' head, INRI. These four letters are an abbreviated Latin version of the inscription as given in the Gospel of John: "Jesus of Nazareth, the King of the Jews," in Latin, "Iesus Nazarenus Rex Iudaeorum." (In Latin "i" and "j" are interchangeable.)

The Gospel of Mark has a shorter version of the story.

The **veil** of the **sanctuary** was torn in **two** from top to **bottom**.
When the **centurion** who stood **facing** him
    saw how he breathed his **last** he said,
      "**Truly** this man **was** the Son of **God**!"
There were also **women** looking on from a **distance**.
Among them were Mary **Magdalene**,
    Mary the mother of the younger **James** and of **Joses**,
      and **Salome**.
These women had **followed** him when he was in **Galilee**
    and **ministered** to him.
There were also many **other** women
    who had come **up** with him to **Jerusalem**.

(18) When it was already **evening**,
    since it was the day of **preparation**,
    the day before the **sabbath**, **Joseph** of **Arimathea**,
    a distinguished member of the **council**,
    who was **himself** awaiting the **kingdom** of **God**,
    came and **courageously** went to **Pilate**
    and asked for the **body** of **Jesus**.
Pilate was **amazed** that he was already **dead**.

Pause after the centurion's profession, for the scene and characters change. Take care with the names of the women.
Magdalene = MAG-duh-lun
Joses = JOH-seez
Salome = suh-LOH-mee
Galilee = GAL-ih-lee

Jerusalem = juh-ROO-suh-lem

The last of the outsiders to attend to Jesus' body.
sabbath = SAB-uth
Arimathea = air-ih-muh-THEE-uh

---

16) The next time reference starts this section, "at noon," and then the cosmic response to the significant event "darkness came over the whole land until three in the afternoon." Many believers mark these three hours on Good Friday.

The words Jesus says are in neither the English of the translation nor the evangelist's ordinary Greek. This was a transliteration into Greek letters of the spoken language or Jesus and his followers: Aramaic. While proclaiming the exclamation accurately is important, far more important is that you proclaim it smoothly and confidently.

The section ends with Jesus' death, as he "breathed his last."

17) Once again, an outsider recognizes the gravity of what has happened. Here is the Roman centurion, the last person whom we would imagine delivering a confession of faith, yet here it is: "Truly this man was the Son of God!"

Then come the faithful and courageous women: Mary Magdalene, and Mary the mother of James the younger and of Joses, and Salome, and, by the evangelist's testimony, "many other women." They stay with Jesus even after his death. Again, outsiders become faithful followers, carrying on the faith through their courage. The Twelve were not faithful to the end, but the women accompanied Jesus up to his hour of death and beyond.

18) The last section of the Passion narrative begins with two time references, the first to the time of day, "when it was already evening," and the second to the Jewish calendar, "the day of preparation" for Passover and "the day before the sabbath."

See below for some details about the cloth that Joseph uses to wrap the dead body of Jesus.

He summoned the **centurion**
  and asked him if **Jesus** had already **died**.
And when he **learned** of it from the centurion,
  he gave the **body** to **Joseph**.
Having bought a linen **cloth**, he took him **down**,
  wrapped him in the linen cloth,
  and **laid** him in a **tomb** that had been **hewn** out of the **rock**.
Then he rolled a **stone** against the **entrance** to the tomb.
Mary **Magdalene** and **Mary** the mother of **Joses**
  watched where he was **laid**.

[Shorter: Mark 15:1–39]

The final unexpected supporter—another outsider turned insider—is Joseph of Arimathea, "a distinguished member of the council," who was "himself awaiting the kingdom of God." Joseph approaches Pilate to ask for the body of Jesus so that he could dress it in a "linen cloth" and put it in the tomb.

The only other mention of a "linen cloth" in the Gospel of Mark is in the mention of the "young man" (see section 9). The word for the garment that the young man left behind, *sindon* (shroud), is the same word for the linen cloth in which Joseph of Arimathea wraps Jesus' dead body. The word is used twice in the story of the young man who runs away, and is used twice here as well.

The narrative ends quickly as the body is laid in the tomb and the tomb closed with a stone. And the two Marys watch.

HOLY THURSDAY: MASS OF THE LORD'S SUPPER

Lectionary #39

READING I   Exodus 12:1–8, 11–14

A reading from the Book of Exodus

Your tone and delivery can reflect what the text is: a prescription for how to celebrate the annual Passover remembrance.
Aaron = AIR-un

The LORD said to Moses and Aaron in the land of Egypt,
   "This month shall stand at the head of your calendar;
   you shall reckon it the first month of the year.
Tell the whole community of Israel:
   On the tenth of this month every one of your families
   must procure for itself a lamb, one apiece for each household.
If a family is too small for a whole lamb,
   it shall join the nearest household in procuring one
   and shall share in the lamb
   in proportion to the number of persons who partake of it.
The lamb must be a year-old male and without blemish.
You may take it from either the sheep or the goats.
You shall keep it until the fourteenth day of this month,
   and then, with the whole assembly of Israel present,
   it shall be slaughtered during the evening twilight.
They shall take some of its blood
   and apply it to the two doorposts and the lintel
   of every house in which they partake of the lamb.
That same night they shall eat its roasted flesh
   with unleavened bread and bitter herbs.

The passage has the appearance of a historical account of what was done on that Passover night, but the instructions are more likely describing what is to be done in the Jewish ritual, where the remembrance of the past is unifying.

READING I In the earliest centuries of Christian worship, this passage from chapter 12 of Exodus was the primary Old Testament reading at the Easter Vigil in most communities. In those early days, the Gospel for the Easter Vigil was the account of the death of Jesus, the Passion narrative. Thus, the fitting Old Testament reading to accompany the Passion was this passage about the Passover lamb, since Christian theology was coming to associate Jesus with the metaphor of the lamb. We still acclaim him under that title, most frequently during the breaking of the bread: "Lamb of God, who takes away the sins of the world." It was not until the end of the fourth or beginning of the fifth century that the Resurrection narrative found its place in the Vigil.

In those earliest centuries there was no Easter Three Days from Holy Thursday to Easter Sunday; there was only the Easter Vigil. Once the Three Days emerged, the Gospel for the Easter Vigil became the Resurrection, for Good Friday the Passion, and for Holy Thursday the Last Supper. As the Gospels shifted, the Old Testament readings shifted with them. The crossing of the Red Sea was matched with the Resurrection, the suffering-servant prophecy of Isaiah to the Passion, and eventually the Passover lamb matched to the Mass of the Lord's Supper. This liturgical tradition has been in place for a millennium and a half, and you will continue the tradition by proclaiming this passage of Exodus 12 on Holy Thursday evening.

The reading is lengthy, and it might be difficult to sustain the full attention of the assembly throughout the whole of the law's

"**This** is how you are to **eat** it:
    with your **loins** girt, **sandals** on your **feet** and your **staff**
        in **hand**,
    you shall eat like those who are in **flight**.
It is the **Passover** of the LORD.
For on this **same** night I will go through **Egypt**,
    striking **down** every **firstborn** of the land, both **man** and **beast**,
    and executing **judgment** on all the gods of Egypt—**I**, the LORD!
But the **blood** will mark the **houses** where **you** are.
Seeing the **blood**, I will **pass over** you;
    thus, when I strike the land of **Egypt**,
    no destructive blow will come upon **you**.

"**This** day shall be a memorial **feast** for you,
    which all your **generations** shall **celebrate**
    with **pilgrimage** to the LORD, as a perpetual **institution**."

The last verse holds up the commemoration as the significant Jewish memorial feast that it has been for millennia.

READING II   1 Corinthians 11:23–26

Be measured and clear with the identifying opening.

This reading tells the Lord's Supper narrative for the feast, since the Gospel reading is the footwashing from the Gospel of John.

A reading from the first Letter of Saint Paul to the Corinthians

Brothers and sisters:
I **received** from the Lord what I also **handed** on to you,
    that the Lord **Jesus**, on the **night** he was handed **over**,
    took **bread**, and, after he had given **thanks**,
    broke it and said, "**This** is my **body** that is for **you**.
Do this in **remembrance** of me."
In the **same** way also the **cup**, after **supper**, saying,
    "This **cup** is the new **covenant** in my **blood**.

detailed prescription of how the Passover lamb is to be chosen, slaughtered, and prepared for the paschal supper. Therefore, choose the parts of the readings that are most important for the Holy Thursday rite and highlight them in your proclamation. These would be the prescription for sharing the meal—"If a family is too small for a whole lamb, it shall join the nearest household"—since the eucharistic sacrifice is similarly to be shared. Also to be emphasized is the clear statement that "It is the Passover of the LORD." Finally, take your time in concluding the reading, for the final verse, from

"This day shall be a memorial feast for you" to "a perpetual ordinance," is significant for what it gives to the theology of our annual Christian observance.

READING II Although many Christians think of the Last Supper narratives of the four Gospels as the oldest recorded evidence of the Eucharist, this passage here from 1 Corinthians is considerably older than they are. The earliest Gospel narrative, Mark, was written around AD 70, but the first letter Paul wrote to Corinth is more

than fifteen years earlier. You can see that the Last Supper account he records here is still older than that, for he begins this section by revealing that "I received from the Lord what I also handed on to you." So, with Paul writing in AD 53 or 54 and noting that this story had been passed along to him as a "tradition," this account of the Last Supper is indeed one of the very oldest pieces of the whole New Testament.

Because tonight's liturgy is the "Mass of the Lord's Supper" and the Gospel narrative is the footwashing of the Gospel of John (a Gospel in which there is no Last Supper),

Do this, as often as you **drink** it, in **remembrance** of me."
For as often as you **eat** this **bread** and **drink** the **cup**,
    you **proclaim** the **death** of the Lord until he **comes**.

Pause briefly before proclaiming this last line.

GOSPEL John 13:1–15

A reading from the holy Gospel according to John

Before the feast of **Passover**,
    Jesus **knew** that his hour had **come**
    to pass from **this** world to the **Father**.
He **loved** his own in the world and he **loved** them to the **end**.
The **devil** had already induced **Judas**, son of Simon the **Iscariot**,
        to hand him **over**.
So, during **supper**,
    fully aware that the Father had put everything into his **power**
    and that he had come **from** God and was returning **to** God,
    he **rose** from supper and took off his outer **garments**.
He took a **towel** and tied it around his **waist**.
Then he poured **water** into a **basin**
    and began to **wash** the disciples' **feet**
    and **dry** them with the **towel** around his **waist**.
He came to Simon **Peter**, who said to him,
    "**Master**, are you going to wash **my** feet?"
Jesus answered and said to him,
    "What I am **doing**, you do not understand **now**,
    but you **will** understand **later**."
Peter said to him, "You will **never** wash my **feet**."

This text not only narrates a unique moment in the ministry of Jesus, it contains an exchange between Peter and Jesus that is very important for the meaning of the action.
Judas = JOO-dus
Iscariot = is-KAIR-ee-ut

Take the time each of their positions and what the exchange itself leads to, both in the historical time when the Gospel was written, and for communities proclaiming and ritualizing the action in our own day.

your proclamation of the Last Supper in 1 Corinthians plays a very important role. From it will the assembly be mindful of the eucharistic tradition celebrated Sunday after Sunday, Holy Thursday after Holy Thursday.

Because the passage is relatively short, you can take your time and assure a clear and powerful reading. Pause after the opening address, "Beloved," as well as before you begin the quoted phrases, "This is my body . . ." and "This cup is the new covenant in my blood." And pause too at the end of repetition of "in remembrance of me."

Finally, note that the final verse of the reading is one of the memorial acclamations of the eucharistic prayers, so proclaim it slowly and deliberately so that it can be recognized as it is proclaimed from its source in 1 Corinthians.

GOSPEL   Some scholars have hypothesized that this gesture by Jesus in chapter 13 of the Fourth Gospel was not simply a rite of service, as it has come to

be interpreted. They suggest that this account captures what had been an initiation and consecratory rite in the community of John's Gospel. A remnant of this initiation theology is here: "Unless I wash [your feet], you have no share with me," for it is by initiation that one has a share in the life of Jesus.

Whatever its origins, this text survives as a unique narrative that accompanies an even more unique ritual. The vulnerability of bending down to wash another's feet is outdone only by the vulnerability of allowing

Jesus answered him,
   "Unless I **wash** you, you will have no **inheritance** with me."
Simon Peter said to him,
   "**Master**, then not **only** my feet, but my **hands**
      and **head** as well."
Jesus said to him,
   "Whoever has **bathed** has no need
      except to have his **feet** washed, for he is clean all **over**;
   so **you** are clean, but not **all**."
For he knew who would **betray** him;
   for this reason, he said, "Not **all** of you are clean."

A new section about service begins here.

So when he had washed their **feet**
   and put his **garments** back on and reclined at **table** again,
   he said to them, "Do you **realize** what I have **done** for you?
You call me '**teacher**' and '**master**,' and rightly so, for indeed I **am**.
If **I**, therefore, the **master** and **teacher**, have washed **your** feet,
   you ought to wash one **another's** feet.
I have given you a **model** to follow,
   so that as **I** have done for **you**, **you** should **also** do."

someone else to wash one's feet. Your proclamation of the narrative in which Jesus performed this humble act for his followers will lend a context by which your listeners can anticipate this unique annual ritual.

The opening merely sets up the context; it need not be emphasized. Starting with the gesture of Jesus that anticipates what is done in the liturgy of Holy Thursday, proclaim more deliberately so that the members of the assembly will recognize this ritual element in its ancient roots.

The dialogue between Jesus and Peter is important for its bearing on the ritual act and the gesture's theological significance, so be careful to distinguish the phrases of the narrative set-up ("Jesus answered," and "Peter said to him," and so on) from the direct discourse. There is no need to worry about time. Those who attend want to be there, and the slight extra time spent for your clear, accessible Gospel proclamation will reward their dedication.

GOOD FRIDAY OF THE LORD'S PASSION

Lectionary #40

READING I   Isaiah 52:13—53:12

A reading from the Book of the Prophet Isaiah

The reading begins with an imperative: See! It is a command to attend to this.

These next few sections take up the humiliations and rejections of the Lord's servant. Carry in your voice the gravity and significance of the suffering of the Lord's servant.

Pause after the question and before the metaphor of the "sapling" to mark the literary change.

These next two sections have been part of the liturgy of the word for Good Friday for centuries, and they have widely and deeply shaped our understanding of the life of Christ.

See, my **servant** shall **prosper**,
  he shall be raised **high** and greatly **exalted**.
Even as many were **amazed** at him—
  so **marred** was his **look** beyond human **semblance**
  and his **appearance** beyond that of the sons of **man**—
so shall he **startle** many **nations**,
  because of him **kings** shall stand **speechless**;
for those who have **not** been told shall **see**,
  those who have **not** heard shall **ponder** it.

Who would **believe** what we have **heard**?
  To whom has the **arm** of the LORD been **revealed**?
He grew up like a **sapling** before him,
  like a **shoot** from the parched **earth**;
there was in him no **stately** bearing to make us **look** at him,
  nor **appearance** that would **attract** us to him.
He was **spurned** and **avoided** by people,
  a man of **suffering**, accustomed to **infirmity**,
one of those from whom people **hide** their **faces**,
  spurned, and we held him in no **esteem**.

Yet it was our **infirmities** that he **bore**,
  our **sufferings** that he **endured**,
while we thought of him as **stricken**,
  as one **smitten** by God and **afflicted**.

READING I   This reading is fairly long and some of your hearers will not be fully attentive through the whole of the proclamation, so, though your reading should be clear from beginning to end, you might be aware of the most poignant parts of the reading so that the tone of your voice might make the hearers hearken.

The most poignant elements of the proclamation are the following: "He was spurned and avoided by people, / a man of suffering, accustomed to infirmity, / one of those from whom people hide their faces, / spurned, and we held him in no esteem." Those in your community to whom this might offer the greatest consolation are those whom others do not notice. Address them as you proclaim these words, for their lives, which to many seem "of no esteem," are close to the Lord's.

Next: "But he was pierced for our offenses, / crushed for our sins; / . . . by his stripes we were healed."

The final verse is that of the servant's vindication. As you prepare for the Good Friday proclamation, commit a part of this verse to memory so that you might make eye contact with the assembly. Those whose lives have been marked by anguish and infirmity between the last Three Days and this

But he was **pierced** for our **offenses**,
    crushed for our **sins**;
upon **him** was the chastisement that makes us **whole**,
    by **his** stripes we were **healed**.
We had all gone astray like **sheep**,
    each following his own way;
but the LORD laid upon **him**
    the guilt of us **all**.

Though he was harshly **treated**, he submitted
    and opened not his **mouth**;
like a **lamb** led to the **slaughter**
    or a **sheep** before the **shearers**,
he was **silent** and opened not his **mouth**.
Oppressed and **condemned**, he was taken **away**,
    and who would have thought any **more** of his **destiny**?
When he was cut **off** from the land of the **living**,
    and **smitten** for the **sin** of his **people**,
a **grave** was assigned him among the **wicked**
    and a burial place with **evildoers**,
though he had done no **wrong**
    nor spoken any **falsehood**.
But the LORD was pleased
    to crush him in **infirmity**.

If he gives his **life** as an offering for **sin**,
    he shall see his **descendants** in a long **life**,
    and the will of the LORD shall be **accomplished** through **him**.

Because of his **affliction**
    he shall see the **light** in **fullness** of days;

The metaphor of the lamb is central to Christian theology and to the Eucharist, with its "Lamb of God, who takes away the sin of the world."

Here begins the light after darkness.

might feel the unity of their lives and that of the Lord's servant, whose wounds and afflictions are proclaimed from your lips.

Because the reading is long, take advantage of the breaks between that the Lectionary pages supply. These breaks are places where a small pause in your proclamation is fitting. If the breaks fall at places that you consider significant in the passage,

use them as opportunities to make eye contact with the people for whom you are the minister of the word in this very important liturgy of the Lord's Passion.

READING II The letter to the Hebrews is not as accessible as other books of the New Testament; it can be hard work to understand. Your task, as proclaimer of God's word on this Good Friday, is

to make this portrait of Jesus, the Son of God, from the letter to the Hebrews ring in the hearts and minds and souls of those in the liturgical assembly. It is a beautiful theology of what Jesus accomplished for humanity by his suffering.

This text is an integral part of the theology of the Three Days and of Good Friday in particular because the suffering in our own lives is not separate from the suffering

through his **suffering**, my servant shall justify **many**,
and their **guilt** he shall **bear**.
Therefore **I** will give him his **portion** among the **great**,
and **he** shall divide the **spoils** with the **mighty**,
because he **surrendered** himself to **death**
and was **counted** among the **wicked**;
and he shall take **away** the sins of **many**,
and win **pardon** for their **offenses**.

READING II   Hebrews 4:14–16; 5:7–9

A reading from the Letter to the Hebrews

Brothers and sisters:
Since we have a great **high priest** who has passed
through the **heavens**,
Jesus, the Son of **God**,
let us hold **fast** to our **confession**.
For we do **not** have a high priest
who is unable to **sympathize** with our **weaknesses**,
but one who has **similarly** been tested in **every** way,
yet without **sin**.
So let us **confidently** approach the throne of **grace**
to receive **mercy** and to find **grace** for timely **help**.

In the days when **Christ** was in the **flesh**,
he offered **prayers** and **supplications** with loud **cries** and **tears**
to the one who was able to **save** him from **death**,
and he was **heard** because of his **reverence**.

The theology of this reading is deep, and the letter to the Hebrews is not an easy book. See the commentary for helpful information.

Like us, Jesus learned from his suffering. Like him, we do not seek out suffering, but endurance when it comes will help us "find grace for timely help."

of the Son, who is able to sympathize. As you prepare for this proclamation, think of your own life and the lives of some of those you know in your parish, and consider the ways the suffering of the people of God does contribute to making the world a better place. We do not seek out suffering, but we accept the inevitability of suffering, and, like the Son, we offer up our prayers and supplications as in our suffering we participate in the Paschal Mystery.

PASSION Scripture scholars tell us that the Gospel of John was written near the end of the first century, more than a half-century after the events that are told in this Passion. Few, if any, of those in the community from which the Gospel of John emerged would have been eyewitnesses to those events. They knew Jesus from their life of faith in the community. That is the same as our experience: having been incorporated into the Church by Baptism, whether as infants or as adults,

and having experienced the life of faith in our community, we participate in the liturgy because there we meet the risen Christ. Even in solemn liturgical moments like the proclamation of two long Passion readings in one week—Mark on Passion Sunday and John on Good Friday—we come back because we know the story and we are part of the story, for we are indeed the body of Christ.

Son though he **was**, he learned **obedience** from what he **suffered**;
and when he was made **perfect**,
he became the source of eternal **salvation** for **all** who
obey him.

PASSION John 18:1—19:42

The Passion of our Lord Jesus Christ according to John

(1) **Jesus** went out with his **disciples** across the Kidron **valley**
to where there was a **garden**,
into which he and his disciples **entered**.
Judas his **betrayer** also knew the place,
because Jesus had often met there with his disciples.
So **Judas** got a band of **soldiers** and **guards**
from the chief **priests** and the **Pharisees**
and went there with **lanterns**, **torches**, and **weapons**.
Jesus, knowing **everything** that was going to **happen** to him,
went out and said to them, "Whom are you **looking** for?"
They answered him, "Jesus the **Nazorean**."
He said to them, "**I AM**."
Judas his betrayer was also with them.
When he said to them, "**I AM**,"
they turned **away** and fell to the **ground**.
So he **again** asked them,
"Whom are you **looking** for?"
They said, "Jesus the **Nazorean**."
Jesus answered,
"I told you that **I AM**.

Ease into the Passion narrative. The narrative itself carries intensity; the proclaimer doesn't need to add any.
Kidron = KID-run

Pharisees = FAIR-uh-seez

Throughout the proclamation, take advantage of these breaks in the text. They will be helpful to you as you speak and to the assembly as they listen.
Nazorean = naz-uh-REE-uhn

The Passion has a number of the typically Johannine "I am" sayings.

Notice the irony, that those who seek to arrest him fall to the ground in worship.

Below are five general theological characteristics of the Passion in the Gospel of John that make its portraits of Christ unique; appreciating these as background for your proclamation will help you with your ministry of proclaiming this account to the Church assembled on Good Friday.

CHRISTOLOGY. The portrait of Jesus in John is moving, striking, and beautiful. In the last of the canonical Gospels to be written, Jesus is depicted with details that reveal his divinity beyond doubt. One of many examples of this high Christology of the Gospel of John is the indication of Jesus' knowledge of all things. At the start of the Passion, the evangelist describes Jesus as "knowing everything that was going to happen to him," an incredible claim about a human being, and then, nearer the end of the Passion, that Jesus was "aware that everything was now finished." By faith, two millennia later, we have no qualms about such a theology of omniscience, but for the early Church this was taking the divinity of Jesus to a level that had not been claimed by the synoptics, Mark, Matthew, and Luke. Be aware of this high Christology as you prepare for the proclamation of the Johannine Passion.

"I AM" STATEMENTS. In a number of places, John has Jesus use simple statements that reveal theologically deep ideas and experiences. Many of these are the most well-known things Jesus ever said, and they start with the simple first-person statement, "I am."

You will readily recognize sayings unique to John's portrait of Jesus, such as "I am the bread of life," "I am the light of the world," "I am the gate for the sheep," "I am the good shepherd," "I am the Resurrection

Only this Gospel adds the detail of the high priest's slave whose ear Peter cuts off.
Simon = SĪ-mun
Malchus = MAL-kus

Annas = ANN-us
Caiaphas = KĪ-uh-fus

This unnamed disciple, "whom Jesus loved," is sometimes called the "beloved disciple." He did not appear in the Gospel until the seond half, but he plays a *major* role in the Passion, death, empty tomb, and appearance accounts.

Peter's "I am not" is the reverse of the statement of Jesus, "I am," that prompted the soldiers and guards to fall to the ground. Both are short statements, but their effect in the story are very different.

So if you are looking for **me**, let **these** men go."
This was to **fulfill** what he had said,
　"I have not lost **any** of those you **gave** me."
(2) Then Simon **Peter**, who had a **sword**, drew it,
　struck the high priest's **slave**, and cut off his right **ear**.
The slave's **name** was **Malchus**.
Jesus said to Peter,
　"Put your **sword** into its **scabbard**.
Shall I not drink the **cup** that the Father **gave** me?"

So the band of **soldiers**, the **tribune**, and the Jewish **guards**
　　seized Jesus,
　bound him, and brought him to **Annas** first.
He was the father-in-law of **Caiaphas**,
　who was high priest that year.
It was **Caiaphas** who had counseled the Jews
　that it was better that **one** man should die
　　rather than the **people**.

(3) Simon Peter and **another** disciple **followed** Jesus.
Now the **other** disciple was **known** to the high **priest**,
　and he entered the **courtyard** of the high priest with **Jesus**.
But **Peter** stood at the gate **outside**.
So the **other** disciple, the **acquaintance** of the high priest,
　went out and spoke to the **gatekeeper** and brought Peter **in**.
Then the **maid** who was the gatekeeper said to **Peter**,
　"You are not one of this man's disciples, **are** you?"
He said, "I am **not**."
Now the slaves and the guards were standing
　　around a charcoal **fire**
　that they had made, because it was **cold**,
　and were **warming** themselves.
Peter was **also** standing there keeping warm.

and the life," "I am the way, the truth, and the life," and "I am the vine, you are the branches." In the Passion narrative, you will find that this construction, "I am," is revelatory even in his arrest. The soldiers approach Jesus, and he asks, "Who are you looking for?" They answer, "Jesus the Nazorean," and Jesus replies, "I am." The evangelist repeats this "I am" twice more in the arrest scene. As you prepare, find a way to subtly emphasize this unique theological element of John.

　PETER. The role of Peter in the Passion is generally contrasted with the role of the

"beloved disciple" in this Gospel, who appears at the table, the cross, and the empty tomb. Because this disciple is not named, proclaim his character as one in whom your listeners might find their own faith experiences, as believers who find difficulties in their first-hand experience and as believers whose faith brings them to new realizations that deepen their lives and give them meaning.

　MARY. Although many believers turn to the Gospel of Luke for a Marian theology, it is in John that Mary appears at the foot of the cross. Most artistic depictions of the

Crucifixion throughout history have been drawn from the Gospel of John, and we know this because of the presence of the beloved disciple. In the other Gospels, there are no male followers at the cross. The scene with Mary and the beloved disciple is brief, yet its theology and meaning are very significant for the tradition, so proclaim the scene with care. As Jesus anticipates his own dying, he leaves the care of his own mother with the beloved disciple. For those today who care for aging relatives, the tender scene with Mary is very important. Proclaim it well.

The questioning by the high priest is
inserted into the middle of Peter's threefold
denial of Jesus. Pause after the questioning
so that assembly recognizes the shift when
the narrative turns back to Simon Peter.
synagogues = SIN-uh-gogz

(4) The high priest **questioned** Jesus
about his **disciples** and about his **doctrine**.
Jesus answered him,
"I have spoken **publicly** to the world.
I have always taught in a **synagogue**
or in the **temple** area where all the Jews **gather**,
and in **secret** I have said **nothing**. Why ask **me**?
Ask those who **heard** me what I said to them.
They know what I said."
When he had said this,
one of the temple guards standing there **struck** Jesus and said,
"Is this the way you answer the high **priest**?"
Jesus answered him,
"If I have spoken **wrongly**, **testify** to the wrong;
but if I have spoken **rightly**, why do you **strike** me?"
Then **Annas** sent him bound to **Caiaphas** the high priest.

Now Simon **Peter** was standing there keeping warm.
And they said to him,
"You are not one of his disciples, **are** you?"
He denied it and said,
"I am **not**."
One of the **slaves** of the high priest,
a **relative** of the one whose **ear** Peter had cut **off**, said,
"Didn't I see you in the **garden** with him?"
Again Peter denied it.
And **immediately** the **cock crowed**.

The cock crowing is an important detail;
read this clearly and pause for its gravity
to be felt.

(5) Then they brought Jesus from **Caiaphas** to the **praetorium**.
It was **morning**.
And they **themselves** did not enter the **praetorium**,
in order not to be **defiled** so that they could eat the **Passover**.

WORSHIP IN JOHN'S GOSPEL. An important yet enigmatic detail of the Passion according to John is the description of the piercing of Jesus' side with a spear, and from his side flowed "blood and water," a detail unique to this evangelist.

The evening before the proclamation of the Passion of John, the Church celebrates the Mass of the Lord's Supper, at which the body and blood of Christ are central. The evening after the Passion of John is the Easter Vigil with its initiation rites with water, oil, hand-laying, and Eucharist. Therefore, as you prepare for proclaiming the Gospel of John for Good Friday, be pointed in highlighting this detail about the "blood and water" flowing from the side of Jesus because of its place as a ritual intertwining between the *blood* and the *water* of Holy Thursday and the Easter Vigil.

1) As a proclaimer, you probably know already that John has some of the longest Gospel stories. The Passion narrative, it is a carefully constructed account, built to make significant theological points. Here in this first section, you see the evangelist's emphasis on Jesus' "I am" statements. This high Christology needs to be proclaimed clearly because it sums up the Gospel to this point. It also brings the Church through the Easter mysteries and the Fifty Days, when the Gospel of John is proclaimed frequently. Throughout the Fifty Days the risen Savior will be manifest to the Church as the face of God in the worshiping assembly, and this opening scene of the Passion of John for Good Friday brings this up close.

2) Take your time here in order to appreciate and proclaim the symbol of the *cup*, a sign of the suffering that Jesus will undergo. His followers want to spare him the suffering to come, yet his question

Pilate = PĪ-lut

More irony, with Jesus, the innocent man accused of a crime in conversation with Pilate, the governor, about the meaning of "kingdom" and "truth."

So **Pilate** came out to them and said,
"What **charge** do you bring against this man?"
They answered and said to him,
"If he were not a **criminal**,
we would **not** have handed him over to you."
At **this**, Pilate said to them,
"Take him **yourselves**, and judge him according to **your** law."
The Jews answered him,
"We do not have the **right** to execute **anyone**, "
in order that the word of Jesus might be **fulfilled**
that he said indicating the kind of **death** he would die.
So **Pilate** went back into the **praetorium**
and summoned **Jesus** and said to him,
"Are **you** the King of the **Jews**?"
Jesus answered,
"Do you say this on your **own**
or have **others** told you **about** me?"
Pilate answered,
"**I** am not a Jew, **am** I?
Your own **nation** and the chief **priests** handed you over to me.
What have you **done**?"
Jesus answered,
"My **kingdom** does not belong to **this** world.
If my kingdom **did** belong to this world,
my **attendants** would be **fighting**
to keep me from being handed **over** to the **Jews**.
But as it **is**, my **kingdom** is not **here**."
So Pilate said to him,
"Then you **are** a king?"
Jesus answered,
"You **say** I am a king.

shows that he sees the will of God in what lies ahead.

Good Friday is the only day of the liturgical year when the bread and the wine are not consecrated. Jesus' question about the cup appears at the right time, for today is the right time to bring up this eucharistic symbol as a reminder of the inevitability of suffering and the uniqueness of Good Friday.

3) The Gospel of John is the only Gospel in which Peter's threefold denial of Christ is rehabilitated later with a threefold profession of love. Take your time in describing the setting as you narrate this scene, for the details—those who question, the fire, the cold weather—add immediacy. The Passion proclamation is not a drama, but it is meant to invite and provoke the imagination of the hearers.

4) One complexity of this Passion is the deceptiveness of appearances. This episode with the high priest and Jesus would be almost comical in its irony, if it were not leading to so tragic an end. Jesus, who has no power or authority, is cross-examining Annas, in whose hands his fate rests. The exchange between Jesus and the high priest is inserted into the story of Peter's denial, and so this end with the crowing of the cock.

There are several authority figures in the Passion, so as you prepare for your proclamation, clarify for yourself who's who among Pilate, Annas, and Caiaphas. This will illuminate your proclamation and make the account accessible to those who hear your proclamation.

5) Again, the roles are reversed, and Jesus, the one with no worldly power is interrogating the one with ultimate power, Pilate. Yet their exchange is on kingship, with the final enigmatic question from Pilate

For **this** I was born and for **this** I came into the world,
   to testify to the **truth**.
Everyone who **belongs** to the truth **listens** to my voice."
Pilate said to him, "What is **truth**?"

(6) When he had said this,
   he **again** went out to the **Jews** and said to them,
   "I find no **guilt** in him.
But you have a **custom** that I release one **prisoner**
      to you at **Passover**.
Do you want me to release to you the King of the **Jews**?"
They cried out again,
   "Not **this** one but **Barabbas**!"
Now **Barabbas** was a **revolutionary**.

(7) Then Pilate took Jesus and had him **scourged**.
And the **soldiers** wove a **crown** out of **thorns**
      and placed it on his **head**,
   and **clothed** him in a purple **cloak**,
   and they came to him and said,
   "**Hail**, King of the **Jews**!"
And they **struck** him repeatedly.
Once more Pilate went out and said to them,
   "**Look**, I am bringing him **out** to you,
   so that you may **know** that I find no **guilt** in him."
So Jesus came **out**,
   wearing the crown of **thorns** and the purple cloak.
And he said to them, "**Behold**, the man!"
When the chief **priests** and the **guards** saw him they cried out,
   "**Crucify** him, crucify him!"
Pilate said to them,
   "Take him **yourselves** and crucify him.

Barabbas = buh-RAB-us

The Gospel of John gives more detail about what Jesus wore during the Passion and about the garments found in the empty tomb.

The Latin of this statement of Pilate, *Ecce homo*, is the title of many works of art that depict Jesus at this moment.

to Jesus: "What is truth?" That's not the kind of question you expect a powerful person to ask a person under arrest.

6) There is some ambiguity here in the Hebrew name, "Barabbas." The prefix "bar-," which means "son of" (as we find in names like "Simon bar Jonah," meaning "Simon, son of Jonah"). Recall Jesus' use of the intimate "Abba" for his heavenly Father. The name "Barabbas" then means "son of the father."

7) When Saint Jerome translated the New Testament into Latin, he rendered Pilate's announcement of Jesus coming out with the crown of thorns and purple cloak as *"Ecce homo!"* with the noun *homo* bearing a deeper meaning. The word does indeed mean a human being, so our modern "Behold, the man" is absolutely correct. But there was the added significance of Jesus, in this moment of degradation and suffering, representing the fate of all humanity.

As you prepare this section, consider those in this faith community and how much they have reflected Gospel values and witnesses. When you proclaim this section and its summary "Behold, the man," bear them in mind and heart.

8) As mentioned above, the Gospel of John was likely the last of the Gospels written, and the Good News had already spread significantly. Here, the inscription on the cross is in Hebrew, Latin, and Greek, revealing that the message has already grown by

I find no **guilt** in him."
The Jews answered,
   "We have a **law**, and according to that law he ought to **die**,
   because he made himself the Son of **God**."
Now when **Pilate** heard this **statement**,
   he became even **more** afraid,
   and went back into the **praetorium** and said to Jesus,
   "**Where** are you **from**?"
Jesus did not answer him.
So Pilate said to him,
   "Do you not **speak** to me?
Do you not know that I have power to **release** you
   and I have power to **crucify** you?"
Jesus answered him,
   "You would have **no** power over me
   if it had not been **given** to you from **above**.
For this reason the one who handed me **over** to you
   has the **greater** sin."
Consequently, Pilate **tried** to release him; but the Jews cried **out**,
   "If you **release** him, you are **not** a Friend of **Caesar**.
Everyone who makes himself a king **opposes** Caesar."

When Pilate heard **these** words he brought Jesus out
   and **seated** him on the **judge's** bench
   in the place called **Stone Pavement**, in Hebrew, **Gabbatha**.
It was **preparation** day for **Passover**, and it was about **noon**.
And he said to the Jews,
   "**Behold**, your **king**!"
They cried out,
   "Take him **away**, take him **away**! **Crucify** him!"

Pilate and Jesus' exchange on weighty matters continues.

Gabbatha = GAB-uh-thuh

the end of the first century, when this was written. So, in our own time, the Gospel continues to be spread in every language, carrying on what the evangelist acknowledges in this scene.

The chief priests complain to Pilate that he wrote "The King of the Jews" instead of "he said, 'I am the King of the Jews,'" the difference between a description and a delusion. The acknowledgment of Jesus' authority is captured in Pilate's reply to the chief priests: "What I have written, I have written." That is a significant moment in the Passion, poignant as we near Jesus'

death. Take your time so that this scene is heard well.

The scene with Jesus' mother and the beloved disciple is as significant as it is brief. The anonymity of beloved disciple in the Gospel of John makes him a figure who might represent any believer in relation to the Mother of God. So take your time in preparing and proclaiming this vignette at the end of John's Passion.

Golgotha = GOL-guh-thuh

The inscription on the cross—in three languages—emphasizes the universality of the salvation Jesus achieved in his life and Passion. This inscription is abbreviated on many crucifixes INRI: (for Jesus; there is no "J" in Latin), "N" (of Nazareth), "R" (for "king," *rex*), "I" (for *iudaeorum,* meaning "of the Jews").

Pilate said to them,
    "Shall I crucify your **king**?"
The chief priests answered,
    "We **have** no king but **Caesar**."
Then he handed him **over** to them to be **crucified**.

(8) So they **took** Jesus, and, carrying the cross **himself**,
    he went out to what is called the Place of the **Skull**,
    in Hebrew, **Golgotha**.
There they **crucified** him, and with him two **others**,
    one on either **side**, with Jesus in the **middle**.
Pilate **also** had an **inscription** written and put on the cross.
It read,
    "**Jesus** the **Nazorean**, the **King** of the **Jews**."
Now many of the Jews **read** this inscription,
    because the place where Jesus was crucified was near the city;
    and it was written in **Hebrew**, **Latin**, and **Greek**.
So the chief priests of the Jews said to Pilate,
    "Do not write 'The **King** of the **Jews**,'
    but that he said, 'I am the King of the **Jews**.'"
Pilate answered,
    "What I have **written**, I have **written**."

When the soldiers had **crucified** Jesus,
    they took his **clothes** and **divided** them into four **shares**,
    a share for each **soldier**.
They also took his tunic, but the tunic was **seamless**,
    woven in **one** piece from the top down.
So they said to one another,
    "Let's not **tear** it, but cast **lots** for it to see whose it will be,"

in order that the passage of **Scripture** might be **fulfilled**
    that says:
    They divided my **garments** *among them,*
        and for my **vesture** *they cast* **lots**.
This is what the soldiers did.
Standing by the **cross** of Jesus were his **mother**
    and his mother's sister, **Mary** the wife of **Clopas**,
    and Mary of **Magdala**.
When Jesus saw his **mother** and the **disciple** there whom he **loved**
    he said to his mother, "**Woman**, behold, your **son**."
Then he said to the **disciple**,
    "Behold, your **mother**."
And from that hour the disciple took her into his **home**.

After **this**, aware that **everything** was now **finished**,
    in order that the **Scripture** might be **fulfilled**,
    Jesus said, "I **thirst**."
There was a **vessel** filled with common **wine**.
So they put a sponge **soaked** in wine on a sprig of **hyssop**
    and put it up to his **mouth**.
When Jesus had **taken** the wine, he said,
    "It is **finished**."
And bowing his **head**, he handed over the **spirit**.

[Here all kneel and pause for a short time.]

Now since it was **preparation** day,
    in order that the **bodies** might not remain
    on the cross on the **sabbath**,
        for the sabbath day of **that** week was a **solemn** one,
    the Jews asked Pilate that their **legs** be **broken**
    and that they be taken **down**.

Because this is the only Gospel that places the mother of Jesus at the cross, proclaim clearly who is present at the cross. Also unique to this Gospel is Jesus' entrusting Mary to the beloved disciple. Clopas = KLOH-pus

hyssop = HIS-up

sabbath = SAB-uth

So the **soldiers** came and broke the legs of the **first**
  and then of the **other** one who was crucified with Jesus.
But when they came to **Jesus** and saw that he was already **dead**,
    they did not break **his** legs,
    but **one** soldier thrust his **lance** into his **side**,
    and **immediately blood** and **water** flowed out.
An **eyewitness** has testified, and his testimony is **true**;
    he **knows** that he is speaking the **truth**,
    so that you **also** may come to **believe**.
For this **happened** so that the Scripture passage might be **fulfilled**:
    *Not a **bone** of it will be **broken**.*
And again **another** passage says:
    *They will **look** upon him whom they have **pierced**.*

Arimathea = air-ih-muh-THEE-uh

After **this**, Joseph of **Arimathea**,
    secretly a **disciple** of Jesus for fear of the Jews,
    asked **Pilate** if he could remove the **body** of Jesus.
And Pilate **permitted** it.
So he came and **took** his body.
Nicodemus, the one who had **first** come to him at **night**,
    also came bringing a mixture of **myrrh** and **aloes**
    weighing about one hundred **pounds**.

The final details about the burial and the cloths in which the body is wrapped are important.
Nicodemus = nik-oh-DEE-muhs

They took the **body** of Jesus
    and **bound** it with **burial** cloths along with the **spices**,
    according to the Jewish **burial** custom.
Now in the place where he had been **crucified** there was a **garden**,
    and in the garden a new **tomb**, in which no one
        had yet been **buried**.
So they laid Jesus **there** because of the Jewish **preparation** day;
    for the **tomb** was close **by**.

End solemnly as you narrate how Jesus' body was laid in the new tomb.

EASTER VIGIL

Lectionary #41

READING I   Genesis 1:1—2:2

Genesis = JEN-uh-sis

A reading from the Book of Genesis

In the **beginning**, when God created the **heavens** and the earth,
   the earth was a formless **wasteland**, and **darkness**
      covered the **abyss**,
   while a mighty **wind** swept over the waters.

Take each day as a mini-reading with its own elements in common with the other days. Pause after each day so that the new world you are proclaiming can sink into the imaginations of those to whom you read.

Then God said,
   "Let there be **light**," and there **was** light.
God saw how **good** the light was.
God then **separated** the light from the **darkness**.
God called the light "**day**" and the darkness he called "**night**."
Thus **evening** came, and **morning** followed—the **first** day.

Our cosmology is different from that of the author of this passage, but for your proclamation you should imagine the world just as it is described so that your words will draw a picture of this world and God's loving care.

Then God said,
   "Let there be a **dome** in the middle of the waters,
      to separate **one** body of water from the **other**."
And so it **happened**:
   God made the dome,
   and it separated the water **above** the dome
      from the water **below** it.
God called the dome "the **sky**."
Evening came, and **morning** followed—the **second** day.

Significant pause between the second and the third days. The text portrays God's providence and generosity.

Then God said,
   "Let the water under the sky be **gathered** into a single **basin**,
      so that the **dry land** may appear."

READING I In most communities the Church's symbols have been more fully emphasized in the liturgy since the Second Vatican Council. One rich symbol that can can always bear a little more emphasis is the Easter fire, a significant fire for a significant moment in the life of the community. This fire, lit and blessed outside the church building, signifies the destruction of what had gone before; it is a sign that the old world is passing away, that the rebirth of the Church is fierce and even a little frightening, that it is also exciting and refreshing.

The first reading of the Easter Vigil is the first Creation account in Genesis, the narrative of God's Creation of the world in six days. A significant fire at the start of the Vigil is a wonderful complement to the reading you will proclaim.

The reading before you is a patterned proclamation, with repeated elements that have been proclaimed in assemblies for centuries, for millennia even. You join the long stream of witnesses to God's providence, and your proclamation should announce God's oversight and loving care of the world. Because of the length and the repetitious style of the text, you should make a significant pause after each day of Creation. (The inclination with a long reading is to rush,

And so it **happened**:
    the water **under** the sky was gathered into its **basin**,
    and the **dry land** appeared.
God called the **dry land** "the **earth**,"
    and the **basin** of the water he called "the **sea**."
God saw how **good** it was.

Then God said,
    "Let the earth bring forth **vegetation**:
    every kind of **plant** that bears **seed**
    and every kind of **fruit** tree on earth
    that bears **fruit** with its **seed** in it."
And so it **happened**:
    the earth brought forth **every** kind of plant that bears **seed**
    and **every** kind of fruit tree on **earth**
    that bears **fruit** with its **seed** in it.
God saw how **good** it was.
Evening came, and **morning** followed—the **third** day.

Then God said:
    "Let there be **lights** in the dome of the **sky**,
    to separate **day** from **night**.
Let them mark the fixed **times**, the **days** and the **years**,
    and serve as **luminaries** in the dome of the **sky**,
    to shed **light** upon the **earth**."
And so it **happened**:
    God made the two great **lights**,
    the **greater** one to govern the **day**,
    and the **lesser** one to govern the **night**;
    and he made the **stars**.
God **set** them in the dome of the sky,
    to shed light upon the earth,
    to govern the **day** and the **night**,
    and to separate the **light** from the **darkness**.

Significant pause between the third and the fourth days. Imagine what you know of the lands and oceans of our planet; capture some of the wonder and passion that comes with knowing how bountiful and varied this world of ours is.

but take your time. The assembly will be more engaged by a strong reading than by a quick reading.)

As you prepare this text, perhaps you can underline or highlight the similar elements in your *Workbook,* using a different color for each. This can help you with the patterned nature of your proclamation: "And God said," "God called," "And so it happened," "God saw that it was good,"

"Evening came, and morning followed." The parts of the reading that are not part of the pattern contain poetic details about the world, so these can include your own appreciation of the created world. Proclaim the reading as if you are seeing the world anew, and share that newness with gathered Church.

READING II This second reading of the Easter Vigil is not as long as the first, but it is still fairly long. Because of the length of the reading, because it is a reading in a series of readings, and because the reading will be proclaimed at this climactic point in the liturgical year, you will need your best skills of proclamation to maintain the assembly's interest and engagement.

God saw how **good** it was.
Evening came, and **morning** followed—the **fourth** day.

Then God said,
"Let the water **teem** with an abundance of living **creatures**,
and on the earth let **birds** fly beneath the dome of the **sky**."
And so it **happened**:
God created the great **sea monsters**
and all **kinds** of swimming creatures with which
the water **teems**,
and all **kinds** of winged birds.
God saw how **good** it was, and God **blessed** them, saying,
"Be **fertile**, **multiply**, and **fill** the water of the **seas**;
and let the **birds** multiply on the **earth**."
Evening came, and **morning** followed—the **fifth** day.

Then God said,
"Let the earth bring forth all **kinds** of living **creatures**:
cattle, **creeping** things, and wild **animals** of all **kinds**."
And so it **happened**:
God made all **kinds** of wild **animals**, all **kinds** of **cattle**,
and all kinds of **creeping** things of the earth.
God saw how **good** it was.

Then God said:
"Let us make **man** in our **image**, after our **likeness**.
Let them have **dominion** over the **fish** of the sea,
the **birds** of the air, and the **cattle**,
and over **all** the wild **animals**
and **all** the creatures that **crawl** on the **ground**."
God **created** man in his **image**;
in the image of **God** he created him;
male and **female** he created them.

Significant pause between the fourth and the fifth days. You can be sure that the "great sea monsters" will catch people's attention!

Significant pause between the fifth and the sixth days. Think of this day as the critical point, for by this time the assembly is starting to catch the pattern. Now we come to the creation of human beings. Animate the reading here, for you are nearing the end, and you want to sustain their listening.

Although this account is suspenseful, most believers know that the story has a happy ending. Given that all know the story, the sacrifice of Isaac can be seen with the theological maning of the inevitable difficulties of human living, of the crossroads all of us, even the most saintly, come to in our days.

Our faith is mediated by the community of faith in which we participate in the liturgy. The will of God is discerned by believers in the context of the faith they share with others. As you prepare to proclaim this reading, be mindful of the times when, in your own life, the will of God has called people to unimaginably difficult decisions. Even those

who are called to Baptism at Easter may have had to make difficult decisions along the way, so keep all these people and situations in mind as you prepare to proclaim this narrative of Abraham, who was called to such a difficult act in his journey of faith.

God **blessed** them, saying:
   "Be **fertile** and **multiply**;
   fill the earth and **subdue** it.
Have **dominion** over the **fish** of the sea, the **birds** of the air,
   and **all** the living things that **move** on the **earth**."

God also said:
   "**See**, I give you every seed-bearing **plant** all over the **earth**
   and every **tree** that has seed-bearing **fruit** on it to be your **food**;
   and to all the **animals** of the land, all the **birds** of the air,
   and **all** the living creatures that crawl on the **ground**,
   I give all the green **plants** for **food**."
And so it **happened**.
God looked at **everything** he had made, and he found it
   very good.
Evening came, and **morning** followed—the **sixth** day.

Thus the **heavens** and the **earth** and all their array
   were **completed**.
Since on the **seventh** day God was **finished**
   with the work he had been **doing**,
   he **rested** on the **seventh** day from all the work
   he had **undertaken**.

[Shorter: Genesis 1:1, 26–31a]

Pause before the summary.

READING II   Genesis 22:1–18

A reading from the Book of Genesis

God put **Abraham** to the **test**.
He called to him, "**Abraham!**"
"Here I **am**," he replied.

Genesis = JEN-uh-sis

**The length of this passage from Genesis is eased by the dialogue. After each bit of dialogue comes a continuation of the narrative. The opening of the exchange comes directly from God to Abraham.
Abraham = AY-bruh-ham**

READING III The newness during the Easter Vigil is the celebration of the Resurrection, the celebration of initiation, the singing of "Alleluia" after weeks of omitting it, and in general the complete renewal of the Church.

This rare ritual moment also calls for some coordination. Consult with the pastor or liturgy director and music director so that you are clear about the transition from the scripture reading to the canticle that follows it immediately.

Like most of the readings of the Easter Vigil, this story is familiar to most in the assembly, so your task is not so much to

hold your listeners in suspense as to emphasize the elements of the reading that are most important to the Easter Vigil. The unique ritual at the heart of the Vigil is the rites of initiation, which begin with Baptism. This reading could not be more appropriate as an anticipation of the baptismal rite of the Vigil. For this reason, highlight the elements

Isaac = Ī-zik

Moriah = moh-RĪ-uh

This next part provides some details of
the context.

The dialogue continues with Abraham's
instructions.

Then the action that follows logically from
the exchange.

This exchange between father and son
is unnerving, because we know what
direction Abraham is following. The
exchange is followed by the details of
the action.

Then God said:
"Take your son **Isaac**, your only **one**, whom you **love**,
and go to the land of **Moriah**.
There you shall offer him up as a **holocaust**
on a **height** that I will point out to you."
Early the next **morning** Abraham saddled his **donkey**,
took with him his son **Isaac** and two of his servants as well,
and with the **wood** that he had cut for the **holocaust**,
set out for the **place** of which **God** had told him.

On the **third** day **Abraham** got sight of the **place** from afar.
Then he said to his **servants**:
"Both of you stay **here** with the donkey,
while the boy and I go on over **yonder**.
We will **worship** and then come **back** to you."
Thereupon Abraham took the **wood** for the **holocaust**
and **laid** it on his son Isaac's **shoulders**,
while he himself carried the **fire** and the **knife**.
As the two walked on **together**, Isaac spoke
to his father Abraham:
"**Father**!" Isaac said.
"Yes, son," he replied.
Isaac continued, "Here are the **fire** and the **wood**,
but **where** is the **sheep** for the **holocaust**?"
"**Son**," Abraham answered,
"God himself will provide the **sheep** for the **holocaust**."
Then the two continued going forward.

When they came to the **place** of which God had **told** him,
Abraham built an **altar** there and arranged the **wood** on it.
Next he tied up his son **Isaac**,
and put him on **top** of the wood on the **altar**.

in the story that are related to water: Moses stretching his hand out over the sea, the Israelites proceeding across the dry sea bed, the death-dealing waters for the Egyptians, and the rejoicing on the seashore.

This moment in the life of ancient Israel is important in its own way, and the life of God continues in communities of faith. Inspire the gathered Christians and those to be baptized as you proclaim this wonderful reading of Israel's rescue by the Lord.

READING IV The fourth reading has three basic parts. Part one describes a marriage and its history, part two compares the spouses' reconciliation to the Lord's promise to Noah after the flood, and part three is a promise to the wife of prosperity and security to come.

After the various texts that the sacred assembly has already heard by this point in the liturgy of the word, this passage represents still another kind of text, a theology in which the Creator's relationship to Israel, in the Jewish tradition, and to the Church, in the Christian tradition, is compared to that of husband and wife. This relationship is not one of uninterrupted bliss. No, the wife described by the prophet was cast off, and

The next exchange we hear with relief.

Then more details, with the ram caught in the thicket.

The final four verses are not from the Lord directly, but from the angel of the Lord. This short speech from the angel is about the promise to Abraham and his descendents, a promise that will be referred to many times in scripture.

Then he reached out and took the knife to **slaughter** his son.
But the LORD's **messenger** called to him from **heaven**,
  "**Abraham**, **Abraham**!"
"Here I **am**," he answered.
"Do **not** lay your **hand** on the **boy**," said the **messenger**.
"Do **not** do the **least** thing to him.
I **know** now how **devoted** you are to God,
  since you did not **withhold** from me your own **beloved son**."
As Abraham looked about,
  he spied a **ram** caught by its **horns** in the **thicket**.
So he went and took the ram
  and offered it up as a **holocaust** in place of his **son**.
Abraham named the site Yahweh-yireh;
  hence people now say, "On the mountain the LORD will see."

Again the LORD's messenger called to Abraham from heaven
  and said:
"I swear by myself, declares the LORD,
that because you acted as you did
in not **withholding** from me your beloved **son**,
I will **bless** you **abundantly**
and make your descendants as **countless**
as the **stars** of the **sky** and the **sands** of the **seashore**;
your **descendants** shall take possession
of the gates of their **enemies**,
and in your descendants all the **nations** of the earth
  shall find **blessing**—
all this because you **obeyed** my **command**."

[Shorter: Genesis 22:1–2, 9a, 10–13, 15–18]

now the husband is turning back to the wife who had been forsaken. The passage then looks to the destruction of the earth in the flood of Noah and to the Lord's promise that it would never happen again.

The theological reason for the passage at the Easter Vigil is as consolation to the people in the steadfastness of God. The Easter Vigil is a liturgy of conquering death

and rebirth in Christ, both for those who will be initiated and the whole community of faith. The consolation offered by this reading will speak to those who have felt that God was far away at times in the past, and for those to be initiated the consolation will be that God will support them and stand by them, as in a Marriage.

The third part of the reading begins with the direct address, "O afflicted one." Pause before you move into this part, for it is an important change. There are some difficult words in that section, with the names of the stones, but the particulars open up in the final two verses to an overarching promise of prosperity and of keeping oppression, fear, and terror at a distance. The Church can

A reading from the Book of Exodus

The LORD said to Moses, "Why are you crying out to me?
Tell the Israelites to go forward.
And you, lift up your staff and, with hand outstretched
    over the sea,
  split the sea in two,
    that the Israelites may pass through it on dry land.
But I will make the Egyptians so obstinate
    that they will go in after them.
Then I will receive glory through Pharaoh and all his army,
    his chariots and charioteers.
The Egyptians shall know that I am the LORD,
    when I receive glory through Pharaoh
    and his chariots and charioteers."

The angel of God, who had been leading Israel's camp,
    now moved and went around behind them.
The column of cloud also, leaving the front,
    took up its place behind them,
    so that it came between the camp of the Egyptians
    and that of Israel.
But the cloud now became dark, and thus the night passed
    without the rival camps coming any closer together
    all night long.
Then Moses stretched out his hand over the sea,
    and the LORD swept the sea
    with a strong east wind throughout the night
    and so turned it into dry land.

Exodus = EK-suh-dus

The readings at the Vigil highlight the important moments and persons in the history of Israel. We heard about Abraham in the second reading, and here we hear about Moses, to whom the Lord speaks directly in the first four verses of the reading.
Moses = MOH-ziz
Israelites = IZ-ree-uh-līts
Egyptians = ee-JIP-shunz
Pharaoh = FAIR-oh

Israel = IZ-ree-ul

The details of Moses' and the Egyptians' actions in the unfolding of the miracle are important. Imagine yourself seeing such an event so that you can inspire those in the assembly to imagine it for themselves.

help in times of need, and the consolation of the passage will speak to those who have looked to the Church at times of difficulty.

READING V   Because most members of the Church did not receive their first Eucharist at their Baptism, the Eucharist is not often seen as the sacrament of initiation that it is. At the Easter Vigil, the Eucharist is celebrated with Baptism and Confirmation, and this order and cohesion is a revival of the awe-inspiring rites of initiation of the early Church.

The reading that you are preparing to proclaim at the Easter Vigil is significant in relation to the sacraments of initiation because it mentions the material elements of Baptism and the Eucharist together (water, bread, and wine), even though the prophet would not have written the passage for this sacramental association.

The water of the opening invitation, "come to the water," is not for washing, which would make a direct metaphorical link to Baptism. The water here is part of a feasting metaphor, as it is addressed to "all

When the **water** was thus **divided**,
the Israelites **marched** into the **midst** of the sea on dry **land**,
with the water like a **wall** to their **right** and to their **left**.

The **Egyptians** followed in **pursuit**;
all Pharaoh's **horses** and **chariots** and **charioteers**
went after them
right into the **midst** of the **sea**.
In the night watch just before dawn
the LORD cast through the column of the fiery **cloud**
upon the Egyptian force a **glance** that threw it into a **panic**;
and he so **clogged** their chariot wheels
that they could hardly **drive**.
With **that** the Egyptians sounded the **retreat** before Israel,
because the LORD was fighting for them **against** the Egyptians.

Then the LORD told **Moses**, "Stretch out your **hand** over the **sea**,
that the **water** may flow **back** upon the **Egyptians**,
upon their **chariots** and their **charioteers**."
So Moses **stretched** out his hand over the **sea**,
and at dawn the sea flowed **back** to its normal depth.
The Egyptians were fleeing **head on** toward the **sea**,
when the LORD **hurled** them into its **midst**.
As the water flowed **back**,
it covered the **chariots** and the **charioteers**
of Pharaoh's whole **army**
which had **followed** the Israelites into the sea.
Not a single **one** of them **escaped**.
But the **Israelites** had marched on dry **land**
through the midst of the **sea**,
with the water like a **wall** to their **right** and to their **left**.
Thus the LORD **saved Israel** on that day
from the power of the **Egyptians**.

Emphasize this fiery cloud, for it is a link with the Easter fire.

The Lord delivers the instructions and Moses follows.

you who are thirsty" rather than to "everyone who needs a bath" or "all you who are dirty." But the proclamation can bear the invitation in both directions, as an invitation of the Lord to those who are thirsty and as an invitation to the waters of Baptism.

The middle part of your proclamation takes up the ruler David, calls the people to the Lord, and calls the wicked and the unrighteous to change their lives. The passage alternates between direct commands—such as "come," "listen," "seek"—more descriptive sentences—such as "I made him a witness," and "my thoughts are not your thoughts." Perhaps as you prepare you can note which parts are commands and which more descriptive so that it will help you recognize the tone to use for each.

READING VI The sixth reading is different from the other readings from the Old Testament because it comes from a book that rarely appears in the *Lectionary for Mass.* It finds its place at the Easter Vigil because it captures a significant moment in the history of Israel, that of the Babylonian captivity, in a concise summary and with hope toward the future in which the people will follow the law of God and live in happiness.

When Israel saw the **Egyptians** lying **dead** on the **seashore**
and beheld the great **power** that the LORD
had shown against the Egyptians,
they **feared** the LORD and **believed** in him
and in his servant **Moses**.

Then Moses and the Israelites sang this **song** to the LORD:
I will sing to the **LORD**, for he is gloriously **triumphant**;
horse and chariot he has **cast** into the **sea**.

The end of the reading leads up to the canticle.

READING IV   Isaiah 54:5–14

Isaiah = ī-ZAY-uh

This first line identifies the speaker as the Lord. Isaiah was prophesying these words to the people.

A reading from the Book of the Prophet Isaiah

The One who has become your **husband** is your **Maker**;
his **name** is the LORD of **hosts**;
your **redeemer** is the **Holy** One of **Israel**,
called **God** of all the **earth**.
The LORD calls you **back**,
like a **wife** forsaken and grieved in spirit,
a **wife** married in **youth** and then cast **off**,
says your God.
For a brief moment I **abandoned** you,
but with great **tenderness** I will take you **back**.
In an outburst of **wrath**, for a **moment**
I hid my face from you;
but with enduring **love** I take **pity** on you,
says the LORD, your **redeemer**.

The Babylonian captivity was a time of over a half-century (587–521 BC) when Israel was conquered, Jerusalem destroyed, and the people of Israel captured and carried off as prisoners to a foreign land, Babylon. Because the holy land was and still is so precious and sacred to the Jews, this displacement of the nation to a foreign country occasioned a huge crisis in their theology

and in their identity. "If we were the people of God," they would have asked themselves, "How could this tragedy have befallen us? How could we have lost the most important gift from God?" The passage from Baruch is from this time of questioning.

The reading is about the conversion of the people, and in this regard its placement at the Easter Vigil is fitting. Though we tend to think of conversion as the change in the

life of an individual, conversion also happens to groups, to communities, and Baruch's word to Israel can be held up at the Vigil as an encouragement to your community for its own conversion.

Emphasize the symbol of light in the last few verses of the passage, for the Easter candle is there burning in the darkened church for all to see. Though the reading

This reference to the flood is fitting, as the community will soon be celebrating Baptism.

This is for **me** like the days of **Noah**,
 when I swore that the **waters** of Noah
 should **never** again **deluge** the earth;
so I have sworn **not** to be angry with you,
 or to **rebuke** you.
Though the **mountains** leave their **place**
 and the **hills** be **shaken**,
my love shall **never** leave you
 nor my covenant of **peace** be shaken,
 says the LORD, who has mercy on you.
O **afflicted** one, **storm-battered** and **unconsoled**,
 I lay your **pavements** in **carnelians**,
 and your **foundations** in **sapphires**;
I will make your **battlements** of **rubies**,
 your **gates** of **carbuncles**,
 and all your **walls** of precious **stones**.
All your children shall be taught by the LORD,
 and great shall be the **peace** of your **children**.
In **justice** shall you be **established**,
 far from the fear of **oppression**,
 where destruction cannot **come** near you.

Pause before you start this section. Practice this section so that your proclamation is smooth and confident.
carnelians = kar-NEEL-yunz

carbuncles =KAR-bung-k*lz

The closing promise brings the passage to a close on a positive note.

READING V   Isaiah 55:1–11

Isaiah = ī-ZAY-uh

This invitation to the table is lovely, as the hearers are welcomed. Proclaim it as an invitation to God's feast.

A reading from the Book of the Prophet Isaiah

Thus says the LORD:
All you who are **thirsty**,
 come to the **water**!

---

does not concentrate on the light until the end, it is still good for you to focus on this symbol in the reading for attentive listeners who might grasp the link.

READING VII There is some complexity in this reading, as you will see. There are some sentences with the first person (using "me," "my," "I"), some in the second person (with "your," "you"), and some in the third person (using "their," "they," "them"). Before you start practicing, it would be good for you to recognize to whom each of the voices refers because it can be difficult to sort out at first sight.

Throughout the entire passage there is the first-person voice, and it consistently refers to the Lord. With "I poured out my fury," for example, it is the Lord who did the pouring.

The beginning of the second line tells us that the Lord is speaking to a human being generally, because it uses the address "Son of man." The first half of the reading is speaking about the Israelites, so here the

You who have no money,
    come, receive grain and **eat**;
come, without **paying** and without **cost**,
    drink wine and **milk**!
Why spend your **money** for what is not **bread**,
    your **wages** for what fails to **satisfy**?
Heed me, and you shall eat **well**,
    you shall **delight** in rich **fare**.
Come to me **heedfully**,
    listen, that you may have **life**.
I will **renew** with you the **everlasting** covenant,
    the **benefits** assured to **David**.
As I made him a **witness** to the **peoples**,
    a **leader** and commander of **nations**,
so shall you summon a **nation** you knew **not**,
    and nations that knew you **not** shall **run** to you,
because of the LORD, your **God**,
    the **Holy** One of **Israel**, who has **glorified** you.

Seek the LORD while he may be found,
    call him while he is near.
Let the **scoundrel** forsake his **way**,
    and the **wicked** man his **thoughts**;
let him **turn** to the LORD for **mercy**;
    to our **God**, who is **generous** in **forgiving**.
For **my** thoughts are not **your** thoughts,
    nor are **your** ways **my** ways, says the LORD.
As high as the **heavens** are above the **earth**,
    so high are **my** ways above **your** ways
    and **my** thoughts above **your** thoughts.

Israel = IZ-ree-ul

The passage alternates back to invitation, this time to seek and call rather than eat and drink.

third person means Israel. So, for example, when the Lord says, "I scattered *them* among the nations," the "them" refers to the Israelites.

A significant change comes about halfway through the passage, where the text reads, "Therefore say to the house of Israel," for from that point on Israel is referred to in the second person ("you"). When the reading continues this is evident, for the Lord says, "Not for your sakes do I act, house of Israel." The "your" and the "house of Israel" are the same, and this is maintained to the end.

This rhetorical complexity is clearer in the text than in the description. Moreover, the passage is quite striking, so taking the time to understand the text will benefit the proclamation. Because of the shift of voice, it might be good in your first practice to read only up to that point. Then, once you have become comfortable with that part, practice the second half. Then put them together with confidence, appreciating the theology of the passage as a whole.

The end of the reading is beautiful, first because of the images of water and the sprinkling of water, which are important in

These metaphors from nature are meant to emphasize God's generosity, and the final gift mentioned is that of God's word, which you yourself share with the assembly at the Vigil.

For just as from the heavens
    the **rain** and **snow** come **down**
and do not **return** there
    till they have **watered** the **earth**,
    making it **fertile** and **fruitful**,
giving **seed** to the one who **sows**
    and **bread** to the one who **eats**,
so shall my **word** be
    that goes forth from my **mouth**;
my **word** shall not return to me **void**,
    but shall do my **will**,
    achieving the **end** for which I **sent** it.

READING VI   Baruch 3:9–15, 32—4:4

Baruch = buh-**ROOK**

The reading begins with a command: "Hear!" Your voice should also carry that tone.
Israel = IZ-ree-ul

A reading from the Book of the Prophet Baruch

Hear, O Israel, the **commandments** of **life**:
    listen, and know **prudence**!
How **is** it, Israel,
    that you are in the land of your foes,
    grown **old** in a foreign **land**,
defiled with the **dead**,
    accounted with those destined for the **netherworld**?
You have **forsaken** the fountain of **wisdom**!
Had you **walked** in the way of **God**,
    you would have **dwelt** in enduring **peace**.

the rituals of the Easter Vigil. There is beauty also in the poetic imagery of the "heart of stone" and "heart of flesh." That faith will keep one's heart from turning to stone is perfectly beautiful.

EPISTLE Paul's letter to the Romans was written almost 2,000 years ago, but its theology of Baptism is so foundational that it can be proclaimed at the Easter Vigil and be heard as if it had been written today.

There are a number of challenges to you as the proclaimer of this significant passage about Baptism. The first challenge is the liturgical occasion at which you are to read this passage, the Easter Vigil. For centuries the Easter Vigil was not celebrated with the whole parish present. It still retained vestiges of its past as the time for initiation, but there were few besides ordained priests

who heard or experienced that. Since Vatican II and particularly since the restoration of the catechumenate and the RCIA, the primary reason for the Vigil was restored, that of initiating new members into the community for the renewal of the life of the Church. This reading about Baptism marks a significant moment in the life of the parish, and the challenge to you is to let Paul's theology be heard clearly.

The first three "where" phrases are dependent on the "learn," and the next two on "know."

Learn where **prudence** is,
  where **strength**, where **understanding**;
that you may know **also**
  where are length of **days**, and **life**,
  where light of the **eyes**, and **peace**.
Who has found the place of **wisdom**,
  who has entered into her **treasuries**?

The One who knows **all** things knows **her**;
  he has **probed** her by his **knowledge**—
the One who established the earth for all **time**,
  and filled it with four-footed **beasts**;
  he who dismisses the **light**, and it **departs**,
  calls it, and it **obeys** him **trembling**;
before whom the **stars** at their posts
  shine and **rejoice**;
when he **calls** them, they answer, "**Here** we are!"
  shining with **joy** for their Maker.
Such is our **God**;
  no **other** is to be **compared** to him:
he has traced out the whole way of **understanding**,
  and has given her to **Jacob**, his **servant**,
  to **Israel**, his beloved **son**.

Since then she has appeared on **earth**,
  and moved among **people**.
She is the **book** of the precepts of **God**,
  the **law** that endures **forever**;
all who **cling** to her will **live**,
  but those will **die** who **forsake** her.
Turn, O Jacob, and **receive** her:
  walk by her **light** toward **splendor**.

Jacob = JAY-kub

The second challenge of the passage is in the second-person ("you") and first-person ("we" and "our") voices of the Letter to the Romans. The challenge for you is to proclaim the reading not as a recital of the theology of first-century Rome but as the theology of your community in your time and your place. There is nothing in the passage to distance your community from the theology Paul sets out.

The third challenge is to be aware of the excitement and vulnerabilities of those waiting to be initiated. The elect and the candidates for reception have been formed over a long period, and this is the night for which they have been waiting. The passage you proclaim will touch their hearts not only because it is a rich theology of Baptism but because they likely pondered this passage deeply in their formation.

In comparison with the seven passages from the Bible that have already been read tonight, the passage from Romans is short. Take your time, be clear, and engage the assembly in their renewal and the elect just before their initiation.

GOSPEL Although the narrative of the Resurrection is extraordinary, after all these many readings it might

Pause here, as you are about to start the final section. The "alien race" are the captors who held the Israelites against their will.

Give not your **glory** to another,
    your **privileges** to an alien **race**.
Blessed are we, O **Israel**;
    for what pleases God is **known** to us!

READING VII   Ezekiel 36:16–17a, 18–28

Ezekiel = ee-ZEE-kee-ul

The passage has two basic directions. Here the Lord is chastising Israel for its disobedience and misconduct.
Israel = IZ-ree-ul

A reading from the Book of the Prophet Ezekiel

The word of the LORD came to me, saying:
    Son of **man**, when the house of **Israel** lived in their **land**,
    they **defiled** it by their **conduct** and **deeds**.
Therefore I poured out my **fury** upon them
    because of the **blood** that they poured out on the **ground**,
    and because they **defiled** it with **idols**.
I **scattered** them among the **nations**,
    dispersing them over foreign **lands**;
    according to their **conduct** and **deeds** I **judged** them.
But when they **came** among the nations **wherever** they came,
    they served to **profane** my holy **name**,
    because it was said of them: "**These** are the people of the LORD,
    yet they had to leave their **land**."
So I have **relented** because of my holy **name**
    which the house of Israel **profaned**
    among the nations where they **came**.
Therefore say to the house of **Israel**:
Thus says the Lord GOD:
    Not for **your** sakes do I act, house of **Israel**,
    but for the sake of my holy **name**,
    which you **profaned** among the nations to which you came.

feel like just another day in the life of Jesus as told in the Gospels. The assembly will have already heard from Paul's letter to the Romans, saying, "We shall also be united with him in the resurrection." The narrative of the Resurrection of Christ is powerful here because, by God's gift in the life of Jesus and in the life of the community of faith before you as you proclaim, is it still the experience in which believers participate. Indeed, before their very eyes at this Vigil, they will

be explicitly tied again to this experience as you celebrate the rites of initiation and the renewal of baptismal promises.

As a story, this passage is broken up by the words of the women to one another, and by the words of consolation from the angel. Take your time with these speeches, for they reveal much about the experience of the disciples then and about the influences on our theology of Baptism and Resurrection today.

Two other details of the Gospel are significant at the Easter Vigil. First, the Resurrection takes place "when the sabbath was over," that is, on Sunday, on the first day of the week. This is key because Sundays are the sustenance of the Church's life. The Easter Vigil is held after dark on a Saturday night because of the ritual tradition, drawn from the Gospels, of meeting on Sunday.

The second detail might depend on whether or not there will be Baptisms at the Vigil and also in whether the newly baptized

The second direction starts here, with the Lord speaking directly to the people of Israel, telling them that this is an opportunity for a new relationship.

From here to the end is a beautiful theology, with poetic images. Practice these last four verses so that you can proclaim them with confidence and hope.

I will prove the **holiness** of my great name,
    profaned among the **nations**,
  in whose midst you have **profaned** it.
Thus the nations shall **know** that **I** am the LORD,
    says the Lord GOD,
  when in their sight I **prove** my holiness through **you**.
For I will take you **away** from among the nations,
    gather you from all the foreign **lands**,
  and bring you **back** to your **own land**.
I will sprinkle clean **water** upon you
    to **cleanse** you from all your **impurities**,
  and from all your **idols** I will **cleanse** you.
I will give you a new **heart** and place a new **spirit** within you,
    taking from your **bodies** your **stony** hearts
  and giving you **natural** hearts.
I will put my **spirit** within you and make you live by my **statutes**,
    careful to observe my **decrees**.
You shall **live** in the land I gave your **fathers**;
    you shall be my **people**, and I will be your **God**.

will be dressed in albs. If so, you might highlight the description of the angel: "his clothing was white as snow." Our ritual actions and symbols were shaped by and are now drawn from the canonical texts that we proclaim.

As you prepare, consider a balance between two things. First, your proclamation comes at the end of a long liturgy of the word, and the assembly will have heard many readings before you step up; second, the Baptisms to follow are tied closely to the experience of the empty tomb. So, without asking too much of the assembly, emphasize the elements that will help them appreciate the initiation rites to follow.

Romans = ROH-munz

The reading starts with the second-person voice, "Are you unaware . . ." Engage the assembly by addressing the passage to them directly.

The theology of death and Resurrection you proclaim is essential to the Vigil.

The union between Christ's death and our death, between Christ's Resurrection and our Resurrection could not be clearer. Proclaim this with confidence.

EPISTLE   Romans 6:3–11

A reading from the Letter of Saint Paul to the Romans

Brothers and sisters:
Are you **unaware** that we who were **baptized** into Christ **Jesus**
　　were **baptized** into his **death**?
We were indeed **buried** with him through baptism into **death**,
　　so that, just as Christ was **raised** from the dead
　　by the **glory** of the Father,
　　we **too** might **live** in newness of **life**.

For if we have grown into **union** with him
　　　through a **death** like his,
　　we shall also be **united** with him in the **resurrection**.
We know that our **old** self was **crucified** with him,
　　so that our **sinful** body might be done **away** with,
　　that we might no longer be in **slavery** to sin.
For a **dead** person has been **absolved** from sin.
If, then, we have **died** with Christ,
　　we believe that we shall also **live** with him.
We know that **Christ**, raised from the **dead**, dies no **more**;
　　death no longer has power over him.
As to his **death**, he died to sin **once** and for **all**;
　　as to his **life**, he lives for **God**.
Consequently, you **too** must think of **yourselves**
　　　as being **dead** to sin
　　and **living** for God in Christ **Jesus**.

GOSPEL   Mark 16:1–7

A reading from the holy Gospel according to Mark

sabbath = SAB-uth

Magdalene = MAG-duh-lun

When the **sabbath** was **over**,
Mary **Magdalene**, Mary, the mother of **James**, and **Salome**
bought **spices** so that they might go and **anoint** him.

The dawn of first day of the week: Sunday morning.

Very **early** when the sun had **risen**,
on the **first** day of the **week**, they came to the **tomb**.
They were **saying** to one another,
"Who will roll back the **stone** for us
from the entrance to the **tomb**?"
When they looked **up**,
they saw that the stone **had** been rolled back;
it was very **large**.

The clothing of the young man, like those who are baptized in our own rites at Easter, is white.

On **entering** the tomb they saw a young **man**
sitting on the **right** side, **clothed** in a white **robe**,
and they were **utterly** amazed.
He said to them, "Do not be **amazed**!
You seek **Jesus** of **Nazareth**, the crucified.
He has been **raised**; he is not **here**.
Behold the **place** where they **laid** him.

The proclamation of the Resurrection, like your proclamation of the Easter Gospel, was a message to be spread. So the young man begins this chain of proclamation that has continued to our day.

Galilee = GAL-ih-lee

"But **go** and tell his **disciples** and **Peter**,
'He is going **before** you to **Galilee**;
there you will **see** him, as he **told** you.'"

EASTER SUNDAY

Lectionary #42/46

READING I   Acts 10:34a, 37–43

A reading from the Acts of the Apostles

Peter proceeded to speak and said:
   "You **know** what has happened all over **Judea**,
   beginning in Galilee after the baptism
   that John **preached**,
   how God anointed **Jesus** of **Nazareth**
   with the Holy **Spirit** and **power**.
He went about doing **good**
   and **healing** all those **oppressed** by the **devil**,
   for God was with him.
We are **witnesses** of all that he **did**
   both in the country of the Jews and in Jerusalem.
They put him to **death** by hanging him on a **tree**.
This man God **raised** on the third **day** and granted
      that he be **visible**,
   not to **all** the people, but to **us**,
   the **witnesses** chosen by God in advance,
   who **ate** and **drank** with him after he rose from the **dead**.
He **commissioned** us to preach to the **people**
   and **testify** that he is the one appointed by God
   as **judge** of the **living** and the **dead**.
To him all the **prophets** bear **witness**,
   that **everyone** who **believes** in him
   will receive **forgiveness** of sins through his **name**."

Pause briefly after each of the two identifications: that of the book of the Bible and that of the speaker, Peter.

See below for the explanation about proclaiming this as if it were a letter rather than as a narrative.
Judea = joo-DEE-uh
Galilee = GAL-ih-lee
Nazareth = NAZ-uh-reth

Jerusalem = juh-ROO-suh-lem

From this verse forward, the reading nearly transcends time, so proclaim it in the stead of Peter.

READING I   Often liturgical readings are either an apostolic letter or a narrative. With a letter, the context comes when the lector says, for example, "A reading from the letter of Paul to the Galatians." With a narrative there is a progressive action. With a letter, the author writes to those addressed as if speaking to them: "Brothers and sisters in Christ," or "Saints of God," for example. Both forms are mentioned here for your preparation, because in today's reading we have a narrative of an action by one of the apostles, Peter, but the action is his speaking to a group gathered in the home of a fellow believer.

In his speech, we find the speaker in the first person plural—"We are witnesses"—and those spoken to—"You know the message God sent"—in the second person plural. As you prepare for the proclamation, therefore, approach this *narrative* reading as if it were a *letter*. It will not take much imagination to deliver the words of Peter to the believers in Cornelius' house as if they are indeed your words to those in your own community, for the Easter faith in this part of the Acts of the Apostles transcends the centuries.

This is a basic history from the lips of Peter about the activity of the Christian faith from the Baptism John announced up to the moment when Peter speaks. This is the longest part of the proclamation. The details are engaging, and you can animate them in your ministry to the assembly. Be clear and colorful in the descriptive elements: "all those oppressed by the devil," "by hanging him on a tree," "us . . . who ate and drank with him after he rose from the dead," the phrase that ends the second part and brings

READING II   Colossians 3:1–4

A reading from the Letter of Saint Paul to the Colossians

Brothers and sisters:
If then you were **raised** with **Christ**, seek what is **above**,
    where Christ is **seated** at the right hand of **God**.
Think of what is **above**, not of what is on **earth**.
For you have **died**, and your life is **hidden** with Christ in **God**.
When Christ your life **appears**,
    then you **too** will appear with him in **glory**.

Or:

READING II   1 Corinthians 5:6b–8

A reading from the first Letter of Saint Paul to the Corinthians

Brothers and sisters:
Do you not know that a little **yeast** leavens all the **dough**?
Clear **out** the **old** yeast,
    so that you may become a **fresh** batch of dough,
    inasmuch as you are **unleavened**.
For our paschal **lamb**, **Christ**, has been **sacrificed**.
Therefore, let us **celebrate** the feast,
    not with the **old** yeast, the yeast of **malice** and **wickedness**,
    but with the **unleavened** bread of **sincerity** and **truth**.

Colossians = kuh-LOSH-unz

As the author wrote to his brothers and sisters, so do you proclaim to yours.

As an assembly of the baptized, the Church celebrates and lives not only its participation in the glorification of Christ, but its participation in the death of Christ as well. The author is clear: "you have died."

Highlight the transformation captured in the metaphor of the yeast and the dough, for these are the central images of the reading. Corinthians = kor-IN-thee-unz

Here is the transformation from the "old yeast" to the "fresh batch of dough."

Here is the metaphor again, but it is made more explicit with the addition of how these are seen in the life of the community.

---

the story up to the Church on the very Easter Sunday on which you proclaim. Address the parish with paschal power on this Easter celebration.

There is a choice of second readings today. Speak with the liturgy coordinator or homilist to find out which reading will be used.

READING II   **COLOSSIANS.** Although many believers think of the Christ-event as something that existed in the past and that we merely remember, this reading for Easter Sunday clearly unites the life of Jesus Christ with the lives of those in the Church now. The Paschal Mystery, so the reading proclaims, is this unity of Jesus Christ and the community of faith, and this is so whether it is the ancient Greek community at Colossae to which this passage was originally addressed or the parish community to which you belong and in which you minister the word of God.

The reading is assigned to Easter Day because this is the feast when the power of the Paschal Mystery in Jesus Christ is most vivid in the hearts and minds of the assembly. Before you get to the specifics of practicing your proclamation, take some time to appreciate the meaning of the short passage, and then consider how you will best minister this word to this parish community.

Notice that the entire reading is completely in the second person, as are most Lectionary passages from New Testament letters. In proclaiming such texts, the best approach is to stand as if in the person and power and conviction of the original author, not imitating, but claiming the power of your Baptism and ministry as they did.

Sunday was and is the "first day of the week."
Magdala = MAG-duh-la

Simon = SĪ-mun

GOSPEL John 20:1–9

A reading from the holy Gospel according to John

On the first day of the **week**,
Mary of **Magdala** came to the **tomb** early in the **morning**,
while it was still **dark**,
and saw the **stone** removed from the **tomb**.
So she **ran** and went to Simon **Peter**
and to the **other** disciple whom Jesus **loved**, and told them,
"They have taken the **Lor**d from the **tomb**,
and we don't know where they **put** him."
So **Peter** and the **other** disciple went out and came to the **tomb**.
They **both** ran, but the **other** disciple ran **faster** than Peter
and arrived at the tomb **first**;
he bent **down** and saw the **burial** cloths there, but did
not go in.
When Simon Peter arrived **after** him,
he went **into** the tomb and saw the **burial** cloths there,
and the cloth that had covered his **head**,
not with the **burial** cloths but rolled **up** in a separate **place**.
Then the **other** disciple **also** went in,
the one who had arrived at the tomb **first**,
and he **saw** and **believed**.
For they did not yet **understand** the **Scripture**
that he had to **rise** from the **dead**.

[The Gospel from the Easter Vigil (Mark 16:1–7, p. 149) may be read in place of this Gospel at any time of the day.]

So, as the author of this short reading addressed these words with power to the believers in Colossae in the first century, you can address it with power to the people to whom you minister the word of God today.

The Paschal Mystery has not diminished in the intervening centuries. The risen Christ is present to the Church today in the sacraments as always. As a minister of the word, you have an important part in this presence. Proclaim with conviction on this Easter Sunday.

1 CORINTHIANS. It might be be a surprise that this reading from 1 Corinthians

was among the most important scriptural passages in the earliest theology of Easter. The single Greek word *pascha* (translated in two words, "paschal lamb") simply meant "Passover," or "paschal," or, later, "Easter." In English we do not have a noun equivalent for *pascha*, and "paschal" is an adjective that modifies something else: mystery, feast, lamb. This has the advantage of connecting the depth of the mystery celebrated on this day, the death and Resurrection of Christ, with the antiphon sung at every Eucharist, "Lamb of God."

Another aspect of this reading that has had an influence on the liturgy is the explicit mention of "unleavened bread." The Roman Catholic prescription for eucharistic bread has long called for unleavened bread in faithfulness to this text. Many of the Eastern Churches, however, do not use unleavened bread for the celebration of the Eucharist for a variety of historical reasons.

Even with all these important matters tucked into this text from Paul, the passage that you prepare is short. (After the many long readings at the Vigil the night before, this passage is *very* short!) The main issue

Lectionary #46

AFTERNOON GOSPEL   Luke 24:13–35

A reading from the holy Gospel according to Luke

That very day, the **first** day of the week,
   two of Jesus' disciples were going
   to a village seven miles from Jerusalem called **Emmaus**,
   and they were **conversing** about all the things
      that had **occurred**.
And it **happened** that while they were conversing and debating,
   Jesus **himself** drew near and **walked** with them,
   but their eyes were **prevented** from recognizing him.
He **asked** them,
   "What are you **discussing** as you walk along?"
They **stopped**, looking downcast.
One of them, named **Cleopas**, said to him in reply,
   "Are you the **only** visitor to Jerusalem
   who does not **know** of the **things**
   that have taken place there in these days?"
And he **replied** to them, "What **sort** of things?"
They said to him,
   "The **things** that happened to **Jesus** the **Nazarene**,
   who was a **prophet** mighty in **deed** and **word**
   before **God** and **all** the people,
   how our chief **priests** and **rulers both** handed him over
   to a sentence of **death** and **crucified** him.
But we were **hoping** that **he** would be the **one** to **redeem** Israel;
   and **besides** all this,
   it is **now** the **third day** since **this** took place.

A number of details in this Gospel reading will connect the story with your assembly. This opening time identification, marking the day as a Sunday, is one.
Jerusalem = juh-ROO-suh-lem
Emmaus = eh-MAY-us

Another common element is that we often do not recognize our fellow believers as manifesting and revealing the presence of Christ to us.

Cleopas = KLOH-pus
This is a summary of the Paschal Mystery delivered to the "only visitor to Jerusalem" who does not know of it.

Nazarene = naz-uh-REEN

Israel = IZ-ree-ul

---

to highlight in your proclamation is the change from the "old yeast" to the "fresh batch of dough," from the yeast of "malice and wickedness" to the bread of "sincerity and truth." This is important because the Church has been reborn in its celebration of the Easter Vigil, and the movement from the Forty Days of Lent to the Fifty Days of Easter (from now until Pentecost) is captured by this metaphor.

GOSPEL The evangelists wrote their Gospels for their own communities of faith. Much like your own community, their communities were filled with unique individuals who together made up a Church unlike any other. The variations in the Gospels are a result of each evangelist's effort to shape the text so that it would be well heard and readily received by their own community, which was unlike any other.

In the narratives of the discovery of the empty tomb, the uniqueness of each evangelist's effort is apparent. Each evangelist

emphasized different elements of the Paschal Mystery based on the experience of the death and Resurrection of Christ in his own Church. For this reason, as you will see, John includes elements that you will not find in the story of the discovery of the empty tomb in Matthew, Mark, or Luke.

Part of the task of proclaiming the Gospel on this Easter Sunday is letting the uniqueness of John's narrative come through. For example, in the other three Gospels, you will not find the foot race

Another common element is the proclamation and interpretation of the scriptures.
Moses = MOH-ziz

The final and perhaps most poignan element is the same meal of bread taken, blessed, broken, and shared, in which the risen Christ is recognized.

Some **women** from our group, however, have **astounded** us:
    they were at the tomb **early** in the **morning**
    and did **not** find his **body**;
    they came **back** and reported
    that they had **indeed** seen a vision of **angels**
    who **announced** that he was **alive**.
Then some of those **with** us went to the tomb
    and found things **just** as the women had **described**,
    but **him** they did not **see**."
And he said to them, "Oh, how **foolish** you are!
How **slow** of **heart** to **believe** all that the prophets **spoke**!
Was it not **necessary** that the Christ should suffer **these things**
    and **enter** into his glory?"
Then beginning with **Moses** and all the **prophets**,
    he **interpreted** to them what referred to him
    in **all** the **Scriptures**.
As they **approached** the village to which they were **going**,
    he gave the impression that he was going on **farther**.
But they **urged** him, "**Stay** with us,
    for it is nearly **evening** and the day is almost **over**."
So he went in to **stay** with them.
And it **happened** that, while he was with them at **table**,
    he **took bread**, said the **blessing**,
    broke it, and **gave** it to them.
With **that** their **eyes** were **opened** and they **recognized** him,
    but he **vanished** from their **sight**.

between Peter and the disciple whom Jesus loved. In John it is a major element in the account and reflects a theology and characters that were important there. (Who wins the race? The beloved disciple is identified elsewhere in the Gospel of John as the youngest of the disciples. He beats Peter to the tomb, but recognizes Peter's authority and, therefore, lets Peter go in first.)

The reason for emphasizing the uniqueness of this Gospel narrative is that, like that ancient community of faith to which John belonged, your parish community also has a unique experience of the Paschal Mystery.

Though Churches celebrating the Eucharist week after week share many common elements—the parts of the Mass, the consecration of bread and wine, and so on—there are many details that happen in no other community as they do in yours, a result of the unique liturgical assembly of people gathered in the power of the Holy Spirit.

AFTERNOON GOSPEL | This Gospel reading from the end of the Gospel of Luke has made an immeasurable contribution to our sacramental theology and to the celebration of the Eucharist. Yet it is also a long Gospel reading, so you will need to use your best and most engaging storytelling skills. There are a couple of characteristics of the reading that will help.

First, the reading has a strong narrative progression, a clear beginning and ending. There are no extended exhortations in the middle of the account, but simply some exchanges to advance the action.

Second, the proclaimer and the listeners have more information than the two disciples on the way to Emmaus. The evangelist

Simon = SĪ-mun

Simon = SĪ-mun

In the season of Easter, the risen Christ is revealed again and again to different people, in different places, as ever when people come together for worship and the sacraments.

Then they said to each other,
    "**Were** not our **hearts burning** within us
    while he **spoke** to us on the way and **opened** the **Scriptures**
        to us?"
So they set out at **once** and **returned** to Jerusalem
    where they found gathered together
    the eleven and those **with them** who were saying,
    "The **Lord** has **truly** been **raised** and has **appeared** to **Simon**!"
Then the two **recounted**
    what had taken place on the **way**
    and how he was made **known** to them in the **breaking** of **bread**.

reveals to us that "Jesus himself drew near and walked with them, but their eyes were prevented from recognizing him." The assembly knows something that two of the main characters do not! You can use this dramatic irony to hold the assembly's attention.

Third, the assembly before you shares a number of things with the two disciples. Like those two, the Church is together on "the first day of the week." Moreover, Jesus explained the scriptures to the disciples, just as in the Sunday liturgy the scriptures are proclaimed and interpreted. Next, and

most important, the risen Christ is with the two on the way to Emmaus just as the risen Christ is present with the Church gathered for Sunday Mass. Finally, the sign in which the risen Christ is recognized is the consecrated bread broken and wine shared. The eucharistic sacrifice is an enduring ritual of the Church in which the risen Christ is both recognized and celebrated.

Deliver these common elements in such a way that they are accessible and recognizable to those in the assembly. It is important that—as the culture changes, as time moves on, as the Church proclaims the Good

News in new places—there are some commonalities uniting the people of God. And in this unity they experience the presence of the risen Christ.

2ND SUNDAY OF EASTER   DIVINE MERCY SUNDAY

Lectionary #44

READING I   Acts 4:32–35

A reading from the Acts of the Apostles

The **community** of **believers** was of one **heart** and **mind**,
  and **no** one claimed that any of his **possessions** was his **own**,
  but they had everything in **common**.
With great **power** the apostles bore **witness**
  to the **resurrection** of the Lord **Jesus**,
  and great **favor** was accorded them **all**.
There was no **needy** person among them,
  for those who owned **property** or **houses** would **sell** them,
  bring the **proceeds** of the sale,
  and put them at the feet of the **apostles**,
  and they were distributed to **each** according to **need**.

READING II   1 John 5:1–6

A reading from the first Letter of Saint John

Beloved:
Everyone who **believes** that Jesus is the **Christ** is begotten
    by **God**,
  and everyone who loves the **Father**
  loves **also** the one **begotten** by him.

The writings of Pope John Paul II about Easter remind us that the power of the Resurrection is no less powerful for us today.

Because it is so contrary to our cultural values, proclaim this final part carefully.

This is a magnificent opening line for the Easter season. We, like Jesus Christ, have been begotten by God.

READING I There are differences in worship during the Easter season. The Church keeps the Easter candle lit throughout the season, the priests and deacons vest in white, and perhaps the newly baptized are catechized about the initiation rites through which they proceeded during the Easter Vigil. Though maybe not as obviously different, the liturgy of the word is also different. One of its changes is that the first reading, almost always from the Old Testament the rest of the year, comes from the New Testament, from the Acts of the

Apostles. The Church proceeds through Acts in order.

Because we are now only one week into the Fifty Days of Easter, the reading you prepare is close to the beginning of Acts, which is the second part of the evangelist Luke's two-part work. In terms of how our Easter faith is manifest in the world, this reading is telling, and you have the opportunity to proclaim Christian faith in the Resurrection of Jesus to the body of Christ, united by the Holy Spirit, that gathers before you as you proclaim.

The values of unanimity and sharing of goods have been part of the tradition since the beginning, but they are contrary to the competitive, acquisitive culture in which we live. Do not flinch in the face of this, but use it as an impetus to take your time and enunciate the apostolic experience clearly.

READING II This passage from the first letter of John has four basic parts, and each has a unique contribution. The first part reveals that our faith is connected to our being begotten by God. The

In this way we **know** that we love the **children** of God
    when we love **God** and obey his **commandments**.
For the love of God is **this**,
    that we **keep** his commandments.
And his commandments are not **burdensome**,
    for whoever is begotten by God **conquers** the world.
And the **victory** that conquers the world is our **faith**.
Who **indeed** is the **victor** over the world
    but the one who **believes** that **Jesus** is the Son of **God**?

This is the one who came through **water** and **blood**, Jesus **Christ**,
    not by water **alone**, but by **water** and **blood**.
The **Spirit** is the one that **testifies**,
    and the **Spirit** is **truth**.

A rhetorical question that you posit as the author of the Letter did.

The answer to that question follows, and the answer contains the significant sacramental matters, water and blood. Be clear as you proclaim these signs.

GOSPEL   John 20:19–31

A reading from the holy Gospel according to John

On the **evening** of that **first** day of the **week**,
    when the **doors** were locked, where the **disciples** were,
    for fear of the **Jews**,
    Jesus came and stood in their **midst**
    and said to them, "**Peace** be with you."
When he had **said** this, he showed them his **hands** and his **side**.
The disciples **rejoiced** when they saw the Lord.
Jesus said to them **again**, "**Peace** be with you.
As the Father has sent **me**, so I send **you**."

Proclaim this time element clearly, for Easter is celebrated for Fifty Days and post-Resurrection appearances are important to the season.

The phrase "Peace be with you" is repeated throughout the passage, a fruit of the liturgy of the community of John's Gospel. (Read below for more.)

---

letters of John carry further the theology of the Gospel of John, and this theology of new birth—as from the account of Nicodemus and Jesus in John 3—is one of the connecting issues.

The second part of the reading connects love of God to obedience to the commandments of God, and this is another link to the Gospel of John.

The conquering of the world in the third part of the reading is realized in Christ's coming in "water and blood." This part also links the letter to the Gospel of John. The

evangelist recorded the piercing of Jesus' side in his Passion, where from his side flowed "blood and water," as we heard on Good Friday.

This passage you prepare is fitting at the start of the Easter season for a number of reasons. First, it relates the life of the Son of God to the season of Easter with two fundamental signs of our sacramental experience: "water and blood." In the sacrament of Baptism, we are washed in the saving waters, and Sunday after Sunday we receive the body and blood of Christ in the Eucharist. Second, the reading links the water and

blood to the testimony of the Holy Spirit. The Holy Spirit calls believers to Baptism, whether or not those called are infants or adults.

GOSPEL   Notice that in the Gospel the Resurrection itself appears at the start of chapter 20, and this passage is just a little after that. The reading starts with a time reference: "It was evening on the day Jesus rose from the dead."

In the same way, the parish gathered at Easter a week ago, and here on the Second

This is "doubting Thomas," he whom
we know for this exchange with
the risen Christ. Take your time with
this important section.

Another time element, one that captures
the weekly gathering, just as we gather to
this day.

And when he had said this, he **breathed** on them and said to them,
   "**Receive** the Holy **Spirit**.
Whose **sins** you forgive are **forgiven** them,
   and whose sins you **retain** are **retained**."

Thomas, called **Didymus**, one of the **Twelve**,
   was not **with** them when Jesus came.
So the **other** disciples said to him, "We have **seen** the Lord."
But he said to them,
   "Unless I see the mark of the **nails** in his **hands**
   and put my **finger** into the **nailmarks**
   and put my **hand** into his **side**, I will **not** believe."

Now a week **later** his disciples were **again** inside
   and Thomas **was** with them.
Jesus came, although the **doors** were **locked**,
   and **stood** in their **midst** and said, "**Peace** be with you."
Then he said to **Thomas**,
   "Put your finger **here** and **see** my hands,
   and bring your **hand** and put it into my **side**,
   and do not be **unbelieving**, but **believe**."
Thomas **answered** and said to him, "My **Lord** and my **God!**"
Jesus said to him, "Have you come to believe because you have
   seen me?
Blessed are those who have not seen and have **believed**."

Now Jesus did many **other** signs in the presence of his disciples
   that are **not** written in this **book**.
But these are written that you may come to **believe**
   that Jesus is the **Christ**, the Son of **God**,
   and that **through** this belief you may have **life** in his **name**.

Sunday of Easter, we continue to celebrate
the Resurrection as narrated in the Gospel
and as experienced in this particular community of faith.

Notice that throughout this Gospel one
finds the phrase "Peace be with you," still
part of the liturgical tradition. Many think
that the phrase found its way into the liturgy
because it was part of the Gospel, but it is
historically more likely that the community
of John's Gospel was using the phrase
"Peace be with you" in its liturgy before the
Gospel itself was written. So the Gospel
phrase, as you proclaim it, is a fruit of the
liturgy, and your proclamation can emphasize these words of the risen Christ so that
some in the assembly will pick up on the
consonance of scripture and worship.

The final paragraph of this passage
sounds like the final passage of the entire
Gospel, and so it may have been at one time.
Because the paragraph has such a sweep-
ing end, proclaim it as such: "through this
belief you may have life in his name."

3RD SUNDAY OF EASTER

Lectionary #47

READING I   Acts 3:13–15, 17–19

A reading from the Acts of the Apostles

Peter said to the **people**:
"The God of **Abraham**,
    the God of **Isaac**, and the God of **Jacob**,
    the God of our fathers, has **glorified** his servant **Jesus**,
    whom **you** handed over and **denied** in Pilate's **presence**
    when he had decided to **release** him.
You **denied** the Holy and **Righteous** One
    and asked that a **murderer** be released to you.
The author of **life** you put to **death**,
    but God **raised** him from the dead; of this we are **witnesses**.
Now I **know**, brothers,
    that you acted out of **ignorance**, just as your **leaders** did;
    but God has thus brought to **fulfillment**
    what he had announced **beforehand**
    through the mouth of all the **prophets**,
    that his **Christ** would **suffer**.
Repent, therefore, and be **converted**,
        that your **sins** may be wiped **away**."

Abraham = AY-bruh-ham

Isaac = Ī-zik

Jacob = JAY-kub

Pilate = PĪ-lut

Read below for how to proclaim this middle section.

The second half of the reading speaks to all of us whose sinfulness contributes to the suffering of the people of God.

READING I   The readings of the Fifty Days narrate the transition from the death and Resurrection, proclaimed in the Three Days, to the Holy Spirit's descent at Pentecost. The events between those two points as told in Acts reveal some of the issues that faced the Church as it was born. One issue in the early Church was between those who supported the advocacy of Peter, who wanted all who joined the Church to observe the Jewish law, and those who supported Paul, the advocate for the non-Jewish Christians.

Both Peter and Paul were Jews, but their discernment about how much of the law would be carried into the nascent Christian faith put them at odds in the beginning, which we know from Acts and from the letter to the Galatians.

All of us, born with an innate tendency to sin, at times choose the wrong over the right. Perhaps you can keep that as a standard from which to proclaim, for all of us at times betray and reject God's law, all of us act out of ignorance. We all need to "repent, therefore, and be converted."

READING II   1 John 2:1–5a

A reading from the first Letter of Saint John

My **children**, I am **writing** this to you
   so that you may not commit **sin**.
But if anyone **does** sin, we have an **Advocate** with the Father,
   Jesus **Christ** the **righteous** one.
He is **expiation** for our **sins**,
   and not for **our** sins **only** but for those of the whole **world**.
The way we may be **sure** that we **know** him
      is to keep his **commandments**.
Those who say, "I **know** him," but do **not** keep
      his commandments
   are **liars**, and the **truth** is not **in** them.
But whoever **keeps** his word,
   the love of God is truly **perfected** in him.

GOSPEL   Luke 24:35–48

A reading from the holy Gospel according to Luke

The two disciples **recounted** what had taken place on the **way**,
   and how **Jesus** was made **known** to them
   in the breaking of **bread**.

While they were still **speaking** about this,
   he stood in their **midst** and said to them,
   "**Peace** be with you."

READING II In the Easter season every year to year, the Church builds up a chain of readings from one of the catholic letters, which are named according to their authors. So during this part of Year B, all of the second readings are from the first letter of John. The three letters of John carry on the theology of the Gospel of John. The reading you prepare now takes up some typically Johannine issues, Christ's atoning sacrifice on our behalf and the necessary correspondence between knowing Christ, following the commandments, obeying the word of Christ, and speaking the truth in the love of God.

For such a short passage, the author has brought together some very deep issues. In this Easter season you, a minister of the word, stand in his place and enliven the Church's appreciation of God's gifts.

Consider the excerpt from this letter as if it had been written to the community to which you will proclaim these words, for their theology of sin and salvation are as important now as they were for those to whom they were sent centuries ago.

GOSPEL This passage from the end of the Gospel of Luke has made an immeasurable contribution to our sacramental theology and to the celebration of the Eucharist. Yet it is a long Gospel reading, so you will need to use your best and most engaging storytelling abilities. There are a couple of characteristics of the reading that will help.

First, the text has a strong narrative progression, a clear beginning and ending. There are no extended exhortations in the

But they were **startled** and **terrified**
and thought that they were seeing a **ghost**.
Then he said to them, "Why are you **troubled**?
And why do **questions** arise in your **hearts**?
Look at my **hands** and my **feet**, that it is I **myself**.
Touch me and **see**, because a **ghost** does not have **flesh** and **bones**
as you can see **I** have."
And as he **said** this,
he **showed** them his **hands** and his **feet**.
While they were still **incredulous** for joy and were **amazed**,
he asked them, "Have you **anything** here to **eat**?"
They gave him a piece of baked **fish**;
he **took** it and **ate** it in front of them.

He said to them,
"These are my **words** that I **spoke** to you while I was still
with you,
that everything **written** about me in the law of **Moses**
and in the **prophets** and **psalms** must be **fulfilled**."
Then he **opened** their minds to understand the **Scriptures**.
And he said to them,
"Thus it is **written** that the Christ would **suffer**
and rise from the **dead** on the third **day**
and that **repentance**, for the forgiveness of **sins**,
would be **preached** in his name
to all the **nations**, beginning from **Jerusalem**.
You are **witnesses** of these things."

Moses = MOH-ziz

Another common element is the interpretation of the scriptures.

Jerusalem - juh-ROO-suh-lem

In the season of Easter, the risen Christ is revealed again and again, to different people, in different places, as always when people come together for worship and the sacraments.

middle of the account, but simply some exchanges to advance the action.

Second, the proclaimer and the listeners have more information than the two disciples on the way to Emmaus. The evangelist tells us that "Jesus himself drew near and went with them, but their eyes were prevented from recognizing him." The assembly knows something that two of the main characters do not! You can use this dramatic irony to hold the assembly's attention.

Third, the assembly before you shares a number of things with the two disciples.

Like those two, the Church has gathered on "the first day of the week." Moreover, the scriptures were proclaimed and explained by the risen Jesus there along the road, just as in the Sunday liturgy the scriptures are proclaimed and interpreted by the homilist.

Next, the risen Christ is with the two on the way to Emmaus as the risen Christ is with these believers gathered for Sunday Mass today.

Finally, the sign in which the risen Christ is recognized is the Eucharist. The eucharistic sacrificial meal is central for the life of the Church.

As you prepare and as you proclaim, deliver these common elements in such a way that they are recognizable to those in the assembly. It is important that—as the culture changes, as time moves on, as the Church proclaims the Good News in new places—there are some commonalities uniting the people of God. And in this unity they experience the presence of the risen Christ.

4TH SUNDAY OF EASTER

Lectionary #50

READING I   Acts 4:8–12

A reading from the Acts of the Apostles

Peter, filled with the Holy **Spirit**, said:
  "Leaders of the **people** and **elders**:
  If we are being **examined** today
  about a good **deed** done to a **cripple**,
  namely, by what **means** he was saved,
  then **all** of you and **all** the people of Israel should know
  that it was in the name of Jesus **Christ** the **Nazorean**
  whom you **crucified**, whom God **raised** from the **dead**;
  in **his** name this man stands before you **healed**.
He is *the stone **rejected** by you, the **builders**,*
  *which has become the **cornerstone**.*
There is **no** salvation through **anyone** else,
  nor is there **any** other name under heaven
  given to the human **race** by which we are to be **saved**."

Peter's address to the authorities and those assembled begins here. Sustain your assembly's interest by taking your time and modulating your voice according to the high and low points of Peter's account.

This familiar metaphor about Jesus, "the stone rejected," is foundational for the Church's beginning and its rebirths through the centuries.

The final verse is powerful. Match its power with a strong voice.

READING I The liturgy of the word in the Easter season is distinct, and one of its changes is that the first reading, in most of the year from the Old Testament, now comes from the New Testament, from the Acts of the Apostles. All three readings on Sundays in the Easter season, then, come from the New Testament. This reading carries on the same issue from last Sunday's reading from Acts, with the apostle Peter indicting those before him for their participation in the death of Jesus.

The passage you prepare would be too long if the whole story were assigned for one Sunday, but a helpful part of the narrative is omitted from the Lectionary, and you will understand your passage better if you read it. In chapter three of Acts, Peter came upon a man lame from birth and healed him in the name of Jesus Christ. It is of this healing that Peter is speaking when he says, "[we] are being examined about a good deed done to a cripple."

Notice that the first part sets the scene for those who will hear the passage you proclaim, and the longer part of the narrative is Peter's words to those before him about the healing and its source in the resurrected Christ. Like Peter, you stand before an assembly, not as antagonistic to you as his was to him, but perhaps an assembly for which the joy of the Easter season has begun to fade now that the Church has been in it for three weeks.

The story of the healing and Peter's fiery speech to the people is a lively one, so be bold with your proclamation. Tell the account in an animated way to lift up those for whom the *laetissimum spatium*, "the span of great joy," as the North African theologian Tertullian said, has started to feel merely routine.

READING II   1 John 3:1–2

A reading from the first Letter of Saint John

Beloved:
See what **love** the Father has **bestowed** on us
   that we may be called the **children** of God.
Yet so we **are**.
The reason the **world** does not **know** us
   is that it did not know **him**.
Beloved, we **are** God's children **now**;
   what we **shall** be has not yet been **revealed**.
We **do** know that when it is revealed we shall be **like** him,
   for we shall **see** him as he **is**.

The many first-person plural pronouns of this short reading, "we" and "us," embrace you and the assembly to which you minister.

Significant pause at the break in the printed text.

GOSPEL   John 10:11–18

A reading from the holy Gospel according to John

Jesus said:
   "I **am** the good shepherd.
A **good** shepherd lays down his **life** for the **sheep**.
A **hired** man, who is **not** a shepherd
   and whose sheep are not his **own**,
   sees a **wolf** coming and **leaves** the sheep and runs **away**,
   and the wolf **catches** and **scatters** them.
This is because he works for **pay** and has no **concern**
   for the sheep.

This simple sentence, which appears twice, is the key to the entire lesson. Proclaim it clearly and confidently.

These two verses are setting up a contrast between the good shepherd and the "hired man." Your tone of voice should be dark as you describe the poor care the sheep receive from the one who does it just for the money.

READING II In the early Church and now in today's Church, the Holy Spirit acts among us to realize the risen Christ in our midst. As this happens, we are awakened to the assurance that we, like the Son of God, are God's children, as this reading makes boldly clear.

Even though you were not the author of this passage from the first letter of John, you, by God's grace, are no less than he as a child of God and an instrument of the word of God in the Church you serve. The repeated use of first-person plural pronouns in the reading puts you and your parish community as the objects of the proclamation, for you and they are indeed loved as God's children.

Even during the Easter season, there are many in the Church who think themselves unlovable to other human beings and, in spite of the testimony of the scriptures, by God. Think of these people as you prepare the passage and as you proclaim. Imagine those who are not able to accept how much God loves them and seek to make clear how much God does indeed love them.

Finally, because this is a short passage, take your time. Be bold with the simple, declarative phrases of the letter, such as "Yet so we are" and "We do know that," and follow each of these with a significant pause. There is no reason to rush. The letter's theological significance and pastoral efficacy are always welcome in the ears of the people of God.

GOSPEL Although the Gospel of John is theologically complex, its grammar is sometimes very simple. Consider the many "I am . . ." statements that appear only in this Gospel: "I am the bread of life," "I am the light of the world,"

Now brighten your tone to reflect this description of the good, caring shepherd who knows those he cares for.

I am the **good** shepherd,
    and I know **mine** and mine know **me**,
    just as the **Father** knows **me** and **I** know the **Father**;
    and I will lay down my **life** for the sheep.
I have **other** sheep that do **not** belong to this fold.
These **also** I must lead, and they will hear my **voice**,
    and there will be **one** flock, **one** shepherd.
This is why the Father **loves** me,
    because I lay down my **life** in order to take it **up** again.
No one **takes** it from me, but I lay it down on my **own**.
I have **power** to lay it **down**, and **power** to take it **up** again.
This **command** I have received from my **Father**."

"I am the gate for the sheep," "I am the Resurrection and the life," "I am the way, the truth, and the life," and "I am the vine, you are the branches." The genius of the fourth evangelist is proved by how familiar these images have become in the life of the Church.

Today you will find another of these deeply theological and grammatically simple statements with "I am the good shepherd," which appears twice in the passage. This Fourth Sunday of the Easter season is Good Shepherd Sunday.

The dark image of the passage is the "wolf," which you might imagine as the "big, bad wolf" of children's literature. This metaphorical wolf is present in the Church in every age, for there are always issues that weigh on the Church and impede our appreciation of God's everlasting love (which the assembly will just have heard of in the second reading).

As you begin the proclamation, recognize that the whole of the reading except the first line is the words of Jesus himself. Take advantage of the line breaks supplied by the

Lectionary. Some of the words of the passage are repeated throughout, so take a deliberate pace. Your assembly will be the more able to receive the word for it.

5TH SUNDAY OF EASTER

Lectionary #53

READING I Acts 9:26–31

A reading from the Acts of the Apostles

When **Saul** arrived in **Jerusalem** he tried to **join** the disciples,
    but they were all **afraid** of him,
    not **believing** that he was a disciple.
Then **Barnabas** took charge of him and **brought** him
      to the apostles,
    and he **reported** to them how he had seen the **Lord**,
    and that he had **spoken** to him,
    and how in **Damascus** he had spoken out **boldly** in the name
      of **Jesus**.
He moved about freely with them in **Jerusalem**,
    and **spoke** out boldly in the name of the **Lord**.
He also spoke and debated with the **Hellenists**,
    but **they** tried to **kill** him.
And when the brothers **learned** of this,
    they took him down to **Caesarea**
    and sent him on his way to **Tarsus**.

The **church** throughout all Judea, Galilee, and Samaria was
      at **peace**.
It was being built **up** and walked in the fear of the **Lord**,
    and with the **consolation** of the Holy **Spirit** it grew in **numbers**.

Jerusalem = juh-ROO-suh-lem
Emphasize the disciples' fear of Saul, their former persecutor. It heightens the drama of the reading.
Barnabas = BAR-nuh-bus

The story of Saul's conversion is familiar, so pronounce this allusion to it clearly.

Speak boldly yourself as you testify to Saul speaking out "boldly," and of the others' attempts to kill him.
Damascus = duh-MAS-kus

Caesarea = see-zuh-REE-uh
Tarsus = TAR-sus
Judea = joo-DEE-uh
Galilee = GAL-ih-lee
Samaria = suh-MAIR-ee-uh

This increase is characteristic of what happens in the Church in every Easter season, so conclude your proclamation with the warmth of this positive paschal message.

READING I The Church proceeds through Acts, the second of the two-part writing from the evangelist Luke, in order. Now, in the middle of the season, we are in the middle of Acts, where Saul is being introduced to the community in Jerusalem.

This reading is important in your own community, for it is likely incorporating some new members who were baptized or received into full communion at Easter.

While it should be an encouragement that others are attracted to the Church, the transitional period is not always easy. Because most Catholics were baptized as infants, their path of faith is different than that of the newcomers. Their profound testimony and strong commitment can overwhelm those who never had to stand up for their faith in such a prominent way.

The reading you proclaim demonstrates that this is nothing new for the Christian community, for the disciples were afraid of Saul, their former persecutor, now claiming to be on their side. The witness of Saul (become Paul) and his fellow believers can be a consolation to those to whom you proclaim. The ending, with the Church being "built up" and growing "in numbers" also reflects the experience of the Easter season.

READING II 1 John 3:18–24

A reading from the first Letter of Saint John

Children, let us love not in **word** or **speech**
    but in **deed** and **truth**.

Now this is how we shall **know** that we belong to the **truth**
    and reassure our **hearts** before him
    in whatever our hearts **condemn**,
    for God is **greater** than our hearts and knows **everything**.
Beloved, if our hearts do not **condemn** us,
    we have **confidence** in God
    and **receive** from him **whatever** we ask,
    because we **keep his** commandments and **do** what pleases him.
And his commandment is **this**:
    we should **believe** in the name of his Son, Jesus **Christ**,
    and **love** one another just as he **commanded** us.
Those who **keep** his commandments remain in **him**, and **he**
        in **them**,
    and the way we **know** that he remains in us
    is from the **Spirit** he gave us.

This opening is so important.

Be prepared to look right at your fellow believers as you address them as your "beloved."

There is no more important link for the Easter season than your proclamation that God commands us to love one another. Do not rush.

READING II In the Easter season, the Church builds up a chain of second readings from one of the catholic letters, which are named according to their author. So during this Year B, all of the second readings are from the first letter of John. This is one of three from John, and they forward the theology of the Gospel of John. The reading you prepare now takes up two keys issues of conversion and Christian life at all times: first, the coherence between our words and our actions and, second, the commandment to believe and love.

As a minister of the word, consider this reading not only in preparation for proclamation, but as instructive for your life. All ecclesial ministers, as public figures in the work of God through the Church, need to live in awareness of the coherence between what they profess and how they live.

The passage's first-person plural pronouns—"we," "our," "us"—sets you and your assembly as the objects for the proclamation, for you and they are indeed loved as God's children. Proclaim the vocative address, "children," with an affectionate glance at the assembly before you.

GOSPEL   John 15:1–8

A reading from the holy Gospel according to John

Jesus said to his disciples:
  "I am the true **vine**, and my **Father** is the vine **grower**.
He takes away every **branch** in me that does not bear **fruit**,
    and every one that **does** he **prunes** so that it bears **more** fruit.
You are **already** pruned because of the **word** that I spoke to you.
Remain in me, as **I** remain in **you**.
Just as a branch cannot bear fruit on its **own**
    unless it remains on the **vine**,
    so neither can **you** unless you remain in **me**.
I am the **vine**, **you** are the **branches**.
Whoever remains in **me** and I in **him** will bear much **fruit**,
    because **without** me you can do **nothing**.
Anyone who does **not** remain in me
    will be thrown **out** like a **branch** and **wither**;
    people will **gather** them and throw them into a **fire**
    and they will be **burned**.
If you remain in **me** and my words remain in **you**,
    ask for **whatever** you want and it will be **done** for you.
By **this** is my Father **glorified**,
    that you **bear** much fruit and **become** my disciples."

These few opening words are the only ones not from the lips of Jesus.

Pause at this natural break in the passage.

Though the Lectionary does not have a break before the second "I am" saying, pause before it so that the assembly will be poised to hear it clearly.

The final section is consoling and supplies a strong ending.

GOSPEL   The Gospels for the seasons of Lent and Easter often draw from the Gospel of John because its theology of who Jesus was in the early community of faith is so fitting for the Church as it anticipates and celebrates the Paschal Mystery even now, these two millennia after the death of Jesus.

One recognizable Johannine element is the evangelist's use of the phrase "I am." In his Gospel John used this many times, and you are familiar with them: "I am the bread of life," "I am the light of the world," "I am the gate for the sheep," "I am the good shepherd," "I am the Resurrection and the life," and "I am the way, the truth, and the life." The inspiration and genius of the fourth evangelist is proved by how significant these images have become in the life of the Church and its foundations.

The Gospel's "I am" sentences appear twice, at the start and halfway through. They are cardinal to the passage, so you should proclaim them emphatically: "I am the true vine, and my Father is the vinegrower," and "I am the vine, you are the branches." The metaphor is lovely as images of the Father, Jesus himself, and the Church today.

Not all of the passage is consoling, because there are two poignant reminders that fruitless branches will not only be cut off, but thrown into fire and burned. The Easter season is basically a time for growth and celebration, so perhaps you might not emphasize the darker elements as much in the Fifty Days as you might at other times.

6TH SUNDAY OF EASTER

Lectionary #56

READING I   Acts 10:25–26, 34–35, 44–48

A reading from the Acts of the Apostles

When Peter **entered**, Cornelius **met** him
  and, falling at his **feet**, paid him **homage**.
Peter, however, raised him **up**, saying,
  "Get **up**. I myself am **also** a human **being**."

Then Peter proceeded to **speak** and said,
  "In **truth**, I see that God shows **no partiality**.
Rather, in **every** nation whoever **fears** him and acts **uprightly**
  is **acceptable** to him."

While Peter was still **speaking** these things,
  the Holy **Spirit** fell upon **all** who were listening to the **word**.
The **circumcised** believers who had accompanied Peter
  were **astounded** that the gift of the Holy Spirit
  should have been **poured** out on the Gentiles **also**,
  for they could **hear** them speaking in **tongues** and
    glorifying **God**.
Then Peter **responded**,
  "Can anyone withhold the **water** for **baptizing** these people,
  who have received the Holy **Spirit** even as **we** have?"
He ordered them to be **baptized** in the name of Jesus **Christ**.

Cornelius = kor-NEEL-yus

This is the start of the universal embrace of the Church, the change that enabled the Church to spread throughout the world.

This mention of the Holy Spirit is important as we near Pentecost.

Address this rhetorical question from Peter directly to your assembly if you can.

READING I It might be difficult for modern Christians to appreciate the gravity of the confession of Peter revealed in this passage from Acts. But in the infant Church, the great struggle was between those who thought all new members, Jewish or not, needed to follow the laws of Judaism (and their advocate was Peter) and those who did not think such adherence to the law was necessary for Gentiles (and their advocate was Paul).

If you have the time, read Acts 10:9–33, the account of Peter's vision, in which he came to see that God did not want to exclude the Gentiles and that the Church could leave behind some of the Jewish practices that Peter had earlier been uncompromising about.

This passage is necessarily a cut-and-paste reading, for the whole narrative would be too long for the liturgy, but it will help your own understanding of what you will proclaim if you look in the scriptures and read the account through.

The key phrases in your proclamation that will help the assembly appreciate Peter's confession are "I see that God shows no partiality" and that those "in every nation" are acceptable to God.

The final two verses link what happens in the account with what happens in the Easter season and, perhaps, with what is happening in your parish as new members are being integrated into the body of Christ. Therefore, address the rhetorical question and Peter's command at the end directly to the liturgical assembly. Try to commit Peter's

READING II   1 John 4:7–10

A reading from the first Letter of Saint John

Beloved, let us **love** one another,
> because **love** is of God;
> everyone who **loves** is **begotten** by God and **knows** God.
Whoever is **without** love does **not** know God, for God is **love**.
In this way the love of God was **revealed** to us:
> God sent his only **Son** into the world
> so that we might have **life** through him.
In **this** is love:
> not that **we** have loved **God**, but that **he** loved **us**
> and sent his **Son** as expiation for our **sins**.

Start off well with this beautiful invitation to your "Beloved, let us love one another."

This is a short passage, but a great inspiration for our faith in God's love for humanity. Do not hurry through such deep theological reflection.

Pause after each sentence, and if possible engage the assembly with eye contact as you proclaim God's love.

question to memory so that you can look up at the members of your parish and perhaps at the newly baptized as you ask: "Can anyone withhold the water . . . ?"

READING II   In the Easter season, the Church builds up a chain of readings from one of the catholic letters, which are named according to their author. During this Year B, all of the second readings are from the first letter of John. This letter is one of three from John, and they carry on the theology of the Gospel of John. The

reading you prepare now takes up some typically Johannine issues, Christ's atoning sacrifice on our behalf and the necessary correspondence between knowing Christ, following the commandments, obeying the word of Christ, and speaking the truth in the love of God.

Even though you were not the author of this passage from the first letter of John, you, by God's grace, are no less than he in being a child of God and an instrument of the word of God in your ministry. The repeated use of first-person plural pronouns in the reading—"we," "us"—puts you and your

community as the objects for the proclamation for you and they are indeed loved as God's children.

There are many in the Church who think themselves unlovable by other human beings and even by God. Think of them as you prepare the passage and as you proclaim. Read this passage to them: "let us love one another." Believe this message in your own experience of love, and share it with those in need in your community of faith.

This is part of the long last discourse of Jesus in the Gospel of John (chapters 14–17). Here all but these first five words are from Jesus' lips.

This section is very familiar and also central to the theology of the Gospel.

GOSPEL John 15:9–17

A reading from the holy Gospel according to John

Jesus said to his disciples:
"As the **Father** loves **me**, so **I** also love **you**.
Remain in my love.
If you **keep** my commandments, you will **remain** in my love,
just as **I** have kept my **Father's** commandments
and remain in **his** love.

"I have **told** you this so that my **joy** may be in you
and **your** joy might be **complete**.
This is my commandment: love one **another** as **I** love **you**.
No one has greater love than **this**,
to lay down one's **life** for one's **friends**.
You **are** my friends if you **do** what **I** **command** you.
I no longer call you **slaves**,
because a slave does not **know** what his master is **doing**.
I have called you **friends**,
because I have told you **everything** I have heard
from my **Father**.
It was not **you** who chose me, but **I** who chose **you**
and **appointed** you to go and bear **fruit** that will **remain**,
so that **whatever** you ask the Father in **my** name he may
give you.
This I command you: **love** one another."

GOSPEL Because the first reading proclaims God's wide embrace—"God shows no partiality"—and the second reading declares that "God is love," the reading that you proclaim already has a great foundation for its powerful theology.

The interplay in the reading is between the invitation to abide in Jesus' love and the imperative to keep the commandments. The nexus of this interplay is at the reading's center: "This is my commandment: love one another as I love you." Because the word "commandment" usually suggests a prohibition, "Thou shalt not," it is important that you recognize that this commandment is positive: "Love!" Keep this in mind as you prepare so that your proclamation of "commandment" can be expansive.

The link between love and commandment is the key part of the proclamation, so, though the Lectionary does not insert a break before "This is my commandment," pause before that line so that the assembly will be poised to receive it. Though the words are among the most well known of the Christian tradition, they can never be proclaimed too often or acted on too much.

Because the whole lesson is from the mouth of Jesus, you should not rush through the passage. Pay attention to the breaks in the printed text as a way to pace yourself.

ASCENSION OF THE LORD

Lectionary #58

READING I   Acts 1:1–11

A reading from the beginning of the Acts of the Apostles

Theophilus = thee-OF-uh-lus

The "I" here is the author of Acts, the evangelist Luke. This opening is the introduction to the whole book of Acts.

In the **first** book, Theophilus,
   I dealt with all that Jesus **did** and **taught**
   until the day he was taken **up**,
   after giving **instructions** through the Holy **Spirit**
   to the **apostles** whom he had **chosen**.
He presented himself **alive** to them
   by many **proofs** after he had **suffered**,
   appearing to them during forty **days**
   and **speaking** about the kingdom of God.
While **meeting** with them,

Jerusalem = juh-ROO-suh-lem

   he **enjoined** them not to depart from **Jerusalem**,
   but to wait for "the promise of the **Father**
   about which you have heard me **speak**;
   for **John** baptized with **water**,
   but in a few **days** you will be baptized with the Holy **Spirit**."

When they had gathered **together** they **asked** him,
   "Lord, are you at this time going to **restore**
      the kingdom to **Israel**?"

Israel = IZ-ree-ul

He answered them, "It is not for **you** to know the **times**
      or **seasons**
   that the Father has **established** by his own **authority**.

If the Ascension of the Lord is celebrated next Sunday, May 28, today's readings are used then in place of those for the Seventh Sunday of Easter.

READING I Notice in this reading that at the start of Acts, the evangelist Luke identifies the person to whom he is writing, as he did at the start of the Gospel. This is Theophilus, which might

have been the proper name of a particular person or might have been a general tag meaning "one who loves [-philus] God [theo-]," and in this way the Gospel and Acts are addressed to all believers through the liturgy of the word.

This is a long first reading, so it will require some storytelling skills to keep the assembly engaged. The reading has three basic parts: an introduction to Acts, an

anticipation of the coming of the Holy Spirit, and the narrative of the Ascension. The reading finds its place here on the solemnity of the Ascension because of this third part.

Luke is the only evangelist to give the "forty days" time indicator for the Ascension, and for the first few centuries of the Church's worship, the story of the Ascension was proclaimed in the Easter season but not according to Luke's timeline. Only at the end of the fourth century does the feast find its

Pause here, for now the text shifts to the topic of the Holy Spirit.
Judea = joo-DEE-uh
Samaria = suh-MAIR-ee-uh

Take your time and be clear with this narrative of the Ascension. The Gospel does not have the Ascension story in it.

The "white garments" are hints of the paschal mystery, reflected in the white vestments worn throughout the Easter season.
Galilee = GAL-ih-lee

But you will receive **power** when the Holy **Spirit** comes upon you,
     and you will be my **witnesses** in **Jerusalem**,
          throughout **Judea** and **Samaria**,
          and to the ends of the **earth**."
When he had **said** this, as they were **looking on**,
     he was lifted **up**, and a **cloud** took him from their **sight**.
While they were looking **intently** at the **sky** as he was **going**,
     suddenly two **men** dressed in white **garments**
          stood **beside** them.
They said, "Men of **Galilee**,
     why are you **standing** there looking at the **sky**?
This **Jesus** who has been taken **up** from you into **heaven**
     will **return** in the same way as you have **seen** him
          going into heaven."

Ephesians = ee-FEE-zhunz

Let the sense lines in the printed text guide you.

This long sentence is poetic in form. Keep the initial idea alive throughout: "that you may know."

READING II Ephesians 1:17–23

A reading from the Letter of Saint Paul to the Ephesians

Brothers and sisters:
May the **God** of our Lord Jesus **Christ**, the Father of **glory**,
     give you a Spirit of **wisdom** and **revelation**
          resulting in **knowledge** of him.
May the **eyes** of your **hearts** be **enlightened**,
     that you may **know** what is the **hope** that belongs to his **call**,
     what are the riches of **glory**
          in his **inheritance** among the **holy** ones,
     and what is the surpassing **greatness** of his **power**
          for us who **believe**,
     in accord with the **exercise** of his great **might**,

place on the fortieth day of the season, or Ascension Thursday, as it came to be known. In some dioceses, the Church celebrates Ascension Thursday, while in others it is on the Sunday after.

   Because the reading has three distinct topics, pause after each so that your hearers can have a moment to absorb that part of the reading. Be most clear and engaging in the third part since it narrates the christological element at the heart of the solemnity of the Ascension.

> There is a choice of second readings today. Speak with the liturgy coordinator or the homilist to find out which reading will be used.

READING II **EPHESIANS 4.** Here Paul begins a reasoned discourse that leads to an undeniable conclusion. In fact, he begins with his conclusion, phrased as a plea: live as one in peace.

This way of life is a consequence of Baptism, where our old selves were buried with Christ. We arose from the waters new beings, capable of knowing and loving Christ and our brothers and sisters, capable of serving in all the ways Christ empowers us to serve with a veriety of gifts.

   Proclaim this beautiful text with the dignity and grace Paul wrote into its words.

   EPHESIANS 1. This is a reading of cosmic scope. Because Christianity has, through the centuries and millennia, become a

which he worked in **Christ**,
raising him from the **dead**
and **seating** him at his **right** hand in the **heavens**,
far above every **principality**, **authority**, **power**, and **dominion**,
and **every** name that is **named**
not only in **this** age but also in the one to **come**.
And he put **all** things beneath his **feet**
and gave him as **head** over **all** things to the **church**,
which is his **body**,
the **fullness** of the one who fills **all** things in every **way**.

Or:

A reading from the Letter of Saint Paul to the Ephesians

Brothers and sisters,
I, a **prisoner** for the Lord,
urge you to **live** in a manner **worthy** of the **call**
    you have received,
with all **humility** and **gentleness**, with **patience**,
bearing with one another through **love**,
striving to preserve the **unity** of the spirit
through the bond of **peace**:
one **body** and one **Spirit**,
as you were also **called** to the one **hope** of your call;
one **Lord**, one **faith**, one **baptism**;
one **God** and Father of **all**,
who is **over** all and **through** all and **in** all.

Notice the first-person identification of the speaker. Since the word is living and active, this first-person speaker in your assembly is yourself. Proclaim the passage with spirited conviction. Address the assembly directly as the "you" of Paul's letter.

From this point to the end, the reading moves away from the language of "I," "we," and "you" pronouns as it talks about the manifestation of God's power in the Resurrection.

world religion, phrases like "far above every principality, authority, power and dominion" might not sound so grand. But in light of the state of the infant Church when this prayer of Ephesians was written, we can see how bold were the conviction and hope of the early communities.

As you prepare for this proclamation, think about this increase in the Church over the years. Although the Church has been beset by difficulties over the centuries, there are also the many contributions that the Church has made: to culture, to education, to the poor and downtrodden, and to so many areas of life that it is, on its best days, a "surpassing greatness" and an "exercise of his great might."

You can see from the first words of the reading that the author was telling this community of his own prayer for it. Even though the passage moves quickly out into its cosmic scope, it starts with the prayer of the author for the community of faith. Your proclamation can be offered to your parish community in the same character of prayer and hope, with, as the reading itself describes, the eyes of your heart enlightened.

But **grace** was given to **each** of us
    according to the measure of **Christ's** gift.
Therefore, it says:
    *He ascended on **high** and took prisoners **captive**;*
    *he gave **gifts** to men.*
What does "he **ascended**" mean except that he also **descended**
    into the **lower** regions of the **earth**?
The one who **descended** is also the one who **ascended**
    far above all the **heavens**,
    that he might **fill** all things.

And he gave some as **apostles**, others as **prophets**,
    others as **evangelists**, others as **pastors** and **teachers**,
    to **equip** the holy ones for the work of **ministry**,
    for building up the body of **Christ**,
    until we all attain to the unity of **faith**
    and **knowledge** of the Son of God, to mature to manhood,
    to the extent of the full **stature** of Christ.

[Shorter: Ephesians 4:1–7, 11–13]

The exaltation of Christ described in this part is lofty. Consider how you would imagine the scene described in the letter, and let your proclamation be strengthened by the visual images.

This reading is proclaimed on the Ascension because it captures the exaltation of Christ as he takes his place at the right hand of the Father. The Ascension is not described explicitly in the text, but it speaks of God raising Christ from the dead for all ages to come.

GOSPEL For quite a long time now, scholars have told us that the original version of the Gospel of Mark ended at Mark 16:8, as the women at the empty tomb flee in fear. Because of this, many editions of the Gospel put the remaining verses in brackets or parentheses. One supposes that the scholars regard the later

date of these verses as a reason for giving them a lower status. But history is not the ultimate criterion of the scriptures.

The books of the New Testament were received by the Church because they embrace the wide spectrum of stories and faith to guide the Church for these many,

GOSPEL Mark 16:15–20

A reading from the holy Gospel according to Mark

Jesus said to his disciples:
  "Go into the **whole world**
  and proclaim the **gospel** to every **creature**.
Whoever **believes** and is **baptized** will be **saved**;
  whoever does **not** believe will be **condemned**.
These **signs** will accompany those who **believe**:
  in my **name** they will drive out **demons**,
  they will speak new **languages**.
They will pick up **serpents** with their **hands**,
  and if they drink any **deadly** thing, it will not **harm** them.
They will lay hands on the **sick**, and they will **recover**."

So **then** the Lord **Jesus**, after he **spoke** to them,
  was taken up into **heaven**
  and took his **seat** at the right hand of **God**.
But they went **forth** and preached **everywhere**,
  while the Lord **worked** with them
  and **confirmed** the word through accompanying **signs**.

Most of the reading is Jesus' proclamation of a mission to the eleven.

many years. And this canon is what the Church holds up as sacred, including verses like these for this Gospel of the Ascension.

As always with the post-Resurrection appearances of Jesus, it happens on Sunday, "the first day of the week." This passage is unique to the Gospel of Mark. In it, we hear signs of faith named. Some of these are familiar from other scripture passages, such as casting out demons and speaking in tongues. But others are mentioned nowhere else, such as picking up snakes and drinking poison.

This Gospel takes its place on the feast of the Ascension for the penultimate verse, which tells us that Jesus "was taken up into heaven and took his seat at the right hand of God." Make sure that you proclaim these final verses most clearly.

7TH SUNDAY OF EASTER

Lectionary #60

READING I   Acts 1:15–17, 20a, 20c–26

A reading from the Acts of the Apostles

Peter stood up in the **midst** of the brothers
—there was a **group** of about one hundred and twenty persons
in the one **place**—.
He said, "My brothers,
the **Scripture** had to be **fulfilled**
which the Holy **Spirit** spoke **beforehand**
through the mouth of **David**, concerning **Judas**,
who was the **guide** for those who arrested **Jesus**.
He was **numbered** among us
and was **allotted** a share in this **ministry**.

"For it is written in the Book of **Psalms**:
*May **another** take his **office**.*

"Therefore, it is **necessary** that one of the men
who **accompanied** us the whole time
the Lord Jesus **came** and **went** among us,
beginning from the baptism of **John**
until the day on which he was taken **up** from us,
become with us a **witness** to his **resurrection**."
So they proposed **two**, **Judas** called **Barsabbas**,
who was **also** known as **Justus**, and **Matthias**.

As Peter addressed believers, so do you. The filling of vacant offices of apostles has continued in the Church as it has grown over time.
This is a long speech by the first apostle, and the historical lens of the perspective is engaging.

Judas = JOO-dus

Be prepared for the names, so that your proclamation will be smooth and confident.
Barsabbas = bar-SAH-bus
Justus = JUS-tus
Matthias = muh-THĪ-us

If the Ascension of the Lord is celebrated today, please see pages 171–175 for the appropriate readings.

READING I We are close to the end of the Easter season, when we have been reading through Acts in order. But this reading is out of order; it comes from near the beginning of the book. We already read about the conversion of Paul from being a persecutor of Christians to being a Christian himself and about the conversion of Peter, who turned from his earlier suspicion of Gentiles in the Church to the revelation that changed his heart and mind to welcoming the Gentiles.

This passage precedes these narratives of Paul and Peter, and it attends more to organizational acts for the building-up of the Church than to internal conversion of human hearts.

These two dimensions of the Church's increase, changes of heart and changes in the institution, are equally important for the spread of the Good News, but narratives of the first type are often more engaging. The reading from Acts that you will proclaim takes up the election of a new person "to take the place in this apostolic ministry" which had been abandoned by Judas when he betrayed Jesus to suffering and death.

Most of the reading is taken up with Peter's words to the believers about what needs to be done in restoring the ministry that had been vacant.

Then they **prayed**,
  "**You**, Lord, who know the hearts of **all**,
  show which one of these two you have **chosen**
  to take the **place** in this apostolic ministry
  from which **Judas** turned away to go to his **own** place."
Then they gave **lots** to them, and the lot fell upon **Matthias**,
  and he was **counted** with the eleven **apostles**.

READING II   1 John 4:11–16

A reading from the first Letter of Saint John

Beloved, if God so loved **us**,
  we **also** must love one **another**.
No one has ever **seen** God.
Yet, if we **love** one another, God **remains** in us,
  and his **love** is brought to **perfection** in us.

This is how we **know** that we remain in **him** and **he** in **us**,
  that he has given us of his **Spirit**.
Moreover, we have **seen** and **testify**
  that the **Father** sent his **Son** as **savior** of the world.
Whoever **acknowledges** that Jesus is the Son of **God**,
  God remains in **him** and he in **God**.
We have come to **know** and to **believe** in the love God **has** for us.

God is **love**, and whoever remains in **love**
  remains in **God** and God in **him**.

Address your assembly as "beloved" just as the author addressed his community.

The final verse is wonderful. End the reading well on this theology of God and love.

READING II In the Easter season, the Church builds up a chain of readings from one of the catholic letters, which are named according to the author. The reading you prepare now takes up some typically Johannine issues, Christ's atoning sacrifice on our behalf and the necessary correspondence between knowing Christ, following the commandments, obeying the word of Christ, and speaking the truth in the love of God.

By God's grace, you are no less than a child of God and an instrument of the word of God in your ministry than the author was. The repeated use of first-person plural pronouns in the reading sets you and your assembly as the objects for the proclamation, for you and they are indeed God's beloved children.

There are many in the Church who think themselves despised. Think of them as you prepare the passage and as you proclaim. Although you may not know these people in your community personally, imagine those who are not able to accept how much God loves them. Read this passage to them: "We are God's children *now*." Believe this message in your own experience of love, and share this with those in need in your community of faith.

GOSPEL   John 17:11b–19

A reading from the holy Gospel according to John

Lifting up his eyes to **heaven**, Jesus **prayed**, saying:
   "Holy **Father**, keep them in your **name** that you have **given** me,
   so that **they** may be one just as **we** are one.
When I was **with** them I **protected** them in your name that you
      gave me,
   and I **guarded** them, and **none** of them was **lost**
   except the son of **destruction**,
   in order that the **Scripture** might be **fulfilled**.
But **now** I am **coming** to you.
I **speak** this in the world
   so that they may share my joy **completely**.
I gave them your **word**, and the world **hated** them,
   because **they** do not belong to the world
   any more than **I** belong to the world.
I do not ask that you take them **out** of the world
   but that you **keep** them from the **evil** one.
They do not belong to the world
   any more than **I** belong to the world.
Consecrate them in the **truth**. Your **word** is truth.
As **you** sent **me** into the world,
   so I sent **them** into the world.
And I **consecrate** myself for them,
   so that they **also** may be **consecrated** in **truth**."

Only this line is not from the lips of Jesus.

Because the passage is long, pause at the breaks in the printed Lectionary's text.

consecrate = KON-suh-crayt

The final part has a lovely parallel between Jesus' relation to the Father and the Church's relation to Jesus.

GOSPEL The Church from which John's Gospel emerged was not without strife, both from without and within. The Gospel offers evidence to us not only of the many people who opposed Jesus during his ministry, but of those who threatened the existence of the community of John. This is important to keep in mind as you prepare for this proclamation. On the positive side, some of the reading makes unity seem like a possibility still, in spite of the factions, yet in other parts, it feels like the divisions are set in stone.

On the positive side are Jesus' prayer for unity, "that they may be one, just as we [Father and Son] are one," his prayer for happiness, "that they may share my joy completely," and his prayer for their holiness, "that they also may be consecrated in truth."

Revelatory of the threats that the community might have been feeling are these: Jesus' prayer "Father, keep them," his indication that "the world hated them," and his prayer that the Father "keep them from the evil one."

Knowing these indicators in the passage can make your proclamation more vibrant because you can see that the blessings and woes of the Church's existence have been part of its life from the beginning. So, as you prepare, consider the prayer of Jesus here as not only a prayer for a community of faith many centuries ago, but as the prayer of Christ for the Church today, for the members of your parish, and, most importantly, for the particular members whom the Holy Spirit has brought together for this Mass.

PENTECOST VIGIL

Lectionary #62

READING I   Genesis 11:1–9

A reading from the Book of Genesis

The whole **world** spoke the same **language**, using the
    same **words**.
While the people were **migrating** in the east,
    they came upon a **valley** in the land of **Shinar** and **settled** there.
They said to one another,
    "**Come**, let us mold **bricks** and harden them with **fire**."
They used bricks for **stone**, and bitumen for **mortar**.
Then they said, "**Come**, let us build ourselves a **city**
    and a **tower** with its **top** in the **sky**,
    and so make a **name** for ourselves;
    otherwise we shall be **scattered** all over the **earth**."

The LORD came down to **see** the city and the tower
    that the people had built.
Then the LORD said: "If now, while they are **one** people,
    all speaking the same **language**,
    they have started to do **this**,
    nothing will **later** stop them from doing
        whatever they presume to do.
Let us then go **down** there and **confuse** their language,
    so that one will not **understand** what another says."
Thus the LORD **scattered** them from there all over the **earth**,
    and they stopped building the city.

The tower of Babel gives the hearers what happened, and there are four basic parts to the story. The first part is introductory setting; pause briefly after it.
Shinar = SHEE-nar

The next section presents the plans the people have for making themselves known.
bitumen = bih-TOO-m*n

The next has the Lord's plans for the people after descending to see the city and its tower.

The final section wraps up the story and gives the status of the population after the Lord intervened to scatter them abroad.

There is a choice of first readings today. Speak with the liturgy coordinator or the homilist to find out which reading will be used.

READING I   GENESIS. The narrative of the tower of Babel appears rather early in the first book of the Bible, and as a metaphor of language and competition the account is well known. Yet some of the details of Babel are less familiar, so as you prepare for this proclamation on the Vigil of Pentecost, read the passage slowly and carefully, gleaning from it the core elements as they relate to Pentecost.

Note that the reading has a few movements in it; it might help you to think of it in four parts before you assemble them. One can see that the account is a description of what happened, with little theological content drawn from the events.

The first part describes the setting in place and in language.

In the second part the author reveals the plans of the people who came to the land of Shinar. They sought not a practical accomplishment but simply to make a name for themselves so that they would not be scattered all over the earth.

Part three reveals that the Lord came to see their accomplishments, the city and the tower in particular, and there we find what the Lord planned for the people, particularly

Babel = BAB-*l

That is why it was called **Babel**,
　　because **there** the LORD confused the **speech** of all the **world**.
It was from that place that he **scattered** them all over the **earth**.

Or:

READING I　Exodus 19:3–8a, 16–20b

A reading from the Book of Exodus

Moses went up the mountain to **God**.
Then the LORD **called** to him and said,
　　"**Thus** shall you say to the house of **Jacob**;
　　tell the Israelites:
　　You have **seen** for yourselves how I **treated** the Egyptians
　　and how I **bore** you up on **eagle** wings
　　and **brought** you here to **myself**.
Therefore, if you hearken to my **voice** and keep my **covenant**,
　　you shall be my special **possession**,
　　dearer to me than all **other** people,
　　though **all** the earth is **mine**.
You shall be to me a kingdom of **priests**, a holy **nation**.
That is what you must tell the **Israelites**."
So Moses **went** and summoned the **elders** of the people.
When he set before them
　　all that the LORD had **ordered** him to tell them,
　　the people all answered **together**,
　　"Everything the LORD has **said**, we will **do**."

Jacob = JAY-kub

The expresson "on eagle wings" is beloved by many; procalim it clearly.

Emphasize "special possession," another beautiful phrase.

regarding their speech. The account does not reveal the reasons for the Lord's response to what the people were doing; it merely tells what the response was.

The final part describes the Lord's scattering of the people.

The role of the Holy Spirit is the building up of the Church, and for this reason the placement of the tower of Babel account here is fitting. The Spirit is not mentioned in the story, but the scattering of the people leaves the opportunity for the Holy Spirit's work in knitting the scattered back into a community united in faith.

EXODUS. It is an ancient tradition—part of the Jewish calendar long before Christianity appeared—that Pentecost was a time for celebrating the covenant, the pact between God and Israel. This theology of covenant was taken up in some early Christian communities, and that theology characterized the Christian Pentecost as well, at least in some places in those first few centuries.

For early Christians, the Easter season was an integral span of Fifty Days, at the end of which a reading about the Sinai covenant was proclaimed, most likely. That the Church has placed this Exodus reading as one of the choices for the Vigil of Pentecost reveals that in the reform of the liturgical

prophesy = PROF-uh-sī

Therefore, **prophesy** and say to them:
>**Thus** says the Lord **GOD**:
O my **people**, I will open your **graves**
and have you **rise** from them,
and bring you **back** to the land of **Israel**.
Then you shall **know** that I am the **LORD**,
when I **open** your graves and have you **rise** from them,
O my **people**!
I will put my **spirit** in you that you may **live**,
and I will **settle** you upon your **land**;
thus you shall know that I am the **LORD**.
I have **promised**, and I will **do** it, says the **LORD**.

Or:

READING I   Joel 3:1–5

Pause slightly before announcing the book. We do not hear from Joel very often.

This passage is vivid.

A reading from the Book of the Prophet Joel

Thus says the **Lord**:
I will pour out my **spirit** upon all **flesh**.
Your sons and **daughters** shall **prophesy**,
your **old** men shall dream **dreams**,
your **young** men shall see **visions**;
even upon the **servants** and the **handmaids**,
in those days, I will pour out my **spirit**.
And I will work **wonders** in the **heavens** and on the **earth**,
blood, **fire**, and columns of **smoke**;

These cosmological images are fascinating. Imagine them for yourself, and proclaim the prophet's words as if you yourself have seen this vision.

two millennia ago, you too are called to proclaim to a new assembly of God's people.

The book of Joel is only three chapters long, just a few pages in most editions of the Bible. This passage for Pentecost captures an important aspect of the role of the Holy Spirit in the life of faith, the animation of flesh by the spirit. The prophet could not say it more clearly: "Thus says the Lord: I will

pour out my spirit upon all flesh," a beautiful and direct theology of the Spirit's work that cannot be repeated too often.

Take your time with this rather short text, and make the imagery come alive for those who hear you proclaim it at this Vigil of Pentecost, for this is the time for the Church to be awakened to the role of the Spirit in our human lives of faith and in the communal life of the assembly in which you worship and minister.

READING II The letter to the Romans came near the end of Paul's writing life, as far as we know, about the year 58 or 59. It was centuries before the theology of the Holy Spirit was developed and the relationship between the Father and the Son and the Holy Spirit discerned, but here we find one of the earliest Christian teachings about the role of the Holy Spirit in the Church. This is fitting for Pentecost, and

the **sun** will be turned to **darkness**,
    and the **moon** to **blood**,
at the **coming** of the day of the LORD,
    the **great** and **terrible** day.
Then everyone shall be **rescued**
    who **calls** on the name of the LORD;
for on Mount **Zion** there shall be a **remnant**,
    as the LORD has said,
and in Jerusalem **survivors**
    whom the LORD shall **call**.

READING II   Romans 8:22–27

A reading from the Letter of Saint Paul to the Romans

Brothers and sisters:
We know that all **creation** is **groaning** in **labor** pains
    even until **now**;
    and not only **that**, but we **ourselves**,
    who have the **firstfruits** of the Spirit,
    we **also** groan within ourselves
    as we wait for **adoption**, the redemption of our **bodies**.
For in **hope** we were **saved**.
Now **hope** that **sees** is **not** hope.
For who **hopes** for what one **sees**?
But if we hope for what we do **not** see, we wait with **endurance**.

The reading is short yet very important in its theology of the Holy Spirit; take your time with the proclamation.

Attend to the significance of the meaning and repetition (and alliteration) of the words in this part—"hope," "saved," "hope," "sees," "hope," hopes," "sees," "hope," and "see."

it also reveals that the *experience* of the Holy Spirit in the life of the Church preceded the theologizing.

Saint Paul reveals here that the Holy Spirit "helps us in our weakness," so—against the culture that says that every accomplishment and every success depends on us as individuals—we know that in the end God will supply what we need. God's will for us is wiser than we are. That is why the celebration of Pentecost is imperative,

so that we know that we individuals are not the final measure of goodness and strength. It is the experience of God's presence in the Church and its sacraments. We do not ignore our personal experience, but, as the baptized, we hold this experience in balance with the communal experience of the liturgy. It will help the members of your parish to appreciate the Spirit's role if your proclamation is made with conviction.

GOSPEL Although the author of the Gospel did not write these words in anticipation of the Christian liturgical year as we know it today, the opening of your proclamation is more than fitting for Pentecost. It is an identification of time for the ancient community of the Gospel of John, and the evangelist marked the time by describing it as "the last day of the festival, the last and greatest day of the feast." Pentecost is not only a one-day celebration,

Pause briefly before beginning the final section for it has the significant theology of the Holy Spirit that makes the reading so fitting for this celebration.

In the **same** way, the Spirit **too** comes to the **aid** of our **weakness**;
for we do not know **how** to pray as we **ought**,
but the Spirit **himself** intercedes with inexpressible **groanings**.
And the one who searches **hearts**
knows what is the **intention** of the **Spirit**,
because he **intercedes** for the **holy** ones
according to God's **will**.

GOSPEL   John 7:37–39

A reading from the holy Gospel according to John

On the **last** and **greatest** day of the feast,
Jesus stood up and **exclaimed**,
"Let anyone who **thirsts** come to me and **drink**.
As Scripture says:
*Rivers of living **water** will flow from **within** him*
who believes in me."

He said this in reference to the **Spirit**
that those who came to **believe** in him were to **receive**.
There **was**, of course, no Spirit **yet**,
because **Jesus** had not yet been **glorified**.

This time indication was not pointing to Pentecost, but in this place it is fitting for this "last and greatest day of the feast" to be proclaimed on the last day of the great festival, Pentecost, at the end of the Easter season.

The Holy Spirit's role is essential in attracting inquirers and potential members to the Church, and the means of their membership is Baptism, the "rivers of living water."

but the closing of the season of Easter. The third-century North African theologian Tertullian called the Easter season the *laetissimum spatium,* that "most joyful span" of time, which closes at Pentecost, the feast for which you prepare this reading. In the words of the Gospel itself, Pentecost is "the last and greatest day of the feast" of the Easter season.

This is one of the shortest Gospel readings in the entire Lectionary. For this reason, pace yourself during the proclamation. Take

significant pauses so that the assembly is reading to hear you as you relate the words of the evangelist.

Because Pentecost is the close of the Easter season, that span during which the Church celebrates and remembers Baptism— *celebrating* at the Easter Vigil or in the weeks of the Easter season itself, and *remembering* those of the members of the Church— the text's mention of "living water" is a good echo of the "living water" that constitutes the Church. Pentecost is the celebration of the birth of the Church in the power of the Holy Spirit.

The Church whose birth and rebirth are celebrated at Pentecost is not some abstract Church, but the community gathered for the liturgy as you proclaim the word. It is the advent of the Holy Spirit that brings the Church together, and in faith we trust that it is the Holy Spirit that gathers this particular community that hears your proclamation. Proclaim the reading clearly, as a testimony to the Holy Spirit's power to realize Christ's presence in the people brought together.

PENTECOST

Lectionary #63

READING I   Acts 2:1–11

A reading from the Acts of the Apostles

When the time for **Pentecost** was fulfilled,
    they were all in one place **together**.
And **suddenly** there came from the sky
    a **noise** like a strong driving **wind**,
    and it filled the entire house in which they were.
Then there appeared to them **tongues** as of **fire**,
    which **parted** and came to rest on **each** one of them.
And they were all **filled** with the Holy **Spirit**
    and began to **speak** in different **tongues**,
    as the **Spirit** enabled them to **proclaim**.

Now there were devout **Jews** from every nation under heaven
    staying in Jerusalem.
At this **sound**, they gathered in a large **crowd**,
    but they were **confused**
    because **each** one heard them **speaking** in his own **language**.
They were **astounded**, and in **amazement** they asked,
    "Are **not** all these people who are speaking **Galileans**?
Then how does **each** of us hear them in his native **language**?
We are Parthians, Medes, and Elamites,
    inhabitants of Mesopotamia, Judea and Cappadocia,

Be clear in this description, for the "tongues as of fire" are a well-known element in artistic depictions of Pentecost.

Jerusalem = juh-ROO-suh-lem

Galileans = gal-ih-LEE-unz

These next few verses contain many proper names; see below for how to prepare for this.
Parthians = PAR-thee-unz
Medes = meedz
Elamites = EE-luh-mīts
Mesopotamia = mes-uh-poh-TAY-mee-uh
Judea = joo-DEE-uh
Cappadocia = kap-uh-DOH-shuh

READING I   You bear a bigger responsibility than usual as you prepare for this reading. Most of the feasts in the liturgical year are reflected in the Gospel reading. But today, the first reading narrates the central event of the feast, the descent of the Holy Spirit. Your proclamation, therefore, needs to be clear and confident since it is the key narrative of the day.

The text can be divided into four parts. The first sets the context and the extraordinary happening begins. The second gives more detail, with the tongues of fire and the gift of the Holy Spirit that manifested itself in the languages. The third is an overview of the variety of people in the crowd. The fourth is the detailed catalogue of places and languages. Imagine the narrative movement in the reading so that you are well aware of the story as it unfolds.

The chain of names near the end calls for some preparation so that your proclamation will be smooth and confident. Worse than mispronouncing one of the cities would be drawing too much attention to any one of them by stumbling over it. Some of the names are simple—"Rome" and "Asia," for example— but others are long—"Mesopotamia"—or uncommon—"Phrygia," for example. But the main point that the assembly should take from the chain of names is simply that there was a great variety of nations and peoples and cultures present for this extraordinary event. Take your time with this list, but do not draw unnecessary attention to them.

In addition to the vocabulary, the narrative is fairly long. The best way to handle a long passage like this is to tell the story in the most engaging, clear, and confident manner possible.

Pontus = PON-tus
Phrygia = FRIJ-ee-uh
Pamphilia = pam-FIL-ee-uh
Egypt = EE-jipt
Libya = LIB-ee-uh
Cyrene = sī-REE-nee
Cretans = KREE-tuns
Arabs = AIR-ubs

Pontus and Asia, Phrygia and Pamphylia,
Egypt and the districts of Libya near Cyrene,
as well as travelers from Rome,
both Jews and converts to Judaism, Cretans and Arabs,
yet we hear them speaking in our own **tongues**
of the mighty acts of **God**."

Corinthians = kor-IN-thee-unz

Notice the parallels created here by Paul, each balancing the word "different" on the one side and "the same" on the other. Pause slightly before each of the pairs so that the hearers can recognize the structure.

The theology of the body of Christ, usually considered in relation to the Eucharist, is here taking up the members of the Church, in Corinth when the letter was written and in your own community today. Proclaim this part of the reading with conviction so that your hearers might appreciate the link between the Eucharistic elements and the assembly in which they celebrate week after week.

READING II   1 Corinthians 12:3b–7, 12–13

A reading from the first Letter of Saint Paul to the Corinthians

Brothers and sisters:
No one can say, "Jesus is Lord," **except** by the Holy **Spirit**.
There are different **kinds** of spiritual **gifts** but the same **Spirit**;
    there are different **forms** of **service** but the same **Lord**;
    there are different **workings** but the same **God**
        who produces **all** of them in **everyone**.
To each **individual** the manifestation of the Spirit
    is given for some **benefit**.

As a **body** is one though it has many **parts**,
    and all the **parts** of the body, though **many**, are one **body**,
        so also **Christ**.
For in one **Spirit** we were all **baptized** into one **body**,
    whether **Jews** or **Greeks**, **slaves** or **free** persons,
    and we were **all** given to drink of one **Spirit**.

Or:

There is a choice of second readings today. Please check with the liturgy coordinator or the homilist to find out which reading will be used.

READING II The letters of Saint Paul constitute the earliest extant Christian literature, for they are older than the Gospels by a few decades. So, even though each of the readings for this Sunday gives some theology of the Holy Spirit, this passage tells how the Holy Spirit was

revealed to Paul at the earliest stage of Christian life.

CORINTHIANS. With this in mind, consider this passage in relation to your own service as a proclaimer of the word of God in the Church. The reading empowers your contribution, for this passage from First Corinthians sees the prompting of gifts in the Church as manifestations of the Holy Spirit in the Church, and, though you may not have been aware of this when you first began your ministry of the word, your contribution

to the Church as a lector is indeed a manifestation of the Spirit working in your community of faith. Therefore, you must be prepared for your ministry in the best way possible, not for your own sake but for the life and health of the Church.

This particular text can be a corrective in the culture where we live, for high priority is given to the rights of the individual here. Yet the Church as a *body*, as a community of faith made up of many individuals, stands in contrast to this exaltation of the individual. The healing that Jesus wrought in his ministry is not given to any of us as

Deliver this passage directly to your assembly as to your "brothers and sisters," for, by Baptism, that is who they are.

The opening sets out the broad scope.

Now the particulars of the flesh . . .

. . . followed by the particulars of the Spirit.

The final line is a positive summary.

READING II   Galatians 5:16–25

A reading from the Letter of Saint Paul to the Galatians

Brothers and sisters, **live** by the **Spirit**
  and you will certainly not **gratify** the desire of the **flesh.**
For the **flesh** has desires **against** the Spirit,
  and the **Spirit** against the **flesh**;
  these are **opposed** to each other,
  so that you may **not** do what you **want.**
But if you are guided by the **Spirit**, you are not under the **law.**
Now the works of the flesh are **obvious**:
  immorality, impurity, lust, idolatry,
  sorcery, hatreds, rivalry, jealousy,
  outbursts of fury, acts of selfishness,
  dissensions, factions, occasions of envy,
  drinking bouts, orgies, and the like.
I **warn** you, as I warned you **before**,
  that those who **do** such things will not **inherit**
    the kingdom of **God.**
In **contrast**, the fruit of the **Spirit** is love, joy, peace,
  patience, kindness, generosity,
  faithfulness, gentleness, self-control.
Against **such** there **is** no law.
Now those who belong to Christ **Jesus** have **crucified** their flesh
  with its **passions** and **desires.**
If we **live** in the Spirit, let us also **follow** the Spirit.

---

individuals, but to us as a community of faith. As that body of Christ, we are able to minister to those in need of healing and support and companionship through life.

As you prepare for this proclamation, keep your own service in mind, and share the joy of the Holy Spirit that you have gleaned from your own work in the Church. Your proclamation for Pentecost can prompt others to consider what their gifts to the body might be.

GALATIANS. Readings like this can be difficult to proclaim at times, for, you are highlighting for those in your assembly, as

Paul did for the members of the assembly at Galatia, the ways that they have failed to live up to their vocation. In this passage, in particular, you are indicting them for following the ways of the flesh and ignoring the ways of the Spirit.

Moreover, you will list the particulars of the "works of the flesh," and they are legion. Paul catalogues nearly twice as many manifestations of the flesh in the community as manifestations of the Spirit.

The reading has five basic parts: the first sets out the big picture, of the opposition between living "by the Spirit" and by

"the flesh"; the second gives the list of the works of the flesh. The third is the single sentence of the consequences of such sinful habits; then the fourth part catalogues the fruits of the Spirit. The last part is Paul's summary and encouragement of the community to live according to the Spirit.

The temptation with such lists is to rush, presuming that no one wants to attend to such a long list or that the items are variations on a theme. But resist that temptation, and insert a poignant pause at each comma in the lists.

The first line has the only words not from the lips of Jesus.

Emphasize the "Advocate" and "Spirit of truth" for they are keys to the feast we celebrate today.

From here on the passage refers to the Spirit only by pronouns. So make sure that this phrase is heard clearly.

GOSPEL John 15:26–27; 16:12–15

A reading from the holy Gospel according to John

Jesus said to his disciples:
"When the **Advocate** comes whom I will **send** you
from the **Father**,
the Spirit of truth that proceeds from the Father,
he will **testify** to me.
And you **also** testify,
because you have **been** with me from the **beginning**.

"I have **much** more to tell you, but you cannot **bear** it now.
But when **he** comes, the Spirit of **truth**,
he will guide you to **all** truth.
He will **not** speak on his **own**,
but he will speak what he **hears**,
and will **declare** to you the things that are **coming**.
He will **glorify** me,
because he will take from what is **mine** and **declare** it to you.
Everything that the Father **has** is mine;
for this reason I **told** you that he will take from what is **mine**
and declare it to **you**."

Or:

Note that there is a choice of Gospel readings today.

GOSPEL **JOHN 15.** Throughout the Fifty Days of Easter, most of the Gospel proclamations have narrated appearances of the risen Christ. Today's Gospel has Jesus addressing the disciples in the long discourse that begins soon after the foot-washing of chapter 13, before the Passion. The reason the Lectionary takes us back to this last discourse is because Jesus speaks of the Holy Spirit, whose coming is anticipated in the words of Jesus here, and celebrated in the Church today.

From a theological viewpoint, it is important that the Spirit was working in the life of Jesus before the Resurrection. Indeed, the Holy Spirit was present with the Father from the beginning of time, at the Creation of the world. And in our own experience, the Spirit is present not only in the joys of life, but in the sorrows and difficulties as well, when it feels like God is far from us.

With the reading, notice that only the first line is outside quotation marks, so it is the only indicator of context.

These words from Jesus were a consolation for the disciples, who knew that Jesus' death was on the horizon. You deliver his message as a consolation to the people of your parish.

JOHN 20. It would be understandable to think that the liturgical phrase "Peace be with you" is a fruit of scriptural passags such as this one, in which Jesus himself speaks the wrods. But once we realize that the Gospels were written down decades after the events told in them, and that their authors incorporated the experiences of their communities as well as the life of

A reading from the holy Gospel according to John

On the evening of that **first** day of the **week**,
    when the doors were **locked**, where the **disciples** were,
    for fear of the **Jews**,
    Jesus **came** and **stood** in their midst
    and said to them, "**Peace** be with you."
When he had **said** this, he showed them his **hands** and his **side**.
The disciples **rejoiced** when they saw the Lord.
Jesus said to them **again**, "**Peace** be with you.
As the **Father** has sent **me**, so **I** send **you**."
And when he had **said** this, he **breathed** on them
    and said to them,
    "**Receive** the Holy **Spirit**.
Whose sins you **forgive** are **forgiven** them,
    and whose sins you **retain** are **retained**."

The time element bears an important clue to the liturgical and theological meaning of the day.

The consonance of this phrase with our liturgy yet today should be emphasized.

This phrase is also important; it is still used in the liturgy.

Jesus, we can guess that phrases like this "Peace be with you" were not only historic words of Jesus, but also that they were liturgical phrases transcribed into the Gospels. So in your proclamation of this passage, consider highlighting the phrase.

It is the gift of the Spirit that brings the assembly together week after week. So the liturgical exchanges and ritual gestures of the early Church that may be reflected in this text are very fitting for proclamation on Pentecost.

The time indication in the text, "on the evening of that first day of the week,"

is important here. It tells us that the Resurrection, which was proclaimed at the start of the Fifty Days on Easter Sunday, and the reception of the Holy Spirit happened on the same day. This helps us understand how the third-century theologian Tertullian could call the Fifty Days "one great Sunday." It also helps us appreciate the endurance of the first day of the week, Sunday, as the day of the liturgy from the beginning. The Sunday assembly is the original gift of the Holy Spirit's work in the life of the Church.

MOST HOLY TRINITY

Deuteronomy = doo-ter-AH-nuh-mee

Lectionary #165

READING I   Deuteronomy 4:32–34, 39–40

A reading from the Book of Deuteronomy

These two imperatives can be addressed as commands to your own assembly as they were to the assembly to which Moses spoke.

The fourth question is complex. Familiarize yourself with it in advance so that you can proclaim it smoothly.

Moses said to the people:
  "**Ask** now of the days of **old**, **before** your time,
  ever since God **created** man upon the earth;
  ask from **one** end of the sky to the **other**:
  Did **anything** so **great** ever **happen** before?
Was it ever **heard** of?
Did a people ever hear the voice of God
  speaking from the midst of **fire**, as **you** did, and **live**?
Or did any **god** venture to go and take a **nation** for **himself**
  from the midst of **another** nation,
  by **testings**, by signs and **wonders**, by **war**,
  with strong **hand** and outstretched **arm**, and by great **terrors**,
  all of which the LORD, your **God**,
  did for you in **Egypt** before your very **eyes**?
This is why you must now **know**,
  and **fix** in your heart, that the LORD is God
  in the heavens **above** and on earth **below**,
  and that there is no **other**.
You must keep his **statutes** and **commandments** that I **enjoin** on
    you today,
  that **you** and your **children after** you may **prosper**,
  and that you may have long **life** on the land
  which the LORD, your God, is **giving** you forever."

Egypt = EE-jipt

The reading closes with a few more verbs of command.

READING I   The Gospel for today mentions the persons of the Trinity, the Father, the Son, and the Holy Spirit. Trinitarian theology began to be clarified in the centuries after the New Testament, as the leaders of the Church debated theological opponents. Your reading bears on today's celebration for Moses' proclamation tells us that the Trinity was at work from the beginning, that is, long before the name "Trinity" emerged.

  There are three literary qualities to this passage to which you should attend. First,

everything after the first verse is from the lips of Moses.

  Second, in Moses' address, the first part and the last part are commands to the people: "ask," "you must know," "you must keep." Address these to your parish community as did Moses to his community.

  Third, between those two sets of commands is a set of three rhetorical questions that can also be addressed right to the congregation.

READING II   It is the Holy Spirit that knits together the body of Christ, the Church, a sign of the presence of God in the world. And all share in this presence as children of God, with the Holy Spirit as the actor in this presence.

  The theology of Paul in the letter to the Romans is not easy. Though this passage is brief, its meaning is profound. Your own conviction about what Paul wrote is necessary for an effective proclamation, so grapple with what the apostle offers here.

Romans = ROH-munz

The Spirit works in bringing us to faith and to the Church. And once here, we share in the salvation won by Christ.

This final verse succinctly expresses basic Pauline theology.

READING II   Romans 8:14–17

A reading from the Letter of Saint Paul to the Romans

Brothers and sisters:
Those who are led by the **Spirit** of God are **sons** of God.
For you did not receive a spirit of **slavery** to fall back into **fear**,
    but you received a Spirit of **adoption**,
    through whom we cry, "**Abba, Father!**"
The Spirit **himself** bears witness with **our** spirit
    that we are **children** of God,
    and if **children**, then **heirs**,
    heirs of God and **joint** heirs with **Christ**,
    if only we **suffer** with him
    so that we may also be **glorified** with him.

This Gospel is relatively short, so don't rush through it. This first part sets the scene for the risen Jesus' address to the eleven disciples.
Galilee = GAL-ih-lee

Here begins the proclamation from Jesus, a missionary statement in which he directs the disciples to go out into the world and make disciples. They did, and the Church is still making them!

The finale is a consolation.

GOSPEL   Matthew 28:16–20

A reading from the holy Gospel according to Matthew

The eleven disciples went to **Galilee**,
    to the **mountain** to which Jesus had **ordered** them.
When they all **saw** him, they **worshiped**, but they **doubted**.
Then Jesus **approached** and said to them,
    "All power in **heaven** and on **earth** has been **given** to me.
Go, therefore, and make **disciples** of all **nations**,
    baptizing them in the name of the **Father**,
    and of the **Son**, and of the Holy **Spirit**,
    teaching them to **observe** all that I have **commanded** you.
And **behold**, I am **with** you **always**, until the end of the **age**."

The final line sums it up. We are participants with Christ in the Paschal Mystery. As proclaimer, recognize that, after Baptism, your own sufferings and glories participate in those of the body of Christ. As you believe this in your heart, you can proclaim this with confidence on Trinity Sunday.

GOSPEL   This Gospel has two basic parts, one setting up the context in narrative form and the other giving the words of Jesus delivered on the mountain. Second, the mission to which

Jesus directs the disciples has a balance of word ("teaching") and action ("baptizing them in the name of the Father, and of the Son, and of the Holy Spirit").

In the Gospel of Matthew, where the evangelist seeks to show the fulfillment of the Old Testament in the life of Jesus, scenes on mountains have a unique gravity. This scene at the end of the Gospel was important for the community the evangelist wrote for, and continues its importance in the Easter season for us now, where the Church discerns its work in the world.

Although this is not the only place in the Bible where the Father, the Son, and the Holy Spirit are named together, it is the only place where the liturgical phrase "in the name of the Father / and of the Son and of the Holy Spirit" is used. Since this appears only in this one place, and does not appear often in the Lectionary, let the Gospel text echo with familiarity.

MOST HOLY BODY AND BLOOD OF CHRIST

Lectionary #168

READING I   Exodus 24:3–8

Exodus = EK-suh-dus

Moses = MOH-ziz

The people's speaking in one voice is a hint of the ritual context.

Israel = IZ-ree-ul

The splashing of blood might seem gruesome, but it forms a the symbolic link with both the second reading and the Gospel.

Again the unified voice of the people.

Pause slightly before you proclaim this final verse.

A reading from the Book of Exodus

When Moses came to the people
    and related all the **words** and **ordinances** of the LORD,
    they all **answered** with one **voice**,
    "We will do **everything** that the LORD has **told** us."
Moses then wrote **down** all the words of the LORD and,
    rising **early** the next **day**,
    he **erected** at the foot of the mountain an **altar**
    and twelve **pillars** for the twelve **tribes** of Israel.
Then, having sent certain young men of the Israelites
    to offer **holocausts** and sacrifice young **bulls**
    as **peace** offerings to the LORD,
    Moses took half of the **blood** and put it in large **bowls**;
    the **other** half he splashed on the **altar**.
Taking the book of the **covenant**, he read it **aloud** to the people,
    who answered, "**All** that the LORD has **said**, we will
        heed and **do**."
Then he took the **blood** and **sprinkled** it on the people, saying,
    "This is the blood of the **covenant**
    that the LORD has **made** with you
    in **accordance** with all these **words** of his."

READING I Sometimes in our life of faith, we can become so accustomed to the stories that we can forget how startling some of them really are. Two sentences in this reading can indeed jar the assembly before you. The first is this description of Moses' action: "Moses took half of the blood and put it in large bowls; the other half he splashed on the altar"; and the second: "Moses took the blood and sprinkled it on the people."

This reading is also strongly linked to the second reading from the letter to the Hebrews, and the link is the same element, the blood of a sacrificed animal. Your proclamation of this text should serve the link with the other two readings of the day, and with the sacramental elements of the Eucharist, the center of today's solemnity.

In addition to the link with the image of blood, there is also the symbolic link with the twelve pillars in the Old Testament reading, which correspond to "the twelve tribes of Israel," and the twelve "pillars" of the Church, that is, the disciples, mentioned in the Last Supper narrative in today's Gospel.

In addition to becoming familiar with the narrative, do your best to emphasize the elements that this reading shares with the two readings to be proclaimed after your ministry.

Study the text closely for a confident proclamation. Here the images are drawn from ritual traditions in ancient Judaism.

The blood imagery of this part is what places this reading on this solemnity. Highlight it so that the assembly can appreciate its significance in relation to the Eucharist.

READING II   Hebrews 9:11–15

A reading from the Letter to the Hebrews

Brothers and sisters:
When **Christ** came as **high** priest
   of the good things that have come to **be**,
   passing **through** the **greater** and more **perfect** tabernacle
   not made by **hands**, that is, not belonging to **this** creation,
   he entered **once** for **all** into the **sanctuary**,
   not with the blood of **goats** and **calves**
   but with his **own** blood, thus obtaining **eternal** redemption.
For if the blood of **goats** and bulls
   and the sprinkling of a **heifer's ashes**
   can sanctify those who are **defiled**
   so that their flesh is **cleansed**,
   how much **more** will the blood of **Christ**,
   who through the eternal Spirit **offered** himself **unblemished**
     to God,
   cleanse our **consciences** from dead **works**
   to **worship** the living **God**.

For this reason **he** is mediator of a **new** covenant:
   since a **death** has taken place for deliverance
   from **transgressions** under the **first** covenant,
   those who are **called** may **receive** the promised
     eternal inheritance.

READING II There is usually a strong link between the first reading and Gospel for any given Sunday, but today, the second reading has a strong connection with the first reading. Both speak of the blood of animals sprinkled in the sacrifice. In the first reading, the blood is a sign of the establishment of the covenant between the Lord and the 12 tribes of Israel, while in the reading you prepare the blood of the sacrificed animal is compared to the blood of Christ.

Although the letter to the Hebrews is incomparably rich in many ways, its language, images, and metaphors are sometimes foreign to our sensibilities these many centuries after it was composed. In this reading you will find references to some elements of the Jewish rites of sacrifice: the high priest, the blood of animals (goats, calves, bulls, and heifers), and the establishment of the covenant.

The best preparation is to become familiar with the meaning of this text. This liturgical year the Church proclaims a series of second readings from the letter to the Hebrews (between the Twenty-seventh and Thirty-third Sundays in Ordinary Time), and you might read those pericopes and their commentaries as part of your preparation.

GOSPEL   Mark 14:12–16, 22–26

A reading from the holy Gospel according to Mark

On the **first** day of the **Feast** of Unleavened **Bread**,
    when they sacrificed the **Passover** lamb,
    Jesus' **disciples** said to him,
    "Where do you want us to **go**
    and **prepare** for you to eat the **Passover**?"
He **sent** two of his disciples and said to them,
    "Go into the **city** and a man will **meet** you,
    carrying a jar of **water**.
Follow him.
Wherever he **enters**, say to the **master** of the house,
    'The **Teacher** says, "Where is my **guest** room
    where I may eat the **Passover** with my **disciples**?"'
Then he will show you a large upper **room** furnished and ready.
Make the **preparations** for us **there**."
The disciples then went **off**, **entered** the city,
    and **found** it just as he had **told** them;
    and they prepared the **Passover**.

While they were **eating**,
    he took **bread**, said the **blessing**,
    broke it, **gave** it to them, and said,
    "**Take** it; this is my **body**."
Then he took a **cup**, gave **thanks**, and **gave** it to them,
    and they all **drank** from it.

The image of the Passover lamb is taken up to suggest that Jesus himself is that lamb sacrificed for humanity.

Here begins the familiar part of the narrative. Believers recognize this ritual action of Jesus with the bread and wine, so take your time in delivering the beloved words.

GOSPEL   The passage before you has two basic parts. The assembly will expect the second part, for it contains the Last Supper narrative of the Gospel of Mark. The challenge to you as proclaimer is in the first part.

When Mark was writing this Gospel, the community was likely a mix of Jewish and Gentile members. Because of this, the narrative reflects some traditions of Jewish

ritual practice and some Christian adaptations of what had originally been a Jewish rite. The first verse has a number of elements from the Jewish tradition, with "the first day of the Feast of Unleavened Bread," and the sacrifice of the Passover lamb.

The next part discusses not time but place, and its background is unclear. Still, the details are engaging, as the two are sent on a room-finding mission by Jesus, who foretells their meeting "a man carrying a jar of water."

Pause before beginning the Last Supper narrative. This is, of course, one of the most familiar stories in the Gospels, for we hear at least the institution narrative each time the eucharistic prayer is prayed. Note that what Jesus says after sharing the cup is much longer than what he says after giving the bread. This is also longer than what is included in the institution narrative of the

He said to them,
  "This is my **blood** of the **covenant**,
  which will be **shed** for **many**.
Amen, I **say** to you,
  I shall not drink **again** the fruit of the **vine**
  until the day when I drink it **new** in the kingdom of **God**."
Then, after singing a **hymn**,
  they went out to the Mount of **Olives**.

eucharistic prayer. For this reason, take your time so that the assembly can catch some of this Gospel's nuances.

Now that the sharing of the blood of Christ with the assembled Church on Sundays has been restored—the baptized and ordained rather than only the ordained as it was for many centuries—the Church's proclamation of what Jesus said after the cup can be appreciated in its fullness, as a reality to be shared. Keep this in mind as you read and prepare for the proclamation.

12TH SUNDAY IN ORDINARY TIME

Lectionary #95

READING I   Job 38:1, 8–11

A reading from the Book of Job

Pause before the first line so that listeners can be poised to hear it.
Job = johb
These descriptions of mighty cosmic deeds call for an assertive voice.

The Lord addressed **Job** out of the **storm** and said:
   Who **shut** within doors the **sea**,
      when it burst **forth** from the **womb**;
   when I made the clouds its **garment**
      and thick **darkness** its **swaddling** bands?
   When I set **limits** for it
      and **fastened** the bar of its **door**,
   and **said**: **Thus** far shall you come but no **farther**,
      and **here** shall your proud waves be **stilled**!

READING II   2 Corinthians 5:14–17

A reading from the second Letter of Saint Paul to the Corinthians

Corinthians = kor-IN-thee-unz

Your tone as you start with this intimate address should catch the attention of the members of the assembly, your "Brothers and sisters."

Brothers and sisters:
The **love** of Christ **impels** us,
   once we have **come** to the **conviction** that **one** died for **all**;
   therefore, **all** have died.
He **indeed** died for all,
   so that those who **live** might no longer live for **themselves**
   but for **him** who for **their** sake **died** and was **raised**.

READING I   The first line sets the context, and it is very important that the assembly recognize from your reading that the Lord is speaking "out of the storm." The assembly's appreciation of the storm is key because it complements the windstorm in the Gospel reading from Mark.

You need to proclaim the text so that it is clearly recognizable as a rhetorical question: Who did all this, this, and this, and then said that?

Read the passage aloud and perhaps consult another lector or a family member if you are uncertain about how to sustain the inquiry. Practice makes perfect, and for lectors, practice means doing so aloud and with others.

READING II   The first letter of Paul to the Corinthians is well known; less frequently proclaimed is the second letter to the Corinthians, from which your proclamation comes.

The sequence of readings from this letter to the Corinthians will continue for two more Sundays. Reading all five selections will help your proclamation, so please look at the second readings from the Seventh, Eighth, Thirteenth and Fourteenth Sundays in Ordinary Time.

The depth of the apostle's words come from the link he makes between the death of Christ, the death of all, and the death of "the old things" that have passed away because

Because the passage is short, you can afford to take a significant pause at the break.

Capture the apostle's hope and strength in the tone with which you proclaim the end of the passage.

Consequently, from now on we regard **no** one according to
     the **flesh**;
   even if we once knew **Christ** according to the **flesh**,
   yet **now** we know him so no **longer**.
So **whoever** is in Christ is a **new** creation:
   the **old** things have passed **away**;
   behold, **new** things have **come**.

GOSPEL   Mark 4:35–41

A reading from the holy Gospel according to Mark

On that day, as **evening** drew on, Jesus said to his **disciples**:
   "Let us cross to the other **side**."
Leaving the crowd, they took **Jesus** with them in the **boat**
     just as he was.
And **other** boats were with him.
A violent **squall** came up and **waves** were breaking over the **boat**,
     so that it was **already** filling up.
Jesus was in the stern, **asleep** on a **cushion**.
They **woke** him and said to him,
   "**Teacher**, do you not **care** that we are **perishing**?"
He **woke** up,
   rebuked the wind, and said to the **sea**, "**Quiet**! Be **still**!"
The wind **ceased** and there was great **calm**.
Then he asked them, "**Why** are you **terrified**?
Do you **not** yet have **faith**?"
They were filled with great **awe** and said to one another,
   "Who then **is** this whom even **wind** and **sea** obey?"

Pause here before moving on.

Look directly at the assembly as you ask this question.

everything is new. Take your time as you proclaim this important text so that it can sink into the minds and hearts of the assembly.

The reading ends on a positive and hopeful note, and you might imagine these sentences ending with exclamation points: "Whoever is in Christ is a new creation!" And "Behold, new things have come!"

Most important is that you take your time. The assembly and you will be strengthened and ennobled by a strong, well-paced proclamation.

| GOSPEL | Notice that the first reading proclaimed a message to Job from the Lord in a storm; it was all about the Lord's power. This reading complements that passage both because of the context of the storm, and also because of the question it ends with: "Who then is this, that even the wind and the sea obey him?"

The first three sentences set the context, before the storm arises. Pause after "And other boats were with him." The next sentence, describing the windstorm, is a short part unto itself, and you might pause before moving on.

The three speeches—the disciples' question to Jesus, Jesus' command to the wind and sea, and Jesus' questions to the disciples—form a unit. And, finally, the last sentence provides the link with the first reading from Job. For this final line, the disciples's awestruck question, you might look into the eyes of the listeners before you as you ask: "Who then is this whom even wind and sea obey?"

13TH SUNDAY IN ORDINARY TIME

Lectionary #98

READING I   Wisdom 1:13–15; 2:23–24

A reading from the Book of Wisdom

The key to the whole reading; pause before you launch into it.

God did not make **death**,
  nor does he **rejoice** in the **destruction** of the **living**.
For he fashioned all things that they might have being;
  and the **creatures** of the world are **wholesome**,
and there is not a **destructive** drug among them
  nor any domain of the **netherworld** on earth,
  for justice is **undying**.
For God **formed** man to be **imperishable**;
  the **image** of his own nature he **made** him.
But by the envy of the **devil**, **death** entered the world,
  and they who **belong** to his company **experience** it.

This part harks back to the Creation account of Genesis.

The reading ends on a darker note.

READING II   2 Corinthians 8:7, 9, 13–15

A reading from the second Letter of Saint Paul to the Corinthians

Brothers and sisters:
As you excel in **every** respect, in **faith**, **discourse**,
  knowledge, all **earnestness**, and in the **love** we have for **you**,
  may you excel in **this** gracious act **also**.

Corinthians = kor-IN-thee-unz

If possible, look at the assembly as you address them with the second-person pronoun, "you."

READING I   As a minister of the word, your work for the community of faith is to deliver the Good News with your well prepared proclamations. At times, however, the Good News comes in a message that people will not welcome. The "good" part of such news is that believers are called to face issues that they often avoid contemplating. Such is the text you are to proclaim today. Its subject is death.

Today's Gospel is about two women who are close to death. The Church matches today's first reading with the Gospel because it too is about death.

Many people in your parish community have been touched by the dying and by death at some time. It may be hard to imagine how many have cared for someone who is dying, how many have witnessed the death of a parent, a child, a loved one. Proclaim these words of wisdom as a consoling message from God. You can do this by being direct, assertive, and compassionate in your delivery.

This assertiveness should start the proclamation, for the first sentence carries the key to the entire passage. Pause between the announcement of the book of Wisdom and the beginning of the reading so that the community is settled to receive the important opening words.

Notice that, unlike the beginning, the final words of the reading are dark. Because other elements in the reading are more hopeful, this last sentence need not be emphasized as strongly as the other parts.

READING II   Take the opening address of Paul to the members of the community at Corinth and use it as you address your assembly. This familial address

The middle portion is embraced by the social issues of the beginning and the ending.

For you know the gracious **act** of our Lord Jesus **Christ**,
    that though he was **rich**, for your sake he became **poor**,
    so that by his **poverty** you might **become** rich.
Not that **others** should have relief while you are **burdened**,
    but that as a matter of equality
    your abundance at the present time should supply **their** needs,
    so that **their** abundance may also supply **your** needs,
    that there may be **equality**.
As it is **written**:
    Whoever had **much** *did not have* **more**,
        and whoever had **little** *did not have* **less**.

The apostle encouraged the early communities to share their possessions, and in 1 Corinthians he indicts the rich in this community for not sharing with those in need.

GOSPEL   Mark 5:21 – 43

A reading from the holy Gospel according to Mark

When Jesus had crossed again in the boat
    to the other side,
    a large **crowd** gathered around him, and he stayed close
        to the **sea**.
One of the **synagogue** officials, named **Jairus**, came **forward**.
Seeing him he **fell** at his feet and pleaded **earnestly** with him,
        saying,
    "My **daughter** is at the point of **death**.
Please, **come** lay your hands on her
    that she may get **well** and **live**."
He went off with him,
    and a large crowd **followed** him and pressed **upon** him.

Here is the beginning of the story of the cure of Jairus' daughter.
synagogue = SIN-uh-gog
Jairus = JĪ-rus

---

will be more personal if you lift up your eyes and address your fellow believers directly as your "brothers and sisters," which by Baptism they are.

Notice that there is a parenthetical insertion in the middle of the first sentence. The basic structure is at the start and end: "As you excel in every respect, my you excel in this gracious act also." But after the first comma, the apostle inserts examples. In order for the complex and powerful sentence to be well received by the assembly, you should be able to make the hearers know by your voice that the inserted portion

is a list of examples. Practice it until you are able to make this clear.

In English the second-person pronoun "you" is the same in both singular and plural forms. In Greek, there is a difference. In the original text, the pronoun is plural, meaning that the apostle was addressing the community, whose members would be supportive of one another, thereby making the community greater than the sum of its parts.

This theology of Church life is fundamental. The remainder of the reading is Paul's demonstration of how such a theology of Church would be realized in day-to-day

life. Paul writes little of the life of Jesus before his Resurrection; therefore, this description of the "gracious act" is precious, and an example for members of the Church who are to support one another. The final quotation is understandable only if you have proclaimed clearly the act of Christ that Paul offers the Church through you.

GOSPEL   This passage contains an example of a clever literary device by Mark. He could have told the two stories of Jairus' daughter and the hemor-

Jesus' movement toward the daughter's healing is interrupted by what happens with the woman. This takes a big section of the text.
Hemorrhage = HEM-er-rij

There was a **woman** afflicted with **hemorrhages** for twelve **years**.
She had suffered **greatly** at the hands of many **doctors**
    and had spent all that she had.
Yet she was not **helped** but only grew **worse**.
She had heard about Jesus and came up **behind** him in the crowd
    and **touched** his **cloak**.
She said, "If I but touch his **clothes**, I shall be **cured**."
Immediately her flow of blood **dried up**.
She felt in her **body** that she was **healed** of her **affliction**.
Jesus, aware at **once** that **power** had gone **out** from him,
    turned **around** in the crowd and **asked**,
        "**Who** has touched my **clothes**?"
But his disciples said to Jesus,
    "You see how the crowd is **pressing** upon you,
    and yet you ask, 'Who **touched** me?'"
And he looked around to see who had done it.
The **woman**, realizing what had happened to her,
    approached in **fear** and **trembling**.
She fell **down** before Jesus and told him the whole **truth**.
He said to her, "**Daughter**, your **faith** has saved you.
Go in **peace** and be **cured** of your **affliction**."

Then comes the return to the first cure, as Jesus continues with Jairus toward his house.

While he was still speaking,
    people from the synagogue official's house arrived and said,
    "Your **daughter** has **died**; why trouble the **teacher** any longer?"
Disregarding the message that was reported,
    Jesus said to the synagogue **official**,
    "**Do** not be **afraid**; just have **faith**."
He did not allow **anyone** to accompany him inside
    except **Peter**, **James**, and **John**, the brother of **James**.

rhaging woman one after the other. But he fit them together in a kind of literary "sandwich," in which the story of Jairus' daughter is the bread and the story of the hemorrhaging woman is the peanut butter and jelly! The two interwoven stories deliver a much richer portrait of Jesus. That Mark intended them to play off one another is revealed by the common use of "twelve years"—the age of the daughter and the duration of the hemorrhage—and by the common use of "daughter" as the girl's relationship to Jairus and as Jesus calls the woman. These elements will help you appreciate Mark's

artistry, but they are too subtle to capture them in your proclamation.

Although the Gospel of Mark is the shortest of the four, it has some wonderful details, and these details will engage the imaginations and faith of the assembly. As you prepare, highlight the engaging descriptive elements. Recall which of these caught your imagination when you first heard the story, and emphasize these for your hearers.

To help the assembly, proclaim the phrase "synagogue official" clearly both times so that the assembly will understand when the reading shifts from the story of the

hemorrhaging woman to the the story of Jairus' daughter.

If you proclaim the full reading, recognize that it is fairly long for a Gospel in Ordinary Time. The temptation for a reader when the passage is long is to speed up. But the better alternative is to concentrate on making the narrative come alive. Here the three parts offer natural breaks. As you prepare, consider them as distinct narrative sections, and highlight within each those elements that will be most gripping for those who hear you proclaim.

When they arrived at the house of the synagogue official,
  he caught sight of a **commotion**,
  people **weeping** and wailing **loudly**.
So he went in and said to them,
  "**Why** this commotion and **weeping**?
The child is not **dead** but **asleep**."
And they **ridiculed** him.
Then he put them all out.
He took along the child's **father** and **mother**
  and those who were **with** him
  and **entered** the room where the **child** was.
He took the child by the **hand** and said to her, *"Talitha koum,"*
  which means, "**Little girl**, I say to you, **arise**!"
The **girl**, a child of **twelve**, arose **immediately** and
  walked **around**.
At that they were **utterly** astounded.
He gave strict orders that **no** one should **know** this
  and said that she should be given something to **eat**.

[Shorter: Mark 5:21–24, 35b–43]

Check the pronunciation on the foreign phrase.
Talitha koum = TAH-lee-thah KOOM

Pause before delivering the final verse.

Lectionary #101

READING I   Ezekiel 2:2–5

Ezekiel = ee-ZEE-kee-ul

The opening lines set up the context for the words that the prophet will mediate to Israel. Emphasize the advent of the spirit and setting the prophet on his feet, for its symbolic value is potent.

Israelites = IZ-ree-ul-īts

Come to a full stop at the end of the line, for there is no following message from the Lord God, as the words might suggest.

A reading from the Book of the Prophet Ezekiel

As the LORD **spoke** to me, the spirit **entered** into me
    and set me on my **feet**,
    and I heard the one who was speaking say to me:
    Son of **man**, I am **sending** you to the **Israelites**,
    rebels who have **rebelled** against me;
    they and their ancestors have **revolted** against me to this
        very **day**.
Hard of face and **obstinate** of **heart**
    are **they** to whom I am sending you.
But you shall say to them: Thus says the Lord **GOD**!
And whether they **heed** or **resist**—for they are a
        rebellious house—
    they shall **know** that a **prophet** has been **among** them.

READING I This reading has a message for you in your ministry and a significant link to today's message from the Gospel of Mark.

First, on the significance of the prophet Ezekiel's words for you and your work in the Church. The Lord called Ezekiel to prophesy to an inhospitable people, to indict the nation Israel for having ignored what the Lord had asked. He was in danger where he delivered the Lord's words, and the words were often not welcome. At times in your ministry, you have probably been assigned readings that were difficult to proclaim, sometimes because in them God calls us to a higher standard. At other times, you are assigned a reading whose words reflect a holiness that is far beyond our own. But the message is to be proclaimed no matter how you feel in delivering it.

Second, on the relation between Ezekiel's message and the passage from the Gospel of Mark. Both Ezekiel and Jesus were bearers of bad news, "bad" in the opinion of those who were uncomfortable with the truth. The words of Ezekiel and of Jesus were harsh against those who were taking advantage of the poor and abandoned, those who had forgotten the covenant with God, and those who passed their days in luxury while others suffered destitution.

In the first reading and in the Gospel, the ways these prophetic words were not welcome are clear. God tells Ezekiel, "I am sending you to . . . the hard of face and obstinate of heart," and this sets up a context for truth-telling that will be taken up in the Gospel as well, where Jesus sees that

Corinthians = kor-IN-thee-unz

The message of the passage shifts after this break, so pause to mark the transition.

Paul writes of the words he received from the Lord, and these words are key to the theology of Paul and of your proclamation.

This final verse a powerful ending of the passage. Proclaim it with strength.

READING II   2 Corinthians 12:7–10

A reading from the second Letter of Saint Paul to the Corinthians

Brothers and sisters:
That I, **Paul**, might not become too **elated**,
　　because of the **abundance** of the **revelations**,
　　a thorn in the **flesh** was **given** to me, an angel of **Satan**,
　　to **beat** me, to keep me from being too **elated**.
Three **times** I begged the Lord about this, that it might **leave** me,
　　but he said to me, "My **grace** is **sufficient** for you,
　　for **power** is made perfect in **weakness**."
I will rather boast most **gladly** of my **weaknesses**,
　　in order that the power of **Christ** may **dwell** with me.
Therefore, I am **content** with weaknesses, insults,
　　hardships, persecutions and constraints,
　　for the sake of **Christ**;
　　for when I am **weak**, then I am **strong**.

his words will not be welcome "in his native place and among his ownkin and in his own house."

READING II   Just after Christmas and Epiphany, the Church began a series of reading from Corinthians, and suspended it for Lent and Easter. Now we have returned to Paul's letters to Corinth, and by now we have moved from 1 Corinthians to 2 Corinthians, the lesser-known of the two long missives. To get a sense of the

apostle's message to this Church in the second letter, you might read the second readings from the Seventh, Eighth, Twelfth, and Thirteenth Sundays (February 19 and 26, June 25, and July 2). Familiarity with his message—to the Church then and the Church now—will strengthen your understanding and in turn your proclamation.

　　Usually the excerpts that we proclaim are compact units with a clearer beginning than we find here. The first sentence refers to revelations described elsewhere, not in this passage. Nevertheless, the main point from Paul to the Corinthians (and now to us)

is about God's love and grace that supply what we need in spite of our weakness, and that is a message that can never be repeated too often. For your ministry of the word is not from yourself, but a gift from God, as is salvation itself, wrought in the life and death of Christ.

　　The words of the Lord quoted by Paul in the middle of the passage are very important, and they set up the rhetoric for the final section. As you read the last few lines written by Paul in the first-person voice—"I am

GOSPEL Mark 6:1–6

A reading from the holy Gospel according to Mark

Jesus **departed** from there and came to his native **place**,
     accompanied by his **disciples**.
When the **sabbath** came he began to **teach** in the **synagogue**,
   and many who **heard** him were **astonished**.
They said, "Where did this man **get** all this?
What kind of **wisdom** has been given him?
What mighty **deeds** are wrought by his **hands**!
Is he not the **carpenter**, the son of **Mary**,
     and the brother of **James** and **Joses** and **Judas** and **Simon**?
And are not his **sisters** here **with** us?"
And they took **offense** at him.
Jesus said to them,
    "A **prophet** is not without **honor** except in his native **place**
     and among his own **kin** and in his own **house**."
So he was **not** able to perform any mighty **deed** there,
     apart from curing a few **sick** people by laying his **hands**
        on them.
He was **amazed** at their lack of **faith**.

---

synagogue = SIN-uh-gog

Emphasize the tension between the family of Jesus by nature and the family of Jesus by faith.
Joses =JOH-seez
Judas = JOO-dus
Simon = SI-mun

These final lines reveal how much his rejection by those in his hometown affected his ability to minister.

---

content . . . I am weak . . ."—take them to heart, for we all face such difficulties, yet by God's grace the weakness becomes our strength. Commit these to memory if you can, so that as you speak these words in the first-person voice of Paul, you can look your hearers in the eye with the conviction of faith and trust in the grace of God in our weakness.

GOSPEL Many early adherents to the faith had to leave behind their closest friends and family members. In Mark, for Jesus and those who follow him, blood connections are not the ones that endure; rather, commitment to following the will of God is what means family in this Gospel. Whenever family members appear on the scene, the evangelist has Jesus give them second place to his true followers, that is, those who follow his word.

In the Gospel of Mark, the two basic social units of Jesus' life in other Gospels, his family and his disciples, are not the ones who stay with him until the end. His closest followers hand him over, betray him, deny him, fall asleep in his most vulnerable moment. Even at the empty tomb, they run away in fear. Even his family is not cast in a good light.

For most Catholics who are baptized as infants, the family plays a formative role in the life of faith. Perhaps you can proclaim this passage more vibrantly if you imagine yourself addressing a group of inquirers in the RCIA.

15TH SUNDAY IN ORDINARY TIME

Lectionary #104

Amos = AY-m*s

READING I   Amos 7:12–15

A reading from the Book of the Prophet Amos

Amaziah, priest of **Bethel**, said to **Amos**,
  "**Off** with you, **visionary**, **flee** to the land of **Judah**!
There earn your bread by **prophesying**,
  but never **again** prophesy in **Bethel**;
  for it is the king's **sanctuary** and a royal **temple**."
Amos **answered** Amaziah, "I was no **prophet**,
  nor have I belonged to a **company** of prophets;
  I was a **shepherd** and a dresser of **sycamores**.
The LORD took me from following the flock, and said to me,
  Go, **prophesy** to my people **Israel**."

Each part introduces a speaker, followed by a message. This is the priest of the temple at Bethel, and he is throwing Amos out.
Judah = JOO-duh
Bethel = BETH-*l
Amaziah = am-uh-ZI-uh
prophesy = PROF-uh-si

The second speaker is the prophet Amos. Proclaim his message with the strength it calls for.

Israel = IZ-ree-ul

READING II   Ephesians 1:3–14

A reading from the Letter of Saint Paul to the Ephesians

Blessed be the God and **Father** of our Lord Jesus **Christ**,
  who has **blessed** us in Christ
  with every spiritual blessing in the **heavens**,
  as he **chose** us in him, before the foundation of the **world**,
  to be **holy** and without **blemish** before him.

Ephesians = ee-FEE-zhunz

READING I The message of the prophet Amos is powerful, for he tried to proclaim the Lord's words to the people of Israel during a time of military success and economic boom. Few wanted to hear the words of the Lord that he mediated, so his presence and his proclamations were not welcome. Here you will find an example of the rejection Amos received.

The reading has two parts, each with an introduction of a speaker, followed by their words. The first speaker is Amaziah, the priest of Bethel. Amos had been prophesying in the temple of Amaziah's ministry, and here Amaziah is throwing him out and telling him to get out of town."

The priest's scolding brings up some details about the prophet, for which we are glad, for we do not know much about him. His message is one of self-effacement, for he tries to tell the priest that his vocation is not of his own choosing: who, me, a prophet? "I was no prophet, nor [member of] a company of prophets." But the Lord called him from his modest occupation, as "a shepherd and a dresser of sycamores," that is, one who prunes or tends the trees. He was called to prophesy the Lord's indictments of Israel, and no one wanted to hear him.

The basic meaning here is that although our vocation is not easy sometimes, we know that the Lord's ways are smarter than our own. For this reading, you as lector can be consoled by Amos' example. Proclaim the message for those in your assembly who are called to difficult work.

Because the reading is long and filled with lofty vocabulary, take advantage of the breaks in the printed text. Pause slightly at each to catch your breath.

In **love** he destined us for **adoption** to himself
    through Jesus **Christ**,
  in accord with the **favor** of his **will**,
  for the **praise** of the glory of his **grace**
  that he **granted** us in the **beloved**.
In him we have **redemption** by his blood,
  the **forgiveness** of **transgressions**,
  in accord with the **riches** of his grace that he **lavished** upon us.
In all **wisdom** and **insight**, he has made **known** to us
  the mystery of his **will** in accord with his **favor**
  that he set **forth** in him as a **plan** for the fullness of **times**,
  to sum up **all** things in **Christ**, in **heaven** and on **earth**.

In him we were also **chosen**,
  destined in accord with the **purpose** of the One
  who **accomplishes** all things according to the **intention**
    of his will,
  so that we might exist for the praise of his **glory**,
  we who **first** hoped in **Christ**.
In him you **also**, who have heard the word of **truth**,
  the gospel of your **salvation**, and have **believed** in him,
  were **sealed** with the promised holy **Spirit**,
  which is the first **installment** of our **inheritance**
  toward **redemption** as God's **possession**, to the praise
    of his **glory**.

[Shorter: Ephesians 1:3–10]

Address this final section, written in the second-person "you," to those you. You can match the positive message of the final lines with a positive and inspiring tone for your delivery.

READING II   This reading has a long version and a short one. Check with the pastor or homilist to know which of the two versions you should prepare.

Because this reading is a hymn of praise, proclaim it at an even pace, taking advantage of the breaks in the printed Lectionary. In this opening of the letter to the Ephesians, which we will read for five weeks, the author did not go into specific details of the life of Christ, the actions of the Spirit, or even particular manifestations of God's power in creation. Rather, the passage is structured by the passage of time, covering in a philosophical reflection the past ("the foundation of the world"), the present ("we have redemption by his blood"), and the future ("the fullness of times," when all things will be summed up).

The challenge is in proclaiming such a lofty philosophical hymn of praise with enough animation to keep those who hear you engaged to the end. At the end, you can address the assembly directly in the second-person voice, "you also," regarding their faith and the Holy Spirit's role in it. You might commit this closing to memory, so that you can address your hearers intimately and directly, as you stand in Paul's place speaking to a new Church many centuries after he originally wrote these words.

GOSPEL   Mark 6:7–13

A reading from the holy Gospel according to Mark

Jesus summoned the **Twelve** and began to send them out **two**
        by **two**
    and gave them **authority** over unclean **spirits**.
He instructed them to take **nothing** for the journey
    but a **walking** stick—
    no food, no sack, no money in their belts.
They were, however, to wear **sandals**
    but **not** a second **tunic**.
He said to them,
    "Wherever you enter a house, **stay** there until you **leave**.
Whatever place does not **welcome** you or **listen** to you,
    leave there and shake the **dust** off your **feet**
    in testimony **against** them."
So they went **off** and preached **repentance**.
The Twelve drove out many **demons**,
    and they anointed with **oil** many who were **sick** and
        cured them.

These are some indications of the itinerant lifestyle of the earliest followers of Jesus. They lived as homeless wanderers, always on the move.

Pause before you begin the section with Jesus' direct instructions.

GOSPEL   In making its point, this passage has three basic purposes: first, to set a context for Jesus' teaching; then, to express this in the words of Jesus himself; and, finally, to show how the Twelve, acting on Jesus' command, ministered to many who were in need.

The ministry of Jesus' early followers was difficult and often unwelcome. For one thing, it was work for itinerants, for those who could be on the move, and, therefore, Jesus instructs them to travel light. Moveover, picking up on the issue that this Gospel shares with the message of the prophet Amos (who was thrown out of town by the local priest), Jesus warns the disciples that there will be places that will not "welcome you or listen to you."

From our point of view, centuries later, it's hard to imagine that the life of Jesus and his followers was so much on the margins of society, but this passage bears clear testimony to the way they had to live, always on the edge of rejection.

The passage ends with a brief summary of the ministry of the Twelve. This is in itself powerful, so do not deliver its concentrated message too quickly.

16TH SUNDAY IN ORDINARY TIME

Lectionary #107

READING I   Jeremiah 23:1–6

Jeremiah = jayr-uh-MĪ-uh

The reading begins with a scathing indictment of Israel's leaders.

Israel = IZ-ree-ul

The rhetoric changes significantly from this point on.

The second half of the reading is filled with consolations for a people that has seen destruction, darkness, and tragedy. As you proclaim, capture the hope in the prophet's words.

Judah = JOO-duh

A reading from the Book of the Prophet Jeremiah

Woe to the shepherds
    who **mislead** and **scatter** the flock of my **pasture**,
    says the LORD.
Therefore, thus says the LORD, the God of **Israel**,
    against the shepherds who shepherd my **people**:
You have **scattered** my sheep and **driven** them away.
You have not **cared** for them,
    but **I** will take care to **punish** your evil deeds.
I **myself** will gather the **remnant** of my flock
    from all the lands to which I have **driven** them
    and bring them back to their **meadow**;
    there they shall **increase** and **multiply**.
I will appoint shepherds for them who will **shepherd** them
    so that they need no **longer** fear and **tremble**;
    and none shall be **missing**, says the LORD.

Behold, the days are **coming**, says the LORD,
    when I will raise up a **righteous** shoot to **David**;
as king he shall **reign** and govern **wisely**,
    he shall do what is **just** and **right** in the land.
In his days **Judah** shall be **saved**,
    Israel shall dwell in **security**.
This is the **name** they give him:
    "The LORD our **justice**."

READING I   Usually readings starting with direct discourse introduce it by identifying the speaker. In the reading you prepare, however, the prophet's words begin with no introduction. After reading the text, you will appreciate why this is so for this passage from the prophet Jeremiah.

The prophet chastises shepherds who have not been good leaders of the flock. The opening word "woe" is often used in the Bible as a sign of impending doom for those who will not amend their ways. The Beatitudes in Luke, for example, are juxtaposed to indictments, and these too begin with "woe." This simple three-letter word bears great meaning in scriptural rhetoric, so be confident using it, where it is the first word.

Jeremiah lived during the tremendous crisis in the history of Israel, the Babylonian captivity, when the temple was destroyed and the people carried off in exile. His words to his people were clearly not welcome: He blamed the cataclysmic events on their misdeeds, and the reading you prepare is his indictment of the leaders of the people, those who have not cared for the people.

The dark tone of the opening is not the last word, for Jeremiah envisions the restoration of Israel under leaders who will care for the people under a righteous king, whom he describes with the metaphor of "a righteous shoot." As the text moves to a vision of the future as it progresses, so should your proclamation reflect the hope of the prophet's proclamation. You stand in his place as the minister giving hope to a people who need it.

Ephesians = ee-FEE-zhunz

This is a poignant line, so deliver it with assurance.

As you proclaim, keep in mind that this reconciliation of hostile enemies can still be realized through the cross of Christ.

The reading ends with a powerful and consoling message of peace.

READING II Ephesians 2:13–18

A reading from the Letter of Saint Paul to the Ephesians

Brothers and sisters:
In Christ **Jesus** you who once were far **off**
   have become **near** by the blood of **Christ**.

For he is our **peace**, he who made both one
   and broke down the **dividing** wall of **enmity**, through his flesh,
   abolishing the law with its **commandments** and **legal** claims,
   that he might create in himself **one new** person in place
      of the **two**,
   thus establishing **peace**,
   and might reconcile **both** with God,
   in one **body**, through the **cross**,
   putting that **enmity** to death by it.
He came and preached **peace** to you who were far **off**
   and **peace** to those who were **near**,
   for through him we **both** have access in one **Spirit** to
      the **Father**.

READING II This passage from Paul's letter to the Ephesians is the second in a series of six readings that began last week and will continue to the Twenty-first Sunday in Ordinary Time. With the *Workbook* in hand, you might look at the excerpts last week and in the weeks ahead for the theological context of the passage you prepare.

It might be difficult to imagine the seriousness of the early Church's dispute over the inclusion of non-Jews (Gentiles) in the

earliest communities. The Church offered refuge in a period of social upheaval, and many came to the fledgling communities not only for spiritual nourishment, but for "daily bread," literally. Those Christians who had followed Jewish practices all their lives, just as Jesus and the first disciples had, sought to maintain their Jewish practices even as Gentiles sought inclusion. Eventually Paul, the "apostle to the Gentiles," persuaded his fellow apostles that "the law with its commandments and ordinances" might not be enjoined on the new members.

This reading is borne of that decisive moment when these two peoples became one people in the Church, for Christ, as the reading says, "has broken down the dividing wall." We, like the early Church, are aware of the many factions and contentions in the Church today, so as you prepare, imagine that the issues of peace and reconciliation that you proclaim will indeed be efficacious in the Church today.

A reading from the holy Gospel according to Mark

The **apostles** gathered together with **Jesus**
    and reported **all** they had **done** and **taught**.
He said to them,
    "Come away by yourselves to a **deserted** place and **rest** a
        while."
People were coming and going in great numbers,
    and they had **no** opportunity even to **eat**.
So they went off in the boat by **themselves** to a deserted **place**.
People **saw** them leaving and **many** came to **know** about it.
They **hastened** there on foot from all the towns
    and **arrived** at the place **before** them.

When he **disembarked** and saw the vast **crowd**,
    his **heart** was moved with **pity** for them,
    for they were like **sheep** without a **shepherd**;
    and he began to **teach** them many things.

The final portion captures the image of the shepherd and sheep that was also in the reading from Jeremiah.

GOSPEL In last Sunday's Gospel, Jesus prepared the disciples for a mission and sent them out. The passage you prepare for today refers to that mission and then moves to the ever-present tension in Mark's Gospel between Jesus and the disciples as they run off to a deserted place and those who seek to find them. It is how we might imagine the life of many public figures today, always looking to escape the cameras and yet always found in what they thought would be a private place.

In a way we can appreciate the account from both sides. Jesus and his disciples were itinerant preachers and healers, and they required some "down time" to pray about the work they were doing. But the people wanted more contact with them, for they were preaching astonishing things that made great sense to the many poor and disenfranchised of first-century Palestine. Mark's Gospel is the one where this tension between Jesus and his friends and the crowds pursuing them is most evident.

It is not an easy text to proclaim with engagement, for it is a short passage without a conclusion. The key rhetorical part is in the final verse, about the "sheep without a shepherd," for this takes up the message your hearers have just heard in the first reading from the prophet Jeremiah.

17TH SUNDAY IN ORDINARY TIME

Lectionary #110

READING I   2 Kings 4:42–44

A reading from the second Book of Kings

Baal-shalishah = BAH-ahl shahl-ih-SHAH
Elisha = ee-LĪ-shuh

Emphasize the numbers, in the accounting of the food and in the number of people to be fed.

Practice distinguishing between the author's advance of the story, and the voices of the characters in it.

A man came from Baal-shalishah bringing to **Elisha**, the man
    of **God**,
    twenty **barley** loaves made from the **firstfruits**,
    and fresh **grain** in the **ear**.
Elisha said, "**Give** it to the people to **eat**."
But his servant **objected**,
    "How can I set this before a **hundred** people?"
Elisha insisted, "**Give** it to the people to **eat**."
For thus says the LORD,
    'They shall **eat** and there shall be some left **over**.'"
And when they had **eaten**, there **was** some left over,
    as the LORD had **said**.

This ending is short. You might linger at the commas a bit so that your listeners hear all the details of the miracle's realization.

READING II   Ephesians 4:1–6

A reading from the Letter of Saint Paul to the Ephesians

Ephesians = ee-FEE-zhunz

Brothers and sisters:
I, a **prisoner** for the Lord,
    urge you to live in a manner **worthy** of the call you have
    received,

READING I Every third summer, during Year B of the three-year Lectionary cycle, there is a span of readings from chapter 6 of the Gospel of John—for more, see the commentary on the Gospel for this day—and this span from John interrupts the sequence of Gospel readings in Year B from Mark. The narrative at the start of John 6, proclaimed today, is a multiplication sign in which loaves and fish feed a crowd of 5,000. This account from the second book of Kings is the same kind of multiplication, here at the hands of "Elisha, the man of God."

The account is only three verses long. "They shall eat and there shall be some left over," says Elisha, and then, "when they had eaten, there was some left over."

Even though the account is short, it is an engaging narrative and a strong reading to precede the Johannine multiplication account. Be mindful of its length and its important link with the Gospel to follow, so that you not proclaim too quickly. The brevity of the account gives you the chance to practice pacing your delivery. Take advantage of the natural line breaks supplied by the Lectionary. It also gives you the chance to

practice letting the members of the assembly know when you are quoting a speaker directly, as here with the words from Elisha, his servant, and from the Lord (speaking through Elisha).

READING II This passage from Paul's letter to the Ephesians continues the series of six readings from the letter that began two Sundays ago and will be continued for a few weeks after this.

These moral qualities to which Paul calls the Ephesians are always good qualities for the community of faith. Pause at each comma so that the virtues are heard clearly.

with all **humility** and **gentleness**, with **patience**,
bearing with one another through **love**,
striving to preserve the **unity** of the spirit through the **bond**
    of **peace**:
one body and **one** Spirit,
as you were also **called** to the one **hope** of your call;
one **Lord**, one **faith**, one **baptism**;
one **God** and **Father** of **all**,
who is **over** all and **through** all and **in** all.

This final section is very important to our baptismal theology centuries later.

GOSPEL   John 6:1–15

A reading from the holy Gospel according to John

The opening merely sets the scene for the work to take place.
Galilee = GAL-ih-lee

Jesus went across the Sea of **Galilee**.
A large **crowd** followed him,
    because they saw the **signs** he was performing on the **sick**.
Jesus went up on the **mountain**,
    and there he sat **down** with his **disciples**.
The Jewish feast of **Passover** was near.
When Jesus raised his **eyes**
    and saw that a large **crowd** was coming to him,
    he said to **Philip**,
    "Where can we buy enough **food** for them to eat?"
He said this to test him,
    because he himself **knew** what he was going to do.

One of the many clues in the Gospel of John of Jesus' all-knowing power.

Paul begged the Ephesians "to live in a manner worthy of the call you have received." These are powerful words, addressed to people he knew and who knew him. He would ask you also to lead a life worthy of the call by which you serve as a minister of God's word. Take his plea to heart, for your ministry of the word is indeed an august and essential work for the Church, one that calls forth the best in you.

The final part of the reading is not only a summary of the short passage, but of the

Church as a medium of God's work in the world. The faith was new when Paul wrote of the oneness of that hope of your call, the oneness of the Lord, the faith, of Baptism, and the oneness of the God and Father of all. By God's grace that unity is still a fundamental hope and object of our faith.

GOSPEL   **The Gospel of Mark is considerably shorter than the other two synoptic Gospels, Matthew and Luke. As you know, each of the liturgical**

years A, B, and C focuses on one of the synoptic Gospels, but because Mark is so short, there is not quite enough text to be stretched over the two spans of Ordinary Time between the end of the Christmas season and Ash Wednesday and between Pentecost and the First Sunday of Advent.

A four-year cycle was seriously considered at the time of the renewal of the Lectionary after the Second Vatican Council so that there would be a year dedicated

Simon = SĪ-mun

Emphasize the details of the numbers: five loaves of bread pluse two fish for 5,000 people!

Philip **answered** him,
   "Two hundred days' **wages** worth of food would not
     be enough
   for **each** of them to have a **little**."
One of his disciples,
   Andrew, the brother of Simon **Peter**, said to him,
   "There is a **boy** here who has five **barley** loaves and two **fish**;
   but what good are **these** for so many?"
Jesus said, "Have the people **recline**."
Now there was a great deal of **grass** in that place.
So the men **reclined**, about five **thousand** in number.
Then Jesus took the **loaves**, gave **thanks**,
   and **distributed** them to those who were **reclining**,
   and also as much of the **fish** as they **wanted**.
When they had had their **fill**, he said to his **disciples**,
   "Gather the **fragments** left over,
   so that **nothing** will be wasted."
So they collected them,
   and filled twelve wicker **baskets** with fragments
   from the five **barley** loaves
   that had been **more** than they could **eat**.
When the people **saw** the sign he had done, they said,
   "This is **truly** the **Prophet**, the one who is to come
     into the **world**."
Since Jesus **knew** that they were going to come and carry him **off**
   to make him **king**,
   he **withdrew** again to the mountain **alone**.

to the Fourth Gospel, but in the end the Council's theologians thought that John would best be proclaimed in the paschal seasons of Lent and Easter, so the Gospel of John did not get a year of its own. The long chapter 6 of John, which narrates a multiplication miracle and a rich theology of the Eucharist, was inserted into the middle of Year B to fill out the year dedicated to the shortest synoptic Gospel. Today is the first time that this insertion of John 6 appears.

Not only are the actions here the same as at the sacrificial meal of the Last Supper as described in Matthew, Mark, and Luke, but the same as in Paul's account of the Eucharist in 1 Corinthians 11:23–26. Because the Gospel of John does not have a Last Supper narrative, the multiplication sign is the locus of John's eucharistic theology. The verb for "gave thanks" is *eucharisteo,* the root of our sacrament of the Eucharist.

TRANSFIGURATION OF THE LORD

Lectionary #614

READING I   Daniel 7:9–10, 13–14

A reading from the book of the Prophet Daniel

As I **watched**:

Thrones were set up
  and the **Ancient** One took his **throne**.
His **clothing** was snow bright,
  and the **hair** on his head as **white** as **wool**;
his **throne** was flames of **fire**,
  with wheels of **burning** fire.
A surging **stream** of fire
  flowed **out** from where he **sat**;
Thousands upon **thousands** were **ministering** to him,
  and **myriads** upon **myriads attended** him.
The court was **convened** and the books were **opened**.

As the **visions** during the night **continued**, I saw
  One like a Son of **man** coming,
    on the clouds of **heaven**;
When he reached the **Ancient** One
  and was **presented** before him,
The **one** like a Son of man received **dominion**, **glory**,
    and **kingship**;
  all peoples, nations, and languages **serve** him.
His **dominion** is an **everlasting** dominion
  that shall not be taken **away**,
  his **kingship** shall not be **destroyed**.

Because the passage is so powerful and full of detail, take a brief pause after each sentence and a longer pause at the break in the printed text.

These numbers are signs of universality.

This Old Testament figure is seen in the Christian tradition as an allusion to Christ.

The final verse reveals what God bestows on Christ, and it is a reign of cosmic proportions. Proclaim it boldly.

READING I   Daniel is one of the four major prophets of the Old Testament, (the others are Isaiah, Jeremiah and Ezekiel). Of these, the Lectionary offers us a great deal from Isaiah, and only a little from Daniel.

The reading you have been assigned is powerful, stunning with its imagery for the feast of the Transfiguration. We seldom hear the readings for the Transfiguration because it is not an obligatory feast. However, when it falls on a Sunday in Ordinary Time, it takes precedence. That is why we are honored with its readings today rather than those for the Eighteenth Sunday in Ordinary Time.

Notice that the passage is cast in the first-person singular voice. Therefore, you stand in the prophet's place. Be bold. Be prophetic as you take up the prophet's vision for your parish.

The literary form of this reading is "apocalyptic," that is, writings that anticipate the end of time. This passage is part of the vision of the Ancient One, and Daniel portrays him with engaging details.

Most readings in the Lectionary call up familiar images: sheep and shepherds, vines and branches, masters and servants. This reading takes up much less familiar images of the scriptural tradition, appearing only in Daniel and the book of Revelation.

The first step in your preparation, therefore, is to prepare your imagination. Read the fascinating portrait of the Ancient One that we received from the prophet, and imagine how Daniel saw him. If you imagine the scene vividly, you will be able to proclaim it vibrantly.

The first- and second-person plural pronouns—"we," "our," "ourselves," "you," and "your"—can be adopted by you and proclaimed anew to the Church before you.

Pause slightly before you deliver this line so that the assembly is poised to recognize the link with the narrative of Jesus' own Baptism.

These final images of light—lamp shining, day dawns, and star rises—are wonderful. Proclaim them forthrightly and clearly.

READING II   2 Peter 1:16–19

A reading from the second Letter of Saint Peter.

Beloved:
We did **not** follow cleverly devised **myths**
    when we made **known** to you
    the **power** and **coming** of our Lord Jesus **Christ**,
    but we had been **eyewitnesses** of his **majesty**.
For he received **honor** and **glory** from God the **Father**
    when that **unique** declaration **came** to him from the
        majestic **glory**,
    "**This** is my **Son**, my **beloved**, with whom I am well **pleased**."
We **ourselves** heard this voice come from **heaven**
    while we were **with** him on the holy **mountain**.
Moreover, we **possess** the prophetic **message**
    that is altogether **reliable**.
You will do **well** to be attentive to it,
    as to a **lamp** shining in a dark **place**,
    until day **dawns** and the morning star **rises** in your **hearts**.

READING II The clearest relation between the three readings is usually between the first and the third readings, but today the second reading complements the others perfectly. Christ's "honor and glory from God the Father" complements the end of the first reading, and the mention of "holy mountain" leads to the Gospel, where Peter, James, and John are led up a "high mountain" by Jesus for the Transfiguration.

The first and third readings mention white garments, and the second reading reminds us of Baptism, quoting from the synoptics' narratives of Jesus' own Baptism, when the voice from heaven said, "This is my Son, my beloved, with whom I am well pleased."

These three readings, with their baptismal images and sayings, is fitting for this feast of the Transfiguration, for the power of the Holy Spirit is at work whenever inquirers are drawn to the Church and whenever the baptized are called to conversion, transformation, transfiguration. The Fifty Days from Easter Sunday to Pentecost are long past now, but echoes of the Easter season abound on the Transfiguration. Let your proclamation make these echoes vivid on this feast.

GOSPEL For centuries the narrative of the Transfiguration has been part of the liturgy of the word during Lent, when the catechumens are in their final stage of formation for Baptism and when the already baptized pare away the sinful accretions that have interfered with the realization of God's love in their lives and in the world. For both catechumens and

Theophanies often take place on a high mountain.

Stress the evangelist's details here.

Elijah = ee-LĪ-juh
Moses = MOH-ziz

Emphasize the words from the cloud, for they echo the words from above that were heard at the baptism of Jesus.

GOSPEL   Mark 9:2 – 10

A reading from the holy Gospel according to Mark

Jesus took **Peter**, **James**, and **John**
    and led them up a high **mountain** apart by **themselves**.
And he was **transfigured** before them,
    and his **clothes** became dazzling **white**,
    such as no **fuller** on earth could **bleach** them.
Then **Elijah** appeared to them along with **Moses**,
    and they were **conversing** with Jesus.
Then Peter said to Jesus in **reply**,
    "**Rabbi**, it is **good** that we are here!
Let us make three **tents**:
    one for **you**, one for **Moses**, and one for **Elijah**."
He **hardly** knew what to say, they were so **terrified**.
Then a **cloud** came, casting a **shadow** over them;
    from the cloud came a **voice**,
    "**This** is my beloved **Son**. **Listen** to him."
Suddenly, looking around, they no **longer** saw anyone
        but **Jesus** alone with them.

As they were coming **down** from the **mountain**,
    he charged them not to relate what they had seen
        to **anyone**,
    except when the Son of **Man** had risen from the **dead**.
So they kept the matter to **themselves**,
    questioning what rising from the **dead** meant.

---

penitents Lent is a time of transformation.

The Gospel of Mark was written about a half-century after the Resurrection, so its stories of Jesus reflect both traditions about the life of Jesus and the traditions of the earliest Christian communities, who saw in the life of Jesus an inspiration for the hardships they faced in their own lives of faith.

The three accounts of the Transfiguration in the synoptic Gospels all depict Jesus in shining white, but each of the evangelists describes this with different words (although many translations don't reflect that). For

Matthew his clothes were "white as light," for Luke "dazzling white," and here in Mark, they were "dazzling . . . as no fuller on earth could bleach them."

The narrative here has four basic parts: the Transfiguration with the apostles nearby, the appearance of Elijah and Moses and Peter's words, the voice from the cloud, and finally the descent and Jesus' command that they tell no one what took place. The Lectionary text offers breaks after each of these parts of the narratives, so pause at each break to mark the transition. If possible, emphasize the baptismal elements, the

garments in part one and the voice from the cloud in part three. The words of the voice from the cloud is not a direct quote from the account of Jesus' Baptism, but many in the congregation will be reminded of it.

The engaging actions of the first three parts are not carried through into the fourth part, which ends with the disciples' silence and puzzlement. Be prepared for this soft ending of a powerful account.

19TH SUNDAY IN ORDINARY TIME

Lectionary #116

READING I   1 Kings 19:4–8

A reading from the first Book of Kings

Elijah = ee-LĪ-juh

Elijah went a day's **journey** into the **desert**,
  until he came to a **broom** tree and sat **beneath** it.
He prayed for **death** saying:
  "This is **enough**, O LORD!
Take my **life**, for I am no better than my **fathers**."
He lay **down** and fell **asleep** under the **broom** tree,
  but then an **angel** touched him and **ordered** him
    to get **up** and **eat**.
Elijah **looked** and there at his **head** was a **hearth** cake
  and a jug of **water**.
After he ate and drank, he lay **down** again,
  but the angel of the LORD came back a **second** time,
  touched him, and **ordered**,
  "Get up and eat, else the **journey** will be too **long** for you!"
He got **up**, **ate**, and **drank**;
  then **strengthened** by that food,
  he walked forty **days** and forty **nights** to the mountain
    of God, **Horeb**.

Elijah's plea is dramatic, so take advantage of it. Pause after his plea.

The same command, but this time with some angelic sympathy for the prophet.

Emphasize this familiar time element.
Horeb = HOH-reb

READING I Even dedicated readers of the scriptures can get bogged down in the historical books because they are at times formidably detailed and filled with unfamiliar characters. The account that you are preparing to proclaim is delightful, however, so put your best narrative skills to work for your fellow believers.

The reading has three parts, all leading in the same direction. Each of the three parts is punctuated with a speech: first as Elijah prays for death and twice as an angel wakes him up and orders him to eat.

Because the Gospel reading is about Jesus' statement that "I am the bread of life," emphasize the words about food and the strength that Elijah found in that food.

READING II This passage from Paul's letter to the Ephesians continues the series of six readings from the letter that began at the Fifteenth Sunday in Ordinary Time and continues for two Sundays more.

Although we do not know all the details of the initiation rites in use when the letters of the New Testament were written, there are clues and remnants of associations among the writings, the theology, and the rituals. Here you find one such remnant at the start of the reading: the "Holy Spirit of God, with which you were sealed." It is a tiny clue, but compelling, so do not rush past it. Though the printed text does not insert a

Ephesians = ee-FEE-zhunz

READING II   Ephesians 4:30—5:2

A reading from the Letter of Saint Paul to the Ephesians

Brothers and sisters:
Do not **grieve** the Holy Spirit of **God**,
   with which you were **sealed** for the day of **redemption**.
All bitterness, fury, anger, shouting, and reviling
   must be **removed** from you, along with all **malice**.
And be **kind** to one another, **compassionate**,
   forgiving one another as God has forgiven **you** in **Christ**.

So be imitators of **God**, as beloved **children**, and live in **love**,
   as Christ loved **us** and handed himself over for **us**
   as a sacrificial **offering** to God for a fragrant **aroma**.

Pause here to mark the transition from the theological to the ethical imperatives.

These last imperatives are wonderful, and they are complemented by the example of Christ himself.

GOSPEL   John 6:41–51

A reading from the holy Gospel according to John

The Jews **murmured** about Jesus because he said,
   "**I am** the bread that came **down** from **heaven**,"
and they said,
   "Is this not **Jesus**, the son of **Joseph**?
Do we not **know** his **father** and **mother**?
Then how can he say,
   'I have come down from **heaven**'?"
Jesus answered and said to them,
   "Stop **murmuring** among yourselves.

There is little movement in the reading, so take advantage of the adversarial exchange that sets up the rest.

From this point to the end, the whole passage is the spoken words of Jesus. Take your time, for the eucharistic theology is deep and rich.

break at the end of that sentence, it is a natural place to pause before moving on.

The next two verses are ethical encouragements to the Ephesians, first listing the things that they must put aside, and then encouraging them toward the good. The final two verses are packed with lovely imperatives—"be imitators of God!" and "live in love!"—that you can proclaim with great conviction, and these are complemented by the example of Christ himself.

The passage you prepare is compact and quite beautiful. Proclaim it well for the inspiration of the Church.

GOSPEL The Gospel of John bears some deep and complex theological ideas in deceptively simple forms. One of these simple forms is found in the "I am" statements that appear only in

this Gospel: "I am the light of the world," "I am the gate for the sheep," "I am the good shepherd," "I am the Resurrection and the life," "I am the way, the truth, and the life," and "I am the vine, you are the branches."

Those instances were in the Gospels for the Easter season, and you will find more of these "I am" sayings in the Gospel passage for today: "I am the bread that came down from heaven," "I am the bread of life," and "I am the living bread that came down

No one can come to me unless the Father who sent me **draw** him,
 and I will **raise** him on the last **day**.
It is written in the **prophets**:
 They shall all be taught by **God**.
Everyone who **listens** to my Father and **learns** from him **comes**
  to me.
Not that anyone has **seen** the Father
 except the one who is from God;
 he has seen the **Father**.
Amen, amen, I **say** to you,
 whoever **believes** has eternal **life**.
I am the bread of **life**.
Your **ancestors** ate the **manna** in the **desert**, but they **died**;
 this is the bread that comes down from **heaven**
 so that one may eat it and **not** die.
I am the **living** bread that came **down** from heaven;
 whoever **eats** this bread will live **forever**;
  and the **bread** that I will **give** is my **flesh** for the life
   of the **world**."

Again, pause at the break, this time to highlight Jesus' words, "I am the bread of life."

from heaven." These are part of Jesus' reflections on the multiplication he had just done (in the text before this excerpt), and this reflection is the foundation for much of the Church's theology of the Eucharist still today.

 Notice that all but three of the lines of the reading are words from Jesus or the people complaining about him. Therefore, be clear as you identify the speakers. The last two-thirds of the text is from the lips of Jesus, so take your time with his words and emphasize the "I am" sayings.

ASSUMPTION OF THE BLESSED VIRGIN MARY: VIGIL

Lectionary #621

READING I   1 Chronicles 15:3–4, 15–16; 16:1–2

Chronicles = KRAH-nih-k*ls

This reading has three parts, story–description–story. The first part of the story appears at the start.
Israel = IZ-ree-ul
Jerusalem = juh-ROO-suh-lem
Aaron = AIR-un
Levites = LEE-vīts
Moses = MOH-ziz

Then comes the descriptive section about the setting for the ark, how it was brought in, and the ritual actions of the assembly as the ark was set in place.
lyre = līr

The last section finishes the story, returning to the ark and its setting among the people.

A reading from the first Book of Chronicles

David assembled all **Israel** in **Jerusalem** to bring the **ark**
    of the LORD
      to the place that he had **prepared** for it.
David **also** called together the sons of **Aaron** and the **Levites**.

The **Levites** bore the ark of God on their **shoulders** with **poles**,
    as **Moses** had **ordained** according to the word of the LORD.

David commanded the **chiefs** of the **Levites**
    to appoint their **kinsmen** as **chanters**,
    to play on musical **instruments**, **harps**, **lyres**, and **cymbals**,
    to make a loud **sound** of **rejoicing**.

They **brought** in the ark of God and set it within the **tent**
    which David had **pitched** for it.
Then they offered up burnt **offerings** and **peace** offerings to God.
When David had **finished** offering up the burnt offerings
    and peace offerings,
    he **blessed** the people in the **name** of the LORD.

READING I This passage is part of a long summary in 1 Chronicles of the reign of King David. The attention that David gave to the ark of the covenant contributes to the Jewish and Christian remembrance of him as caretaker of worship and promulgator of temple traditions.

The link between this reading and the solemnity of the Assumption might be obscure, so your confident proclamation would be helped by appreciating the ark as the center of Israel's worship. This focus on the ark, which held the stone tablets of the Ten Commandments, as the locus of the covenant between God and Israel was adopted by the Christian tradition as a precedent for its focus on Mary's womb as the locus of the incarnate life of Jesus Christ. The covenant is an alliance with God, sealed in blood, a symbol that establishes a real relationship. And so it is with Mary, the icon of God's salvation wrought in the Messiah.

The Litany of the Blessed Virgin Mary is a well-known part of Catholic popular devotion, and one of the titles accorded Mary in the Litany is "Ark of the Covenant." This is probably what led the Church to place this reading from 1 Chronicles on the feast of the Assumption.

READING II The theological tradition about the Assumption of Mary is that Mary was exempt from the pain of death because of her holiness. The passage from Paul's first letter to the Corinthians is fitting because Mary, who was without sin, was spared the wages of sin.

Note that the Corinthians passage, indeed the whole letter, has nothing explicit about the Mother of God; the theology of Mary developed centuries later. In a way,

Corinthians = kor-IN-thee-unz

Address this directly to the assembly before you, your "brothers and sisters" in Christ.

Be careful to pronounce the word "immortality" clearly and correctly.

Pause before and after the text in italics. The questions are directed to "death."

READING II 1 Corinthians 15:54b–57

A reading from the first Letter of Saint Paul to the Corinthians

Brothers and sisters:
When that which is **mortal** clothes itself with **immortality**,
 then the **word** that is **written** shall come **about**:
 *Death is swallowed up in **victory**.*
 ***Where**, O death, is your **victory**?*
 ***Where**, O death, is your **sting**?*
The sting of **death** is sin,
 and the **power** of sin is the **law**.
But thanks be to **God** who gives **us** the victory
 through our **Lord** Jesus **Christ**.

GOSPEL Luke 11:27–28

This entire Gospel passage is a brief exchange between a woman and Jesus. Pause after identifying the Gospel of Luke.

Pause again before the woman's words and before Jesus' reply.

A reading from the holy Gospel according to Luke

While **Jesus** was **speaking**,
 a **woman** from the **crowd called** out and said to him,
 "Blessed is the womb that **carried** you
 and the **breasts** at which you **nursed**."
He replied,
 "**Rather**, **blessed** are those
 who **hear** the word of God and **observe** it."

the proclamation of this passage makes its message as applicable to the Church today as to the Blessed Virgin Mary. Paul mentions the mother of Jesus only once in his body of letters, in the letter to the Galatians. And there she is not even mentioned by name: "God sent his Son, born of a woman, born under the law." But by the time of the Gospel of Luke, the narrative tradition about Mary had grown, and yet later, the Council of Ephesus defined her as the Mother of God. This development of the doctrine of Mary reminds us that the Church is ever growing, ever learning from its experience of living

the Christian life together. Your ministry of the word in the assembly contributes to that growth and experience.

GOSPEL Luke, in presenting the indispensable role of Mary as the icon of election within God's Chosen People, sees her as a model and prototype of all believers who hear the Word and keep it. For you, a minister of the word in the Church, this can be a message of congratulations and support, a rallying cry to let you know how essential for salvation are the

word and those who proclaim the word.

Note that in Luke Jesus does not say, "Blessed are those who *read* the word," but "Blessed are those who *hear* the word." In the liturgical tradition, the sensory experience of the liturgy of the word has always been primary. We might study the scriptures in the quiet of our homes in preparation for the Sunday liturgy or in a school of theology in preparation for ministry, but study is not the privileged experience in our tradition. The privileged experience of the word in the Church is found in proclaiming and hearing.

ASSUMPTION OF THE BLESSED VIRGIN MARY

Lectionary #622

READING I   Revelation 11:19a; 12:1–6a, 10ab

A reading from the Book of Revelation

The reading has three parts. The first is a short beginning that sets up the apocalyptic vision.

The second part is the vision, and it occupies most of the reading. This part describes the woman, then the dragon, and the woman and her son. This is the part that will take the most practice in your preparation.

God's **temple** in heaven was **opened**,
  and the ark of his **covenant** could be seen in the temple.

A great sign appeared in the **sky**, a **woman** clothed with the **sun**,
  with the **moon** beneath her **feet**,
  and on her **head** a crown of twelve **stars**.
She was with **child** and wailed aloud in **pain** as she **labored**
      to give **birth**.
Then **another** sign appeared in the sky;
  it was a huge red **dragon**, with **seven** heads and ten **horns**,
  and on its heads were seven **diadems**.
Its **tail** swept away a third of the **stars** in the sky
  and hurled them down to the **earth**.
Then the dragon **stood** before the woman about to give **birth**,
  to **devour** her child when she gave birth.
She gave **birth** to a son, a **male** child,
  destined to rule all the **nations** with an iron rod.
Her child was **caught** up to **God** and his **throne**.
The woman **herself** fled into the **desert**
  where she had a place **prepared** by God.

READING I   The book of Revelation has been at times ignored and at other times studied too closely. Between the sixteenth century (1570) and Vatican II (1962–1965), the book was rarely proclaimed in the Sacred Liturgy, yet many groups over the centuries who thought that the world was soon coming to an end have studied each syllable of the book, often to erroneous and dangerous ends. What can keep the book from being either forgotten or taken too literally is the regular proclamation of it in the assembly and sound preaching on it. For this your ministry is central.

As you prepare for this proclamation, you might experiment with different styles for one that suits such an apocalyptic image. You do not want to be so dramatic as to have young children flee to the parking lot, but you also do not was to be so understated as to obscure the terrible beauty of the text. You might try a few different methods of proclaiming this reading with a friends, family member, or fellow lector to find a good voice for your proclamation.

The passage was not written about Mary, but through the centuries the tradition has applied the "woman about to give birth" to the historical figure of Jesus' mother,

The last part starts at the first-person "Then I heard a loud voice . . ." Here you can speak with confidence as the one who has heard the voice. The "now" of this last verse tells us that this saving narrative is not something of the past, but that the "kingdom of our God" and the "authority of his Anointed One" are still at work. Bring this to life with your proclamation.

Then I heard a loud **voic**e in heaven say:
"**Now** have **salvation** and power come,
    and the **kingdom** of our **God**
    and the **authority** of his **Anointed** One."

READING II   1 Corinthians 15:20—27

Corinthians = kor-IN-thee-unz

A reading from the first Letter of Saint Paul to the Corinthians

You address the assembly before you as "brothers and sisters" as Paul addressed his letter to Corinth.

Brothers and sisters:
Christ has been **raised** from the **dead**,
    the **firstfruits** of those who have fallen **asleep**.
For since **death** came through man,
    the **resurrection** of the dead came **also** through man.
For just as in **Adam** all **die**,
    so **too** in **Christ** shall all be brought to **life**,
    but each one in proper **order**:
    Christ the **firstfruits**;
    then, at his coming, those who **belong** to Christ;
    then comes the **end**,
    when he hands **over** the Kingdom to his God and **Father**,
    when he has **destroyed** every **sovereignty**
    and every **authority** and **power**.
For he must **reign** until he has put all his **enemies** under his feet.
The **last** enemy to be destroyed is **death**,
    for "he subjected **everything** under his **feet**."

Here is the key line of Paul's argument: "in Christ shall all be brought to life."

The reading finishes with this cosmic vision of Christ.

Mary. That tradition is what brings this reading to the Lectionary for this day.

READING II The Church's dogma of the Assumption doesn't say whether Mary died or not. Pope Pius XII left that an open question. Most theologians say she did depart from this life (the Dormition)

but that her death was a peaceful transformation and glorification, without the "punitive" and bitter character that death has for the rest of humanity. For this reason, the passage from Paul's first letter to the Corinthians is fitting because Mary, who was without sin, was spared the wages of sin.

First Corinthians supports the theological tradition about Mary's sinlessness, even though she is not mentioned in the passage.

God kept Mary from sin, so this celebration is one of God's life in humanity, and as Mary was saved from sin and death by God's grace, so does God rescue all believers from sin.

Paul's letter here has nothing explicit about the Mother of God. The theology of Mary developed centuries later, but in a way this theology of this text is as applicable to the Church today as to the Blessed Virgin

GOSPEL   Luke 1:39–56

A reading from the holy Gospel according to Luke

Mary set out
  and traveled to the **hill** country in **haste**
  to a town of **Judah**,
  where she entered the house of **Zechariah**
  and greeted **Elizabeth**.
When Elizabeth heard Mary's **greeting**,
  the infant **leaped** in her womb,
  and **Elizabeth**, filled with the Holy **Spirit**,
  cried out in a loud voice and **said**,
  "**Blessed** are you among **women**,
  and **blessed** is the fruit of your **womb**.
And how does this happen to **me**,
  that the mother of my Lord should come to me?
For at the moment the sound of your **greeting** reached my **ears**,
  the **infant** in my womb **leaped** for joy.
Blessed are you who believed
  that what was **spoken** to you by the Lord
  would be **fulfilled**."

And Mary said:
  "My **soul** proclaims the **greatness** of the Lord;
    my spirit **rejoices** in God my **Savior**
    for he has looked upon his lowly **servant**.
  From this day all **generations** will call me **blessed**:
    the **Almighty** has done great **things** for me,
    and **holy** is his **Name**.
  He has **mercy** on those who **fear** him
    in every generation.

The opening sets two scenes; the first is the description of Mary's journey.
Judah = J<u>OO</u>-duh

Zechariah = zek-uh-RI-uh

The second scene is the greeting of the two women. Linger over this part, for it is a tender scene.

This verse contributed to the traditional prayer, the Hail Mary, so proclaim this sentence with clarity. Pause after "the fruit of your womb" before you continue.

Take a significant break after Elizabeth's proclamation ends, for there are only three words of transition from Elizabeth's words to Mary's: "And Mary said."

This praise hymn of Mary is very important in the liturgical tradition; pause at each break in the printed text.

Mary. (Paul mentions the mother of Jesus only once in his body of letters, in the Letter to the Galatians. And there she is not even mentioned by name: "God sent his Son, born of a woman, born under the law.") But the time of the Gospel of Luke the narrative tradition about Mary had grown, and the Council of Ephesus later defined her as the Mother of God. This development of the doctrine of Mary reminds us that the Church is ever growing, ever learning from its experience of Christian life together.

Your ministry of the word in the assembly contributes to that growth and experience. The theology of death, of which Mary is an example to all believers, is a key aspect of the Church's teaching and of your proclamation on this solemnity.

GOSPEL This proclamation has three parts: a narrative about the visitation, a proclamation of Elizabeth about Mary and her child, and a canticle from Mary. The three parts are wrapped up by the final summary verse: "Mary remained with her about three months and then returned to her home."

The narrative describes the women's meeting and the leaping of Elizabeth's child (John the Baptist) in her womb at Mary's

Abraham = AY-bruh-ham

Pause at the end of Mary's hymn before closing the passage with the narrative summary.

He has shown the **strength** of his **arm**,
　　and has **scattered** the proud in their **conceit**.
He has cast down the **mighty** from their **thrones**,
　　and has **lifted up** the lowly.
He has filled the **hungry** with **good** things,
　　and the **rich** he has sent away **empty**.
He has come to the **help** of his servant **Israel**
　　for he has **remembered** his promise of **mercy**,
　　the promise he made to our **fathers**,
　　to **Abraham** and his children for **ever**."

Mary **remained** with her about **three months**
　　and then returned to her **home**.

greeting. Although this scene with Mary and her relative Elizabeth appears in only one Gospel, it has shaped Christian tradition immensely; it has been rendered in art frequently over the centuries. Few museums with collections of European art would be without at least one painting of the scene depicted in this Gospel for the solemnity of the Assumption.

The esteem that the Church has accorded the text here—one passage contributing to the Hail Mary ("Blessed are you among women and blessed is the fruit of your womb") and another to the canticle sung at Vespers (Evening Prayer) every day (the Magnificat)—cannot be overestimated. The challenge as you proclaim is to have the assembly catch the familiarity of these passages yet also hear them anew.

This is a long Gospel reading. As you prepare, recognize and mark the different movements in the text. If you can anticipate where the account will move the assembly, your confidence will contribute to a good proclamation. Take your time. Be confident without being dramatic.

20TH SUNDAY IN ORDINARY TIME

Lectionary #119

READING I   Proverbs 9:1–6

A reading from the Book of Proverbs

The pronouns "she" and "her" refer to the personified wisdom.

Wisdom has built her **house**,
    she has set up her seven **columns**;
she has **dressed** her meat, **mixed** her wine,
    yes, she has spread her **table**.
She has sent out her **maidens**; she calls
    from the **heights** out over the **city**:

This invitation to "whoever is simple" is a little stiff. Lighten it with a warm delivery.

This verse is connects this reading to the Gospel, so emphasize it in your reading.

"Let **whoever** is **simple** turn in **here**";
    to the one who lacks **understanding**, she says,
"**Come**, eat of my **food**,
    and drink of the **wine** I have **mixed**!
Forsake **foolishness** that you may **live**;
    advance in the way of **understanding**."

READING II   Ephesians 5:15–20

Ephesians = ee-FEE-zhunz

Address those before you as your own "brothers and sisters" in Christ, for by Baptism that is who they are. If you can do it comfortably, make eye contact as you deliver this address.

A reading from the Letter of Saint Paul to the Ephesians

Brothers and sisters:
Watch **carefully** how you **live**,
    not as **foolish** persons but as **wise**,
    making the **most** of the opportunity,
    because the days are **evil**.

READING I The book of Proverbs is one of the wisdom books of the Old Testament, one of those collections of sage advice for the people of Israel. The passage that you prepare is about the life of wisdom. And this is quite literal, for in the passage wisdom is personified as a woman, a woman who has built her house and sends out servants to invite people into that home.

Theologians of the Gospels have supposed that Jesus himself, when texts speak of him as all-knowing, is a fulfillment of this personified wisdom from the Old Testament. In the Gospels we find Jesus telling stories in which the characters do much as wisdom does here, sending out servants to bring in all takers of his hospitality.

This passage is matched to a passage from the Gospel of John in which Jesus also speaks of bread and wine. Because of this, be most clear as you proclaim wisdom's invitation: "Come, eat of my food and drink of the wine I have mixed."

Notice that the six lines after the first (in which wisdom is identified as the house-builder) all begin with the pronoun "she," referring to wisdom. Because the role of women in many biblical passages is not so clear, proclaim this description of wisdom with confidence and conviction.

READING II Notice that the verbs of the passage are commands to the readers or hearers, orderig them to act

Be careful with this long sentence.

Therefore, do not continue in **ignorance**,
  but try to **understand** what is the will of the **Lord**.
And do not get drunk on **wine**, in which lies **debauchery**,
  but be filled with the **Spirit**,
  addressing one another in **psalms** and **hymns** and
    spiritual **songs**,
  singing and **playing** to the Lord in your **hearts**,
  giving thanks **always** and for **everything**
  in the name of our Lord **Jesus** Christ to God the **Father**.

GOSPEL   John 6:51–58

A reading from the holy Gospel according to John

On these "I am" statements of the Gospel of John, see the Introduction.

Jesus said to the **crowds**:
  "I am the **living** bread that came down from **heaven**;
  whoever **eats** this bread will live **forever**;
  and the bread that **I** will give
  is my **flesh** for the life of the **world**."

Pause before and after this description of those disputing and their question about Jesus' extraordinary claim.

The Jews **quarreled** among themselves, saying,
  "How can this man give us his **flesh** to eat?"
Jesus said to them,
  "Amen, amen, I **say** to you,
  unless you **eat** the flesh of the Son of **Man** and **drink** his **blood**,
  you **do** not have life **within** you.

The theology of the Eucharist is drawn from these words of Jesus in John. Proclaim them in their sacramental richness and beauty.

Whoever **eats** my flesh and **drinks** my blood
  has **eternal** life,
  and I will **raise** him on the last **day**.

(or not act) in certain ways: "watch carefully," "do not continue," "try to understand," "do not get drunk," "be filled with the Spirit." This last command is a wonderful way for you to engage your listeners, particularly those who serve in music ministry. The imperative is to "be filled with the Spirit," but the clear result of being Spirit-filled is singing psalms and hymns, making music, and giving thanks.

Notice that the second half of the reading is one sentence. Because the first line of that second half is negative, describing what

dfshould *not* be done, you can treat the comma after "debauchery" as if it were a period. Pause before you counter the negative with the positive encouragement of the faithful.

Proclaim these imperatives, especially those in the second half, as your own ministry encouraging your peers to participate in the active worship of giving thanks by singing. But be prepared for the length of the encouragement, and know ahead of time how you will maintain vocal variety so that the sentence will not sound laborious.

GOSPEL   Year B is the year of the Gospel of Mark, but Mark is the shortest of the four. The Gospel of John does not have a liturgical year dedicated to it, but its high Christology is appropriate to the seasons of Lent and the Easter season, where the Church places many passages from the fourth Gospel. The brevity of Mark's Gospel offers space for four readings from chapter 6 of the Gospel of John, where there is a wonderful theology of the Eucharist. The Gospel proclamation that you prepare is one of these passages from chapter 6 of the Gospel of John.

Pause for emphasis before this last line.

For my **flesh** is true **food**,
    and my **blood** is true **drink**.
Whoever eats my **flesh** and drinks my **blood**
    remains in me and I in **him**.
Just as the living Father sent **me**
    and I have life **because** of the Father,
    so also the one who **feeds** on me
    will have life **because** of me.
This is the bread that came down from **heaven**.
Unlike your **ancestors** who ate and still died,
    whoever eats **this** bread will live **forever**."

The passage interjects a question from the people, but nearly all the rest is the words from Jesus, in which he speaks of those who eat his flesh and drink his blood. As baptized Christians, we are not as astonished at these words as those who originally heard them must have been. As you prepare for this reading, imagine how those original followers of Christ might have felt as they heard this. We have the advantage of long-developed eucharistic theology to help us understand and appreciate what Jesus means here, but that developed theology is a fruit of a passage such as this and centuries of reflection on it.

Much of the passage is Jesus' words speaking of himself, employing the first-person: "I am the living bread," "I will raise him," and "I have life because of the Father." Proclaim these extraordinary words of Jesus boldly, capturing the high theology of the Eucharist that the evangelist has given to the Church.

21ST SUNDAY IN ORDINARY TIME

Lectionary #122

READING I   Joshua 24:1–2a, 15–17, 18b

A reading from the Book of Joshua

Joshua gathered together all the tribes of **Israel** at **Shechem**,
    summoning their **elders**, their **leaders**,
    their **judges**, and their **officers**.
When they stood in ranks before **God**,
    Joshua **addressed** all the people:
    "If it does not **please** you to serve the LORD,
    decide today whom you will **serve**,
    the gods your **fathers** served beyond the **River**
    or the gods of the **Amorites** in whose **country** you are
        now **dwelling**.
As for **me** and my **household**, we will serve the LORD."

But the people answered,
    "Far be it from **us** to forsake the LORD
    for the service of **other** gods.
For it was the LORD, our **God**,
    who brought **us** and our **fathers** up out of the land of **Egypt**,
    out of a state of **slavery**.
He performed those great **miracles** before our very **eyes**
    and **protected** us along our entire **journey**
    and among the **peoples** through whom we **passed**.
Therefore we **also** will serve the LORD, for he is our **God**."

Review the proper names carefully as you prepare so that you can proclaim with confidence. Although this is a story, most of the passage is from the mouths of Joshua and the people who respond to him. These opening lines set the scene.
Joshua = JOSH-oo-uh
Israel = IZ-ree-ul
Shechem = SHEK-um
Here is Joshua's challenge to the people.

Amorites = AM-er-īts

And here is how the people respond to him and the salvation history of Israel.

Egypt = EE-jipt

READING I Usually there is a strong narrative or theological link between the first reading and the Gospel, but today the link is not so clear. Nevertheless, the final part contains the people's response to Joshua's words, and they dedicate themselves to the Lord our God as they make clear that they would not forsake the Lord for other gods.

The phrase "other gods" might sound foreign to us, but think about the many things that are prized so highly by some believers that they compete with their dedication to the faith. In that way, the goals of the culture of acquisition and narcissism in which we live are like the "other gods" in the text from Joshua. If you keep this in mind, perhaps your proclamation will be more vital.

READING II Most times as we listen to a well-delivered proclamation during Mass, we find that the message of an ancient story seems to transcend time and place. Once in a while, however, a text is proclaimed in which the changes in society and the world make the difference between now and the ancient culture of early Christianity more than clear.

READING II   Ephesians 5:21–32

Ephesians = ee-FEE-zhunz

While this opening section encourages listeners to care for one another and the community, it is followed by evidence of the social difference between life in twenty-first-century North America and the Mediterranean world of the first century.

A reading from the Letter of Saint Paul to the Ephesians

Brothers and sisters:
Be **subordinate** to one another out of **reverence** for **Christ**.
Wives should be subordinate to their **husbands** as to the **Lord**.
For the husband is **head** of his wife
      just as **Christ** is head of the **church**,
      he **himself** the savior of the **body**.
As the **church** is subordinate to **Christ**,
      so **wives** should be subordinate to their **husbands**
            in **everything**.
Husbands, love your **wives**,
      even as **Christ** loved the **church**
      and handed himself **over** for her to **sanctify** her,
      cleansing her by the bath of **water** with the **word**,
      that he might present to himself the church in **splendor**,
      without **spot** or **wrinkle** or **any** such thing,
      that she might be **holy** and without **blemish**.

The rhetoric toward the husband is lovely, cast in the image of the body.

So **also** husbands should love their **wives** as their own **bodies**.
He who loves his **wife** loves **himself**.
For no one hates his own **flesh**
      but rather **nourishes** and **cherishes** it,
      even as **Christ** does the **church**,
      because we are **members** of his **body**.

The passage so familiar in the rite of Marriage, here applied to Christ and his Church.

*For this reason a **man** shall leave his **father** and his **mother***
      *and be **joined** to his **wife**,*
      *and the **two** shall become one **flesh**.*
This is a great **mystery**,
      but I speak in reference to **Christ** and the **church**.

[Shorter: Ephesians 5:2a, 25–32]

The longer version of today's passage has a mix of both dimensions, for there are some parts in which the beautiful imagery of Christ and the Church is arresting and some where the the unequal address to husbands and wives makes clear that this text bears the imprint of the first-century Mediterranean world. Perhaps the beauty of the message will be obscured by the social differences, but you can do your best to highlight the beauty in your proclaiming.

The shorter version opens with a terrific imperative. Proclaim this with great conviction. The imperatives to husbands are complemented by the example of Christ, as he is "cleansing her by the bath of water with the word." This link of the "water" and "word" is a clear reference to Baptism.

GOSPEL   From the Seventeenth Sunday in Ordinary Time until today, the Lectionary inserted a set of readings from chapter 6 of the Gospel of John. This Gospel pericope that you prepare is the last of the readings from John 6 before the Church again takes up Mark.

GOSPEL John 6:60–69

A reading from the holy Gospel according to John

Many of Jesus' **disciples** who were **listening** said,
  "This **saying** is **hard**; who can **accept** it?"
Since Jesus **knew** that his disciples were **murmuring** about this,
  he said to them, "Does this **shock** you?
What if you were to see the Son of Man **ascending**
  to where he was **before**?
It is the **spirit** that gives life,
  while the **flesh** is of no **avail**.
The words I have **spoken** to you are **Spirit** and **life**.
But there are **some** of you who do not **believe**."
Jesus **knew** from the **beginning** the ones who would not **believe**
  and the one who would **betray** him.
And he said,
"For this **reason** I have told you that **no** one can **come** to me
  unless it is **granted** him by my **Father**."

As a **result** of this,
  many of his disciples **returned** to their former way of life
  and no longer **accompanied** him.
Jesus then said to the **Twelve**, "Do you **also** want to leave?"
Simon **Peter** answered him, "**Master**, to **whom** shall we go?
You have the **words** of eternal **life**.
We have come to **believe**
  and are convinced that **you** are the **Holy** One of **God**."

The disciples' response, "Who can accept it?" sets up the discourse of Jesus to follow.

The characteristically Johannine opposites, "spirit" and "flesh."

The final words of Peter are strong. Your delivery should match them in strength.

As a minister of the word, you might have wondered how you can deliver a word from the Lord that has felt empty and without power in the face of the disappointments and failures of life. This reading you prepare delivers a stark truth, that such dire straits are not new and that God is greater even than this failure and sadness. Peter, the leader of the disciples, recognized the universality of human weakness and the consolation that might be found in Christ: "Master," he says in your voice, "to whom shall we go?"

From our point of view the future is uncertain, but God is ever-faithful, more than any of us as individuals and even more than the Church as a whole. Trusting in God and in the faithful with whom you worship, proclaim the message of consolation to those who need it.

22ND SUNDAY IN ORDINARY TIME

Lectionary #125

READING I   Deuteronomy 4:1–2, 6–8

Deuteronomy = doo-ter-AH-nuh-mee

The entire text is from the lips of Moses except for this opening line. Pause before you begin so that the assembly will know who is speaking and to whom he is speaking.
Moses = MOH-ziz
Israel = IZ-ree-ul

A reading from the Book of Deuteronomy

Moses said to the **people**:
 "Now, Israel, **hear** the statutes and decrees
   which I am **teaching** you to **observe**,
   that you may **live**, and may enter in and take **possession**
     of the land
   which the LORD, the God of your **fathers**, is **giving** you.
In your **observance** of the commandments of the LORD,
     your **God**,
   which I **enjoin** upon you,
   you shall not **add** to what I command you nor **subtract** from it.
Observe them **carefully**,
   for thus will you give **evidence**
   of your **wisdom** and **intelligence** to the **nations**,
   who will **hear** of all these statutes and say,
   'This great **nation** is truly a **wise** and **intelligent** people.'
For what great nation **is** there
   that has gods so **close** to it as the LORD, our God, is to **us**
   whenever we **call** upon him?
Or what great nation has **statutes** and **decrees**
   that are as **just** as this whole **law**
   which I am setting **before** you **today**?"

This is a quotation within Moses' speech. The tone of your voice should make this clear to the hearers.

These are rhetorical questions, meant to convince the Israelites of God's care and providence. Proclaim them as such.

| READING I | Notice a few literary characteristics of this reading. First, except for the first line, the entire passage is direct discourse, Moses speaking to the Israelites. The author of the book framed it in the first person: "This [is the] whole law which I am setting before you today."
   Second, because of that first-person, the passage is in the present tense, not "Moses did set the law before you," but "I am setting it before you." This allows the passage to be proclaimed and heard with immediacy and energy. |

Third, within Moses' discourse is what other people will say about the nation Israel when it observes the law. So there is a speech within a speech, and your proclamation needs to communicate such changes of speaker.
   Finally, the last two verses are rhetorical questions that Moses placed before the Israelites. And you, proclaiming Moses' words, can pose them as real questions about God's closeness and the justice of the law.

The vocabulary of the passage is clear, but there are a few words that we do not use in ordinary conversation very often: "statutes," "decrees," "enjoin." So practice this passage so that you can proclaim it with confidence.
   This reading from Deuteronomy is paired with a Marcan Gospel reading that also takes up the issue of the law. So your thoughtful, clear delivery will enable the assembly to appreciate the link between the two readings.

READING II James 1:17–18, 21b–22, 27

Because this is the first in the series of readings from the Letter of James, be clear as you announce the book from which the passage comes.

A reading from the Letter of Saint James

Dearest brothers and sisters:
All **good** giving and every perfect **gift** is from **above**,
    coming down from the Father of **lights**,
    with whom there is no **alteration** or **shadow** caused by **change**.
He willed to give us **birth** by the word of **truth**
    that we may be a kind of **firstfruits** of his **creatures**.

The imperative forms of the verbs call for direct engagement, if possible, with eye contact.

Humbly **welcome** the word that has been **planted** in you
    and is able to save your **souls**.

Be **doers** of the word and not **hearers** only, **deluding** yourselves.

Here are the actions that James' commends to those who would be "doers." You too commend them to your community.

Religion that is **pure** and **undefiled** before God and the Father
    is **this**:
    to care for **orphans** and **widows** in their affliction
    and to keep oneself **unstained** by the world.

GOSPEL Mark 7:1–8, 14–15, 21–23

A reading from the holy Gospel according to Mark

This passage has three parts: First, Pharisees challenging Jesus; second, Jesus answers them; third, Jesus teaches the crowd.
Pharisees = FAIR-uh-seez
Jerusalem = juh-ROO-suh-lem

When the **Pharisees** with some **scribes** who had
    come from **Jerusalem**
    gathered around **Jesus**,
    they **observed** that some of his **disciples** ate their meals
    with **unclean**, that is, **unwashed**, **hands**.

READING II This reading has great significance for you as a minister of the word, as it declares that God gave us birth "by the *word* of truth," that implores you to welcome the word that "is able to save your souls," and that you not merely hear the word but "be doers of the *word*." Such wisdom was not addressed specifically to ministers of the word, but it has a particular depth for you, which you can use to energize your proclamation.

The first part points to the theological foundation, to the Father as the source of all things. Pause at the break in the printed text.

This second part, also of two sentences, begins with a command: "Humbly welcome . . ." This is followed by another command: "be doers of the word . . ." These commands should be addressed directly to the people hearing your delivery. If possible, make eye contact as you encourage them with such commands.

The second part encourages not merely words but action, so this last verse gets specific about these actions: "to care for orphans

and widows," and to remain unstained by the world. At the time of this letter, being a widow did not only mean being a woman whose husband had died. It was a technical term for the ministry that these women served in the Church.

GOSPEL The opening section of this passage has Mark's explanation of the law, perhaps because he knew that the Gentiles were not in the community were not familiar with the requirements of

The evangelist explains the law to the Gentiles of his community.

—For the **Pharisees** and, in fact, **all** Jews,
    do not **eat** without **carefully** washing their **hands**,
    keeping the **tradition** of the **elders**.
And on coming from the **marketplace**
    they do not eat without **purifying** themselves.
And there are many **other** things that they have
        traditionally observed,
    the **purification** of cups and jugs and kettles and beds.—

Pause here at the change of speakers.

So the Pharisees and scribes **questioned** him,
"Why do **your** disciples **not** follow the tradition of the **elders**
    but **instead** eat a meal with **unclean** hands?"
He responded,

The evangelist quotes Jesus who quotes Isaiah.
Isaiah = ī-ZAY-uh

"Well did **Isaiah** prophesy about you **hypocrites**, as it is written:
    This people honors me with their *lips*,
        *but their **hearts** are far from me;*
    in ***vain*** do they worship me,
        *teaching as doctrines **human** precepts.*
You disregard God's **commandment** but cling to
        human tradition."

The speaker does not shift but the audience does, from the religious leaders to the crowd.

He summoned the crowd **again** and said to them,
"**Hear** me, **all** of you, and **understand**.
Nothing that enters one from **outside** can **defile** that person;
    but the things that come out from **within** are what **defile**.

"From **within** people, from their **hearts**,
    come evil thoughts, unchastity, theft, murder,
    adultery, greed, malice, deceit,
    licentiousness, envy, blasphemy, arrogance, folly.
All **these** evils come from **within** and they **defile**."

The final verse is the thesis of the entire account. Deliver it clearly and as such a summary.

the law. So here are some particulars about washing hands, washing food, washing cups and jugs and kettles. You can deliver the Pharisees' question as the summary that it is, and then pause before the next section.

Jesus answers with his own interpretation of the law, quoting the prophet Isaiah. Deliver this quotation so that the assembly can catch that the Pharisees' question and Jesus' answer draw from the same source, the Old Testament.

After his answer to the the Pharisees, he turns to speak to the crowd. Pause at this shift.

Here in this third part, your proclamation can take on a gentler tone, for he is no longer chastising the religious leaders, but teaching the crowd about the source of human defilement. Notice the list of vices that he names; pause slightly after each so that the assembly can follow clearly and understand the gravity of these sins that come from the heart. After the list comes the summary, that evil comes from within. Deliver it so that it is recognizable as the finale.

23RD SUNDAY IN ORDINARY TIME

Lectionary #128

READING I   Isaiah 35:4–7a

Isaiah = ī-ZAY-uh

The reading starts with imperative verbs:
Be strong! Fear not! Proclaim them boldly.

The second and third parts are quite
poetic. This section focuses on the healing
of human beings. Pause after this part,
before you launch into the final section.

Think of the rejoicing when people living
in a parched and barren land hear the
sound of rain and see puddles and pools.
Picture that in your mind and heart as you
proclaim Isaiah's wonderful images.

A reading from the Book of the Prophet Isaiah

Thus says the LORD:
    Say to those whose hearts are **frightened**:
        Be **strong**, fear **not**!
    Here is your **God**,
        he comes with **vindication**;
    with divine **recompense**
        he comes to **save** you.
    Then will the **eyes** of the blind be **opened**,
        the **ears** of the deaf be **cleared**;
    then will the lame **leap** like a **stag**,
        then the **tongue** of the mute will **sing**.
    Streams will burst forth in the **desert**,
        and **rivers** in the **steppe**.
    The **burning** sands will become **pools**,
        and the **thirsty** ground, springs of **water**.

READING I   This reading from Isaiah is poetic. Employ your best skills to see to it that the community shares in the prophet's vision.

The reading has three parts. First, the prophet's encouragement to those who are afraid; second, the changes in human beings that will accompany God's coming; and third, the changes in nature that will also accompany God's coming. You might take the first part as an encouragement of your own ministry, for when the prophet prompts another to "say to those whose hearts are frightened," so do proclaimers of the word encourage those who are broken and afraid. You likewise encourage your hearers, prompting them also to strengthen those who are afraid.

The poetic images of parts two and three are just lovely, and, mindful of the transformative power of God's life in your own journey, you can proclaim them with conviction and joy. This text is matched with the passage from the Gospel of Mark because the second healing, "the ears of the deaf [shall] be cleared," is what actually happened at Jesus' touch.

Pause after the predictions of the healings so that the hearers are poised to hear the images from nature in the third part. They are filled with hope for the restoration of the world at God's hand.

READING II   James 2:1–5

A reading from the Letter of Saint James

My brothers and sisters, show no **partiality**
    as you adhere to the **faith** in our glorious Lord Jesus **Christ**.
For if a man with **gold** rings and fine **clothes**
    comes into your **assembly**,
    and a **poor** person in **shabby** clothes **also** comes in,
    and you pay **attention** to the one wearing the **fine** clothes
    and say, "Sit **here**, please,"
    while you say to the **poor** one, "Stand **there**," or
        "Sit at my **feet**,"
    have you not made **distinctions** among yourselves
    and become **judges** with evil **designs**?

Listen, my beloved brothers and sisters.
Did not God **choose** those who are **poor** in the world
    to be **rich** in faith and **heirs** of the kingdom
    that he **promised** to those who **love** him?

Deliver this opening address directly to the assembly.

These detailed descriptions are engaging.

Here are two rhetorical questions. Make the answers to the inquiries obvious by your tone.
Again, if possible, deliver the direct address to those listening to you.

READING II   This reading is the second of five passages from the letter of James. The letters of the New Testament are spread out over the three-year Lectionary cycle, so such a series from any particular book only appears once every third year. Last week's selection was from the first chapter of James, and this is the start of chapter two.

You might read through the other four passages of James that are proclaimed during this span of Ordinary Time to help you appreciate the letter's contribution to the Church, its theology, and its worship.

In James' teaching about favoritism in the assembly—whether his ancient assembly or the congregation before you as you proclaim this almost two millennia later—you find "a person with gold rings and fine clothes" and "poor person in shabby clothes." And the letter-writer imagines how each of them might be treated by the usher in that time and in ours.

Notice, that the author has set the passage up with an alternating structure, something like "on the one hand" and "on the other hand." The first pairing is the particular appearance of each; the second is how they would be seated in the assembly; and the third opens the focus to a rhetorical question about the ways of God with regard to the "poor in the world" and the "rich in faith."

Practice the reading so that you can deliver it with animation.

GOSPEL   Mark 7:31–37

A reading from the holy Gospel according to Mark

Again Jesus left the district of **Tyre**
   and went by way of **Sidon** to the Sea of **Galilee**,
   into the district of the **Decapolis**.
And people brought to him a **deaf** man who had a
     speech impediment
   and **begged** him to lay his **hand** on him.
He took him **off** by himself **away** from the crowd.
He put his **finger** into the man's **ears**
   and, **spitting**, touched his **tongue**;
     then he looked up to heaven and **groaned**, and said to him,
   "Ephphatha!"—that is, "Be **opened**!"—
And **immediately** the man's ears were **opened**,
   his **speech** impediment was **removed**,
   and he spoke **plainly**.
He ordered them not to tell **anyone**.
But the **more** he ordered them not to,
   the **more** they proclaimed it.
They were exceedingly **astonished** and they said,
   "He has done **all** things **well**.
He makes the **deaf hear** and the **mute speak**."

Be careful with the place names. It is as important that you deliver them with confidence as it is that you deliver them exactly right. Pause after the geographic setting to mark the switch toward Jesus and the deaf man.
Tyre = tīr
Sidon = SĪ-dun
Galilee = GAL-ih-lee
Decapolis = dih-KAP-uh-lis

An unusual word. See below for more on its pronunciation and place in the tradition.
Ephphatha = EF-fah-thah

Pause at the end of the miracle, before the summary verses.

GOSPEL   The story of healing the deaf man with the speech impediment appears in three parts. The first simply sets the scene geographically. There are four proper names in this one verse. Check the pronunciation guide so that you can proclaim them smoothly and confidently.

The second part is the healing miracle itself, which begins as a crowd brings the man to Jesus, who takes him off "by himself away from the crowd." The third part brings Jesus back to address the crowd and details their reaction to this astounding sign.

In the early and medieval period, the Aramaic word that you find in your reading, "Ephphatha," was taken into the Gospel's Greek and then into Church Latin, even though Aramaic, Greek, and Latin have different alphabets. In our English translation of this passage, the word remains in its original language. You might facilitate your preparation by imagining the "ph" as an "f," so that the word would be "Effatha."

The most engaging element of the reading is the middle part, the healing itself, with its description of the physical contact between Jesus and the man. Such mediation of God's curative power in human life is at the heart of our sacramental theology and practice, so, as you prepare, concentrate on this part, and see how engaging you can make the story of the healing of the deaf man at the hands of the Savior.

24TH SUNDAY IN ORDINARY TIME

Lectionary #131

READING I   Isaiah 50:4c – 9a

Isaiah = Ī-ZAY-uh

A reading from the Book of the Prophet Isaiah

> The Lord **GOD** opens my **ear** that I may **hear**;
> and I **have** not rebelled,
>   **have** not turned back.
> I gave my **back** to those who **beat** me,
>   my **cheeks** to those who **plucked** my beard;
> my **face** I did not **shield**
>   from **buffets** and **spitting**.
>
> The Lord **GOD** is my **help**,
>   **therefore** I am not **disgraced**;
> I have **set** my face like **flint**,
>   **knowing** that I shall **not** be put to **shame**.
> He is **near** who upholds my **right**;
>   if **anyone** wishes to **oppose** me,
>   **let** us appear **together**.
> **Who** disputes my right?
>   Let **that** man confront me.
> **See**, the Lord **GOD** is my **help**;
>   **who** will prove me wrong?

These physical indignities are detailed and engaging; do not rush through them.

Pause here as the thought shifts from his description of suffering to the vindication and help the prophet found in the Lord.

Finally, pause before you begin these rhetorical questions. Deliver them as true questions for those who hear you.

READING I   Awareness of the literary characteristics of this text will help you prepare for proclaiming. First, note that only the first line of the passage is outside the quotation marks, so this is the prophet identifying from whom the words that follow have come, namely, the "servant of the Lord," that is, the suffering servant.

Second, the rest of the reading is a confession of what has happened to the servant, and all of this is done in the first-person style: "The Lord God opens *my* ear," "*I* have not rebelled," and so on. As a minister

of the word, you are speaking the words from the prophet, words that are centuries old. But, by their embrace in the scriptures of the Church, these are also the words of the community of faith.

While we do not know the suffering of Isaiah's servant of the Lord, no believer, indeed no human being, is exempt from suffering. So we participate in Isaiah's prophecy simply by our humanity. Therefore, mindful of how suffering has been part of your days, and of how the presence of God and the

ministry of fellow believers have supported you in such times, you can be bold in proclaiming with confidence these confessions of suffering from the lips of the suffering servant, mediated in the inspired texts of the prophet.

The final part has three rhetorical questions, and, having confidently delivered the parts about the servant's suffering and vindication, you can offer these to those who hear your courageous proclamation. Not an easy reading, but one that will offer much to your community of faith.

Those to whom you proclaim are your brothers and sisters by Baptism. Address the opening to them directly, making eye contact.

This line is a rhetorical question, leading to a directed answer: "Of course not!"

The final line restates the practical example in the theological vocabulary of faith and works.

READING II   James 2:14–18

A reading from the Letter of Saint James

What **good** is it, my brothers and sisters,
    if someone says he has **faith** but does not have **works**?
Can that faith **save** him?
If a brother or sister has **nothing** to wear
    and has no **food** for the day,
    and one of you says to them,
    "**Go** in peace, **keep** warm, and **eat** well,"
    but you do not give them the **necessities** of the **body**,
    what **good** is it?
So **also** faith of **itself**,
    if it does not have **works**, is **dead**.

Indeed someone might **say**,
    "**You** have faith and **I** have works."
Demonstrate your faith to me **without** works,
    and **I** will demonstrate my faith to you **from** my works.

READING II This very passage was and is involved in the great debates about what brings salvation. Is it God's gift alone, to which we assent by *faith?* Or does God attend to what we do, such that we earn our salvation by *works?* Catholics believe that salvation in Jesus Christ is pure gift, and yet the Lord crowns his gifts by rewarding us in heaven for our charity.

The passage from James makes the unique observation that, faith is essential, yes, but can there be faith without expressions of it in works and actions?

From a literary point of view, the passage has some unique elements. First, it quotes what a hypothetical someone might say in two places. So be clear here when you are quoting "one of you" and "someone."

Second, the passage has three rhetorical questions. Be aware that the questions are coming so that you not be surprised.

Finally, the letter transcends time. Its details about the Church's ministry of clothing and food are as contemporary now as they were in James' day. So proclaim the

passage directly to your assembly as if it had been written specifically to them.

GOSPEL This passage appears only halfway through the Gospel of Mark, yet the evangelist was already alerting the Church to the pain and service that came into the life of Jesus, that comes into the Church, the body of Christ, and that comes into our individual lives of faith as well.

GOSPEL   Mark 8:27–35

A reading from the holy Gospel according to Mark

Jesus and his disciples set out
   for the villages of Caesarea Philippi.
Along the way he asked his disciples,
   "Who do people say that I am?"
They said in reply,
   "John the Baptist, others Elijah,
   still others one of the prophets."
And he asked them,
   "But who do you say that I am?"
Peter said to him in reply,
   "You are the Christ."
Then he warned them not to tell anyone about him.

He began to teach them
   that the Son of Man must suffer greatly
   and be rejected by the elders, the chief priests, and the scribes,
   and be killed, and rise after three days.
He spoke this openly.
Then Peter took him aside and began to rebuke him.
At this he turned around and, looking at his disciples,
   rebuked Peter and said, "Get behind me, Satan.
You are thinking not as God does, but as human beings do."

He summoned the crowd with his disciples and said to them,
   "Whoever wishes to come after me must deny himself,
   take up his cross, and follow me.
For whoever wishes to save his life will lose it,
   but whoever loses his life for my sake
   and that of the gospel will save it."

Caesarea = see-zuh-REE-uh
Philippi = fih-LIP-i

1 Notice that the two questions are the same except for the subjects.

Elijah = ee-LĪ-juh

Be clear and direct as you proclaim Peter's confession of Jesus as Messiah.

The exchange with Peter is interrupted for the Passion prediction. The openness of this is contrary to the "secret" of his being the Messiah.

Satan = SAY-t*n

This last section broadens from that ancient conversation between Jesus and Peter and is applicable to people of faith today. Deliver this with conviction, and, if possible, make eye contact with those lines that you find most profound.

As you review this passage, notice how much of it is in quotation marks, with an exchange between Jesus and the disciples, another between Jesus and Peter, and the third with Jesus addressing the crowd.

For clarity, mphasize the subjects of the first two questions, so that the assembly catches the shift from "Who do *people* say that I am?" to "But who do *you* say that I am?" After this second inquiry, we get the terse and powerful confession of Peter's faith: "You are the Messiah."

Mark's Gospel is where we find the "messianic secret," namely, places where Jesus is trying to keep his identity from being known, as here. This closes the section, so take a breath before you continue.

The exchange with Peter is interrupted for the Passion prediction. When Peter appears again, his recognition of Jesus as the Messiah is counterbalanced by his rebuking Jesus, and this is characteristic of the portrayal of Peter in Mark, where each step ahead in courage or understanding is followed by a step back.

The final two verses broaden the theology of suffering to all followers of Jesus. You might commit some of this last part to memory, so that you can deliver it directly to those who hear you.

25TH SUNDAY IN ORDINARY TIME

Lectionary #134

READING I   Wisdom 2:12, 17–20

A reading from the Book of Wisdom

The **wicked** say:
Let us beset the **just** one, because he is **obnoxious** to us;
    he sets himself **against** our doings,
        reproaches us for **transgressions** of the law
        and **charges** us with violations of our **training**.
Let us **see** whether his words be **true**;
    let us find **out** what will happen to him.
For if the **just** one be the son of **God**, God will **defend** him
    and **deliver** him from the hand of his **foes**.
With **revilement** and **torture** let us put the **just** one to the **test**
    that we may have **proof** of his **gentleness**
    and **try** his **patience**.
Let us **condemn** him to a shameful **death**;
    for according to his own **words**, God will take **care** of him.

The entire passage is from the mouths of "the wicked," so that this opening line must be delivered clearly or the assembly will be perplexed by the remainder of the reading.

READING I   This is a unique passage from the Lectionary, unique and difficult, for you can see that all of it is the book of Wisdom offering the words of the wicked. "The righteous one" is described by the wicked, and hatefully, too. He "is obnoxious to us," "sets himself against our doings," and "reproaches us for transgressions of the law."

The author did not have Jesus in mind when he wrote of the "righteous one" long before Christ's birth, yet the Christian tradition believes in Jesus as the fulfillment of

such a passage. So this text's plots by the wicked to "put the just one to the text" and "condemn him to a shameful death" are paired with the Gospel reading, where Jesus teaches that "the Son of Man will be handed over to men and they will kill him." The wicked of the book of Wisdom precede those who seek Jesus' suffering and death in the Gospel of Mark. Keep this in mind, for it will help you to understand the purpose of including this text in the Lectionary.

Notice that all the words of the wicked are in first-person plural pronouns: "we," "us," and "our." Contrary to what is usually the best way to proclaim such a literary form, namely, as if you were speaking from your own experience, you do not want to do this here (after all, you are not one of the wicked). You do want the plans of the schemers to be understood by the assembly, but proclaim the text with a certain distance.

READING II James 3:16 — 4:3

A reading from the Letter of Saint James

Beloved:
Where **jealousy** and selfish **ambition** exist,
    there is **disorder** and every foul **practice**.
But the wisdom from **above** is first of all **pure**,
    then **peaceable, gentle, compliant**,
    full of **mercy** and good **fruits**,
    without **inconstancy** or **insincerity**.
And the fruit of **righteousness** is sown in **peace**
    for those who **cultivate** peace.

Where do the **wars**
    and where do the **conflicts** among you **come** from?
Is it not from your **passions**
    that make war within your **members**?
You **covet** but do not **possess**.
You **kill** and **envy** but you cannot **obtain**;
    you **fight** and wage **war**.
You do not **possess** because you do not **ask**.
You **ask** but do not **receive**,
    because you ask **wrongly**, to spend it on your **passions**.

James describes these human tendencies, but follows with their opposites, the gifts from above.

The significant sentence of the reading. Proclaim it clearly, without hurry.

Pause before you deliver these two rhetorical questions.

READING II   This is a hard passage to proclaim, not because of its rhetoric or structure, but because, in delivering the words of James to your community, you will be asking hard questions of them: Where do the wars and conflicts among you come from? "Is it not from you passions that make war within your members?" Consider how, as a minister of the word, you can deliver these not as an accusation, but from the standpoint of a participant in the community of the baptized which, though saved by God's gift of love in Jesus Christ, still lapses into sin.

The message of James is prophetic in our time, for many of us live in disputatious places, where conflicts lead to arguments and even violence, emotional and physical. But James is clear that "the fruit of righteousness is sown in peace for those who cultivate peace."

The first reading is from the book of Wisdom, and the passage from James speaks of "wisdom from above." This wisdom is juxtaposed to its opposites, "jealousy and selfish ambition," "disorder and every kind of foul practice." Consider how to deliver these words not as a scolding, but from the point of view of one who, like those before you, is nurtured by God's goodness, but also lives in a world that is sometimes scarred by fighting.

GOSPEL Mark 9:30–37

A reading from the holy Gospel according to Mark

Jesus and his disciples **left** from there and began a **journey**
    through **Galilee**,
  but he did not wish **anyone** to know about it.
He was **teaching** his disciples and **telling** them,
    "The Son of **Man** is to be handed **over** to men
    and they will **kill** him,
    and three days after his **death** the Son of Man will **rise**."
But they **did** not understand the **saying**,
    and they were **afraid** to **question** him.

They came to **Capernaum** and, once inside the house,
    he began to **ask** them,
    "What were you **arguing** about on the **way**?"
But they remained **silent**.
They had been discussing among themselves on the way
    who was the **greatest**.
Then he sat **down**, called the **Twelve**, and **said** to them,
    "If anyone wishes to be **first**,
    he shall be the **last** of all and the **servant** of all."
Taking a **child**, he placed it in the their **midst**,
    and putting his **arms** around it, he said to them,
    "Whoever receives one **child** such as this in my **name**,
        receives **me**;
    and whoever receives **me**,
    receives not **me** but the One who **sent** me."

Galilee = GAL-ih-lee

This is a prediction of the Passion, so characteristic of the Gospel of Mark.

The narrative changes here, so pause.
Capernaum = kuh-PER-n*m

GOSPEL Unlike in the First Gospel, Matthew, in which the disciples of Jesus are more favorably portrayed, in the Second Gospel, Mark, they are not always exemplary. The bickering of the disciples that you will deliver in your proclamation is one of those episodes in which the followers of Jesus are less than perfect.

The passage has four sections that call for different proclamation styles. First, setting the context and the Passion prediction; second, the revelation about the argument the disciples were having; third, Jesus'

response to that revelation; and fourth, the teaching of Jesus with the child in his arms.

Your confident proclamation will be stronger if you know the turns in the story ahead of time.

Some biblical scholars speak of the Gospel of Mark as a "Passion narrative with a long introduction," for not only is the Passion such a significant portion of the Gospel, but, leading up to the Passion and cross, the evangelist hints often at the inevitability of what Jesus faces. So with the Passion prediction here and the disci-

ples' incomprehension, both characteristically Marcan.

As you prepare, notice that each of the four elements in this passage begins with setting a context and then offers with a saying by Jesus. The opening Passion prediction is followed by Jesus' discovery of the disciples' argument about who is greatest. The end of the passage is gentler, hopeful, consoling, and can be clearly imagined by those who hear you proclaim. Because the earlier content is grim, take up a compassionate tone as you deliver the brighter message at the end.

OCTOBER 1, 2006

26TH SUNDAY IN ORDINARY TIME

Lectionary #137

READING I   Numbers 11:25–29

A reading from the Book of Numbers

The LORD came down in the **cloud** and spoke to **Moses**.
Taking some of the **spirit** that was on Moses,
    the LORD **bestowed** it on the seventy elders;
    and as the spirit came to **rest** on them, they **prophesied**.

Now two men, one named **Eldad** and the other **Medad**,
    were not in the **gathering** but had been left in the **camp**.
They **too** had been on the list, but had not gone out to the **tent**;
    yet the spirit came to rest on them **also**,
    and they **prophesied** in the camp.
So, when a young man quickly told **Moses**,
    "Eldad and Medad are **prophesying** in the camp,"
    Joshua, son of **Nun**, who from his youth had been Moses'
        aide, said,
    "Moses, my lord, **stop** them."
But Moses answered him,
    "Are you **jealous** for my sake?
Would that **all** the people of the LORD were **prophets**!
Would that the LORD might bestow his spirit on them **all**!"

You might imagine this opening scene for yourself, so that it will sound vivid to those who hear you.
Moses = MOH-ziz

The actions of Eldad and Medad stir up concern among the people.
Eldad = EL-dad
Medad = MEE-dad
prophesied = PROF-uh-sīd

This concern is captured in the voice of this young man.
prophesying = PROF-uh-sī-ing

Joshua is seeking to ease the concern, but in the end we hear Moses, through you, recognizing the work of the Lord even in this unusual action.

READING I As you begin your preparation, learn the proper names in this passage from the book of Numbers so that you will proclaim them confidently. None is especially difficult.

Also regarding pronunciation, be aware of the distinction between the two words "prophecy" and "prophesy"; the first is a noun, referring to the message proclaimed by a prophet, and it is pronounced "PROF-uh-see." The second is a verb, less common,

meaning the act of proclaiming a prophecy, and it is pronounced "PROF-uh-sī," rhyming with "sigh" or "tie."

There are a number of speakers in this reading, and each of their speeches carries a different content and feel. Be familiar with each speech so that you know what tone to employ as you begin to proclaim their words. For example, you might imagine the young man delivering incredible news to Moses, almost as if he is saying, "You won't *believe* what's going on down in the camp!"

Joshua's words are a command: "My lord Moses, stop them!" And Moses's question and words of consolation to Joshua are hopeful.

The expression of a wish beginning with the phrase "Would that . . ." is not as common today as it once was. To get the right tone, you might practice as if you were saying, "If only all the people . . ."

In spite of the complexities in the passage, it delivers an important reminder to all

Notice the form of these verbs of command. Imagine them with exclamation points: Come now! Weep! Wail! Behold!

The poetic images that are as applicable today as when they were first written.

The social justice dimension from the Lord's words is evident.

The passage does not end on a consolatory note. Consider how best to end the passage.

READING II   James 5:1–6

A reading from the Letter of Saint James

Come now, you **rich**, **weep** and **wail** over your impending
       miseries.
Your **wealth** has rotted **away**, your **clothes** have become
       moth-eaten,
    your gold and silver have **corroded**,
    and that corrosion will be a testimony **against** you;
    it will **devour** your flesh like a **fire**.
You have stored up **treasure** for the last days.
Behold, the **wages** you **withheld** from the **workers**
    who harvested your **fields** are crying **aloud**;
    and the cries of the **harvesters**
    have reached the **ears** of the Lord of **hosts**.
You have lived on earth in **luxury** and **pleasure**;
    you have **fattened** your hearts for the day of **slaughter**.
You have **condemned**;
    you have murdered the **righteous** one;
    he **offers** you no **resistance**.

God's people, namely, that not all new and surprising things are to be mistrusted and stopped. Sometimes new messages, actions, and ideas are the life of God in us.

READING II This passage is the last of five that the Church will hear from James here in Year B of the Lectionary's three-year cycle. In literary terms, some of the images of the reading are beautifully specific, and they will engage the imaginations

of those hearing you. Also, notice the imperative forms of some of the verbs: "Come now," "weep and wail," and "behold."

The passage you are assigned can be difficult to deliver in a world like ours. We live in a culture where wealth and the acquisition of material goods are held up as supreme values, as if the one who is the richest in the end is the one who wins. Our formation in the faith contradicts this message of the world, and you are the bearer of this contradictory message in the letter of James.

Do not tone down the strong words of James. It is very important when the Church's values against the world in which it lives are proclaimed boldly and courageously. (But don't go to the opposite extreme, wagging your finger and glaring at the best-dressed in the congregation as you deliver the word!) Yet this is your vocation for this assembly, to offer this world-indicting message with courage.

GOSPEL   Mark 9:38–43, 45, 47–48

A reading from the holy Gospel according to Mark

At that time, **John** said to **Jesus**,
"**Teacher**, we saw someone driving out **demons** in your name,
    and we tried to **prevent** him because he does not **follow** us."
Jesus replied, "Do **not** prevent him.
There is **no** one who performs a mighty **deed** in my name
    who can at the **sam**e time speak **ill** of me.
For whoever is not **against** us is **for** us.
Anyone who gives you a cup of **water** to drink
    because you belong to **Christ**,
    amen, I say to you, will surely not lose his **reward**.

"Whoever causes one of these **little** ones
        who **believe** in me to **sin**,
    it would be **better** for him if a great **millstone**
    were **put** around his neck
    and he were thrown into the **sea**.
If your **hand** causes you to sin, cut it **off**.
It is **better** for you to enter into life **maimed**
    than with **two** hands to go into **Gehenna**,
    into the unquenchable **fire**.
And if your **foot** causes you to sin, cut it **off**.
It is **better** for you to enter into life **crippled**
    than with **two** feet to be thrown into **Gehenna**.
And if your **eye** causes you to sin, pluck it **out**.
Better for you to enter into the kingdom of God with **one** eye
    than with **two** eyes to be thrown into **Gehenna**,
    where 'their worm does not **die**, and the fire is not **quenched**.'"

Most of the Gospel is a speech from Jesus, so proclaim this opening exchange well to set the scene for Jesus' words to follow.

All good things come from God.

Although these images are grave and frightening, they are also provocative because of their specificity.
Gehenna = geh-HEN-nah

A grim ending, no doubt; but the vocabulary animates the imagination.

GOSPEL   As you prepare for your proclamation of this reading from the Gospel of Mark, consider the first reading from the book of Numbers, for it describes a precedent for what happens in the first part of this Gospel passage and for God's ways in human communities.

Notice that in this passage, after John speaks to Jesus about the one who had been casting out demons, the remainder of the long reading is from the lips of Jesus. Be prepared for this so that your voice will carry his words and teaching for the distance.

Although there is a positive message in the reading when Jesus says that anyone who gives a cup of water will be rewarded, the remainder of the passage is darker. Though they are God's word to us, Jesus' words here are not an easy to proclaim, for they contain the unimaginable actions of cutting off one's hand or foot if these cause one to stumble. Better, he says, "to enter into life maimed . . . [or] crippled." Sometimes such caustic sayings are followed by others that soften the shock, but not here. The final image is of the fires of hell.

Because the words of the Gospel are usually strengthening and compassionate, this self-inflicted punishment recommended by Jesus for those who might sin might be hard to proclaim directly. But your role as the proclaimer of God's word is to deliver the words as clearly and directly as you can, whatever its content.

27TH SUNDAY IN ORDINARY TIME

Lectionary #140

READING I   Genesis 2:18–24

Genesis = JEN-uh-sis

Emphasize the LORD God's attentiveness to the man's state, for this will console those who are lonely.

A reading from the Book of Genesis

The LORD God said: "It is not **good** for the man to be **alone**.
I will make a suitable **partner** for him."
So the LORD God **formed** out of the **ground**
   various wild **animals** and various **birds** of the air,
   and he **brought** them to the man to see what he would **call**
     them;
   whatever the man **called** each of them would be its **name**.

The act of naming is deep in the tradition and scriptures.

The man gave names to all the **cattle**,
   all the **birds** of the air, and all wild **animals**;
   but **none** proved to be the suitable **partner** for the man.

Pause at the end of the section, for the creation of the woman and its specific elements are sharply drawn.

So the LORD God cast a deep **sleep** on the man,
   and while he was asleep,
   he took out one of his **ribs** and closed up its **place** with **flesh**.
The LORD God then built up into a **woman** the rib
   that he had **taken** from the man.
When he brought her to the man, the man said:

The man's summary of the Lord's creative act.

"**This** one, at last, is **bone** of my **bones**
   and **flesh** of my **flesh**;
   this one shall be called '**woman**,'
   for out of 'her **man**' this one has been **taken**."

A cardinal verse for the whole Catholic theology of Marriage as a sacrament of unity.

That is why a man **leaves** his father and mother
   and clings to his **wife**,
   and the **two** of them become **one flesh**.

READING I The Bible opens not with one account of Creation, but two. The first is the story of the six days of Creation and the seventh day of rest. The second is the one you will proclaim, the account of Adam and Eve.

The full narrative is quite long, and the excerpt you prepare is fairly long itself. You will need to stir up your best narrative skills to keep the assembly attentive as the story progresses.

Although the reading does not appear often in the Lectionary cycle, people are perhaps more familiar with it as a choice for the first reading at weddings. The last line, "a man leaves his father and his mother and clings to his wife, and the two of them become one flesh," is foundational for the theology of Marriage as a sacrament of unity.

There are a few elements to notice as you prepare. First, the reading has a lot of dramatic action: the LORD God's forming animals from the ground and bringing them to the man, in the deep sleep that comes upon the man, and the forming of the woman from the rib of the man.

Next, the actions are followed by the man's summation of the great act of the Lord's creation, and then comes the author's summary verse about the two becoming one. The weight of these summaries will be appreciated more if the drama of the creation of the two people are well delivered. Pace yourself, for the reading is relatively long.

READING II Hebrews 2:9–11

A reading from the Letter to the Hebrews

Brothers and sisters:
He *for a little while* was made ***lower*** than the **angels**,
   that by the **grace** of God he might taste **death** for everyone.

For it was **fitting** that he,
   for whom and **through** whom all things **exist**,
   in bringing **many** children to **glory**,
   should make the **leader** to their salvation **perfect**
     through **suffering**.
He who **consecrates** and those who are **being** consecrated
   all have **one origin**.
Therefore, he is not **ashamed** to call them "**brothers**."

Hebrews = HEE-brooz

The three verses of the reading are dense kernels of truth. Proclaim them deliberately and smoothly.

Pause at each break in the printed text.

This phrase about Jesus as "the leader to their salvation" is delightful. Pause at the end of the verse for some breathing room.

This last line posits the association of humanity with Jesus as children of God the Father.

GOSPEL Mark 10:2–16

A reading from the holy Gospel according to Mark

The **Pharisees** approached Jesus and asked,
   "Is it **lawful** for a **husband** to **divorce** his **wife**?"
They were testing him.
He said to them in reply, "What did **Moses** command you?"
They replied,
   "Moses **permitted** a husband to write a bill of **divorce**
   and **dismiss** her."

The adversarial exchange between the Pharisees and Jesus is long. Be clear in identifying the speakers so that the assembly can follow easily.
Pharisees = FAIR-uh-seez
Moses = MOH-ziz

READING II Last week the Church finished a series from the letter of James, so today it turns to the letter to the Hebrews. Perhaps you can be more emphatic than usual as you announce the book from which the text is proclaimed. The series from Hebrews will continue until November 19.

Although the passage is only three verses long, it is not short, and there are various theological elements to consider as you prepare this reading. First, the opening is cosmological, casting Jesus within our sight, yet juxtaposed to the angels and humanity.

In the second section, Jesus is described as "the leader to their salvation," for he is indeed the one who has cleared the path to God for the rest of humanity, made perfect in order to give us access to the life of God which he won for us.

Like the earlier parts, the final section is deep, but here the family of humanity is depicted in relation to Jesus and to one another as children of God. Because the theology is heavy here, the language of these passages is not the easiest to proclaim well. But it will bear fruit for those who hear, for by it the members of your parish will be refreshed in recognizing what they have gained in Jesus and in one another. Try to lighten the complex ideas with an animated proclamation.

GOSPEL This long reading from the Gospel of Mark has two basic parts, and in theology, literary style, and even context, the parts are not closely related to one another.

The first, longer part bears teachings from the mouth of Jesus about marriage,

Here is the text from the Book of Genesis that was proclaimed in the first reading.

But Jesus told them,
  "Because of the **hardness** of your **hearts**
  he wrote you this **commandment**.
But from the **beginning** of creation, *God made them **male***
    *and **female**.*
*For this reason a man shall **leave** his father and mother*
  *and be **joined** to his wife,*
  *and the **two** shall become **one flesh**.*
*So they are no longer **two** but **one flesh**.*
Therefore what **God** has joined **together**,
  no human **being** must **separate**."
In the house the disciples **again** questioned Jesus about this.
He said to them,
  "Whoever **divorces** his wife and marries **another**
  commits **adultery** against her;
  and if **she** divorces her **husband** and marries another,
  she commits **adultery**."

Pause here for the narrative shifts significantly, in place and meaning.

And people were bringing **children** to him
    that he might **touch** them,
  but the disciples **rebuked** them.
When Jesus saw this he became **indignant** and said to them,
  "Let the children **come** to me;
  do not prevent them, for the kingdom of God **belongs**
    to such as **these**.
Amen, I **say** to you,
  whoever does not accept the kingdom of God like a **child**
  will not **enter** it."

The final lines of Jesus and the gestures toward the children are beautiful.

Then he **embraced** them and **blessed** them,
  placing his **hands** on them.

[Shorter: Mark 10:2–12]

divorce, and adultery. Much of Catholic teaching about the indissolubility of the sacrament of Marriage is founded in this teaching of Jesus: "What God has joined together, no human being must separate." As you see, he teaches in the face of Pharisees who approach to question him about the law on divorce, one of the many occasions when the Jewish leaders seek to trip up Jesus.

The opening exchange is about what Moses taught on these topics, and Jesus cites the Hebrew Scriptures. Notice that most of this long part is a dialogue between Jesus and the Jewish leaders. Find a verbal way to signal the difference between the narrative elements moving the account forward— such as "They said" or "But Jesus told them"—and what each of the sides says.

Unlike the first part, the second has action to complement Jesus' teaching. Make clear the difference between the disciples'

attitude toward the people and Jesus' desire to receive the children. The final gesture of Jesus in the reading—taking the children in his arms, laying hands on them, and blessing them—is a lovely gesture that gives the long passage a warm ending, which is important after the rather sharp exchange of the first part.

28TH SUNDAY IN ORDINARY TIME

Lectionary #143

READING I   Wisdom 7:7–11

A reading from the Book of Wisdom

I **prayed**, and **prudence** was given me;
  I **pleaded**, and the spirit of wisdom **came** to me.
I **preferred** her to **scepter** and **throne**,
and deemed riches **nothing** in comparison with her,
  nor did I liken any priceless **gem** to her;
because all **gold**, in view of **her**, is a little **sand**,
  and before her, **silver** is to be accounted **mire**.
Beyond **health** and **comeliness** I loved her,
and I chose to have **her** rather than the **light**,
  because the splendor of her **never** yields to sleep.
Yet all good things **together** came to me in her **company**,
  and countless **riches** at her **hands**.

READING II   Hebrews 4:12–13

A reading from the Letter to the Hebrews

Brothers and sisters:
Indeed the word of **God** is **living** and **effective**,
  sharper than any two-edged **sword**,
  penetrating even between **soul** and **spirit**, **joints** and **marrow**,
  and able to discern **reflections** and thoughts of the **heart**.

Read below for the key to understanding the pronouns "I" and "her" in the passage.
  scepter = SEP-ter

mire = mīr

Hebrews = HEE-br<u>oo</u>z

Short readings give you the opportunity to practice the pace of your proclamations. There is no reason for you to race through these few verses.

READING I The key to understanding and proclaiming this reading is in the pronouns. The original Hebrew word for "wisdom" is a feminine noun, so the pronoun "her" throughout the reading is referring to the "spirit of wisdom" in the opening verse, in "the spirit of wisdom came upon me."

The first-person singular pronoun refers to the receiver of the gift of wisdom, a member of the Jewish community from which this reading was born, of course; and you, the proclaimer of this passage, stand in the place of that ancient author. As a baptized member of the community of faith, you have access to the life of grace and to the gifts of the Holy Spirit, so the "I" and "me" of the reading is not you exactly, but they can be truly proclaimed boldly from your mouth.

The figure of wisdom from the Old Testament literature was later applied to Jesus himself. So in the Gospel for today, a man runs up to Jesus and addresses him as "good teacher." This is Jesus the personification of wisdom, who taught his disciples and followers the truth about God and the world.

Your ministry in the Church and your observation of the world in which the Church lives enable you to speak forthrightly in this passage. In a culture where—as the reading lists them for its own time—wealth, health, and beauty were preoccupations, the author set forth understanding and wisdom as far more valuable than gold and silver. So we today, in another place and time, again find material possessions prized far above understanding and wisdom. Proclaim this word of truth so that the word of the Lord can stand against the culture yet again.

No creature is **concealed** from him,
but everything is **naked** and **exposed** to the eyes of him
to whom we must render an **account**.

GOSPEL   Mark 10:17–30

A reading from the holy Gospel according to Mark

As Jesus was setting out on a **journey**, a man ran up,
knelt down before him, and asked him,
"Good **teacher**, what must I **do** to inherit eternal **life**?"
Jesus **answered** him, "**Why** do you call me **good**?
No one is good but God **alone**.
You know the commandments: *You shall not **kill**;*
*you shall not commit **adultery**;*
*you shall not **steal**;*
*you shall not bear false **witness**;*
*you shall not **defraud**;*
*honor your **father** and your **mother**."*
He replied and said to him,
"**Teacher**, all of **these** I have observed from my **youth**."
Jesus, looking at him, **loved** him and said to him,
"You are lacking in one thing.
Go, **sell** what you have, and give to the **poor**
and you will have treasure in **heaven**; then come, **follow** me."
At that statement his face **fell**,
and he went away **sad**, for he had **many** possessions.

Consider the reading in its three parts. The first is the exchange between this good, rich man and Jesus.

Imagine the man's feelings as he went away. Pause after this.

READING II   This is the second of a series of seven readings from the letter to the Hebrews. The letter does not identify its author, but for centuries it was thought that the author was the apostle Paul.

During that period, artwork of the apostle often showed him with a sword in his hand, pointed toward the ground. (Often paired with him in such depictions is Peter, holding a set of keys.) The symbol of the sword comes from this passage of Hebrews. Even though historical studies of the New Testament have shown that the book is not

from the hand of Paul, the symbol has remained with him.

This reading is powerful not only because of its image of the "two-edged sword," but also because of the power it attributes to the word of God. As a minister of the word, you would do well to attend to this reading closely, not only for the particular occasion for which you prepare, but as an inspiration for your own work in the Church. The gravity with which the reading speaks of the word should empower you for how your own proclamation nurtures the Church.

The reading is short, only two verses from Hebrews. So take your time and do not speed through the proclamation. Pause after the line identifying the book, again at the natural break between the verses, and, as ever, at the end of the passage, just before you deliver the closing "The word of the Lord."

GOSPEL   We live in a place where wealth is held up as the highest achievement. Whoever has the most wins, says the culture, yet the values of the Gospel and the Church that proclaims this

The second part has more familiar elements, images, and phrases.

The final part offers some hope for those who have abandoned the familiar for their vocation. Peter speaks up on behalf of the disciples and the followers of Jesus, and Jesus' answer here is not as hard to hear.

Jesus looked around and said to his **disciples**,
   "How **hard** it is for those who have **wealth**
   to enter the kingdom of **God**!"
The disciples were **amazed** at his words.
So Jesus **again** said to them in **reply**,
   "**Children**, how **hard** it is to enter the kingdom of **God**!
It is easier for a **camel** to pass through the eye of a **needle**
   than for one who is **rich** to enter the kingdom of **God**."
They were **exceedingly** astonished and said among themselves,
   "Then **who** can be **saved**?"
Jesus **looked** at them and said,
   "For human **beings** it is **impossible**, but not for **God**.
All things are possible for **God**."
Peter began to say to him,
   "We have given up **everything** and followed you."
Jesus said, "**Amen**, I say to you,
   there is **no one** who has given up **house** or **brothers** or **sisters**
   or **mother** or **father** or **children** or **lands**
   for **my** sake and for the sake of the **gospel**
   who will not receive a **hundred** times more **now** in this
      present age:
   houses and **brothers** and **sisters**
   and **mothers** and **children** and **lands**,
   with **persecutions**, and eternal **life** in the age to **come**."

[Shorter: Mark 10:17–27]

Gospel are the complete opposite of this: "Sell what you have, and give to the poor." Jesus does not say, "Sell *most* of what you have," which would be a hard enough message to proclaim, but he tells the man in today's reading to sell everything. In our culture, this man would be *the* man, for, the Gospel tells us, "he had many possessions."

   The long reading has three basic sections. The first part is a dialogue between Jesus and the rich man. The second part is Jesus' teaching the disciples and the disciples' perplexity at his message. And the third part is an exchange between Peter and

Jesus. The three parts are related by the issue of what one needs to abandon in order to follow one's call. But the delivery of each part should be unique.

   Part one has the rich man eagerly run up and kneel before Jesus. He is a good, dedicated man, one who has kept the commandments. But Jesus tells him to sell everything, for there will be treasure in heaven; then come, follow him. As you deliver this invitation and then the verse that describes the man's reaction, imagine the heaviness of the man's soul.

   The difficulty of Jesus' message persists through the second part, with the familiar elements of the "camel [passing] through the eye of a needle," and that for God "all things are possible."

   Fortunately, the proclamation finishes with a more consolatory word, namely, that those who have given up will receive from God in abundance.

   This is a hard word to proclaim. Prepare well and deliver it clearly.

29TH SUNDAY IN ORDINARY TIME

Lectionary #146

READING I Isaiah 53:10–11

Isaiah = ī-ZAY-uh

Make a full stop.

This message is grave, so again pause before continuing. Let the message sink in.

Emphasize the metaphor of light, for it is a rich symbol in the scriptures.

A reading from the Book of the Prophet Isaiah

The LORD was **pleased**
    to **crush** him in **infirmity**.

If he gives his **life** as an offering for **sin**,
    he shall see his **descendants** in a **long** life,
    and the **will** of the LORD shall be **accomplished** through him.

Because of his **affliction**
    he shall see the **light** in fullness of **days**;
through his **suffering**, my servant shall justify **many**,
    and their **guilt** he shall **bear**.

READING I The reading you prepare is among those that are usually proclaimed in Lent, yet we hear them now, halfway between last Lent and next. Both the second reading and the Gospel with which it is matched speak of the suffering of those who would follow Jesus.

From a theological point of view we know that our salvation was gained in the life, Passion, and death of Jesus of Nazareth,

God's only Son. As baptized members of the Church we participate in the suffering of all humanity. We do not seek suffering, but it makes its way into all human life.

The prophet Isaiah was not knowingly prophesying or writing in particular about Jesus of Nazareth, of course, for he wrote centuries before Jesus was born of Mary. But as Christians we read Isaiah with a new lens.

Although you may not personally know all of those to whom you will proclaim this reading, you can be sure that most of them have been touched by hardship, whether physical, emotional, social, financial, or spiritual. No life is spared hardship, so take it as your vocation to unite the lives before you with the suffering of the servant about whom Isaiah prophesied, the one who, as Jesus himself fulfilled this message, has indeed borne the guilt of many.

READING II   Hebrews 4:14–16

A reading from the Letter to the Hebrews

Brothers and sisters:
Since we have a great **high** priest who has passed
    through the **heavens**,
  Jesus, the Son of **God**,
  let us hold **fast** to our **confession**.
For we do **not** have a high priest
  who is **unable** to sympathize with our **weaknesses**,
  but one who has **similarly** been tested in **every** way,
  yet without **sin**.
So let us **confidently** approach the throne of **grace**
  to receive **mercy** and to find **grace** for timely **help**.

This middle verse is the key. Make sure the hearers are able to recognize that Jesus Christ understands the weakness of being human in our world.

This is an imperative, "let us . . . ," so make it inviting to those with whom you worship.

GOSPEL   Mark 10:35–45

A reading from the holy Gospel according to Mark

James and **John**, the sons of **Zebedee**, came to **Jesus** and said
    to him,
  "**Teacher**, we want you to **do** for us whatever we **ask** of you."
He replied, "What do you wish me to **do** for you?"
They answered him, "**Grant** that in your glory
  we may sit **one** at your **right** and the **other** at your **left**."
Jesus said to them, "You do not **know** what you are **asking**.
Can you drink the cup that **I** drink
  or be **baptized** with the baptism with which **I** am baptized?"

Let the hearers know clearly who is speaking, and distinguish between the lines that set context and those that come from a speaker.

The passage you prepare is short. The main thing to keep in your mind as you prepare and as you proclaim is to take your time and proclaim clearly.

READING II   Your best proclamation of this reading will come with familiarity with its meaning. So even before you practice it orally, study what it is saying to the Church. Then deliver it "as the reading says, "confidently."

GOSPEL   This reading has two basic parts. The first (and longer) part is an exchange between Jesus and the brothers James and John. There is a volley of speeches here, so use your skills to distinguish between what is from the mouths of the speakers and what is from the hand of the evangelist.

The second part (or the only part, if you choose the shorter version) has an introductory line from the evangelist and then a lengthy speech from the lips of Jesus. This section is quite beautiful and should be proclaimed with utmost conviction.

For the past few weeks, Jesus in Mark's Gospel has delivered words to his followers that were difficult for them, and now difficult for us, to hear and receive. The "cup" in this

Pause after this part, for the passage shifts its focus from the brothers to Jesus.

Gentiles = JEN-tils

This powerful message is wonderfully located at the end of the long passage. Take your time and be sure that the assembly has every chance to hear it.

They said to him, "We **can**."

Jesus said to them, "The cup that **I** drink, **you** will drink,
    and with the baptism with which **I** am baptized, **you** will
        be baptized;
    but to sit at my **right** or at my **left** is not mine to **give**
    but is for those for whom it has been **prepared**."

When the **ten** heard this, they became **indignant**
    at James and John.

Jesus **summoned** them and said to them,
"You **know** that those who are **recognized** as rulers over
        the Gentiles
    lord it over them,
    and their **great** ones make their **authority** over them **felt**.

But it shall not be so among you.

Rather, whoever wishes to be **great** among you will be
        your **servant**;
    whoever wishes to be **first** among you will be the **slave** of all.

For the Son of Man did not come to be **served**
    but to **serve** and to give his **life** as a **ransom** for **many**."

[Shorter: Mark 10:42–45]

passage is a symbol of the suffering that Jesus himself found in his ministry and in the path to his death. As baptized Christians who come to the table, we share in the cup as we share in his suffering and the suffering of the vocation of the baptized Christian.

As you proclaim the Gospel, make eye contact with the assembly before you as you pose to them the question that Jesus put to his followers: "Can you drink the cup that I drink, or be baptized with the baptism which

which I am baptized?" And as you proclaim their answer, "We can," pronounce it in a way so that your words clear representing the community's willingness to follow the way of Jesus.

The passage is relatively long, and the best lines are in the last few verses. Be most emphatic and measured as you move into the last five lines of the passage.

30TH SUNDAY IN ORDINARY TIME

Lectionary #149

READING I   Jeremiah 31:7–9

A reading from the Book of the Prophet Jeremiah

> **Thus** says the LORD:
> Shout with **joy** for **Jacob**,
>   **exult** at the head of the **nations**;
>   proclaim your **praise** and say:
> The LORD has **delivered** his people,
>   the **remnant** of **Israel**.
> **Behold**, I will bring them **back**
>   from the land of the **north**;
> I will **gather** them from the ends of the **world**,
>   with the **blind** and the **lame** in their **midst**,
> the **mothers** and those with **child**;
>   they shall **return** as an immense **throng**.
> They **departed** in **tears**,
>   but I will **console** them and **guide** them;
> I will **lead** them to brooks of **water**,
>   on a **level** road, so that none shall **stumble**.
> For I am a **father** to Israel,
>   **Ephraim** is my **first-born**.

Jeremiah = jair-uh-MĪ-uh

Make sure that this line is heard clearly, for it is the only part that identifies the LORD as the speaker. See the commentary for thoughts on how to deliver these imperatives.
Jacob = JAY-kub
Israel = IZ-ree-ul

The Lord gathers together people who are broken, in trouble, weighed down, and tired, then and now.

Ephraim = EE-fray-im

READING I   As you begin preparing for your proclamation, notice that the first line identifies the speaker, the LORD, and the rest is what the speaker says. Because of this, pause slightly after you announce the book from which the reading comes so that the community is poised to hear the first words of the text.

The reading is in three sections, divided by breaks in the printed text in the Lectionary.

In part one, the verbs are all in the imperative form, that is, they are verbs with which the Lord is telling the people what to do: "Shout," "exult," "proclaim your praise and say."

During the deportation and captivity of the Israelites, many died or were killed by their captors. That context might seem like the ancient history that it is, but in all of our communities there are many people who feel bedraggled, abandoned, lonely, and despairing, no matter what their appearance may

be as they gather with the community for the liturgy. So know that as you deliver these words of the prophet Jeremiah, you stand in his footsteps and address those who long for relief in difficult lives. Your ministry with this reading is supremely important.

Among those who return from deportation are the "blind." Emphasize this word, because it connects this reading with the Gospel, in which a blind person is cured.

Hebrews = HEE-brooz

See below for the comments on this letter's theology. It is rich and deep, but also mysterious two millennia after its composition.

The point here is that Christ, like us, was subject to weakness. This is the key part of the reading for the assembly.

Aaron = AIR-un

Melchizedek = mel-KEEZ-ih-dek

READING II   Hebrews 5:1–6

A reading from the Letter to the Hebrews

Brothers and sisters:
Every **high** priest is **taken** from among men
    and made their **representative** before **God**,
    to offer **gifts** and **sacrifices** for **sins**.
He is able to deal **patiently** with the **ignorant** and **erring**,
    for he **himself** is beset by weakness
    and so, for **this** reason, must make sin offerings for **himself**
    as well as for the **people**.
No one takes this honor upon **himself**
    but only when called by **God**,
    just as **Aaron** was.
In the same way,
    it was not **Christ** who glorified **himself** in becoming high priest,
    but **rather** the one who **said** to him:
        *You are my **son***: *this day I have **begotten** you;*
    just as he says in **another** place:
        *You are a priest **forever** according to the order*
            *of **Melchizedek**.*

READING II   Though the letter to the Hebrews and this passage from it are deep in meaning, its context feels foreign to us. Rendering this passage accessible will take some concentration and practice on your part.

　　The two quotes in the second part are important to the rhetoric of the ancient author, and you need to make clear to the assembly that these are from another voice.

So be clear with "the one who said to him," introducing the first quotation, and with "as he says in another place" for the second.

GOSPEL   It is a common notion among believers that what we do in worship is a fruit of what we find in the scriptures. But scholars have found that rather than worship being a fruit of the Bible stories, the New Testament stories of Jesus were more likely fruits of worship in the

first-century communities of faith. This is important with this reading. We might think that Bartimaeus' cry, "Son of David, have pity on me," contributed to the liturgical phrase, "Lord, have mercy." It is more likely that the community of Mark's Gospel used a phrase like "Lord, have mercy," or "Son of David, have pity," in its worship before the Gospel was written, and that the evangelist adopted that phrase from his community's

GOSPEL   Mark 10:46–52

A reading from the holy Gospel according to Mark

As Jesus was leaving **Jericho** with his disciples and
     a sizable **crowd**,
  Bartimaeus, a **blind** man, the son of **Timaeus**,
  sat by the roadside **begging**.
On hearing that it was Jesus of **Nazareth**,
  he began to cry out and say,
  "**Jesus**, son of **David**, have **pity** on me."
And many **rebuked** him, telling him to be **silent**.
But he kept calling out all the **more**,
  "Son of **David**, have **pity** on me."
Jesus **stopped** and said, "**Call** him."
So they **called** the blind man, saying to him,
  "Take **courage**; get **up**, Jesus is **calling** you."
He threw aside his **cloak**, sprang **up**, and **came** to Jesus.
Jesus said to him in reply, "What do you want me to **do** for you?"
The blind man replied to him, "**Master**, I want to **see**."
Jesus told him, "Go your **way**; your **faith** has **saved** you."
Immediately he **received** his sight
  and **followed** him on the way.

Jericho = JAIR-ih-koh

Bartimaeus = bar-tih-MAY-us
Timaeus = tim-AY-us

Make these cries from Bartimaeus ring in
the ears of those hearing you. The first is
shouted and the next "calling out all the
more"!
Nazareth = NAZ-uh-reth

The words of Jesus are commands.

The blind man's supplication, "I want to
see," is moving.

---

life and put it on the lips of the blind man in
this Gospel.

   As proclaimer of this Gospel, you can
profit from knowing this because, just as his
community's worship revealed the life of
Christ to Mark, so does the worship of your
community reveal the life of the body of
Christ to you and the people around you. If
possible, as you proclaim the line, "Jesus,

son of David, have pity on me," let it res-
onate with those who listen so that some
will catch the echo.

   The connection between Bartimaeus'
saving and healing encounter with Jesus
and the parish's living as the body of Christ
is an utterly important reality. The more you
can do as a minister of the word to have
people recognize this connection, the better.

   Although the narrative is not very long,
the Lectionary text supplies two breaking
points in the account. Pay attention to these
for the action shifts slightly from one to
another, and they offer you a chance to
catch your breath.

ALL SAINTS

Lectionary #667

READING I   Revelation 7:2 – 4, 9 – 14

Revelation = rev-uh-LAY-shun

The complexity of this unusual passage might prompt you to speed through it, but resist that inclination. Study the passage, as below, and deliver it clearly and with confidence.

A reading from the Book of Revelation

I, **John**, saw another **angel** come up from the **East**,
    holding the **seal** of the living God.
He cried out in a loud **voice** to the four **angels**
    who were given **power** to damage the **land** and the **sea,**
        "Do not damage the **land** or the **sea** or the **trees**
        until we put the **seal** on the **foreheads** of the servants
            of our **God**."
I heard the **number** of those who had been marked with the seal,
    one **hundred** and forty-four **thousand** marked
    from every **tribe** of the children of **Israel**.

This crowd of 144,000 robed in white is a symbol of the Church; do not rush through the details.
Israel = IZ-ree-ul

After **this** I had a vision of a great **multitude**,
    which no one could **count**,
    from every **nation**, **race**, **people**, and **tongue**.
They stood before the **throne** and before the **Lamb**,
    wearing white **robes** and holding **palm** branches in their **hands**.

For those who know that the white robes are a sign of initiation, be clear where the white robes are mentioned.

They cried out in a loud **voice**:
    "**Salvation** comes from our **God**,
        who is **seated** on the **throne**,
    and from the **Lamb**."
All the angels stood around the throne
    and around the **elders** and the four living **creatures**.
They **prostrated** themselves before the throne,
    worshiped **God**, and exclaimed:

READING I As a lector studying this passage, you might think that this text has little relation to your own faith life. There are some symbolic clues that can help you appreciate that this sometimes enigmatic text is not as remote as you might think.

Consider a few of the important symbols of this passage: the 144,000, the white robes, the blood of the Lamb.

The number 12 is a symbol of universality in much of the Bible. Consider the 12 tribes of Israel, for example, or even the 12 disciples. The number was not meant exclusively as a historical fact, but as an embracing symbol of all. So when, the author here writes of the 144,000, this is a kind of hyper-inclusiveness, for 12 x 12 = 144: universality times universality times a thousand!

Now consider the white robes. When each of us is baptized, whether as an infant or an adult, we are robed in white, a symbol

of newness and the new life into which we have been reborn. The white robes in this passage mean that the multitude in white robes have been baptized into the people of God.

Finally, what about the paradox the author brings in here? "[T]hey have washed their robes and made them white in the blood of the Lamb." (It was no easier then than now to get blood stains out of white

"**Amen. Blessing** and **glory, wisdom** and **thanksgiving,**
    honor, power, and **might**
        be to our God for**ever** and **ever. Amen.**"
Then one of the **elders** spoke up and said to me,
    "Who **are** these wearing white **robes,** and where did they **come**
        from?"
I said to him, "My **lord, you** are the one who **knows.**"
He said to me,
    "**These** are the ones who have **survived** the time
        of great **distress;**
    they have **washed** their robes
    and made them **white** in the blood of the **Lamb.**"

The paradox of the blood-washed white robes is a brilliant literary device.

READING II   1 John 3:1–3

A reading from the first Letter of Saint John

Beloved:
See what **love** the Father has bestowed on **us**
    that **we** may be called the **children** of **God.**
Yet so we **are.**
The reason the world does not know **us**
    is that it did not know **him.**
Beloved, we are God's children **now;**
    what we **shall** be has not yet been **revealed.**
We **do** know that when it is revealed we shall be **like** him,
    for we shall **see** him as he **is.**
Everyone who has this **hope** based on **him** makes himself **pure,**
    as he is pure.

The passage is short, so your reading can be measured and well proclaimed. The first- and second-person pronouns enable you to speak to the assembly intimately, sharing with them in being the "we" and "us" of God's children.

Pause here so that your use of "Beloved" in addressing the assembly comes through with meaning and engagement.

clothes.) The Lamb is Christ, and these people in white robes, like the Church today, are the body of Christ. The juxtaposition of the blood and the white robes tells us that some members of the community of the book of Revelation were martyred.

    The details of these symbols will make the reading more engaging for you so that you, in turn, can be clear and intentional when you proclaim the reading to the liturgical community you serve. Revelation is a great work, so the Church saves it for the end—of the Bible and the liturgical year!

READING II This is a beautiful reading; take its message to heart so that you can communicate it boldly to the Church. It is quite brief, so there is absolutely no need to hurry through it.

    The language of "we" and "us" is present because the author of the letter was speaking for and with his faith community, and together they were "children of God." This is no different for yourself and your faith community, for you, like that community of John's letter, are indeed "children of God."

    Remember that when this was written the Christian movement had not yet spread far, so when the author writes that "the world does not know us," that was literally true. In the intervening centuries, the faith has grown into one of the major world religions. The world does indeed "know us," meaning Christians, and "know him," meaning Christ, even those who are not themselves Christians. You can read this solemnly, however, for the Church and Christ always need to be better known.

GOSPEL   Matthew 5:1–12a

A reading from the holy Gospel according to Matthew

When **Jesus** saw the **crowds**, he went up the **mountain**,
    and after he had sat **down**, his **disciples** came to him.
He began to **teach** them, saying:
    "**Blessed** are the poor in **spirit**,
        for **theirs** is the Kingdom of **heaven**.
    Blessed are they who **mourn**,
        for **they** will be **comforted**.
    Blessed are the **meek**,
        for **they** will inherit the **land**.
    Blessed are they who hunger and **thirst** for **righteousness**,
        for **they** will be **satisfied**.
    Blessed are the **merciful**,
        for **they** will be shown **mercy**.
    Blessed are the clean of **heart**,
        for **they** will **see** God.
    Blessed are the **peacemakers**,
        for **they** will be called **children** of God.
    Blessed are they who are **persecuted** for the sake
            of **righteousness**,
        for **theirs** is the Kingdom of **heaven**.
    Blessed are **you** when they **insult** you and **persecute** you
        and utter every kind of **evil** against you **falsely** because of **me**.
    Rejoice and be **glad**,
        for your **reward** will be **great** in **heaven**."

After these opening lines, the remainder is in Jesus' words, to the end.

Because the passage is familiar and the literary form patterned, take your time.

Pause here, for the style and content shift slightly for the ending.

This final verse is not a "beatitude" as the other verses are. But its imperatives ("rejoice" and "be glad") are important.

Pause at the break, for the salutation the author uses to address his community at the beginning of the next section—that is, "Beloved"—is touching. A pause will help the assembly be poised to hear you address them as the author addressed his community: "Beloved, we are God's children now."

GOSPEL │ Many of those to whom you will proclaim this word of God are indeed "poor in spirit," "meek," "merciful," and "peacemakers." They, like all the saints, have had their lives shaped by the Gospel.

As proclaimer of the Gospel of the beatitudes, you can make the familiar text from Matthew a key ingredient for this solemnity. Though it is never a good idea to presume that one is a saint, more believers probably err on the side of thinking that their lives have no holy quality than on the side of presumption. With the clarity and strength of your proclamation, let those in the assembly know that holiness is not distant from the way they themselves live.

Proclaim with conviction, with trust in God's grace, having practiced the message, and believing that God's word is efficacious.

ALL SOULS

Lectionary #668

READING I · Wisdom 3:1–9

A reading from the Book of Wisdom

The **souls** of the **just** are in the hand of **God**,
  and no **torment** shall **touch** them.
They **seemed**, in the view of the **foolish**, to be **dead**;
  and their passing **away** was thought an **affliction**
  and their going **forth** from us, utter **destruction**.
But they are in **peace**.
For **if** in the sight of **others**, indeed they be **punished**,
  yet is their **hope** full of **immortality**;
chastised a little, they shall be greatly **blessed**,
  because God **tried** them
  and found them **worthy** of himself.
As **gold** in the furnace, he **proved** them,
  and as sacrificial **offerings** he took them to **himself**.
In the time of their **visitation** they shall **shine**,
  and shall **dart** about as **sparks** through **stubble**;
they shall judge **nations** and rule over **peoples**,
  and the **LORD** shall be their King **forever**.
Those who **trust** in him shall understand **truth**,
  and the **faithful** shall abide with him in **love**:
because **grace** and **mercy** are with his **holy** ones,
  and his **care** is with his **elect**.

The opening line is strong and central to the passage.

This beautiful line should be delivered as slowly and clearly as possible.

The metaphorical images here, of shining sparks in stubble, are unique.

The reading closes as beautifully as it began.

The readings given here are suggestions. Any readings from the Lectionary for the Commemoration of All the Faithful Departed (#668) or the Masses for the Dead (#1011–1016) may be used.

READING I This reading from the wisdom literature of the Old Testament is proclaimed frequently at Catholic funerals, for it offers a frame for the theology of purgatory, as well as distinguishing those who are remembered on this day, All Souls, from those who are remembered the day before, All Saints.

Although the Church has a process of canonization that marks as saintly those whose lives we commemorate in the liturgy, those who manifested God's gifts and love in their days on earth. The saints are not only holy, their holiness was known to others. There are many more souls about whose holiness we do not know. Some of these are surely saints now, and some of these will be accepted into God's kingdom later.

In your assembly there are people who are concerned for the souls of their beloved dead. For them you can mark and emphasize the elements of the reading that give hope: "they are in peace," "their hope [is] full of immortality," "they shall be greatly blessed," "they shall shine," and "the faithful shall abide with him in love."

All Souls focuses on the dead, and, in a culture where sickness and death are kept out of sight, such a commemoration is rare and countercultural. It provides consolation to many believers, and for this reason it is important in the unfolding of the liturgical year.

READING II   Romans 5:5–11

A reading from the Letter of Saint Paul to the Romans

Brothers and sisters:
Hope does not **disappoint**,
    because the love of **God** has been poured **out** into our **hearts**
    through the Holy **Spirit** that has been **given** to us.
For **Christ**, while we were still **helpless**,
    died at the appointed time for the **ungodly**.
Indeed, only with **difficulty** does one **die** for a **just** person,
    though perhaps for a **good** person
    one might even **find** courage to **die**.
But God **proves** his love for us
    in that **while** we were still **sinners** Christ **died** for us.
How much **more** then, since we are now **justified** by his **blood**,
    will we be **saved** through him from the **wrath**.
Indeed, **if**, while we were **enemies**,
    we were **reconciled** to God through the **death** of his **Son**,
    how much **more**, once **reconciled**,
    will we be **saved** by his **life**.
Not only **that**,
    but we **also** boast of God through our Lord Jesus **Christ**,
    through whom we have now received **reconciliation**.

Or:

These opening lines are filled with brightness. If you can, deliver them while engaging the assembly before you with eye contact.

The middle section is a rich theology. It is central to Paul's message of salvation in the letter to the Romans.

The reconciliation theology of the final two verses is key to this feast.

READING II   **ROMANS 5. On the feast of All Souls the Church remembers the dead and repeats our hope in God for the salvation of all. These two elements, the remembrance of the dead and the hope of good things from God, are central to this day, and this reading from Paul to the Romans sums up this theology sharply and beautifully.**

After looking at the assembly directly when you address those before you as your "brothers and sisters," proclaim the opening lines with its wonderful theology of the love of God. This is a fact of faith that believers can never bring to mind and heart often

enough: "The love of God has been poured out into our hearts." This is the work of the Holy Spirit, as Paul wrote. If you can, commit this opening sentence to memory, and speak it with conviction and with love for those to whom you minister.

The middle section of the reading brings forth the generosity of Christ, who died not only for the just but for sinners as well. This is the longest part of the reading, and, to proclaim it with conviction, you might pray about it and appropriate it to your own experience.

After the second break, the focus is on the reconciliation of humanity in Christ, on how in spite of the darkness and division of sin, Christ brings humanity together, the living and the dead. On this day as the living remember and pray for the dead, those known and those forgotten, this reconciliation toward the union of all humanity in Christ is central.

This is not a light text. Study the passage and proclaim it well, for its message will be consoling to those who hear you proclaim it.

READING II   Romans 6:3–9

A reading from the Letter of Saint Paul to the Romans

Brothers and sisters:
Are you **unaware** that we who were **baptized** into Christ Jesus
    were **baptized** into his **death**?
We were indeed **buried** with him through baptism into **death**,
    so that, just as Christ was **raised** from the dead
    by the **glory** of the Father,
    we **too** might **live** in newness of **life**.

For if we have grown into **union** with him through a **death**
    like his,
    we shall also be **united** with him in the **resurrection**.
We know that our **old** self was **crucified** with him,
    so that our **sinful** body might be done **away** with,
    that we might no longer be in **slavery** to sin.
For a **dead** person has been **absolved** from sin.
If, then, we have **died** with Christ,
    we believe that we shall also **live** with him.
We know that **Christ**, raised from the **dead**, dies no **more**;
    death no longer has power over him.

The reading starts with the direct second-person voice. Address the passage to your listeners directly.

The theology of death and resurrection you proclaim here is key as the Church remembers its dead.

The union between Christ's death and our death, between Christ's Resurrection and our own could not be clearer. Proclaim this with confidence and consolation.

ROMANS 6. Paul's letter to the Romans was written almost two thousand years ago, but its theology of Baptism is so foundational that it can be proclaimed and heard in the assembly as if it had been written by a contemporary. There are two challenges to you as the proclaimer of this passage about Baptism.

The first challenge comes from the liturgical context of All Souls. At each Christian funeral, the body is covered with a funeral pall and placed next to the Easter candle. These symbols represent the Baptism by which the Christian was united to Chist, and on this experience the Church's theology hangs. For those in your community who are concerned about the souls of their beloved dead, this foundation of salvation in Baptism and this person's being joined to the death and Resurrection of Christ in Baptism are important.

The second challenge of the passage is in taking seriously the second- and first-person voices of the letter to the Romans. The challenge is that you proclaim the reading not as a recital of the faith of first-century Rome but as the faith of your community in your time and your place. There is nothing in the passage to distance your community from the faith Paul captured here.

The Church's theology of purgatory can be received two ways. The harsh side is that of waiting out an eternity of punishment and chastening until one is welcomed into God's reign. The consoling side is that all baptized Christians have been joined to the life of Christ, and the balance is weighted toward hope because of Christ's love for all.

Only this line is not from the lips of Jesus. Pause before beginning so that this context is understood.

The key lines of the proclamation are these last three. Take your time and, if you can, engage the assembly with eye contact.

GOSPEL John 6:37–40

A reading from the holy Gospel according to John

Jesus said to the **crowds**:
"**Everything** that the Father **gives** me will **come** to me,
　　and I will not reject **anyone** who comes to me,
　　because I came **down** from heaven not to do my **own** will
　　but the **will** of the one who **sent** me.
And **this** is the will of the one who **sent** me,
　　that I should not lose **anything** of what he **gave** me,
　　but that I should **raise** it on the last **day**.
For **this** is the will of my **Father**,
　　that everyone who **sees** the Son and **believes** in him
　　may have eternal **life**,
　　and I shall **raise** him on the last **day**."

GOSPEL　In the Gospel of John, this section appears in the discourse where Jesus reveals himself as the "bread of life." (His words, "I am the bread of life," appear just before this passage.) That discourse follows a multiplication miracle in which Jesus takes the five loaves and two fish from a boy and feeds about five thousand people. Then comes the passage you will proclaim, which is followed by the eucharistic theology of the Gospel of John. John's gospel does not have a Last Supper with bread and wine, as do the others, so the eucharistic teachings come here in this chapter 6. This context helps understand the passage you proclaim and its relation to All Souls.

Just before this passage, Jesus had explained to the crowd that, just as God had sent manna from heaven to nourish those near starvation, so now has Jesus come down from heaven to nourish those on the brink of death. And this is the link with the feast of All Souls, for here Jesus says that he was sent so that "I should not lose anything of what he [the Father, who sent him] gave me."

Because All Souls recalls those who have died and who might not have gained salvation at death, this theology of Christ's not losing anything is at the heart of this Catholic day of remembrance. The Church trusts in God's love and in the salvation wrought in Christ's life and death, so that all will be united with him in resurrection as we all are united with him in death.

The final lines are of consolation. Commit them to memory, if you can, and proclaim them to those before you who might worry about their dead.

31ST SUNDAY IN ORDINARY TIME

Lectionary #152

READING I   Deuteronomy 6:2 – 6

Deuteronomy = doo-ter-AH-nuh-mee

Pause before you start the reading, for only in this first verse are the speaker and his audience mentioned.
Moses = MOH-ziz

In anticipation of the Gospel reading for this day, the key words are "statutes," "commandments," and "enjoin." Knowing that they are echoed in the Gospel, proclaim them with some emphasis.
Israel = IZ-ree-ul

The image of "a land flowing with milk and honey" is a treat. Proclaim it as such.

A reading from the Book of Deuteronomy

Moses spoke to the **people**, saying:
   "**Fear** the LORD, your **God**,
   and **keep**, throughout the **days** of your lives,
   all his **statutes** and **commandments** which I **enjoin** on you,
   and thus have long **life**.
Hear then, Israel, and be **careful** to observe them,
   that you may **grow** and **prosper** the more,
   in **keeping** with the **promise** of the LORD, the God
      of your **fathers**,
   to give you a **land** flowing with **milk** and **honey**.

"**Hear**, O Israel! The LORD is our **God**, the LORD **alone**!
Therefore, you shall **love** the LORD, your **God**,
   with all your heart,
   and with **all** your soul,
   and with **all** your strength.
Take to **heart** these words which I **enjoin** on you today."

READING I Notice that all but the first few words of the passage are from Moses, as he speaks "to the people." Because the identification of the speaker and the audience is in this short introduction, pause slightly after you announce the book of Deuteronomy so that the assembly is poised to hear the opening words.

The reading has three basic parts for you to attend to as you prepare. The first part demonstrates Moses' blessing on the people. Faith is instilled deeply in those who practice it from infancy, as this text suggests.

Part two reveals what will come to those who observe the law, the commandments. In some communities of the early Church, the metaphor of the "land flowing with milk and honey" was taken so seriously that neophytes were given milk and honey to drink as a celebration of their arrival in the Promised Land, that is, the saving embrace of the Church. Some scholars of early Christian worship think that in still other communities milk and honey were

part of the eucharistic table. Whatever their use then and now, this is a vital metaphor, so pronounce it clearly and with animation.

The final part is Moses' summary. As you take up his words, "Hear, O Israel . . ." deliver them to your people as if they were the Israelites who heard them centuries ago. His words about the commandments round off the passage, for the opening part centered on them, and here too at the end.

Take a significant pause between the three sections, for your own sake, but also for the benefit of those hearing you.

Hebrews = HEE-brooz

In this opening section, the former priests are mentioned first, to which the priesthood of Jesus is compared. Pause at the end of the section as a transition marker.

In each of the reading's three sections the rhetoric relies on the juxtaposition of the former priests and the high priest Jesus Christ.

As before, the former is laid out first, and the perfection of the son, the new priest, follows at the end.

READING II   Hebrews 7:23–28

A reading from the Letter to the Hebrews

Brothers and sisters:
The **levitical** priests were many
    because they were prevented by **death** from remaining in **office**,
    but **Jesus**, because he remains **forever**,
    has a **priesthood** that **does** not pass away.
Therefore, he is always able to **save** those who approach God
        through him,
    since he **lives** forever to make **intercession** for them.

It was **fitting** that we should have such a **high** priest:
    holy, **innocent**, **undefiled**, **separated** from **sinners**,
    higher than the **heavens**.
He has no need, as did the **high** priests,
    to offer **sacrifice** day after day,
    first for his **own** sins and then for **those** of the **people**;
he did that once for **all** when he **offered** himself.
For the law appoints men subject to **weakness** to be **high** priests,
    but the word of the **oath**, which was taken **after** the law,
    appoints a **son**,
    who has been made **perfect forever**.

READING II   This is the fifth of a series of seven readings from the letter to the Hebrews. If you can spare a little time in preparation and especially if you have not proclaimed a passage from this letter before, read through the four earlier and two succeeding passages so that you can put the passage you will proclaim in the context of the Church's selections from the rich theology and liturgical meaning of the letter to the Hebrews.

GOSPEL   The Gospel of Mark was written as the temple in Jerusalem was being destroyed by the Roman occupiers in Palestine. The cultic practices of the Jews and the Mosaic law were under attack by foreign enemies. Passages such as this in Mark reflect the state of Judaism and Palestine at the time when the evangelist was writing the Gospel, about the year 70, more than they reflect what was happening there during the life of Jesus.

Although the first three Gospels frequently portray many confrontations between Jesus and other interpreters of the Mosaic law, the Pharisees and scribes in particular, narratives such as this reveal Jesus' own knowledge and appreciation of the law, in spite of times he violated it in order to help people in need.

Notice that the reading is a conversation between one of the scribes and Jesus, tossing scripture quotations back and forth. Take your time as you move from one speaker to the next.

GOSPEL Mark 12:28b–34

A reading from the holy Gospel according to Mark

One of the **scribes** came to Jesus and asked him,
    "**Which** is the first of all the **commandments?**"
Jesus replied, "The first is **this:**
    Hear, O Israel!
    The **LORD** *our* **God** *is* LORD **alone***!*
    You shall **love** *the* LORD *your* **God** *with* **all** *your heart,*
    with **all** *your soul,*
    with **all** *your mind,*
    and with **all** *your strength.*
The second is **this:**
    You shall love your **neighbor** *as* **yourself***.*
There is no other commandment **greater** than these."
The scribe said to him, "Well **said**, teacher.
You are right in saying,
    'He is **One** and there is no **other** than he.'
And 'to love him with **all** your heart,
    with **all** your understanding,
    with **all** your strength,
    and to love your **neighbor** as **yourself**'
    is worth more than all burnt **offerings** and **sacrifices**."
And when Jesus **saw** that he answered with **understanding**,
    he said to him,
    "You are not **far** from the kingdom of **God**."
And no one dared to ask him any more **questions**.

Stress the first commandment as you proclaim it here, for Jesus is here quoting what was just proclaimed in the first reading.
Israel = IZ-ree-ul

Be assertive with the mention of the scribe, for the crux of the passage rests on the religious leader, often posed as an adversary, sanctioning Jesus' teaching.

Notice too that in the words of both Jesus and the scribe there are quotations within quotations. The scribe actually quotes Jesus who had quoted the law, so there are three layers in one spot: the words of the law, in the words of Jesus, as quoted in the words of the scribe. (It is far more clear than this unpacking makes it sound.) Be forthright as you proclaim Jesus' and the scribe's interpretation of the law as written here by the evangelist.

32ND SUNDAY IN ORDINARY TIME

Lectionary #155

READING I   1 Kings 17:10–16

A reading from the first Book of Kings

In **those** days, Elijah the **prophet** went to **Zarephath**.
As he **arrived** at the entrance of the **city**,
  a **widow** was gathering **sticks** there; he called out to her,
  "**Please** bring me a small **cupful** of water to **drink**."
She left to get it, and he called out after her,
  "**Please** bring along a bit of **bread**."
She answered, "As the LORD, your God, **lives**,
  I have nothing **baked**; there is only a **handful** of flour in my **jar**
  and a little **oil** in my **jug**.
Just **now** I was collecting a couple of **sticks**,
  to go in and **prepare** something for **myself** and my **son**;
  when we have **eaten** it, we shall **die**."
Elijah said to her, "**Do** not be afraid.
Go and do as you **propose**.
But **first** make me a little **cake** and **bring** it to me.
Then you can prepare something for **yourself** and your **son**.
For the LORD, the God of **Israel**, **says**,
  'The **jar** of flour shall **not** go empty,
  nor the **jug** of oil run **dry**,
  until the **day** when the LORD sends **rain** upon the earth.'"

Elijah = ee-LĪ-juh
Zarephath = ZAIR-uh-fath
Speeches fill this story, with these first two from Elijah in the imperative mode, requesting the widow to act on his behalf: "Please bring me . . ."

Each of the characters, Elijah and the widow, has a long speech in the middle of the passage. These six lines are from her.

And these are from the prophet. Notice that the final part of this speech is quoted speech from "the LORD, the God of Israel." Be careful so that the assembly can follow the narrative and the alternating speakers.

READING I   The care of widows and orphans in the earliest days of Christianity was a ministry of consequence, and one to be greatly admired and taken up in prayer and preaching again and again. This reading you will proclaim is a narrative about the prophet Elijah and his experience on meeting a poor widow.

The narrative before you is unique and engaging. Be sure to emphasize the word "widow" each time it appears, for it is the link between this account and the Gospel reading. The narrative from 1 Kings has its twists and turns, so you might ask for help from a fellow lector or a family member in testing out ways to make the account come alive for your hearers.

Because the passage has a number of speeches, be especially clear in identifying who is speaking. The woman speaks only once, but her part is long, and it reveals a lot about the situation of many of the disenfranchised in the society where she lived.

The summary reveals the miracle that the prophet foretold. Proclaim this with emphasis and conviction.

She **left** and did as Elijah had **said**.
She was able to eat for a **year**, and he and her son as **well**;
    the **jar** of flour did **not** go empty,
    nor the **jug** of oil run **dry**,
    as the LORD had foretold through **Elijah**.

READING II   Hebrews 9:24 – 28

Hebrews = HEE-brooz

These first few verses describe what Christ did not do, which opens up to the positive aspects of the redemption wrought in his suffering and death.

The final sentence of the passage is fairly long and complex. Prepare thoroughly and be ready for what the author has done, so that your delivery will be smooth and confident.

A reading from the Letter to the Hebrews

Christ did not enter into a sanctuary made by **hands**,
    a copy of the **true** one, but heaven **itself**,
    that he might **now** appear before **God** on our **behalf**.
Not that he might offer himself **repeatedly**,
    as the **high** priest **enters** each year into the **sanctuary**
    with **blood** that is not his **own**;
    if **that** were so, he would have had to **suffer** repeatedly
    from the **foundation** of the **world**.
But **now** once for all he has **appeared** at the end of the **ages**
    to **take** away sin by his **sacrifice**.
Just as it is **appointed** that human beings die **once**,
    and after this the **judgment**, so also **Christ**,
    offered **once** to take away the sins of **many**,
    will appear a **second** time, not to take away **sin**
    but to bring **salvation** to those who eagerly **await** him.

READING II | Although the letter to the Hebrews is incomparably rich in many ways, its language and metaphors can be quite foreign to our sensibilities these many centuries after it was composed. The best way for you as lector to bring this text alive is to be familiar with its meaning.

This is the sixth in a series of seven readings from the letter to the Hebrews. Read through the five earlier passages and the one remaining so that you can put the message you will proclaim in the context of the Church's selections from the letter to the Hebrews.

The passage is set up in a rhetorically beneficial way, with the description of what Christ's appearance did not do coming first, followed by the positive aspects of the redemption won in Christ's sacrifice and death. In the New Testament period, there was a general expectation that Christ's second coming was imminent. In reading this text, you can take up the expectation of the author of the letter anew.

The final verse is the summary: Christ offered himself to redeem us from sin, and he will return to save those who wait for him. While you do not want to be overly enthusiastic in your proclamation, this is great news, so be prepared to deliver it with power and depth. You can indicate with a glance that you and your assembly are among those who are eagerly awaiting him, and your voice can capture what such eagerness would sound like.

GOSPEL   Mark 12:38 – 44

A reading from the holy Gospel according to Mark

In the course of his teaching Jesus said to the **crowds,**
  "**Beware** of the **scribes,** who like to go around in long **robes**
    and accept **greetings** in the **marketplaces,**
    seats of honor in **synagogues,**
    and **places** of honor at **banquets.**
They **devour** the houses of **widows** and, as a pretext
    recite lengthy **prayers.**
They will receive a **very** severe condemnation."

He sat **down** opposite the treasury
    and **observed** how the crowd put **money** into the treasury.
Many **rich** people put in large sums.
A **poor widow** also came and put in two small **coins** worth
    a few **cents.**
Calling his disciples to himself, he said to them,
"**Amen,** I say to you, this poor **widow** put in **more**
    than all the **other** contributors to the **treasury.**
For **they** have all contributed from their **surplus** wealth,
    but **she,** from her **poverty,** has contributed all she **had,**
    her **whole** livelihood."

[Shorter: Mark 12:41 – 44]

The key characters that unite this Gospel reading with the first reading from 1 Kings are the widows. For this reason emphasize the words "widows" and "widow" as they appear in the Gospel.

This lesson from Jesus can be delivered slowly and deliberately.

GOSPEL Notice the key role of widows in this long passage from Mark. They are mentioned as a group in the first half, and then an individual widow approaches the treasury in the second half. She becomes the key figure for what Jesus taught then and for what we as Church consider now.

In early Christianity, widows were women whose husbands had died, just as we use the word now, but they were also members of a dedicated and enrolled ministry in the Church, alongside bishops, priests, and deacons. It is unfortunate, in a way, that this august ministry has not survived into the Church today, for widows are indeed the vivifying force in many parishes, especially active in corporal works of mercy and charitable self-giving. Perhaps you can read about them in 1 Peter as a background for appreciating how the group of widows and then the one widow function in this Marcan passage you will proclaim.

The widow is the unifying element between the two parts. Each part has a distinct location: Jesus was teaching in the temple in the first part, and in the second, he is seated opposite the treasury. You can pause between the parts and take up the second half with freshness, especially as you near the end, with the lesson Jesus draws from the impoverished generosity of the poor widow and her two small coins.

33RD SUNDAY IN ORDINARY TIME

Lectionary #158

READING I   Daniel 12:1–3

You need not emphasize this opening too much.

The end of the world is often portrayed with dark images like these.

But the prophet's words do not end on this dark note.

Have your voice capture the hopeful message and bright imagery. Commit this part to memory so that you can address the assembly with eye contact as you bring the passage to a close.

A reading from the Book of the Prophet Daniel

In those days, I, **Daniel**,
    heard this word of the LORD:
"At **that** time there shall arise
    Michael, the great **prince**,
    guardian of your **people**;
it shall be a time **unsurpassed** in **distress**
    since nations **began** until that time.
At **that** time your people shall **escape**,
    everyone who is found **written** in the **book**.

"**Many** of those who **sleep** in the dust of the **earth** shall **awake**;
    some shall live **forever**,
    others shall be an everlasting **horror** and **disgrace**.

"But the **wise** shall shine **brightly**
    like the **splendor** of the **firmament**,
and those who lead the many to **justice**
    shall be like the stars **forever**."

READING I   Near the end of the liturgical year, the Church turns to readings about the end of life and the end of time. This has a twofold implication for those who hear the scriptures on these last Sundays before Advent. Listeners are brought to consider the end of the world and also to consider how well prepared they are for their own last days. Your ministry for this proclamation is not an easy one, for words about death and the end are difficult, even when the basic theological meaning of this passage is warm and consoling.

In the creed each Sunday we profess that we believe in the communion of the saints, and that communion includes the living and the dead. This passage you prepare considers the waking up of those who sleep, that is, those who have died. Though we tend to think of salvation as individual, the tradition more often speaks of it in this communal sense, embracing not only the community of faith in our time, but the community of faith of *all* time.

As you review the passage, notice that the darker elements come first, with the words about great distress. The final part of the reading weighs on the other side of the balance, with the wise shining brightly and so forth. Be sure to match this hopeful message with a positive, bright proclamation.

Hebrews = HEE-br<u>oo</u>z

The meaning of "this one," meaning Christ, is discussed in the commentary.

READING II   Hebrews 10:11–14, 18

A reading from the Letter to the Hebrews

Brothers and sisters:
Every priest stands **daily** at his **ministry,**
  offering **frequently** those same **sacrifices**
  that can **never** take away **sins.**
But **this** one offered **one** sacrifice for sins,
  and took his seat **forever** at the right hand of **God;**
  now he waits until his **enemies** are made his **footstool.**
For by **one** offering
  he has made perfect **forever** those who are being **consecrated.**

Where there is forgiveness of **these,**
  there is no longer **offering** for sin.

READING II After six second readings from the letter to the Hebrews, we come to the seventh and last. If you have not proclaimed Hebrews before or if you do not feel familiar with the New Testament book, you might page through the *Workbook* to read and consider the passages that have been assigned over the past six weeks. (They began on October 8.)

It is helpful to understand the rhetoric of the ancient author. He was making the point that we are saved, indeed "consecrated" in the language of the passage, by the *one* sacrifice of Christ, the high priest. And that makes all other sacrifices obsolete.

The more comfortable your are with the ancient rhetoric and its deep theology, the more confident your proclamation of the passage will be.

GOSPEL Year after year, the end of this long span of Ordinary Time gives believers a chance to think about the end of the world and the end of their own lives.

At the time when Mark was writing the Gospel for his community, it seemed that the world was indeed ending. His society was in disarray, with many people displaced

GOSPEL   Mark 13:24–32

A reading from the holy Gospel according to Mark

Jesus said to his **disciples**:
"In **those** days after that **tribulation**
the sun will be **darkened**,
    and the **moon** will not give its **light**,
and the **stars** will be falling from the **sky**,
    and the powers in the **heavens** will be **shaken**.

"And **then** they will see 'the Son of **Man** coming in the **clouds'**
    with great **power** and **glory**,
    and then he will send out the **angels**
    and **gather** his **elect** from the four **winds**,
    from the end of the **earth** to the end of the **sky**.

"Learn a **lesson** from the **fig** tree.
When its branch becomes **tender** and sprouts **leaves**,
    you know that **summer** is near.
In the **same** way, when you see **these** things happening,
    know that he is near, at the **gates**.
Amen, I **say** to you,
    this **generation** will not pass **away**
    until **all** these things have taken **place**.
Heaven and **earth** will pass away,
    but my **words** will **not** pass away.

"But of that **day** or **hour**, **no** one knows,
    neither the angels in **heaven**, nor the **Son**, but only
      the **Father**."

Notice that only this line is not in quotation marks. The remainder is from the lips of Jesus. Pause before you begin so that the assembly is poised to hear who is speaking and to whom.

See below for some thoughts on how to proclaim these cosmological and apocalyptic elements.

Sometimes such dark passages in the Lectionary end on a consoling note. Not today! The uncertainty about the time of the end is as ominous as the topic itself.

---

from familiar surroundings and ways of living. Many were driven from their homes and families, and many were left in dire straits. The time of suffering about which the evangelist wrote was not just from his theology or his imagination; it was before his eyes day after day.

The content of the passage is cosmological and apocalyptic. The evangelist related the strife in human life to events in the cosmos—the sun, moon, stars, and powers in the heavens.

Although you do not want to proclaim the passage with such ferocity that your hearers start looking outside to see if there are any stars falling in the parking lot, you also do not want to proclaim the passage so

mildly that your hearers do not face up to the inevitable end of life, when God will be all in all. Find the appropriate level for your voice with such a unique passage. If possible, practice with a family member or fellow minister. Another's assessment of how we match content with style is usually much better than our own.

OUR LORD JESUS CHRIST THE KING

Lectionary #161

READING I   Daniel 7:13–14

A reading from the Book of the Prophet Daniel

As the **visions** during the night **continued**, I saw
    one like a son of **man** coming,
        on the clouds of **heaven**;
    when he reached the **Ancient** One
        and was **presented** before him,
    the one like a Son of man received **dominion**,
        glory, and **kingship**;
    all **peoples**, **nations**, and **languages** serve him.
His **dominion** is an **everlasting** dominion
    that shall not be taken **away**,
    his kingship shall **not** be destroyed.

Pause significantly after identifying the book, for this opening line is an essential ingredient in the passage.

The more vividly you have the Ancient One and the one like a Son of man in your mind, the more vivid will your proclamation be.
ancient AYN-shent
dominion = doh-MIN-yun

READING II   Revelation 1:5–8

A reading from the Book of Revelation

Jesus **Christ** is the faithful **witness**,
    the **firstborn** of the **dead** and **ruler** of the kings of the **earth**.
To him who **loves** us and has **freed** us from our sins by his **blood**,
    who has made us into a **kingdom**,
        priests for his God and **Father**,
    to him be **glory** and **power forever** and **ever**. **Amen**.

The reading opens with an extraordinarily wide scope and claim about the kingdom of God wrought in the redemption of Jesus Christ.

READING I   Although we are at the end of the liturgical year, the visions of the readings for today—and the reading from Daniel that you prepare in particular—match up with the end-of-the-world readings of Advent, at the start of the liturgical year.

This is a short reading bearing a potent message, so take your time. Imagine the Ancient One and the one like a Son of Man for yourself so that your proclamation will inspire your hearers to imagine what he looked like on "the clouds of heaven." There

is an arresting image at the end of the reading, with all peoples, nations, and languages united to serve the one like a Son of Man. His advent is one of communion, bringing together all people.

READING II   The community from which the book of Revelation was born was under threat and persecution. This context is perhaps one reason why many minority faith-groups turn to it when they feel under attack by the dominant cultures around them. The blood-drenched white

robes of the army in this book reveal the suffering of its members. With this in mind, we can appreciate how the thought of the coming reign of Jesus Christ would have given them the hopeful vision you will proclaim.

Your best preparation for proclaiming this passage is to realize its extraordinary and true claims. As you draw the assembly in with your imperative voice, "Behold," you need to be firm in your own acceptance of the vision.

Be bold with your proclamation, for this scene is powerful and calls for a confident

Maintain a measured delivery; the reading is brief but its vision is grand.

Behold, he is **coming** amid the **clouds**,
and **every** eye will **see** him,
even those who **pierced** him.
All the peoples of the earth will **lament** him.
Yes. **Amen**.

See below for an explanation of this verse. Proclaim this last verse with unswerving conviction.
Alpha = AL-fuh
Omega = oh-MAY-guh

"I am the **Alpha** and the **Omega**," says the Lord God,
"the one who **is** and who **was** and who is to **come**,
the **almighty**."

GOSPEL   John 18:33b–37

A reading from the holy Gospel according to John

There are more changes of speaker than there are breaks in the printed text. As you prepare, imagine that there is a break each time the speaker shifts, and therefore pause at each change.

Notice that all of Pilate's contributions are questions. He seeks the truth from the one he will hand over to be killed.

Pilate said to **Jesus**,
"Are **you** the King of the **Jews**?"
Jesus answered, "Do you say this on your **own**
or have **others** told you **about** me?"
Pilate answered, "**I** am not a Jew, **am** I?
Your own **nation** and the chief **priests** handed you over to me.
What have you **done**?"
Jesus answered, "My **kingdom** does not **belong** to this world.
If my kingdom **did** belong to this world,
my **attendants** would be **fighting**
to keep me from being handed **over** to the Jews.
But as it **is**, my kingdom is not **here**."
So Pilate said to him, "Then you **are** a king?"
Jesus answered, "You **say** I am a king.
For **this** I was born and for **this** I came into the world,
to testify to the **truth**.
Everyone who **belongs** to the truth **listens** to my voice."

Jesus' closing sentence on truth is the last word of proclamation in this liturgical Year B, so match its depth with your delivery.

delivery. The reading is not long, so make full pauses at the breaks in the printed text. Finally, commit the final verse to memory, and engage the assembly, however large or small, with direct eye contact. Be bold as you deliver the alphabetic sweep (Alpha and Omega are like our A to Z, beginning to end) and the time span of the Lord God (is . . . was . . . and is to come). Be bold!

GOSPEL All three readings for this last Sunday of the liturgical year are about kingship and dominion, about

the realization of God's will in the world through those he has sent, the one like a Son of Man and the Ancient One of the Book of Daniel, and Jesus Christ in the second reading and the Gospel.

The wonderful yet difficult literary characteristic of this passage from John is its dialogue between two rulers, the govenor of the nation and Jesus, whose dominion is all of creation. (Perhaps you can highlight the lines of Pilate and those of Jesus in different colors in your *Workbook* so that you can more easily catch what is at stake in the theology of the Gospel of John.)

Two practical suggestions as you study the dialogue. First, each change of speaker is preceded by a curt identification: "Pilate said to Jesus," "Jesus answered," "Pilate answered," and so on. Pause slightly before each of these so that the exchange can be understood clearly by those who hear your delivery. Because the words of Jesus are so profound, perhaps you can deliver them with slightly more gravity.